D1459653

The Atomic Bomb of Love

Written by An Yong-Jun
Translated by Peter S. Kim

The KIATS Press

On the Publication of the English Version of
Sarangui Wonjatan [The Atomic Bomb of Love]

Within a short time span, the Korean Church has experienced tremendous growth and a distinct development in its theology. In particular, the passion for missions that has carried over from the early years of Korean Christianity is one of several important characteristics that have distinguished the Korean Church in its role as a catalyst for the worldwide growth of Christianity in the 21st century. Furthermore, our predecessors in the faith who led the Korean Church in its early days have passed on to us a special legacy, expressing their passion and commitment in the form of sermons, essays, fiction, poetry, and artwork. Through such works we are given the opportunity to connect with their lives and their faith.

The Korea Institute for Advanced Theological Studies (KIATS) has striven to rediscover this legacy, and to allow international access to such a valuable inheritance cultivated by our faithful predecessors. One result of this effort is the publication of The Korean Christian Leaders Series and The Korean Christian Classics Series begun in January, 2008. The Korean Christian Leaders Series is a collection of the written works of church leaders who represent various facets of Korean Christianity. Each monograph in this series is published in two volumes: one in Korean and the other in English. The Korean Christian Classics Series is a multi-volume compilation of classic texts that were previously unavailable to the general public. Each volume contains a facsimile of the original text, accompanied by an English translation and a modern Korean version. In selecting the texts for these two series, priority is placed on works that carry greater spiritual and literary value, and selections are made on the basis of painstaking comparisons and examinations of each author's body of work. In the case of Christian leaders who made an impact on the Korean Church and society but have not left behind any writings, we have compiled secondary sources and biographical materials into representative monographs.

As one step in the task of compiling the literature of Korean Christianity and making it available internationally, we are publishing an English translation of *Sarangui Wonjatan* [The Atomic Bomb of Love]. Rev. Son Yang-Won was a man who embodied Christian agape love through his life and faith. He risked his life in resisting Shinto worship during Japan's colonial rule of Korea, and he adopted the communist who had killed his two natural sons, desiring to make him his ministry successor. Finally, while defending the faith during the Korean War, he was shot and killed by communist soldiers, thus joining the ranks of the martyrs. This book contains a moving account of the life and the faith of Son Yang-Won.

KIATS has been working since the winter of 2007 to make Rev. Son's legacy known outside Korea. Firstly, in 2008, we published Cha Chong-Soon's *Aeyangwon-gwa Son Yang-Won Moksa* [Aeyangwon and Martyr of Love: Son Yang-Won] in Korean and English; secondly, in April of 2009, on the 100th anniversary of the founding of Seongsan Church where Rev. Son ministered, we compiled a selection from Son's hand-written papers and published them in Korean and English volumes; finally, we are presenting this re-publication of the well-loved *Sarangui Wonjatan* with a first-time publication of its English translation, *The Atomic Bomb of Love*.

Our wish is that this book will bring even more people, both within Korea and overseas, in touch with the life and the faith of one of the spiritual giants of Korean Church history. In particular, we anticipate that, through this travelogue of the life and faith of Pastor Son Yang-Won, readers will discover the foundations of the growth and the zeal of the Korean church, and will appreciate anew the depth of the spiritual legacy left by our predecessors in the faith. In addition to rediscovering and ruminating on the inheritance of Korean Christianity, we hope that readers will encounter the fundamental truths and teachings of global Christianity.

November, 2009
Kim Jae-Hyun
Director, The Korea Institute for Advanced Theological Studies

The Atomic Bomb of Love

The KIATS Press
Seoul, Korea, 2009

The Korea Institute for Advanced Theological Studies

The Korea Institute for Advanced Theological Studies (KIATS) was founded in 2004 for the purposes of cultivating Christian leaders across generations; compiling the written legacy of Korean Christianity and making it available to a global readership; promoting mutual understanding and communication between Christians in the East and the West; and providing a transdenominational space for the nurturing of churches and believers.

KIATS emphasizes "people, infrastructure, and network." KIATS seeks out those who "steal a glance at the secret of heaven and realize it on earth" and nurtures their vision to undertake research on Christianity with a global perspective. By supplying resources for the study of Korean Christianity" KIATS helps provide Korean Christians with the means to undertake church and theological research. Also, by forming connections between Asian and Western Christianity, KIATS strives to be a bridge to facilitate common growth.

Publishing Date: November 15, 2009
Published by The KIATS Press, Seoul, Korea
Publishing Director: Kim Jae-Hyun
Translator: Peter S. Kim
Cover Design: Lee Kyung-Hwa
ISBN: 978-89-93447-08-8
Printed and bound in Korea

Dedicated to

Westside Presbyterian Church
(Mississauga, ON Canada)

Where three generations dream and dance together;
A loving community, disciples of Jesus changing the world.

Westside Presbyterian Church
(Senior Pastor: Rev. Park Hun-Seung)

CONTENTS

Foreword

Part I

Part II

Foreword

If there were two great wonders of the 20th Century, it would be the appearance of destructive atomic bombs and the reemergence of constructive love for humanity.

If the result of thousands of scientists consuming the resources worth tens of millions of dollars and spending a long period of time was this wondrous thing of destruction, then how can we not say that the reemergence of love for humanity is the great crown of construction that was borne by the period of thousands of years and the life of faith of tens of years!

It is said that Rome was not built in a day.

The reason that I rejoiced upon receiving this good news in America was that I believed Korea would contribute greatly to the kingdom of God that is to come in the future. That's why, after returning home, I did a thorough research of which the result is this small book.

There were three things that encouraged me while I was writing this book.

First, it was the book The Bell of Nagasaki by Mr. Nagai which was translated by Lee Seung-Tak. The author writes at the end of the book, "As long as there is such thing as an atomic bomb, war is nothing but humanity's act of self-destruction. Those on gun platforms who are crying on the field of atomic bombardment cry out to the world. Stop the war! Cooperate with each other with love only! Those on gun platforms prostrate themselves in ashes and plead to God. Please, turn this gun platform into the last field of atomic bombardment on earth... etc." These words became the fuel for the fire being ignited.

Second, it was the newspaper article by President Truman of the United States in the title of "Resolving all the problems of the world through faith" which emphasized the role of religious life. He stated, "I believe that if human beings uphold the principles of the ancient prophets and the Sermon on the Mount, then all the problems of the world today could be solved. If there is a danger to the religious life of our citizens, it is the tendency to take our religious inheritance for granted. Religion is not of polity or something remains inside a building but something that resides in the center of the human heart. Unless people live with faith and practice of faith, religion never becomes vital energy...etc." These words became the flower on silk.

Third, it was the program of ideological conversion executed by the highest council of the citizens' Bodo league and the program of defection executed by the department of defense. By all means, I wish that it is not superficial conversion brought on by the lack of options or fraudulent defection brought on by the disadvantageous situation. Rather, I wish that there will be justice and love that could guide them.

These provided whipping to the running horse.

This book is not a biography. Biography promises the future.

This book is not a novel. It is based on facts to be considered a novel.

Shall I say that it is a reflective writing that illustrated what a life of faith is about?

I wish that this book, as a great bell of justice that rings throughout the wicked world, becomes the declaration of war unto the evil empire on its retreat home.

This book is the first step in tracing the contributions of our predecessors who were martyred during Japan's colonial rule. I ask anyone who has information about this living historical fact to record it in detail and contact me.

May this effort offer even the smallest comfort to those who awaited martyrdom in prison but were released and still remain living, spared for the sake of God's work yet to be done here on earth. And may it also comfort those saints and prayer warriors of Yeosu Aeyangwon, abandoned by the world but always faithful, and those saints who remain hidden like flowers in the woods.

It is not to idolize them or make factions around them. It is only because I could not keep the grace and providence of God that was demonstrated through them buried.

Jesus said, "You are the salt of the earth. But if the salt loses its saltiness, how can it be made salty again? It is no longer good for anything, except to be thrown out and trampled by men." Again he spoke, "You are the salt of the earth. But if the salt loses its saltiness, how can it be made salty again? It is no longer good for anything, except to be thrown out and trampled by men. "You are the light of the world. A city on a hill cannot be hidden. Neither do people light a lamp and put it under a bowl. Instead they put it on its stand, and it gives light to everyone in the house. In the same way, let your light shine before men, that they may see your good deeds and praise your Father in heaven" (Matthew 5:13–16).

I don't know how many times I cried while writing this book. It would not be an understatement to say that it began in tears and ended in tears.

It greatly pains me to know that, in order for me to write this book, Korea Presbyterian Seminary with which I was helping out had to come to a halt and this caused much inconvenience for the warriors of faith who study in evenings and on weekends. But I had to move ahead resolutely having promised the future.

By all means, I pray that God blesses this poor writer in me and wish the power of love of this atomic bomb of love spreads to wherever the news of the might of atomic bombs reached.

An Yong-Jun

the blood of a sinner like me

I thank the Lord for choosing me, among so many believersm to have privile caring for these beautiful treasures.

3. I thank the Lord for letting me offer up my eldest and the most beloved of my three boys and three girls.

Part I

hey say it is precious to have a son who is martyred. Still more, thank the Lord that my two sons were martyred together.

5. They say it is blessing [enough] to believe in Jesus and die a peaceful death, but I thank the Lord for letting my sons be shot th death while carring out the work of evangelism.

My sons were preparing to study abroad in the U.S. But I thand the Lord,

ecause my heart is relieved to know that they went to heaven, a better place than Am

think the Lord for giving me a loving ead my enemy to repentance and emb

I am thankful, believing that the martyrdom of my two sons will bear countless uit of heaven, a better place than America.

9. I thank the Lord for allowing me to recognize God's love even in adv and for granting me faith to overcome.

Explanatory Notes

1. Part One of *Sarangui Wonjatan* was first published in 1949, and Part Two in 1952. A two-volume edition was then published in 1980 and went through fifteen printings due to high demand. Each edition included a new foreword by Rev. An Yong-Jun, but there were no revisions to the main text.

2. We express our thanks to Sung Kwang Publishing and CEO Lee Seung-Ha for permitting KIATS to undertake an English translation of *Sarangui Wonjatan*.

Before the Wind Began to Blow

Chapter 1

"What did your family prepare?"

"Us? We made kimbop, fried anchovies, and sweet rice cakes... Oh by the way, I asked Mr. Park, who was driving out to town with his truck, if he could get us ten apples. Guess how much I had to pay for them!"

"How much?"

"A *won* for 10 apples!"

"Oh my gosh!" exclaimed Ok-Sun and Yea-Sun. They were a couple of fourth graders at Seongsan Primary School, a chartered school of Aeyangwon. They were eagerly looking forward to the school picnic, which was in two days, like a pair of brides who have just learned of their wedding dates.

"Rev. Son said he would come tomorrow, but I don't know if he would be there for sure."

"Well?"

"Without him, it would not be as fun!"

"I know! Remember how much fun it was last autumn? Ha, ha, ha!"

"Oh, it was so much fun. Did you see how he reacted when a pine cone fell on his bald head? He was jumping up and down, just freaking out!"

The two girls broke out in a frenzy of laughter. It was something that happened last autumn at the school picnic. The group had arrived at the forest, which was at the bottom of Mount Gaemi-Sil, a place that belonged to Aeyangwon, Yeosu, and was known for its numerous chestnut trees. A well-ripened chestnut fell squarely on the head of Rev. Son, which was covered neither with a hat nor a string of hair. The girls were laughing because they just had remembered how Rev. Son jumped up and down, crying "Oh, oh, I am dying!" and pretending to cry like a kid.

Rev. Son attended as many of these events as he possibly could, and made the children joyful and happy with many different kinds of pranks. This incident, too, he probably planned it out from the beginning—He was standing up at first, but when the chestnut fell on his head, he grabbed his head and began to sit, stand, run, and cry "woo, woo." This made the whole group laugh until their stomachs began to hurt.

"I am not going if Rev. Son does not go," said Yea-Sun with a sad glow. Yea-Sun first came to Aeyangwon with her mother when she was only four years old because her mother had contracted Hansen's disease and was forced out by their family. She died some time after arriving at Aeyangwon, but Yea-Sun, even though she herself had no disease, had been staying here for eight years because she was completely abandoned by her father, who had now married a new wife. She often sang the following song, which she either composed herself or learned from someone else. Singing this song gave her great comfort, but it had the effect of bringing people to tears.

1. The sun is setting upon the sea, far away from here.
   Children that were picking clams are scurrying home now.
   Young birds of the sea that were dancing over the waves
   Travel ten *li* back to their nests deep in the island.

2. Night winds seem so lonely here on the beach.
   Even the crescent moon so pretty finds its way home,
   But what about me, a girl who left her hometown eight years ago?
   When can I go back home?

This young student was one of many who lived at Aeyangwon and felt so lonely in their hearts for having to carry stories unspeakable and kept private from others. For Rev. Son, this girl's predicament of having to live at Aeyangwon despite being disease-free was hard to bear.

"I prayed to God last night that he would come and I know that he will probably come because I saw him with a smile when he arrived."

"Yea-Sun, come and have dinner," called her mother.

"Okay!" said Yea-Sun. "Why don't we pray so that he would come for sure?" said Yea-Sun turning to Ok-Sun.

Ok-Sun, as she stood watching Yea-Sun jog away, was startled by a voice, saying, "Clean your room, Ok-Sun!"

The mothers of the girls were not their real mothers. Though not of genealogical relation, they became mothers to the girls at Aeyangwon out of love within this household of the heavenly family.

1. Standing on the charming hill surrounded by a white beach and a blue sea,
   It is a blessing of God.
   Sun rising above the beautiful scenery of the naval station is indeed glorious,
   Seongsan School reflects our spirit of courage and valor.

2. Beyond the mountains, islands, horizons,
   We are aboard the ship that looks for the port of hope.
   The sound of the bell on the top of Mount Zion tells we are the students of
      Seongsan.
   Compass is our treasure in the limitless ocean.
   We move ahead, the star of truth, our Seongsan School.

3. Broaden your knowledge like an ocean and purify your minds like white sands.
   Friends, let us forge ahead, forward, forward.
   On this rough road, the lighthouse flickers.
   Oh, shine your light, Seongsan, Seongsan, Seongsan School.

Belting out this song, the female students marched in the front and the male students marched in the back of the group in a straight formation through Gate Makmun, across the stream, past the "Chicken Head" and over the levee. It was the procession of the students of Seongsan Primary School, a charter school of Aeyangwon, on their way to a picnic. They were marching dressed in colorful new clothes, carrying their lunch pails and with their water canteens strapped over their shoulders. This procession of the students included among them those with disfigured faces, those that limped along, and those without a limb among them, and it was led by a teacher with a bald head. It must have been quite a sight and an occasion of laughter for healthy onlookers. There were male teachers as well as female teachers, but the one who followed everyone else all the way in the back was the principal of this school, a minister who was himself only a little taller than the students. He wore a fedora and a regular suit. The only pieces of his appearance fitting for the field trip was a water canteen strapped over his shoulder and socks pulled all the way up to his knees and over his dress pants. Of course, the parents of the students were part of the procession as well.

Onlookers, who regarded the procession with more mockery than jealousy, included adults with wooden racks on their backs, a girl with a baby on her back, children picking rice kernels who stood from afar, and people waiting for a train at the Sinpung Train Station.

The high sky ended at the peak of Mount Gaemi-Sil and the autumn wind was blowing over the field. Leaves were falling, startled at the sound of birds; a few remaining persimmons on the vine, now red enough to eat, were signaling the imminent arrival of winter. Such beautiful scenery was a day of joy for the students on march and about which the outside world knew nothing. It was so-called "the day of venturing out into the world."

Though the sun rises and the stars come out for the three hundred sixty five days of the year and all twelve months, people still prefer the mornings in which flowers bloom and the nights in which the moon is up in the clear sky; they despise the days of rain and wind. Likewise, the day of venturing into the world was one of the happiest days of all the days of the year to these children. If the day of the diagnosis of their disease was the day of curse, if the day of leaving one's home was the first day of wandering, this day represented a day of returning to one's hometown. Though this day of curse eventually turned out to be a day of blessing and the day of wandering the first day of salvation for these people, who could force them to ignore the longing that they had for the past! All the teachers, students, men, and women had had different circumstances and situations just as they looked different in the appearances of their faces and limbs.

"Let's sing, 'It is so beautiful,'" said the female teacher who was leading the group out in front, and soon all the people began to sing along. Among the students who were singing this song and that hymn, there were more than a few that said, "Hah, I prayed for the pastor to come, and he is here! The pastor is following us. It will surely be fun!" Why did they keep looking back? Were they worried that the pastor might not follow them?

> If going over that high and steep mountains means seeing my mother,
> I would fly with my two wings and get there to see her.
> There may be no high mountain where my mother is,
> But it is this disease of leprosy, like an enemy, that blocks my way.
> If crossing that river and that sea means seeing my mother,
> I would swim with all my might and get there to see her.
> There may be no river or sea where my mother is,
> But it is this disease of leprosy, like an enemy, that blocks my way.

This was the song that a few children in front began to sing upon arriving at the top and sitting down on the boulder, where they could see the mountain and the sea. Though this was only one of the songs they sang all the time, but their eyes still welled up with tears, almost without them knowing it.

This was the top of Mount Gaemi-Jul. They had left at 9 o'clock in the morning and traveled the distance of about ten *li* within the span of two hours. Once the marching formation reached the bottom of the mountain, more time was spent playing and picking chestnuts. In climbing the tree to the top, many slipped and fell more than several times. Some dirtied their clothes and had their shoestrings cut when slipped.

Rev. Son was in the midst of the students, holding the hands of even those who were reluctant to let him, pulling and pushing them onward. This was because they were aware of the nature of their illness and they did not want to be a bother to Rev. Son. However, Rev. Son still chose to hold their hands ever so tightly and in this moment, the children felt as if they were holding hands with their biological fathers or mothers. During those days, even biological parents would send their children with leprosy to this place because they did not want to care for them. The children must have thought, "How could Rev. Son who did not give birth to me love me like this!" Rev. Son must have thought, "How could I love these children to whom I did not give birth."

"Let us have lunch now. Please go and find suitable places to sit down. Our principal will say the grace for all of us," a voice called out. Immediately, all those who were chirping like little birds became as silent and as still as rocks. In the quiet, each person felt that the prayer they heard was only for him or her.

God our Father! You created the universe, granted us this nature and ordained four seasons so that we could live in thanksgiving to you. But human affairs only reflect the ignorance that is the end result of sin. Lord, in this moment, help us so that we may open our spiritual eyes one more time. Let this be an opportunity for us to listen to your voice, the holy Lord. Our shepherd, who provides for all our needs so that we would not be in want, make us lie down on green pastures. Lead us beside still waters. We are grateful to you for reviving our souls and leading us to the path of righteousness for the sake of your name. We ask you to protect us so that we would not be harmed in the valley of the shadow of death. Prepare a table before us in the presence of our enemies. In this hour, you put us in the wondrous palm of your hand and there is nothing other than thanksgiving, praise, and joy in what we see, hear, and feel. Oh, Lord! Once again I thank you for giving us the food for our bodies. Let the food we take not be for merely satisfying our appetite or the hungry stomach, but let it for our spiritual power that we need in living for your glory and seeking your kingdom and righteousness. We give you thanks and pray in the holy name of our Lord, Jesus Christ. Amen.

As soon as the prayer ended, all the students scattered quickly and efficiently in many different directions like an army of ants.

"Well, I forgot to pack my lunch. Who'd like to share food with me?" said Rev. Son, the principal who had said grace a moment ago. However, there was not even one person who said, "Come this way and please eat with us." Was it because the food was scarce? Was it because no one wanted to share? Of course not. They were all prepared to offer him everything they had. But the reason for not readily offering their food to Rev. Son was because they knew what they were. However, regardless of what people were thinking, Rev. Son went after the food that the ugliest of all the patients had brought. Making the patient share his lunch with him even by force, Rev. Son offered water that he had brought with him in return.

Some said, "Oh, no. What if he contracts the disease by doing that?" Another responded by saying, "Well, that's nothing. Rev. Son even goes into intensive care units and touches the patients on their sores and lays his hands on their heads in prayer," as they recollected on Rev. Son did in the room of the late Mr. Hwang. Still, some cried out, "Now,

I could die happy after seeing Rev. Son honor us by eating with us," satisfied that they had entertained an angel. In this way, all ate lunch while praising and delighting in Rev. Son.

To the south, Namhae Island could be seen like a levee across the wide-open sea. A pair of sailing ships could also be seen gliding gently by the island. In the clear blue sky, a few seagulls could be seen chasing the rear of the ship. Cool autumn wind was rallying the golden waves to break against the sides of the ship. The sea, when seen from the back of Aeyangwon, seemed so close that it looked like it was its front yard.

"Pastor, while you are eating, would you care to hear the students sing?" asked Mr. Lee, a classical singer.

"Yes, why not? Who wants to do it? Please go ahead!" nudged Rev. Son.

"Okay. Bok-Sun, why don't you try it?" called Mr. Lee. "I can't," declined Bok-Sun shyly. And yet, she was nudged on by others to do it for Rev. Son and was told that she would regret it later if she didn't. So, Bok-Sun grudgingly stood up to sing. "The Whole Land of Korea, the Peninsula, the Land of Beauty, the Hill that God Gave Us," sang Bok-Sun with all her might. When the song ended, people erupted in applause. Even the teachers and students who were eating at another place came running to where she was.

Bok-Sun arrived at Aeyangwon last spring. She was in the fourth grade when she was diagnosed with Hansen's disease. Her parents committed her to Aeyangwon for treatment. However, people could not tell just from her appearance that she had the disease. In addition to her smooth voice, her face was radiant and she was a good student as well. Since she had grown up in a non-Christian family, she did not know much about Christianity at first. However, recently she became interested in memorizing the Bible, praying, and singing hymns, to the delight and admiration of other students and her teachers.

"By the way, Pastor, is it true that the people in society are forbidden from singing the song 'The Whole Land of Korea, the Peninsula, the Land of Beauty?'" asked Mr. Jo, the musician who had snuck beside the pastor.

"Yes, of course. Besides that song, there also are many hymns that have been prohibited. For example, Hymn No. 204 "A Mighty Fortress is Our God" and Hymn No. 224 "Onward Christian Soldiers" are censured also."

"Oh my, what kind of world has it become!"

The conversation revolved around the policy of cultural reengineering that the imperial Japan employed in importing Shintoism into Korea, as well as trying to convert Koreans into the citizenry of Japan's empire in the wake of Japan's victory in the Chinese-Japanese War. Particularly, the religious oppression against Christians in Korea was implemented systematically and had brought about the General Assembly, the highest ecclesial body of governance, officially approving Shinto worship. The page 9 of the minutes of the 27th General Assembly, which was held in 1938 reads,

The motion by Mr. Park, the representative of the alliance of three presbyteries (Anju, Pyeongseo, and Pyeongyang) to approve Shinto worship and issue an official declaration thereof was ratified.

The Declaration

We hereby approve Shinto worship as an act of national loyalty and agree to observe it with due diligence on the basis that Shintoism is not a religion and as such does not violate the doctrines of Christianity. Therefore, we ratify the resolution to participate in Shinto worship with earnestness as the citizens of the Japanese Empire in this time of extraordinary circumstances.

Signed
September 10, 1938
Hong Taek-Ki
Moderator of the General Assembly, Joseon Presbyterian Church

As it can be gleaned from the above record, not only had the colonial government succeeded in coercing the church, it had also gone one step further and ordered the Bible to be altered and songs to be removed from the hymnal, thereby striking with the hand of aggressive persecution.

What was worse than this was the circus of sycophantic church leaders who had volunteered to edit the Bible and the hymnals in an apparent effort to align themselves along the oppressive policy, thereby selling themselves out. Such leaders had feared the Japanese more than God. The only place where the restrictions of the government were yet to take root was Aeyangwon. Aeyangwon, as a part of the consortium of mission and evangelism ministries of the Southern Presbyterian Church, was first established in Yangrim, Gwangju in 1909. As a group treatment center for Hansen's disease patients, it had been relocated to the present location in 1925. The institution had come a long way from the time when it had first started with 9 patients, now boasting the number of about a thousand. Because of the institution's dual purpose of aiding patients in their lives and guiding them in faith, the fact that people were trying to live by faith had to come as a shock to most people. Some were able to return to the society after a successful round of treatments, but a majority of patients spent the rest of their lives at Aeyangwon. Children who were separated from their parents, those that had to leave their friends and families behind, and the living dead filled with anger and contempt at being abandoned by the society composed the constituency of Aeyangwon. However, the marks of the disease on their faces, arms, and legs became the basis of which they belonged together as friends without prior histories, as brothers and sisters that came from different parents, and as families not listed on the official registry. In faith, it was possible for them to become one big family. It was not an artificial body of people as in the general assembly, presbytery, or even the church. Many participated not only in the early-dawn prayer meetings, family prayer meetings, and workplace prayer meetings, but also in the overnight prayer meetings.

To the people of Aeyangwon, the reading of the Bible and the practice of prayer represented something more valuable than food and medicine. They were committed to living and dying in prayer. They prayed whenever they opened their eyes and whenever they closed their eyes. These prayers ranged from the prayers of repentance resulting from the tragedies in their lives, but also the prayers of earnest supplication for the salvation of their families, relatives, and even the society that had abandoned them. The most recent focus of their prayers had been to intercede night and day for the Korean Church, which seemed to be on the verge of apostasy due to its acquiescence to Shinto worship. The two individuals of true faith, namely Dr. Robert M. Wilson, who dedicated his life to this ministry of service from the very beginning, and Rev. J. Kelly Unger, the missionary in charge of the church of this community, had made the critical decision to bring Rev. Son to Aeyangwon, who was embroiled in the controversy with the Gyeongnam Presbytery for his refusal to participate in shrine worship, and had given him the responsibility of training the community in matters of faith. It is therefore most likely that the Southern Presbyterian Church missionaries, who ran the educational institutions later shut down by the authorities in 1937 because of the issues of shrine worship, operated the schools out of the same principles.

"Pastor, how was the revival meeting this time?" asked Miss Kim, a teacher.

"Well, it was very interesting. One thing that I am especially grateful for is how the authorities could not do anything to me when I took down the flag of Japan that was displayed right behind the pulpit prior to the start of the revival. They took me into custody a few times but nothing could be done when they saw that my reasoning made sense."

"What did you say to them?"

"A flag is something to display in front of a house to show one's respect for their country, or something used by a ship to disclose its nationality. However, a flag is not something to be displayed inside a church so that people could bow to it. It is the same thing as bowing to one's nameplate. Paying respect to the flag should only be done by those that are truly patriotic. What good is it if drunkards can become patriots and evil economic policies can be seen as doing the work of compatriots and if traitors with concubines can be seen as revolutionaries? Therefore, one should not ask people to do such an act. It might soon bring about the ruin of Japan. I don't know about the society in general, but in Christianity, there is a strong possibility that it could amount to idol worship, which is a violation of the Ten Commandments. I told them that I could not comply even if it meant that I am not allowed to participate in the revival. Though I regard what happened entirely as the intervention of God, the fact that it was a village police station that I was dealing with and that there was a rapport between the chief of police and the church's elder might have had something to do with it. They allowed me to go on with the revival as scheduled but said, "The church should never call a preacher like that ever again for a revival meeting. Ha, ha.""

Rev. Son laughed. Those that were listening to the story also broke out in laughter, but more for the reason that they saw a child-like innocence in Rev. Son who managed to blurt out an awkward laughter out of telling the story of the revival meeting. On the other hand, it was a way of implicitly acknowledging their gratitude for Rev. Son's work of evangelism on behalf of the disabled such as themselves and giving thanks to God for answering their prayers in working things out for him.

"Let us sing 'The Whole Land of Korea, the Peninsula' with all our might," suggested Miss Kim in response to the encouragement everyone gained from Rev. Son's words.

The group broke out in singing, responding, "Now, let us sing more powerfully."

> The whole land of Korea, the peninsula, the land of beauty;
> The hill that God has given us.
> The whole land of Korea, the peninsula, the land of beauty;
> The hill that God has given us.
>
> God calls workers to this hill from many different directions,
> For there is a lot of work to be done.
> Who will respond to the call today?
> Let us go to work. Let us go.
> We received God's call for the whole land of Korea.
> Let us go to work in the peninsula, the land of beauty.

This hymn, sung by a group of disabled people unto the whole land of Korea and unto the ocean outstretched in front of them, was more of a cry that petitioned God for more workers.

The male teachers felt it. The female teachers felt it. The adults felt it. The students felt it. Everyone felt it. Who knew that the sweet sound of this song would bring a fresh wind over Korea and the world, thereby raising a mighty wave? Who knew except God who is truly the one and only!

From the Wind, to the Wind

> The warm wind of spring,
> The hot wind of summer,
> The cool wind of autumn,
> The nose-slicing wind of winter,
> It is the representative wind of the four seasons.
> The gently blowing wind of spring,
> The whipping wind of rain,
> The wind of autumn that shakes down the leaves,

The wind of winter that makes snow fall,
It is the working wind of the four seasons.

The wind from the east,
The wind from the west,
The wind from the south,
The wind from the north,
It is the pride of the east, west, south, and north.

The blowing wind of the morning,
The resting wind of the night,
The angry wind of the daylight,
The sleeping wind of the late night,
It is the wind of a man's heart
That blows whimsically to the tune of morning and evening.

The wind falling from the above,
The wind rising from the below,
The wind that blows from the land,
The wind that rests on the sea,
Is it the wind of help that blows from the sky, sea, and land?

You are in trouble if you think all winds are the same.

The wind of faulty democracy incurs the embarrassment of the heavens.
The wind of a misguided seminary produces a red leader.
The wind of meaningless dogmatic arguments famishes the flock.
The wind of foolish theologians causes the flock to wander aimlessly.
The wind of Shinto worship preserves the lives of shameless shepherds.
The wind of the shepherd disguised like a sheep increases the number of the
    sheep in hell.
The wind of the ecclesial misuse of power renders the Korean Church
    powerless.
The wind of the greedy church in taking over the enemy property buries the
    name of Jesus to the ground.
The wind of lifeless church politics tarnishes the glory of God.

The wind of success rather than repentance buries the saints in prison to the ground.

The wind of sermons lacking the power of the Holy Spirit causes the flock to die of hunger.

The wind of subscribing to trends without criticism causes women to rot.

The wind of unexamined freedom brings down the moral code of old.

The wind of the greedy middlemen causes the number of cigarette sellers to increase.

The wind of inadequate inspection turns the train into a den of peddlers.

The wind of blind greed produces communists.

The wind of worthless pride turns fellow Koreans into enemies.

Do you know why all these things are true in both the north and south of Korea? Don't you know?

God is the wind that cannot be cheated.

Jesus is the wind that is truly alive.

The Holy Spirit is the wind that groans.

The Wife's Entreaty
Chapter 2

"Look, Mr. Jo! Please be patient! Everything will be resolved in the near future!"

"Well, I understand it. But I am just relaying what the director has told me. What can I do?"

"But you can put in a good word for us, can't you?"

"I have been talking to him..."

This was an exchange between Mr. Jo, a messenger from Director Ando, and Mrs. Son, the wife of Rev. Son.

With the police department's order of eviction in hand, Mr. Jo was trying to directly negotiate a deal on behalf of Director Ando. The truth, however, was like the saying "The junior mourner seems to be in a greater mourning than the chief mourner" in the sense that Mr. Jo's hatred towards the family of Rev. Son was greater than that of Director Ando.

'Scumbags! From where are they going to get help? When the American pastor was here, they had their ways and their stubborn demands were met. But it is surely different now. The age of Japan has dawned and things are different now...' Mr. Jo thought to himself.

To Mr. Jo, the sum of Rev. Son, his family, the people of Aeyangwon was worth less than two pennies. However, he opted to operate covertly, enlisting insidious strategies to cover up his blunt arrogance.

Of all the things that bothered him, Mr. Jo disliked being called "Mr. Jo" whenever he came to visit the household of Rev. Son, instead of Hayama, which he preferred. Being addressed as Hayama made him feel better than being called "Mr. Jo." Despite Rev. Son's Japanese name Omura, people continued to call him "Rev. Son" just as they refused to call Mr. Jo Hayama. Mr. Jo's inkling of goodwill toward Rev. Son's family, however rarely it happened, inevitably turned into coldness whenever he was addressed as Mr. Jo. Hayama, who was once complimented for his fluency in Japanese when Director Ando told him, "You speak like a native Japanese," was always uncomfortable around Rev. Son's family as they spoke so freely in Korean at home whenever he happened to visit them. He attributed such behavior to the ignorance of the family, especially that of Mrs. Son, in not being able to master the Japanese language. What he could not understand though was why they continued to resist Shinto worship. As long as they did as they were told, they would live without much bother here at Aeyangwon. However, they continued to remain obdurate without giving an inch. Furthermore, he could not understand their stubbornness in refusing to bow to the flag of Japan and bow to the emperor in the direction of the east, bowing in the direction at the forty five degree angle signified a citizen's morning greeting to the Japanese emperor. He thought that it would be easier to find a way to not breathe than to find a way out of this ritual. He wondered why they would put their lives on the line over such a minor requirement—why the reckless stubbornness? He thought, "Didn't I keep telling them until their ears hurt that this is not a religious act but a mere civic act?" "I myself have been going to church for five years and I see that this issue is a matter of keeping good manners. Even if they do not like doing it, can't they at least try to pretend that they are doing it?" The family's obstinate loyalty to dissecting the minute right from wrong showed him that there was nothing that he could do to resolve this dilemma. "If they had been flexible in the past, it would not have come to this and they would not have to beg him for help," Mr. Jo said to himself in the mist of many

shifting thoughts. In his estimation, there was no one that was as smart
and wise as him. In his mind, everyone else was a fool that could not
correctly discern the time of the day, a fool that was digging his own
grave, and a fool that was running into a fire with a bundle of twigs on
his back.

"Anyhow, I will try to put in a good word, but at the same time, please
go back and bring about a quick resolution to this," said Mr. Jo as if it
was his magnanimity he was displaying.

"We offer our loyalty as the citizens of the empire. Proclaim the
king of the country," recited Mr. Jo as he departed in the direction of
Aeyangwon. He took the joy in thinking, "Those idiots cannot even
memorize the 'allegiance of the empire's citizens.'" He whistled and
looked to the sky. The clear sky did not have a speck of cloud. And he
felt a renewed sense of the Japanese pride.

However, to Mrs. Son, who did not take her eyes off seemingly happy
Hayama on his way out until he had finally faded away from her view,
everything was a nuisance. Talking about being bothered all the time!
Once or twice are manageable! "But this is getting insane," she must
have thought. Every time, she had to fight the urge to say everything
she wanted to say to him. Even if she knew that it was best to leave this
place once for all, there was no other place to go and no one beckoned
her family to come. She remembered that it was their protest of
Shinto worship which had brought the family to come and live here at
Aeyangwon in the first place. "Is there anywhere else that is better?"
Mrs. Son thought to herself.

"Dong-In, please wake everyone up so that we can go to the prayer
meeting," said Mrs. Son as she rallied the children to the prayer meeting
earlier than usual. Afterwards, she went to the Sinpung Train Station to
wait for the earliest train to Yeosu. "What a weird dream! Something is
sure to happen today!" thought Mrs. Son as she recalled the appearance

of Rev. Son dressed in white and seated in a neat place in the dream that she had the previous night. Her gaze was fixed on a spot that was already brightened by the morning sun. The smoke rising from chimneys was signaling that the families of Aeyangwon had already finished their morning prayers and had begun making breakfast. Dong-Su, who was on her back, did not make a sound. He must have fallen asleep.

It was the morning of July 20, 1941. Mrs. Son was wondering whether there was any news of Rev. Son, who had been taken into the police's custody as soon as he had returned home from attending the Wednesday worship service on September 25, 1940. Since then, she had not heard from him, and this made it almost impossible for her to wait any longer. Some said that Rev. Son would be released because there was no specific crime that he committed. Whenever she heard people saying that, she was relieved somewhat. However, she would become greatly concerned whenever someone said that Rev. Son would be indicted rather than being released due to the worsening circumstances of the time.

At first, she did not even know what it meant to be indicted, but now she knew that it meant being tried in the court. The sound of the word "indictment" made her shudder because she did not know if there was any legitimate reason for her husband to be tried in the court of the worldly people. Whenever she became immersed in such thought, she did not know what to do. However, already ten months had passed. Not knowing what kind of decision was being made in her husband's case made her all the more worrisome. The unusual dream that she had had prompted her to be on her way to find out if everything was right.

"Where should I go to ask about his condition? Who should I seek out?" thought Mrs. Son. Once she was on board the train, she began recalling the specifics of her husband's case. Because the case was being handled by the Police Department of South Jeolla Province and as

such had a high level of confidentiality attached to it, there was no way
for Mrs. Son to find out anything about her husband's situation–even
though she knew that he was retained at Yeosu Police Department when
he was arrested over ten months ago. She only knew, by the change of
clothes that she brought him and the flea-infested clothes that she took
back, that he was alive. Though she was now on her way to find out
more about his condition, she was yet to figure out whom she needed
to ask or to whom she needed to turn. "Should I go to the person who
makes the meals for those in jail? Should I go to the detective Song's
house? Should I go and visit the house of Mr. Park, the police officer?
Should I go to the pastor of the Yeosu Church for information? Should
I go to Elder Yang? Or should I go directly to the police intelligence
unit? I am going to Yeosu no matter what, but I don't know where to
turn for help. Once I visited Detective Song but I did not find him to be
friendly. I don't think going to the house of the jail's cook would work
either. Even if I go visit the pastor or Elder Yang, I don't think that they
can do anything for me since they are in the same situation as I am. The
intelligence unit is a much more fearful place to visit. I would try to talk
to the person in charge of the intelligence unit. But since I do not know
how to speak Japanese, the language of the enemy, there is nothing I
can do.

While she was wrestling with these thoughts, the train had reached
Mipyeong already. The next station was her destination. Since she could
not reach any decision, her mind was filled with nervousness. Despite
such nervousness, the reason that she wanted to meet her husband was
to make sure that he was all right. His life in jail, his health, and his
future certainly concerned Mrs. Son, but more importantly, it was the
state of his faith that worried her the most.

It was true that, when he was in Suncheon several days ago, she had
heard that Rev. Son would be released shortly because he had given into
the pressure of accepting Shinto worship. Upon hearing this, she prayed

in the back room of her house throughout the night. "Did he really give in? Is this just a voice of deception? Was the message misconstrued?" wondered Mrs. Son. If this were true, the news of his release would not be as pleasing as the news of his indictment.

While immersed in these thoughts, the train stopped at Yeosu Station. Mrs. Son got off the train along with a long wave of merchants. At once, she walked to the house of Detective Song. As expected, he was rude and did not divulge any information about Rev. Son. Without any other recourse, she turned to the house of the cook in charge of making the meals for those in the jail. He also did not have any information for her, except that he had been getting private meals for the last fourteen days.

'Private meals? I tried to arrange private meals for him for more than nine months but he refused to take them. Why suddenly accept private meals now?' Though it was initially good to hear that he has been getting private meals, now she just did not know what to make of it. She began to wonder if he might have been given this privilege because he had compromised his faith. The cook did not know anything other than this detail. With this piece of information, Mrs. Son came to the police station and sought Detective Song out.

"I hear that he is getting private meals now. What happened?"

After a long pause, the detective began speaking, "Isn't this what you wanted?"

"Well, yes but for what reason was this privilege allowed?" asked Mrs. Son.

"His health has been failing and it looks like his end is near. That's why private meals are being allowed in," answered the detective.

Upon hearing the words "weak" and "end," Mrs. Son asked, "When is it going to end?" There was no answer to the question. As she was waiting for a reply, Dong-Su began to whine perhaps due to hunger. So, she turned him around to the front and quickly breastfed him.

After thinking for a long time, Detective Song said, "Go to that caterer and pay for the meals."

Thinking that something would be decided between that day and the next, she did not ask more questions but went to the caterer to pay for the meals.

"If I pay this up, when do you think a decision will come down?" asked Mrs. Son to the caterer. She was told that it could be tomorrow or the day after tomorrow. While paying for the balance of fourteen *won*, the child who ran errands for the caterer recognized Mrs. Son and followed her out on her way out. Then the child led Mrs. Son to a place hidden from the view of others and whispered to her ear, "Rev. Son is leaving the Yeosu Police Station tomorrow and he needs a change of clothes." Mrs. Son was hopeful to hear that something was definitely going to happen the next day, but she still did not know whether he was going to be released or indicted. "Let it be according to God's will," sighed Mrs. Son. Then she returned to her house at Aeyangwon in Sinpung. The news that Mr. Jo had visited her twice that day awaited Mrs. Son upon her return.

It was July 21, 1941. The morning train did not fail to arrive at Yeosu Station. A big crowd of people was there to buy fish as usual. The sea, which was situated to the left of Yeosu Port, seemed never so bluer; Mount Jonggo right in front of the train station seemed never so higher. A mother had a baby on her back and her two sons were holding hands with their two younger siblings near the platform. It was unclear if they got off a train or waiting to get on a train. They seemed to be waiting for someone. This was Mrs. Son and the rest of the family. Yesterday, Mrs. Son returned to Aeyangwon. Because she did not know what was happening to her husband, today, she had decided to go visit him with the rest of her family.

Since it was 7 o'clock in the morning, Mrs. Son knew that many were yet to come to work at the government building. The family tried to walk slowly but they arrived at the police station in no time. The gates to the police station were shut.

"Mother, when is father coming out?" asked Dong-Jang.

"He will be out soon," said Mrs. Son, trying to hold back the tears. Ten minutes passed. Suddenly, the wife of Elder Yang showed up. She said that he had seen Mrs. Son earlier that day and had brought her something to eat. As soon as Mrs. Son had finished thanking her for food, she saw Detective Song walking toward her. Mrs. Son greeted him.

"Did you settle the account for the meals yesterday?" asked the detective.

"Yes!"

"Well, good," said the detective as he tried to enter the building.

"Wait a minute, please give these clothes to him," requested Mrs. Son. The detective took the bag that had the clothes and told her to go and wait at the train station. She felt disappointed because she thought she could have asked him more questions. Soon, she begrudgingly walked back to the train station. As she kept on waiting, it felt like an eternity.

There were a whole lot of people waiting for the 10 o'clock morning train bound for Mokpo. "I don't understand why so many people bother to travel at all. I guess if everyone were like me, then the train company would never make a dime..." thought Mrs. Son. The only time she would take a train was whenever she needed to come to Yeosu to buy a few things. She was surprised to see so many people waiting for the train making all the local stops. "I could never get used to riding a train even if I was paid to do it," thought Mrs. Son as she recalled the longest trip by train that she once had to endure. Once she took the train from Busan and got on a different train at Daejeon. Then she had to stop at Suncheon for a while before she got on a connecting train to Sinpung. She had to do this while she had a terrible headache and was exhausted from looking after all her belongings for the trip.

"Look over there!" cried Dong-In. Mrs. Son turned around and saw several rotund detectives and Rev. Son with his hands free of handcuffs walking toward her!

"Doesn't not being handcuffed mean that he is released? Then why are the detectives accompanying him?" Mrs. Son wondered out loud.

He seemed to have had his head shaved just like little children. His shaved head made him look even shorter. Seeing Rev. Son with fat detectives by his side made Rev. Son look like a child standing next to grown-ups. Rev. Son was wearing the laundered shirt and white dress pants that she had brought him. His face was even whiter than the color of the clothes and his body was literally just a mere shell of himself, as he had suffered a major sickness. Even the manner of his walking seemed as if he would fall to the wayside any minute.

"Is that truly my husband that was taken into the police custody without having a chance to say much?" thought Mrs. Son as she tried to keep herself from burst into tears. When she looked to her side, she saw that Dong-In and Dong-Sin were already crying with their heads down and Dong-Hee was taking out her handkerchief.

"No, this is not the time to cry. This is the moment of life and death. Before I cry, I must help him live. His soul! His soul! His soul," thought Mrs. Son as she clenched her teeth. In that moment, Dong-Jang was pulling his mother forward because he was happy to see his father. Only Dong-Su, who was on her back and sleeping, was quiet.

The crowd was stealing a look at the detectives and Rev. Son as if they were looking at what they were not supposed to. However, that was not a problem for her now. She could not bring herself to approach her husband, who was being escorted by the detectives. She could not tell if she was allowed to do so or not.

"Yes, I must save him. His soul! His soul!" Mrs. Son kept repeating as she approached the place where Rev. Son was standing. One of the detectives went away to go buy the tickets and Detective Song to whom she handed over the clothes earlier that day struck up a conversation with another person as if he wanted to allow the couple a private moment.

"This is it. This is a God-given moment. I must save him. His soul!" thought Mrs. Son as she pushed the tears down her throat.

"Where are you being taken?"

"To Gwangju…"

At the sound of the word "Gwangju," she slipped her hand between her back and the blanket with which she wrapped her baby around her waist and took out a Bible. She did so faster than an army officer pulling out a pistol out of the holster to shoot at the enemy.

Pointing down on the Bible, she said, "My dear pastor, you know this, right?" Before he could even look at it, she added, "You know the words of the wife of Rev. Ju, right? If you agree to Shinto worship, you don't deserve to be my husband. Don't forget that. Your soul will not see salvation." The words reflected Revelation 2:10 (Do not fear what you are about to suffer. Beware, the devil is about to throw some of you into prison so that you may be tested, and for ten days you will have affliction. Be faithful even to the point of death, and I will give you the crown of life). Upon hearing these words, there was a smile on the pale face of Rev. Son. Tears welled up in his eyes.

He said, "Don't worry. Just pray for me!"

Hearing these words from his mouth, Mrs. Son could finally cry. These were the tears of assurance. It was not clear when the wife of Elder Yang arrived. But she was there witnessing the scene and she also had tears in her eyes.

Mrs. Yang also knew these words by her heart because she had memorized the verse in the past. "Be faithful until death, and I will give you the crown of life."

Dear Church, the Bride

Sisters, mothers, and the women of the land,
The golden faced Yankee-women,

In this land without flowers,
In this unadorned country.
Oh, how fair you are like the brides with flowers, picture-perfect, and beautiful
    markings on your cheeks,

Do you suppose that Joan of Arc was able to deliver France out of trouble
    because she could dance well?
Do you suppose that Monica was able to lead Augustine to repentance because
    she had permed her hair?

Do you suppose that Mencius was compelled to study
Because of her mother's lipstick?
Do you suppose Baekbeom Kim Koo was compelled
By the red-manicured nails of his mother or his wife?
Do you suppose that's why he led the liberation movement?

Oh, sisters, mothers, and the women of this land,
Do you really want the equality of men and women?
Do not prepare yourselves for the life of concubines.
Throw away your study that only leads to illegitimacy.
You should move forward as exemplary mothers and good wives and innocent
    virgins.
Who is going to disdain you or oppress you or look down on you?

You can perm your hair
If with it your minds become clear of confused and vain thoughts.
You can wear a lipstick
If it is not the color of blood that you suck out of stupefied men.

You can do manicure and it will not be a sin
If you don't scrape the chest of the man wanting to return to his wife with your

fingers.
You can embellish your cheeks in any way you want
If they are not anesthesia for stimulating sex.

You can dance all you want
As long as it is not to the flattery of crazy people.

Sisters, mothers, and the women of this land,
Is it true that the rise and fall of a nation can be gleaned from its women?
Display your individuality abundantly.
However, do not do anything that is immoral–even a little bit.

Do you think every fad transported in by a ship is good?
Do you think everything traditionally Korean is bad?

Oh, the bride of Christ, the Church of Korea!
Are you a good mother or an evil stepmother?
Are you a faithful wife or an adulterous wife?
Are you an innocent girl or a depraved girl?
Are you Ruth or a Samaritan woman?

Since your husband of Japanese sandals has left
How hard has it been for you to look after a husband with Western shoes!

Do you think that the Church of Korea had fallen in the past
   because it did not have E. Stanley Jones?
Well, did it not have President Mr. Magino?
Do you think it failed because it did not have J. H. Mackay?
Well, did it not Mr. Domida?
Do you think that the church was ignorant because E. Brunner had not come?
Well, did not Mr. Kagawa come?

Is there any difference between a drunkard father disciplining his own child,
And a teacher with a cigarette in his mouth disciplining a student,
And worrying about the state of the nation sitting in a restaurant,
And worrying about the nation while lying in the house of a concubine,

And pasturing a flock in a church that the Holy Spirit has left?

Repent, the Church of Korea!

Don't you know that you bear the burden of the church divisions, in-fightings, powerlessness,

The Daegu Incident, the Jeju Incident, the Yeosu Incident,

The problem of the 38th Parallel, and the rise and fall of the Korean race?

Get rid of man-made strategies.

If you want to be Nineveh, then become Jonah.

If you fear Sodom and Gomorrah, then become a truly righteous person.

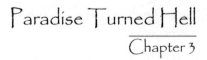

After dinner, few gathered at Elder Park Chun-Gap's house, which was situated in a sequestered location. It was a spring evening with only the stars high up in the sky. Only the sound of dogs from a distant town echoed through the evening. This place was as silent as the interior of a grave. People had gathered in secrecy in a small and light-dimmed room.

Following the departure of Director Wilson and Rev. Unger and the arrival of the Japanese director, Mr. Ando at Aeyangwon, the administrative office had also changed hands. Naturally, they were not Christians. No longer was Aeyangwon a paradise that ensured the freedom of faith. On more than a few occasions, conscientious believers had objected the forced observance of the pledge to the Japanese empire during a worship service or a prayer meeting. However, since Christian worship was banned without it, they had reluctantly given in to the demand. Seven of the church leaders, nonetheless, were not going to give up without a fight.

There was even an incident as this one.

A team of detectives and investigators were dispatched by the Yeosu Police Department to Aeyangwon in a brazen attempt to scrutinize the sermons of Rev. Son immediately following his arrest. They called up several members of the church leadership and interrogated them about the sermons that Rev. Son had preached in the past.

"What do you believe?" the investigators asked the leaders.

"We believe as Rev. Son does," replied the church leaders. The interrogation also covered other doctrinal beliefs such as the church's understanding of the end times, the Second-Coming of Christ, and the final judgment.

"If that's true, will Japan be subject to the judgment of fire?" quipped the investigators.

"Of course, it will most definitely be judged," the leaders answered without a hint of hesitancy.

"Do you mean that even the emperor will be subject to the judgment?" It was the final and ultimate question designed to test them.

"Yes. If the emperor does not believe in Jesus, he will be burnt to a crisp!" answered Elder Jeong Gi-Jae readily.

"What?" the detectives yelled even before Elder Jeong could finish what he was saying. The staff of Aeyangwon and the leaders of the church were sweating through the moment. The detectives looked as if they were ready to pounce on the elder. The only reason he was spared of the beating was because he was a leper. Instead, they were throwing a fit, jumping up and down with their faces turning red.

"What a disrespectful bastard you must be to say something like that about the emperor!"

"Hey look, if my answer is disrespectful, why would you ask me for my opinion in the first place?" answered Elder Jeong as he looked at them defiantly. His lips may be twisted, but what he said was not.

Anyhow, this incident showed the strength of the church members' faith. To them, the demand of Director Ando was not even considered a problem deserving of their attention. That was the reason for conducting a secret meeting of the church leaders without the Japanese director's awareness. After the prayer, Elder Park began to speak.

"First of all, we must deal with the situation of the family of Rev. Son urgently. From what I hear, I figure Rev. Son will soon be indicted. In addition, Director Ando has been pressuring Mrs. Son to vacate the residence through an intermediary. It is a miserable situation. What shall we do?" However, no one volunteered any comment in response.

"It would be great if we have a financial resource to draw from or are healthy in our bodies like others. But since we are not, with the congregation's approval, we should use the fund of seven hundred *won* that we have been saving and give it to Mrs. Son," said Deacon Kim, the church treasurer.

"That is a great idea. But do you think that it would be easy to have the congregation agree to it? Rather than going through that route, let's give it to Mrs. Son first and then help the people understand it. I don't think there would be anyone who would find fault with it," said Elder Shin.

"But can we withdraw the fund that easily?" said someone.

"That's not difficult to do. Since the account is still under the name of Elder Shin and not all the details about the church finances have been reported, if we hurry, we can make it work," said the treasurer confidently.

"Then, why don't we do it tomorrow and give it to Mrs. Son?" the group rendered the decision without any objection.

At that moment, they heard a sound from outside. Everyone was startled. Deacon Kim, who was the boldest of the group, went outside the house to check it out. However, he found no one.

"Who was it?" the group asked Deacon Kim upon his return.

"There was no one," said Deacon Kim. Relieved, the group resumed the meeting.

"By the way, how can we evade the pledge to the empire that the authorities are pushing down our throat?" asked Deacon Kim Bong-Im. He was the one who burned his own leg with an iron and feigned an injury so that he would not have to attend the worship of the east.

"Well, since we cannot have a worship service without it, how can we possibly evade it?" said Elder Park worriedly.

"Then, is it right for us to give in to the external pressures, compromise our faith, and live without standing up for our values?" replied Deacon Kim angrily. But no one could respond to the question or even calm him down because everyone felt the same frustration. Silence continued for a moment. There was a sound of footsteps coming from afar. It was the church members on their way to pray all night at the church.

"Even if we give the seven hundred *won* to Mrs. Son, it would all be spent on moving to Gwangju and getting a couple of rooms somewhere. Then what shall we do?" said Elder Shin as he changed the subject. Those who felt they could not afford to miss the worship of the east, Shinto worship, and the pledge of the empire tried to argue for a change of position even if it was temporary.

"I thought about that too. But it will be hard for us to continue our support. Even if we go out to the outside world, we could hardly make any money," sighed Deacon Jang.

"Let us do it this way, then," whispered Deacon Kim Su-Nam. As the group began attending to his words, there was once again a sound of someone's footsteps from the outside. Again, everyone was startled. Deacon Kim ran out of the house at once. It was hard for him to see in the dark, but it looked like someone was running away. He wondered, "Who could it be?" and he looked around the house to make sure that there was no one else.

"Who was it?" the group asked Deacon Kim as he entered.

"I don't know. I thought I saw someone moving away, but I cannot be sure."

"Can it be Mr. Jo," asked one of them.

"Well..." murmured another.

Now, after breakfast, the church leaders were forced to line up in the hospital patient confinement room as if they were prisoners.

"So, what kind of meeting did you have last night?"

"What do you mean a meeting? What meeting?"

"Please speak truthfully. If you readily admit it, I will forgive you all."

"..." No one responded.

"Do you think that I would not know just because you refuse to speak?" yelled Director Ando. His previous experience as the police chief was put to good use in treating the church leaders like criminals.

"Didn't you all meet up at Park's house yesterday?" said Director Ando. This made everyone startled. They realized now that the director was on to something.

Elder Park spoke admittedly, "Yes, we met to discuss church business."

"What church business? What was it about?" asked the director.

"It was about what we have to do in the future," said the elder.

"What do you mean what you have to do in the future?" shot back the director.

"It was about how we could lead the church. Since Rev. Son has not been with us for a long time, we were worried about the church."

"What? Since Rev. Son is not here? Didn't I tell you before? Instead of Rev. Son, Rev. Heo will be here after two weeks! Is that all you talked about?" said the director.

At that very moment, the door to the office was opened and Mr. Seong-Guk, an office clerk, brought the name card of a guest that wanted to see the director. Immediately, the group turned their gaze to Mr. Jo. After taking a look at the name card, Director Ando told the group to remain seated and continue to think about what he was saying. Then, he walked over to his office. Mr. Jo followed him out as well.

"It seems like they know everything," said Elder Jeong.

"Well, I guess someone spied on us last night and reported to him."

"It doesn't matter if someone has told on us or not. Well, now that we're here, we should take this chance to say what we really want to say to the director," suggested Elder Shin. Everyone seemed to be in agreement.

"Director, there are a few things that we want to ask you about," said Elder Park to the director, who came back in after about twenty minutes.

"What is it?" replied Director Ando with a hint of contempt.

"It is about the pledge that you make us do during a worship service or a prayer meeting. Can't you raise the awareness of patriotism in some other way?"

The director became angry at the suggestion. He said in response, "You are talking about that again? I have spent the last two months explaining it. It was two months ago that the decision was made. Please don't let me repeat the same thing. If you really don't want to abide by the policy, you always have the choice of leaving."

With the exception of Elder Park, no one in the group could respond to these words anymore. How can they respond to the challenge of leaving Aeyangwon? Though no one wanted to spend the rest of their lives here, it had already been more than ten years since each of them had come here due to their misfortune. It had now singularly become their home, their hometown, and their paradise. But the loss of their freedom of faith had turned the paradise of the past into the hell of today. It was not that difficult for them to leave. However, once in the outside world, they might have to live as beggars. Were they going to put living in faith before living as beggars? Or were they going to accept living in hell for the security of livelihood? This was the biggest challenge facing them.

The spring passed. Most flowers also withered. It was the season in which barleys in the field were able to grow one more inch and the leaves of the trees were turned from bluish green to a real dark green. Though the spring shower that had been pouring until yesterday had stopped, the lingering clouds continued to weigh heavily on the minds [of the people] that morning. It was a little cold. The train station hid its rear between the desolate mountain and the field of barleys waving like a sea. Many people were waiting for the train on the platform of Sinpung Station that did not even have a waiting room. Which were the ones that were sending their loved ones off? Which were the ones that were leaving?

"Mrs. Son, please do not worry too much."

"Yes!" said a middle aged woman with an infant on her back and two young children by her side.

"I have already contacted Deacon Lee and I am sure that he has found a house for you. Also, someone would be waiting at Gwangju."

"Thank you so much." It was an answer laden with heaviness.

"I am also relieved to know that Dong-In has come to accompany you there." As this conversation continued, Dong-In was carrying on more conversations with others. Among his remarks was the following: "As I told you last night, I will become a minister in the place of my father in the future. I will come here to work for all of you." The seriousness of his facial expression showed his resoluteness.

"Of course, you will. But since I am already old, I don't know if I will be alive to see you come back," said Deacon Lee, who was much advanced in age.

The entourage was obviously the remaining family of Rev. Son. The send-off party represented the people of Aeyangwon. However, there were those in the group who had already decided to leave Aeyangwon and go somewhere else as well.

At that moment, a sound of whistle came from the direction of Yeosu. At once, the crowd turned toward the direction of the sound.

"Mrs. Son, I will go to Gwangju to see you in the near future," said Miss Hwang, who was considered to be a sister in faith to Rev. Son. No one knew who started to sing first, but soon others followed.

God be with you till we meet again,
By his counsels guide, upon you,

With his sheep securely fold you,
God be with you till we meet again.
Till we meet, till we meet,
Till we meet at Jesus' feet
Till we meet, till we meet,
God be with you till we meet again.

The group sang the song and cried at the same time as it greeted the arriving train.

Restore the Paradise Which Has Now Become the Hell

The fallen angel is Satan,
The fallen paradise is hell,
The fallen heaven is the world of evil.

He said, "Heaven is in your heart."
A heart that sins is a heart of a serpent.
It is not an overstatement to say that a sanctuary that sins is a sanctuary of the devil.
No one will argue with the statement that a pastor who sins is a sort of a poisonous snake.
Have you ever seen a theologian from the old to the present who confesses, "I am a heretic"?
The ability to differentiate between truth and falsehood can only come about as the product of perseverance through persecution.
Would anyone not declare with his open mouth and throat to be an orthodox theologian?

The early church tried to wash off the blood of Jesus through oppression.
The contemporary church crucifies Jesus all over again with its so called "New theology– liberalism of ecumenists."
Since they all claim to be orthodox, how can the flocks know the truth?
However, they cannot deceive the Holy Spirit.
Even the fox that transforms into a human could not hide its tail.

You, the blind patients, you who have rejected doctors and obsess over
medicine bottles!
Is it really the construction of a heaven?
Or is it the expansion of the world of the devil?
Why does the call for ecumenism sound like the sound of wolves?
Are you poisonous snakes?
Or are you Adam and Eve that were kicked out of Garden of Eden?
Are you planning to build the tower of Babel?

Go ahead and try building it as you wish.
Go and attend all kinds of international events.
God who is living will look down on you.

Therefore, the Church of Korea!
Are you the true church of God?
Or are you the party of the devil that does not stop committing sin?
Before you curse at the words of Reconstructionists,
You should reflect on your conduct once again.
Before you can call for the division of a denomination,
You should inspect the path of your denomination.
Before you dance to the tune of ecumenism,
You should commit yourself to a mental hospital.
The disease of Shinto worship has not been cured yet.
The chronic ailment that was deepened during the time of Shinto worship has
not been cleansed.

When the gospel entered the Church of Korea,
The nationalists who were ready to forsake Jesus and go fishing slipped in like
a shadow at the same time.
When the seminaries were being built for the development of leaders, atheists
also slipped in.
If the seminary that used to be taught by the red communist is said to exist in
South Korea,
Then wouldn't the Church of Korea laugh and say that it is a lie?
But don't you really know that they are so many red communist shepherds out
there?

Theological liberals, ecumenists, and red communists are all neighbors.

The devil of the Japanese Shintoism has now slipped into a cloak of ecumenists.
Atheists are more honest in this regard, humanly speaking.

Repent! Leave the way of sinfulness.
Do not be deceived by the serpent again.
Restore the paradise that has now become a hell.
Before the day is done,
The Holy Spirit awaits for one more soul.

"Hey, Rev. Son, this is the transcript of the conversation that you and I had. I am going to read it. Listen," said Detective Garube. This detective, who had visited from the police headquarters of the South Jeolla Province, began to read the transcript excitedly.

Because they made revisions to it daily as they read through it, the process of finalizing the report had gone on for eight long days. This report, which spanned five hundred pages, was to become the basis of Rev. Son's indictment. As if a weight had been lifted off his shoulders now that this was almost done, the detective pulled out a cigarette, put it in his mouth and lit it.

"Rev. Son, you've worked very hard. Now that it is all done, I need you to put your thumb print right here," said the detective.

"What is the purpose of the thumb print?" asked Rev. Son in response.

"It just means that the statement you gave is true," said the detective.

Stunned at those words, Rev. Son said, "Is that right? Then I cannot."

"What?" The detective screamed. The cigarette fell from his mouth.

"Those statements are not mine," replied Rev. Son.

The detective screamed as he got up abruptly, "Are you out of your mind? Rev. Son (the word "Son" means "hand" in Korean) or Rev. Foot, whatever you are! Did ten months in prison make you lose your mind?"

"What, then, are you *saying* these statements are *mine*?" said the detective. He looked as if he was ready to strike Rev. Son.

"No, that's not what I mean. These statements are neither mine nor yours," said Rev. Son.

As the detective maintained an intense gaze at Rev. Son, he struck the desk with his hand, and said, "What a mindless moron! Are you actually saying these words or are you just eating them up?" With his face completely flushed, he finally asked, "Then, whose words are these?" It was not clear which of the two was in the right mind. There was not even a slight change in Rev. Son's facial expression. However, his appearance showed the frailty of a weakened body. He seemed small, fragile, and feeble that if he was kicked, he would be lifted in the air and travel more than ten *li* before falling to the ground. He had disheveled hair and beard that was overgrown.

"Yes, those are all God's words," said Rev. Son coldly.

The detective slapped him in his face and said, "All right, you bastard. Are you saying that you are God?" Though he was ready to slap Rev. Son again, he could not because Rev. Son did not even flinch. The detectives that were sitting on the other side of the room were looking at the two men attentively.

"I am not saying that I am God. I'm only saying that I spoke on God's behalf. Don't get so worked up and instead get me a Bible. I will show you what I mean," said Rev. Son in a gentle voice.

"Okay, fine, tell me what you mean," said the detective as he handed Rev. Son the same copy of the Bible that was given to him whenever he had requested it in the past. Rev. Son then proceeded to find the verses that he needed and read them aloud one by one.

The annexation of Korea by Japan in the guise of the partnership between two countries in 1910 A.D. had effectively colonized Korea and its 30,000,000 citizens. The loss of the national sovereignty had also translated into the loss of domestic independence and freedom. There had never been a nation in the past that was subject to the harshness of a foreign rule and forced colonial acculturation to the degree that Korea suffered at the hands of the Japanese government. Japan committed acts of unprecedented exploitation, oppression, and genocide. Its cultural reengineering program intended the obliteration of not only ethnic heritage, cultural resources, but also the people's Korean names. The final phase of this oppression involved the explicit revocation of religious freedom.

Japan enticed, lied to, and intimidated its colonial subjects by claiming that Japan was the chosen nation of gods and that the Japanese emperor was a divine being and that Shinto worship was a mere civic ceremony. As the crisis of faith reached its breaking point, the forefathers of faith committed themselves to defend their faith to the point of dying as martyrs and began protesting on the ideals of truth and justice. To some, it may have been another systematic demonstration, but it was more of a protest of individuals acting out of their faith.

One of such protesters was Rev. Son. Upon his arrival at Aeyangwon, he preached against the policy of the Japanese government through all his venues. He did his best to instill the strength of faith within the unfortunate people of Aeyangwon.

Ever since he was taken into the custody of the police on November 25, 1940, he had been persevering through ten months of interrogation, and had been cooperating with the detectives of the Yeosu Police as well as Detective Garube of South Jeolla Province in giving his statements. This was partially due to the reason that, whereas he had many chances to witness his faith to non-believers in all kinds of situations, he had always felt bad in not having the opportunity to reach out to police officers, prosecutors, and prison officials. To him, the opportunity presented itself in his arrest to witness Christ to the detectives. That's why he took the time to spell out his views of the Bible, God, the world, the nation, the end time, and the return of Christ in completing the report with a prayerful heart. Therefore, he admitted not only his offense, but also those statements that could be used against him insofar as they were useful in clarifying the truth and sharing the gospel. All the while, however, Detective Garube thought that Rev. Son complied so well because he was either a gullible human being or that his interrogation tactics were effective. The detective was so satisfied with the progress of work that was done in the last eight days and was thrilled to put an end to the report. No wonder, he was so upset to hear the words, "Those are God's words... I cannot put my thumb print on them."

At the end, it did not really matter if he had given his thumb print or not. After all, this was a world where a fist was far more effective than a law and this was a police station where reasoning was useless. The charge was entered and the indictment was rendered.

There was a chance that Rev. Son could have been released due to his failing health by the prosecutor's discretion. But Rev. Son's firmness of faith forced him to complete the full sentence of a year and a half as charged.

Once, Prosecutor Yoda inquired to one of the prison wardens that had escorted him, "Do you think that there is a chance of his rehabilitation? Has his attitude improved at all? Does he observe well Shinto worship?"

The warden answered, "Yes, not only does he observe Shinto worship, but he has also shown progress in terms of his conduct." However, overhearing the exchange, Rev. Son quickly shot down the report of the warden by saying, "No, I have never observed Shinto worship."

Upon hearing this, the prosecutor looked at the warden and Rev. Son alternately. The prosecutor must have thought, "What a fool he must be. Let's say what the warden says is not true. It still is an advantage for him to agree to it, but this guy does the very opposite, flatly denying the truth of it. What kind of a man is he?" The prosecutor did not know how to respond to Rev. Son's words and his face turned red. Only Rev.

Son was imperturbable.

Already much time had passed since Rev. Son came to the Gwangju Prison and the sentence of a year and a half was nearing its end. It had been almost thirty months since he was taken from home. He must have wanted to find out very badly about the well being of his parents who were in their eighties. He also missed his wife, children, and friends who were waiting for the completion of his sentence. He could have given in a little bit to Prosecutor Yoda's interest in seeing some progress in his attitudes. After all, Prosecutor Yoda was ready to release him if there was even a semblance of change in his position. But now, he was offended by Rev. Son's remark. As he flipped through the documents that he had brought, he decided to give it one more try.

"It has already been three years since you left home. I am sure that you are dying to see your parents, siblings, and children. You want to return home badly, don't you? Your sentence is almost fulfilled and this ordeal is almost over. When you get out of here, please get rid yourself of the past stubbornness and help out with promoting the religious interests of people," said the prosecutor in a compassionate appeal. But these words did not register with Rev. Son at all.

"Thank you for being concerned about me in so many ways. But I think you are overstating your case when you say, 'Get rid of the past stubbornness,'" said Rev. Son, his face a little flushed.

"Huh, huh, you haven't learned anything in three years," responded the prosecutor with a dose of condescension.

"That's right. Didn't I tell you when you interviewed me a year and a half ago? The faith of Christianity becomes brighter only through persecution. Therefore, for you to imprison me is beneficial to me. It is a great blessing. I did not suffer for nothing. Only your effort in imprisoning me has been futile," said Rev. Son.

The prosecutor was dumbstruck by what he heard. "Stop yapping. If you continue to talk like that, you can forget about getting released.

Even after the current sentence, you will be sent to a long-term penitentiary," said the prosecutor angrily. Now, his admonition turned into a threat. "You will only get out when you are reformed," said the prosecutor contemptibly.

Rev. Son answered, "To you it is a matter of reform, isn't it? To me it is a matter of faith." He was amused by the clever comparison that he made. He tried not to laugh but remain cool.

"Stop talking non-sense. Do you think that you can say anything? If you do, you will be shipped out to the penitentiary," threatened the prosecutor.

"It's all good for me. To go home is to live with Christ. To go to a penitentiary is to live with Christ. Does it matter where I go since I live with Christ?" replied Rev. Son.

"You look like you will die any minute now. From where do you get the strength to keep yapping like that?" said the prosecutor contemptibly as he waved Rev. Son to return to his cell.

This was how Prosecutor Yoda came to conclude that it was best for Rev. Son to be further detained at a penitentiary. Penitentiary was the place where people were imprisoned indefinitely until they were reformed in their ideology and was a kind of prison for those imprisoned for life.

"Whatever will be, will be. If it means that God is glorified, then I will gladly abide by it," thought Rev. Son. As he began walking back to his cell, he said to the warden, "Hey, warden, I thank you so much for acknowledging me as your fellow human being in front of the prosecutor. But I said what I said because it is of absolute importance to me. Please understand. To me, it is not a problem of being released. To me, it is a matter of faith. Had I remained silent in that moment, it would have come to me as a crisis of faith." Rev. Son said, as both an apology and an explanation.

"I just could not bear to see a saint like you rotting in prison anymore.

That's why I said what I said. I said those things on your behalf because I knew that you would not bring yourself to say those things. And I thought I could help you to get released by saying those things. Since it was a matter of life and death for you, I don't find it regrettable about what I said in front of the prosecutor," replied the warden apologetically. In fact, his action was in agreement with many wardens who had much respect for Rev. Son.

Consequently, though May 17, 1943 was supposedly the date of the completion of his sentence and release, Rev. Son was instead transferred to Gyeongseong Penitentiary.

From Yeosu Police Station to Gwangju Prison, from Gwangju Prison to Gyeongseong Penitentiary, from Gyeongseong Penitentiary to Cheongju Penitentiary, he was moved around the prison system. In this way, he was taken from his family and isolated from the society, living the life of a prisoner for five long years until the liberation of Korea. However, he did not find his life during those years to be the life of suffering and restriction. Rather, he spent the years in prison in thanksgiving, prayers, and doing the work of evangelism. Let us turn to the letters that Rev. Son had written while in prison and get a glimpse of what his life in prison had been like.

Letter Dated June 13, 1942

Dear Dong-In (at Beomiljeong, Busan)

I cannot express how glad I am to hear that you are still healthy and sound. I also receive with joy the news that Deacon Park is fine. Please make sure you greet him for me. I thank God and believe that it is God's will that you have been able to relocate along with your friends. However, please do not ever forget that, while it is good to work at a factory for the time being, this is the stage of your life when you need to devote yourself to study. You can still earn money in the future. But it is so hard to pick up studying again once you lose that chance. For everything, it is crucial to not miss the timing. Since it is already late to enroll in a school, you can work until next year, but make sure that you study whenever you have time. Many great sages of the old were too poor to devote themselves to study alone. They had to till the ground during the daytime and read books at night. Still, many achieved great success this way. In the same way, you should start with prayer and read the Bible, which gives you the foundation. Then find good books and study on your own. Again, don't forget to waste the golden opportunity you have for your study. If you lose the timing, you will have regret as your future payment. Furthermore, more than anything, it is beneficial to work on one's faith and character. You should not sin. To sin is to be a slave to sin. If you succumb to sin, you can never become a great man of faith. Sin should be stopped in its track from an early age. The habits of sin that were learned at an early age will inevitably remain impervious to change at an old age. I earnestly pray and wish that you heed to your father's words and act accordingly. Dong-In, work hard to become the good person that I expect you to be. More than a wish that you treat your parents with good clothes and good food in the future, I wish that you grow up to be a great person.

Letter Dated August 13, 1942

Dear Dong-In (at Beomiljeong, Busan)

(Omitted)... I am comforted by the letters you send me time to time and I am thankful for this. But when I heard that you send home twenty *won* out of the twenty-three *won* that you earn monthly, I wondered, "How can he afford to feed and clothe himself?" Please try not to be overly thrifty. It is now a time in your life when you should grow much by eating well. Please be wise to eat well and keep yourself healthy…

Letter Dated November 5, 1943

Dear Father in Manchuria

To see a leaf of a paulownia tree fall to the ground is to recognize the arrival of fall everywhere (一葉落知天下秋). It is a wise sage's saying that by paying attention to detail, one is able to understand even bigger things of the world. It is the time to work hard to gather the harvest before the late fall turns into a cold winter.

Though I cannot prostrate myself before you and show my care, I greet you, father. May God's grace that is deep and wide be upon your body and spirit, and may God give you eternal peace and perpetual blessing. I want to know about the well being of my youngest brother, Eui-Won, and his household. I hear that the condition of the wife of my second brother, Mun-Jun, has been improving. I am grateful that God has alleviated the burden of my burdens. The news of my second brother coming to meet me on January 4 of next year brings much joy to my heart and I look forward to that day with the fullness of hope. Thousand years of the old seem like a day. But the time I have spent in earnest waiting seems like an eternity. Father, do not worry about your disobedient son, not even a little. The prayers of my parents, brothers, wife, and children have been answered by God. I have been eating well. One ball of rice and a cup of salty soup taste like the food of holy men and the cake of angels. The best taste belongs to a mouth of one with a good appetite. My parents and siblings worry about me being hungry and naked, but would God who even clothes the lilies of the field and feeds the birds in the air not feed his own son and workers that work hard? Since I have always been a man who needed only a small portion of food, I am satisfied with the kind of food here. Since I have always been short in height, this blanket here covers me from head to feet. I cannot ask for more than these as a member of the empire.

My prayer for you, father, and my wife and children is that you recognize the blessing of being able to be content no matter what. I can even see you and the family in my dream being overwhelmed by worries and various trials to the point of becoming sick. That has become my worry. As clouds are formed to give rain and dew in the cold turns into frost, the thoughts of the flesh become worries and these worries crystallize into an illness. The thoughts of the spirit lead to self-sufficiency and the life of self-sufficiency bears all encompassing contentment. Worry is the cause of an illness and the greatest sin of all sins. However, mortals don't seem to understand this truth. I have not seen a better son than self-sufficiency. Therefore, it was not only once or twice that I cried the tears thanksgiving whenever I had food or clothing. There are so many that struggle in living the life of a soldier in the front line. Since there are various sufferings that stem from the worries of the heart and the flesh, please persevere in patience. There is a saying that has been passed down through generations: "It depends on how you control your mind. Like the wind that blows through a willow tree, you should give in to others. But you should win over yourself. There can be no enemy for someone who controls him or herself." This saying is so true. A person's mind changes depending on how he or she guides it. Like the breeze that blows through a willow tree, one should accept all kind of trials with gentleness. If a person defeats and controls his or her desire of the flesh, and boldly moves forward, things will go his or her way even in the midst of the greatest challenge. Therefore, there are people who view life through the dichotomous lens of optimism and pessimism. However, instead of the two extremes, it is only right to respect life in all its diversity and colorfulness. As the four seasons are all different, as the joy and sorrow of each of the seven types of love for human beings is defined and categorized, as there is a time to be joyful and a time to be sad, as there is a time to laugh and a time to cry, I also believe in the coming day of light. For that reason, even in the darkest night, it is only right that I eagerly wait for the dawn of the glorious morning.

Father! Brothers! What is most precious to us and what we need the most is patience. There is nothing among all the things of the world that can be achieved without a trial. It is not only true for us, but also true for all people. Our nation is not the only one that suffers like this.

The entire world is going through sufferings. There might be a little difference among what people have to endure, but it is usually the same kind of suffering. How can we then excuse ourselves and cavort to the pleasures of daydreaming and mirage?

I ask you, father, and the family to entrust everything to the Lord and find peace.

Letter Dated February 2, 1943

To the members of Mount Okjong

(Omitted)... That daylight comes when night passes is a given. It is also a given that warm spring comes when winter passes. In the same way, we must live through the night in order to welcome the bright day. We must brave through the coldness of winter in order to embrace the warm spring... The ungrateful complains even after obtaining the whole world. To the one who finds self-sufficiency in one ball of rice and one cup of water shall be given a joy of contentment... For this reason, give all your cares to the Lord and be joyful in all things always. Worry is the cause of all diseases and joy is the antidote for all diseases.

I hear that my sister, Yang-Seon, will come to visit sometime in April. If she has a justifiable reason, she will be able to see me. However, since

May 17 is my day of release, I would like to ask her to wait one more month and joyfully meet me in front of the prison on that day. Please do not needlessly waste time and money in coming here earlier than that. If she prays for me in faith, it will suffice...

Letter Dated June 8, 1943

Dear Father (at Beomiljeong, Busan)

(Omitted)... How surprised and concerned were you on May 17, a day you had been looking forward to so eagerly? With what words can I possibly comfort you? I cannot but ask you to be consoled in the same unwavering faith that Abraham and Job had.

On May 20, it was decided that I was to be transferred to the Prevention Penitentiary. It was due to my confession that I absolutely adhere to the teachings of the Bible. In order to file a suit, I requested a hearing to the Appeals Court on June 2. Rather than expressing my complaints or seeking an exemption from my suffering, I wanted to testify to the truths of the Bible. Perhaps if I get to Daegu on the 20th of this month or by the end of the month, the process will be finished sometime in August and I will be transferred to the Gyeongseong Penitentiary.

Letter Dated July 9, 1943

Dear Dong-In (at Beomiljeong, Busan)

How hard it must be for you to bear on your shoulders the responsibility of caring for your grandfather, mother, and younger siblings and looking after the family in my place! I cannot imagine the toil of your labor. But I know that God has greater blessings to give you than those that He had granted Ninomiya Kinjiro for his sacrificial work in looking after his parents and siblings by chopping wood in the daytime and making sandals in the nighttime. You have noted in your letter several shortfalls that you could not reveal to me previously. Though I do not understand well how exhaustingly busy your life at the factories, the fact that you were writing the letter at midnight is evidence of that. I am filled with gratitude for your actions of love. I read with tears the letter which you have written in tears thinking about me.

My earnest request to you is for you to comfort your grandfather and carry out the sonly duties of checking on his well being both in the morning and night and I trust that you will do well the things that I could not do.

I have peace in knowing that you will do much more than what I ask. And from your salary of two *won* and twenty *jeon*, I can tell that you are an exemplary worker and I am thankful for that.

Letter Dated August 18, 1943

My Dear Wife (at Beomiljeong, Busan)

What a terrible suffering you must be in. It is worrisome to know that your high fever is serious in this hot weather and your physical ache has been intensified due to your illness. However, be comforted by the fact that God's love and truth transcends even the weather and environment. Not only is God's love reflected in the warm seasons during which flowers bloom and birds sing, but God's love also remains constant even in the season of frequent snow and wintry cold. Not only is God's love apparent in the season of harvest and the fall month of September, but also in the season of hot summer heat and drought. Not only are we commanded to sing of God's love while enjoying the finest food inside a magnificent mansion, but we are also to sing of God's love in the cold, hunger, pain, and suffering of in this life inside a small cottage.

I beseech you to be joyful always and to be thankful in all things. I trust and am assured that your faith will help you overcome the burden of your illness.

Listen, my beloved, the suffering of Job is more precious to me than the splendor of Solomon, and the patience of Job is more beautiful to me than the wisdom of Solomon. That is because the wealth and the wisdom of Solomon became the bridge to his corruption in the end, but Job's hardships and patience ultimately produced his glory. One's glory is determined by his or her end and true wisdom is in averting evil and wickedness.

Peace and joy is the antidote to all ills. Please give all your concerns to the Lord and I pray that you will soon be able to be healthy again.

Letter Dated September 25, 1943

Dear Father (at Beomiljeong, Busan on the three-year anniversary)

I cannot stop beseeching for God's great favors to be upon your health and well being and entrust to the Lord the peace and good of my wife and children and all the family members. Though your son is carrying on his life here inside the prison, I am thankful that God has kept me safe and healthy in God's embrace and grace for the past three years.

Dear Father, today is September 25. Exactly four years ago at 9 p.m. on this night, I was taken from home. When I reached the Yeosu jail, it was forty minutes past midnight. I have been a prisoner since then. Now, I am given an order of further detention at another Penitentiary and will soon be leaving Gwangju. I ask the Lord for a peace of mind.

As I am inside the prison far away from home,
I am faced with the depth of the night, the prison cell, and grief in my
heart.
Despite the depth of the night, the prison cell, and grief in my heart,
I am filled with joy because the Lord is with me.

Four years of life inside the prison walls is a long time,
But it seems like a day because the Lord is with me.

I trust that the Lord will protect me,
As he has protected and kept me in peace for the past four years.

God who was with Joseph and Paul in the old is with me today. I
leave for Gyeongseong believing and being assured that God who keeps
me secure will keep you, my wife, and my children secure. I just moan
at the old age of you, father. When I saw you on January 4 for the
first time in three years, I was saddened by how old you had become.
I wondered whether it was my fault or the fault of the passing time. I
realized that it was my fault and became penitent. I realized that you
have become all but dried up in your body trying to teach and raise me
right and I am a disobedient son for being in prison. Please forgive me
for being unworthy as your son and grace me with your love that is as
wide as an ocean. I earnestly beseech you to give your concerns to the
Lord and find peace in him. I can never stop praying like this to God.
My prayer is as follows:

Dear God, though my father's eyes have dimmed in seeing the world
of wickedness, I ask you to brighten his eyesight to see the glory of
heaven. Though his hearing in hearing the sound of men has weakened,
make his hearing better in listening to the voice of the Lord. Though
his steps have become slow, let his steps be quickened in walking the

paradise of Eden. In this way, let him commune with you, thereby living a life of spiritual fellowship, rather than communing with men. Let him start living the life of heaven here on earth.

This is how I ask of the Lord each day. I beseech you to find satisfaction in living spiritually for the rest of your life. Didn't the great sage, Confucius, become a person of transcendence at the age of seventy? I prostrate before you and ask.

Letter Dated July 27, 1945

Dear Dong-In (at Beomiljeong, Busan)

Do not let your mind be affected though there is scarcity of food and clothing. It is better to have a right frame of mind than to eat well. It is more important to be clothed in right conduct than to be dressed in good clothes. Though one may be mistreated for not having money and one may suffer because there is no food, it is only fitting for a righteous man to be upright than befriending money or food. Therefore, everything depends on the perspective that one takes. Good and bad exist in the mind of a person. Do not bemoan the scarcity of possessions. Transcendence comes from extreme poverty. All evil and immorality are borne of the fullness of stomach and idleness. Repentance and an upright spirit are borne of the suffering of hunger, cold, and poverty.

Moreover, we are not the only ones that are experiencing the scarcity of things. This is the time of worldwide tribulations. Instead of falling into the pit of anguish, worry, and sorrow, seek the growth of life and the way of truth at this time. Since one cannot have wealth just by having the desire for it and the matters of life and death are not decided by the human will, just give all your cares to the Lord and be joyful always and live a life of gratitude in all things as you discern the ways of the Lord from walking peacefully with him. This is the way of a Christian. Who cannot be joyful when things are going well? To live a Christian life is to be grateful and joyful in the midst of trials and tribulations. Do not try to flee from suffering. Instead, overcome by persevering. Those who try to flee from the suffering would grow all the more worrisome. Those that persevere would be full of joy in discovering the truth. There's a paradise in the heart that perseveres. One who perseveres is stronger than a warrior that overcame all his enemies.

A Young Evangelist

Chapter 5

"Hello, please come on in, Deacon Seo."

"How are you, Mrs.?"

"Have you come alone? Is Young-Hae not coming?"

"No. He told me to go ahead because he will be late."

The greeting was between Mrs. Son, the wife of Rev. Son, and Deacon Seo. Dong-In and Dong-Sin also greeted him as they came in. Deacon Seo had come to the house to attend the Sunday worship service.

Deacon Seo willingly gave up his thriving furniture retail business because he did not want to comply with Shinto worship. After that, he began to regularly go up to the mountain to pray. He was a man of great faith and an apostle of tears.

Ever since Mrs. Son had come to Busan along with Dong-In and Dong-Sin, he did not want to go to conventional churches because he felt like the Holy Spirit had left them a long time ago. However, since he could not miss worshipping on Sundays, he would, from time to time, visit this house where a few believers would gather to worship. After a short silent prayer, he began speaking again.

"Has there been any correspondence from Rev. Son?"

"Yes, as a matter of fact, a letter arrived the day before yesterday."

"Is he all right?"

"Yes," said Mrs. Son as she pulled out a postcard stamped with a seal of approval from in between the pages of a Bible. Deacon Seo received the postcard from Mrs. Son, and began to read the message:

Though the good season of flowering blossoms is fair, tender and good to the eye, the fatigue of the springtime–the kind of fatigue that even makes a cat lethargic enough to stop chasing after a mouse that is fooling around right in front of its view–is unbearable. For me to hear that you have to go up the mountain to draw water is painful, since I know how much you suffer from the springtime fatigue. I am in shock to hear the news of the death of Brother Ju, who particularly loved me. It is such earth-shattering and leg-shaking news. Please send my condolences to his old parents and wife on my behalf. However, do you know what the illness was and where he died? Was it at his house? Or was it at the big house (prison)? Please find out and let me know. I received all the things that you have sent me, except the socks. Socks are not allowed here. You can use the remaining soaps at home. This is sufficient for me. Does my father wear the shoes that my brother, Mun-Jun had gotten for him? Please look after him. Caring for one's parents should not be done based on the calculation of the blessing that one would receive from doing so. Caring for one's parents should be done out of the sense of responsibility that it is only right for the children to take care of their elderly parents and out of duty by asking, "Who will respect and care for them, if I don't?" I am so sorry to hear that you suffer from a cold all the time because of the inadequacy of the house. If you are not feeling well, please send me your reply through Dong-In.

After he had finished reading the message, Deacon Seo turned to Mrs. Son and asked her, "Who is Brother Ju?"

Mrs. Son teased him saying, "Don't you already know?"

"Well, no, I don't," answered Deacon Seo again. "Well, is it a cousin of Rev. Son?"

"Ha ha, we are all cousins before God our Father."

"Oh, is it Rev. Ju Gi-Cheol?"

"Yes, ha, ha..."

"Ha, ha, ha..." laughed Deacon Seo as he asked for the postcard again. Dong-In and Dong-Sin, who were standing outside, came in upon hearing the laughter. They did not know what was going on.

Deacon Seo read the words of the postcard again in a clear and loud voice, "I am in shock to hear the news of the death of Brother Ju, who particularly loved me. It is such earth-shattering and leg-shaking news. Please send my condolences to his old parents and wife on my behalf. However, do you know what the illness was and where he died? Was it at his house? Or was it at the big house (prison)? Please find out and let me know."

With tears in his eyes, Deacon Seo said, "Rev. Son, who is at the big house (prison), does not know that Rev. Ju also died at the big house." Mrs. Son cried also. She knew that it was very much possible for her husband to meet the same fate in the future as Rev. Ju.

"How do you think that he found out it?"

"Well..." wondered Mrs. Son.

This is how Rev. Son was able to find out about Rev. Ju's death. When the problem of Shinto worship had first surfaced, the trio of Rev. Ju Gi-Cheol, Rev. Han Sang-Dong, and Rev. Son Yang-Won had prayed together and decided to carry on the protest against it in both the northern and southern regions of Korea. However, they had all been taken into the police custody a year ago and had lost contact with each other. Then, he received a letter from Elder Son, his father.

"(Omitted)... Your uncle, Choi Gwon-Neung, went back home on April 19 and your brother, Ju Gi, also went back home on April 20 at 9 p.m. He leaves his old mother who is 82 years old and four children that are minors..."

Choi Gwon-Neung refers to Rev. Choi Bong-Seok, and Ju Gi refers to Rev. Ju Gi-Cheol. The phrase "went back home" means that they were martyred. As soon as Rev. Son heard of the news, he wrote the letter they had just finished reading above.

The sound of intermittent coughing that could be heard from the other room was the sound of Elder Son, who did not fail to pray for his son in prison as well as the faith of the family by tying a rope on the ceiling. It was he that notified Rev. Son of the news of Rev. Ju's death by mail.

In that moment, someone called out, "Dong-In." It was Young-Hae. He said, "To walk here is like going on a hike."

"Well, don't you like it better than exercising?" replied Dong-In. As soon as Ju Young-Hae entered, Deacon Seo quietly held up the letter and said, "Rev. Son heard about the death of your father and sent this letter." As Deacon Seo read the letter line by line, tears flowed down from Young-Hae's eyes. The images of his deceased father, his grandmother who was in her eighties, and his mother who used to love him like her own child, and himself who had been lodging at the house of the factory manager, passed by in his mind like a revolving lantern.

Ju Young-Hae had been living from day to day while working with Dong-In and Dong-Sin at the factory. When he first received the news of his father's death, he spent the whole night crying and grieving. Now that he was reading the letter, the grief came over him again and made him cry.

Dong-In and Dong-Sin who were standing next to him cried also. Dong-Hee and Dong-Su were sitting with a blank look in their faces.

This Sunday, Bokdong-yi is waiting for the young evangelist, gathered in this deep part of the woods here at Beomneth-gol along with fifteen others, who were present at last Sunday's worship. It has been already ten Sundays and counting since they started meeting for Sunday worship. Now, the weekly gathering feels like a real church and Sunday school. After Sunday breakfast, the young evangelist attends the worship service with the adults at his house. Then after lunch, he runs to this part of the woods at Beomneth-gol. He is none other than the young Son Dong-Sin. Ever since he was young, he has asked his grandmother, who used to go up to the mountain to pray, to take him along with her. He even tried to tie a string between his shirt and the shirt of his grandmother before going to sleep so that he could go with her. When he was a little grown and in public elementary school, he refused to pay respect to the emperor and observe Shinto worship despite numerous appeals from his principal. Ultimately, he was expelled from the school along with his brother, Dong-In. He is still the same in his faith. Whenever he thinks about the failure of the Korean church in giving into Shinto worship, he worries if his father who is in prison, his family who has been struggling, and he as well would eventually forsake their faith. This apprehension exists because it seems to him that the Holy Spirit has left the church.

His desire in wanting more than a house church and carrying out the work of evangelism led him to the woods of Beomneth-gol. Mostly the congregants are the children, who work at a factory nearby. Without even telling his family, he had started this gathering.

"Did you memorize all the Bible verses that I taught you last Sunday?" asks Bokdong-yi, to Su-Nam.

"Yes, I memorized them, though not so fluently," answers Su-Nam.

"Me, too. I almost memorized it all," [answers Bokdong-yi.] Then, he begins reciting, "Blessed are the poor in spirit for theirs is the kingdom of heaven..." Meanwhile, Dong-Sin reaches the top of the mountain where the children are gathered.

"Let's pray together," says Dong-Sin as he starts the worship service. He prays as follows: Dear our Father in heaven! We thank you for your grace in allowing us the holy Sabbath so that we can worship you. You have placed us in this evil and hostile world so that we could glorify you. But instead, we value ourselves more than you and live apart from you. Have mercy on us and give us the freedom of faith. Also, give us your grace so that we can overcome the world just as our Lord overcame the world. In the name of Jesus, we pray.

It is a prayer that is not fitting for a child. In fact, anyone who understands the circumstances of the time cannot help but recognize that this is much more than just a prayer.

"Let's read Matthew chapter 5 verses 13 through 16," says Dong-Sin as he begins reciting the passage from his memory.

"You are the salt of the earth; but if salt has lost its taste, how can its saltiness be restored? It is no longer good for anything, but is thrown out and trampled under foot. You are the light of the world. A city built on a hill cannot be hid. No one after lighting a lamp puts it under the bushel basket, but on the lamp stand, and it gives light to all in the house. In the same way, let your light shine before others, so that they may see your good works and give glory to your Father in heaven."

Everyone is not surprised by the proficiency with which Dong-Sin recites the passage because they already know that Dong-Sin has memorized the whole Bible. Gil-Su, who has come out to the gathering for the first time, is alone in amazement.

As he recites the passage, Dong-Sin has a flashback to a moment when Ms. Hwang asked him about two weeks ago, "Where do you go every Sunday afternoon?" Since he could not avoid answering the question, Dong-Sin confessed, "I go to the woods of Beomneth-gol to teach the Bible to the children that gather there." Ms. Hwang doubtfully asked, "What can a person like you teach?" Dong-Sin replied, "Well, I can make them recite the Bible that I have memorized." Ms. Hwang said, "Recite the Bible you have memorized?" "Yes, you are absolutely right," interjected Deacon Seo, sitting next to him.

When Dong-Sin says, "Why don't we review what we memorized last Sunday before putting today's Scripture to memory?" everyone starts reciting in unison:

"Blessed are the poor in spirit, for theirs is the kingdom of heaven.

Blessed are those who mourn, for they will be comforted. Blessed are the meek, for they will inherit the earth. Blessed are those who hunger and thirst for righteousness, for they will be filled. Blessed are the merciful, for they will receive mercy. Blessed are the pure in heart, for they will see God. Blessed are the peacemakers, for they will be called children of God. Blessed are those who are persecuted for righteousness' sake, for theirs is the kingdom of heaven. Blessed are you when people revile you and persecute you and utter all kinds of evil against you falsely on my account. Rejoice and be glad, for your reward is great in heaven, for in the same way they persecuted the prophets who were before you."

While they are reciting the passage, the image of his father, Rev. Son, who is in prison, comes to his mind along with the martyrs, Rev. Choi Gwon-Neung and Rev. Ju Gi-Cheol. He understands that the part which says, "Blessed are those who are persecuted for righteousness' sake, for theirs is the kingdom of heaven. Blessed are you when people revile you and persecute you and utter all kinds of evil against you falsely on my account. Rejoice and be glad, for your reward is great in heaven, for in the same way they persecuted the prophets who were before you," to be referring relevantly to the church and its warriors of faith. After having the children recite the passage several times, Dong-Sin tells them to memorize a new passage.

The worship service continues without a sermon. Now, it is time for the offering and everyone gives what they can.

"How shall we use the offering that has been collected?" asks Dong-Sin after the service is over.

"Let us give it to the same beggar to whom we gave money to last Sunday," suggests Bokdong-yi.

Su-Nam opposes the idea by saying, "Let's not give it to just one person."

Another person suggests, "If we give the money to several people, they may not know the reason why we do this. I think that it will be best to give it to one person who is in a dire strait as a way of carrying out evangelism."

Su-Nam says, "Yes, there is that need, too. But since it is an offering given to glorify God who watches us in the secret, let's not deliberate too long. Let's us give it to the first person that we meet who is in need." People agreed that Su-Nam's suggestion makes sense, too.

All these suggestions made sense to Dong-Sin and he could not side with any one person. So, Dong-Sin suggests, "Let's do as the majority says."

"We agree," says everyone.

Then, they vote by raising their hands. Six people vote with Bokdong-yi, eight people vote with Su-Nam, and Gil-Su, who has come out to the gathering for the first time, abstains.

Bokdong-yi laughs and says, "Well, I lost! Ha, ha, ha."

This can be a foreshadowing of democracy to come. Or this can be more than democracy. It can be the practice of God-as-the-Lord faith. Anyhow, it has already become dark. From faraway, smoke rising up from the chimneys of the houses in the town below can be seen. People must be making dinner.

The Second Diaspora
Chapter 6

It was towards the end of January, 1944. Dong-In, who was riding a train on the Gyeongbu(Seoul-Busan) Railroad line, was looking outside the window. As he watched the scenery of mountains and fields that revolved like a slow moving whirlwind, he could not erase from his mind the image of his father with whom he had visited at Cheongju Penitentiary, pale and dressed in tattered red clothes—not even for one moment. Dong-In thought,

"Father, yes, that's the dad I know. He has served a sentence of three years, moving from the Yeosu Police Station to Gwangju Prison. Since he had served his sentence of three years, he could have been released. But he has been prophesying that Japan would ultimately fall if it maintains the same course of action. Also, he has been carrying out the work of evangelism and calling for the repentance of people without bending his faith a little bit. Now, the authorities have decided that they could not release him. It has been more than a year since he was moved to the Cheongju Penitentiary. However, when I saw him yesterday, I could not find even a small measure of bitterness in him. Instead, with his words, he encouraged me regarding my faith as well as that of the whole family. His words... 'If you don't see me again in this life, let us meet each other before the throne of God.'"

In his mind, his father in prison he had just seen seemed much holier than the father he remembered at Aeyangwon, church, and home.

"Father! But what about me? What about me? Me?" thought Dong-In as he cried.

He could not stop crying, thinking, "My sins of yesterday...no, the temptations I'd gone through... More than that, how much would what I did bother my father who is very much holy? How sad would God the Father be? Did I crucify Jesus again?"

He bemoaned, thinking, "I was told to do it and I did it because I wanted to see my father. But everything was a lie of the devil... Oh, no."

Dong-In felt as if Hell was looking squarely at him and the sound of the train was the sound of a bat beating him. There were perfectly good reasons for feeling like this.

Having cleared his schedule of everything, Dong-In came to Cheongju wanting to meet his father, one he had not seen for more than five years. The only contact between him and his father had been through written correspondence. Now that he was here, his heart was palpitating with excitement. The person in charge of the prison was trying to be kind to Dong-In. He asked,

"Would you agree to do Shinto worship?"

"I can't," said Dong-In.

"Ha, ha, ha, ha," laughed the person for a long time. Then, he went on to give a long speech:

"Your father cannot do agree to Shinto worship because he is stubborn and old-fashioned. However, a young person like you—a young man who will one day become a great person—should not be uninformed. Think about it for a moment. Your father alone objected to Shinto worship. On the outside, your father still seems to be opposing it. But the fact is, he has been slowly changing on the inside. I cannot say for how long. But within six months, he will become enlightened. I can see that from the reflections the people have been writing in our prison. For example, people praise with all kinds of words the tenacity with which the empire's army has been fighting difficult battles. For people to follow all the policies of the empire of Japan is to support the army. They write that the institutions such as Shinto shrine and the pledge to the emperor are not inherently religious but are civic ceremonies designed to promote nationalism, courage, and patience. How is it that you don't see it that way, even when you are out there? We know this because all these policies have been shaped and enforced by the cultural department of the government and not by the religious department of the Ministry of Home Affairs. Don't you see Mr. Moderator of the General Assembly, Mr. Moderator of the Presbytery and Reverend so-and-so all carrying on their work for the church and the presbytery while observing Shinto worship and the pledge to the emperor? I personally would like to think that the reason that you are defiant is because your father has taught you wrong, or maybe because you have a strong sense of nationalism within you. Your defiance is due to the misguided attitude that is preventing you from wanting to cooperate with Japan. However, at this juncture in time, I cannot allow anyone to carry out the work of nationalist movement under the guise of religion. It is the time to crack down on anyone, regardless of gender and age, who disobeys. Therefore, it is best not to think so superficially but think of the circumstances of the day. That's why I ask you to do this *only once* as a token of unity and determination in making a collective breakthrough in this time of national emergency. Do not think so deeply about the meaning of it. Just try it once. And if you don't like it, you don't have to do it again. Again, I encourage you to do it out of the sense of cooperation as a citizen of the empire."

After this long sermon, the man lit a cigarette, and said, "And I feel ashamed for not being able to quit smoking. I applaud the position of Christians regarding smoking. It is good to refrain from smoking since it is bad for the body. However, there is nothing in the Bible that prohibits smoking, is there?" asked the person.

"No, there is none."

"Well, I'm sure they prohibit it anyway because it is not good for their health. In fact, I used to smoke two packs of cigarettes a day not too long ago. But now, I go through one pack of cigarette in two days. Though I do not believe in Jesus, I should quit smoking, just like Christians," said the person as he put out the cigarettes. And he looked around to find something.

"Well, will you go and try it?" asked the person.

"..." Dong-In remained silent.

"Huh, did you not understand what I said? You can try it just once and stop if you do not like it. Again, do it as a token of unity and determination in making a collective breakthrough in this time of national emergency," explained the person.

Lastly, he said, "If you cannot believe what I say, then I cannot allow you to see your father." This statement hit Dong-In like a thunderbolt out of nowhere. His desire to see his father made him to go to the shrine and made a half-hearted gesture of bow. When he did that, instead of a rebuke, he heard a compliment, "Since I know where you stand, I will allow you to meet your father."

Dong-In felt like he was successful in deceiving the guy. But he was taken back to the office. The person wrote something on a piece of paper and said to Dong-In, "You should copy what is written."

"Why are you asking me to do this?" asked Dong-In.

"It is really nothing. I just want to keep it as a reminder for the future. Just in case when your father gets released from the prison having recognized the authority of the Japanese nation, I want to show it to him and say, 'Your son has already done this ahead of you.'"

Dong-In hesitated for a long time before telling himself, "Just do it half-heartedly." And he copied the words, "Dear father, just as the chief says, I have realized that Shinto worship is indeed a civic ceremony. I felt it was appropriate to do it as a sign of my cooperation in this time of national emergency."

This was how Dong-In got to see his father. Upon reading the letter that his father gave him, he felt as if his whole face and body was on fire. His legs were trembling, too.

"Woe is I. Why did I play that wretched game in order to see my father? Why did I cheat God? Why did I cheat that guy? Oh, my! How did I become prey to the trap of the devil? Oh, no. Oh, no..."

He could not help but bow his head and cry because he felt unworthy to see his grandfather, father, and mother again. Moreover, he felt unworthy to see God whenever it might be that he would go to heaven. He felt unworthy to meet Jesus. At this thought, he felt dizzy as if he was falling downward tens and hundreds of miles from a cliff.

The old Japanese man sitting next to him asked, "Hey, are you sick? Should I give you some medicine? Or has something wretched happened to you?" Dong-In did not say anything in response to the probing questions because he did not have any courage to say anything. When the old man stopped questioning him, having felt slighted by Dong-In's lack of response, someone called out, "What is your destination?"

It was not such a friendly voice. When he turned around, he found a transit police officer. He looked Japanese.

The residual anger from having been tricked by the chief of the publicity department almost compelled him to get into a shouting match with the transit police officer. Dong-In somehow managed to stay unresponsive except continuing to cry.

"Why are you crying," the harsh voice asked again. Regarding the silent defiance, the Japanese old man blurted out complainingly in Japanese, "Untomo suntomo iwandesuyo (He does not say anything.)" It was not clear whether he wanted to help Dong-In's case or not.

"Hey, what is your destination?" asked the police officer as he demanded to see the train ticket. "Let me see your ticket."

Because he did not pull the ticket out of his pocket, Dong-In mustered all his strength to say, "I am going to Busan."

"Huh? Where? I cannot hear you. Say it clearly. Show me your ticket," replied the police officer as he asked for the ticket again.

"I am going to Busan," said Dong-In as he snapped out of it.

"What business do you have there?" asked the police officer.

"I am going home," said Dong-In after a long pause.

"Where have you been?" asked the officer.

"I am on my way home from Cheongju," said Dong-In.

"For what did you visit Cheongju?" The officer continued his non-stop questioning.

"I went to visit my father," answered Dong-In as he teared up again.

"Why are you crying? So, what does your father do?" asked the officer.

Dong-In said to himself in his mind, "Is this a question that I should answer truthfully or deceivingly?" Then a rebuking voice in his head said, "Do you want to fall prey to that temptation again?" and made him immediately come to his senses.

So, Dong-In said out loud, "He is at Cheongju Penitentiary." It was the first step in repenting over his sin of trying to pretending to have observed Shinto worship in front of the chief of the publicity department. No, he was repenting ultimately the sin of deceiving himself and God.

"I see. That's why you were crying. So, your father is at a really nice place!" sneered the officer. The old Japanese man and the other passengers began looking at each other in a unified agreement over the revelation.

"Come and follow me," said the officer. He led Dong-In to the engineer's room to continue the conversation.

"What kind of work do you do?"

"I am a worker at a factory in Bumiljeong, Busan. We make cans."

"Why is your father imprisoned at the penitentiary? If he has engaged in a useless ideological struggle, he should be shipped out to Russia," said the officer. The statement was a half-question and a half-admonition.

"No, my father is not a communist. He is a pastor," said Dong-In.

The officer was surprised to hear the word 'pastor.' Then he changed his expression and said, "Why, isn't there a communist among pastors?"

Dong-In explained, "It was because of his refusal to observe Shinto worship." In answering, Dong-In felt refreshed inside. Unexpectedly, it was the detective who seemed to be surprised by the retort.

"I see. There are pastors that still oppose Shinto worship?" said the officer. He then went on to say, "What a great father you have. Your father is as useful as a much needed medicine."

Dong-In felt it was now appropriate to say, "That's definitely a sin. Clearly, that is a sin. My father..."

The officer interrupted Dong-In in the middle of the sentence and interjected, "That's right. It is a sin to not acknowledge one's devotion to the nation."

"No, observing Shinto worship is a sin before God," clearly answered Dong-In.

"What? Say it again!" shouted the officer.

"Shinto worship is definitely a religious act and as such is an abomination before God. It does not matter that people claim it to be a civic ceremony..." Dong-In sounded a little agitated. And he broke out in tears again.

"What are you, at a funeral home? Why are you crying again? I should look into your belongings," said the officer as he started doing a body search. He seemed to show a condescending attitude toward him. He probably thought, "Nanda gono aonisaiga (Immature son of a gun!)." Then the officer found the letter that Dong-In had on him. The message of the letter that his father gave him during the visitation was as follows:

> Do not ever observe the pledge to the emperor and Shinto worship, for they are sins before God and the violation of the very first and the second

commandments. *Do* observe the Sabbath on Sundays. Participate in house prayer meetings and early-dawn prayer meetings. Do your best to read the Bible. Give tithes. Care for and obey your grandfather.

After reading the letter, the officer sneered, "You have a good father." He went on to say, "You can only survive if you observe the pledges to the nation." After saying a few things in admonition, writing down his name and address and confiscating the letter, the officer dismissed Dong-In and told him to go back to his seat.

Dong-In came back to his seat, feeling as if he was robbed of a precious treasure. However, he felt a tinge of satisfaction.

The train was moving steadily. He felt like he could now control his tears.

"Will you agree to be drafted?"

"Yes, it is the citizen's duty to do so."

"If you go, you will have to observe Shinto worship. Will you still go?" said the detective as he looked straight into Dong-In's eyes. This was the North Busan Police Station. Some time after he had come back from Cheongju, Dong-In was called in for questioning. His glance caught the sight of a familiar piece of paper on the desk of the chief of the intelligence unit. As he took a closer look at the paper, Dong-In realized that it was his father's letter that was confiscated on the train back home.

"That, I cannot do," answered Dong-In.

"Why not?" said the detective. His voice was coarse.

"I cannot do it because it violates God's commandment," Dong-In answered.

"Stop talking nonsense. All the citizens of the empire are mandated to do it. Aren't you a citizen of the Japanese empire?" rebutted the detective.

"Even though I am a Japanese citizen, I cannot go against the command of God," replied Dong-In.

While the questioning was going on, the chief signaled for the detective to come out. The detective went out and came back in a little later. "Think about it a little more. The affairs of the world are not so simple..." said the detective. After explaining to and giving him a long admonition, the detective dismissed him to go back home until he was called back.

When the subpoena came, the whole family had become worried as if something so grave has happened and sent Dong-In to the Busan Police Station as they earnestly fasted and prayed for him. The reason why Dong-In was released quicker than expected was because the chief of the intelligence unit thought that once conscripted, he would have no choice but to observe Shinto worship. The chief's crafty strategy was to get Dong-In by the means of conscription. Regardless of the reason, the whole family rejoiced in Dong-In's return on that day just like the early believers had rejoiced in the safe return of Peter from prison.

The prayer of the family for Dong-In was, "God, if Dong-In gets conscripted, he would surely be subjected to the sin of idol worship. Please help him to avoid this test, even if it meant he would contract leprosy." The family prayed like this because Dong-In had received the order for a physical as part of the conscription process. Whether this was a blessing or curse could not be clarified, but he did pass the physical with flying colors.

The scenery of the city of Busan with its many houses and the picture of several boats floating on the sea just beyond it was just the same as what the brothers enjoyed on their way to the factory in the morning and on their way back home in the evening. Now, however, since passing the physical, it looked all different for some reason.

Some might consider passing all the requirements as something to boast about. However, for Dong-In, it was a kind of death sentence.

But the decision had already been made and he could not avoid it now. He wished that he had a serious illness. But something like that does not happen just because a person wishes for it. He thought about killing himself. But that was a sin. "How about running away?" he thought. But that might mean freedom for Dong-In but suffering for the family. The police would surely harass his mother and family in order to discover his whereabouts. "What shall I do? What shall I do?" he pondered. Moreover, this war was immoral to start with. It was a war of imperialism. How could he fight against the forces of allies, which were fighting for a just cause? Now that he had passed the requirements, wasn't he as good as a Japanese soldier? Also, how could he survive without observing Shinto worship? He could not again compromise his faith. These spontaneous thoughts bothered Dong-In.

It was July of 1945. The quietness of Busan was severed by the sounds of bombs falling. The urgency of the time would surely put the order of conscription into effect any day now.

A day passed. Another day passed. Each day passing seemed like a year. All the households that had received the orders for conscription were in mourning. Having informed of his family, Dong-In put everything aside and went into the deep woods of Namhae to fast and pray. It was his way of trying to receive a sign from God.

Upon returning from praying, Dong-In said, "Mother...," but he could not continue.

"What is it?" asked his mother as she washed the nose of Dong-Su. Dong-Sin looked up to his brother. Since Dong-In was speechless after calling her, she asked again, "What is it? How come you are so quiet after coming back from your prayers?"

While praying to God for three days, Dong-In in fact had received a sign from God, but the hesitation came from his inability to bring it up to his mother and siblings and not from needing more time to think about it. On the night after coming back from praying to God, Dong-In finally decided to talk about it, after the night prayer meeting had ended. But he still did not know how to continue once he had called for his mother's attention. He just hung his head.

"You look like you have something to say. Why aren't you speaking? Is it something that you cannot tell your own mother?" asked his mother.

"No, it is not something that I cannot tell you. It's just that it is difficult to follow through with it. That's why," said Dong-In.

"Whether it is something difficult or easy to say, why aren't you able to tell me about it? Don't you need to tell me because it is something difficult to say?" asked his mother.

"The answer that I got from my prayers is that, the family…" said Dong-In as he burst into tears immediately upon completing these words.

"I see what you are trying to say. You wanted to say that it is best to disperse the family!" said the mother as she displayed a calm demeanor.

"Yes," said Dong-In. After a pause, he continued, "It would be different, if I had never given into the pressure…"

As Dong-In sobbed louder, Dong-Sin and Dong-Hee also began to cry. Soon, Dong-Jang and Dong-Su, who had not a clue as to why their siblings were crying, had joined them. Their mother had her gaze fixed on the flickering light of the gasoline lamp. A teardrop fell from her eyes and onto the light of the lamp.

Upon being asked to vacate the parsonage in Yeosu, their mother had moved the family to Gwangju with the hope of looking after the incarcerated Rev. Son. Since the family could not stay in Gwangju any longer due to her refusal to keep a kamidana (a Japanese mini-shrine) in their house, they had to move down to Busan leaving their imprisoned father behind. Now due to the inevitable conscription and the unavoidable Shinto worship, the family was on the verge of being dispersed. Could this be possible? Where would they go upon getting dispersed? The time had become too dangerous. Every day, there was a siren warning of an impending bombing. That was why Dong-In had been crying upon bringing up the topic. It was fitting to describe the situation as a "problem-after-problem."

At this moment, someone called out, "Hey, Dong-In, a light is coming from your house." It was Mr. Choi, who was in charge of the district, giving him a warning.

"What?" Dong-In looked around, and saw that the curtain was keeping the door ajar. Every day, this exercise of keeping the lights out had continued.

After making sure the curtain was properly in place, their mother began to speak, "Dong-Sin and Dong-Hee, listen. I am sure that you heard what Dong-In said too. However, instead of deciding what to do on my own, I want you to think about what Dong-In said since both of you are of maturity."

Dong-Jang, who was sitting right next to the mother, suddenly broke out in singing, "My Jesus, as Thou Wilt..." He was singing the hymn which was the favorite of the family in a rambling manner. From time to time, they used to sing the hymn after praying in tears during the prayer meetings.

"Well, since our oldest brother would have to observe Shinto worship once he gets conscripted, I do not think it is in God's will," said the siblings. Instead of discussing the actual issue of getting dispersed, they were worried about the difficulty of evading Shinto worship. Dong-Hee remained silent.

"Then, let's separate," concluded Mrs. Son. She thought, "I have already given up my husband to the Lord. I have left Gwangju, too. We cannot sin in order to carry on this life of the flesh. The one who sins is not my child. Didn't I tell my husband at Yeosu Station that he would not be my husband if he gives in to Shinto worship? It is time for me to put into action what I always taught my children! God will surely protect us."

At that very second, "I am dying, Dong-Hee" said Ms. Hwang as she entered the house. She had apparently come in response to the letter that said, "Dong-In had passed the requirements for conscription." "God must be asking me to pray more," she said.

"What... how did you? Why did you *come* to Busan when it is being bombed all the time? We live here but you don't, you know," asked Mrs. Son with a mixed reaction of delight and curiosity.

"They tried to stop me from coming here at one point, and I thought I was just going to die. Anyhow, Dong-In, I read your letter. Did you come back from praying?" said Ms. Hwang without answering Mrs. Son's question.

"Why did you come? In the midst of all this bombing?" asked Mrs. Son again.

"It is because I did not want to die alone. I had wanted to come ever since I got the letter from Dong-In. When I asked around yesterday, I was told that Busan was being bombed. I felt so anxious inside to be apart from you. I thought that I wanted to be with you all even if it meant that I would die. I left early this morning and I have just arrived..." said Ms. Hwang.

The family was in tears upon hearing these words.

Mrs. Son thought, "Let us die together."

Others try to flee from Busan in the name of evacuation or seeking refuge. But Ms. Hwang had come to Busan in the midst of all this bombing!

In the past, whenever Ms. Hwang came, Dong-Jang would come over to her and sit on her lap. But this time, Dong-Jang did not act as he usually did. So, Ms. Hwang, sensing that something might be wrong, asked, "What's wrong?"

No one said anything in response.

Finally Mrs. Son opened her mouth and said, "It's good that you came, Ms. Hwang. We were just discussing what to do now that Dong-In has passed all the requirements for conscription. Dong-In came back after praying in Namhae and reported to us that he has received God's calling. God told him to disperse the family. That's what we were talking about."

"What?" said Ms. Hwang. Now she could see why the mood of the family was so heavy. However, it was something very much unexpected for her to hear.

"To disperse the family...," thought Ms. Hwang. She had been there for the family always. She had tried her best to help this family when they moved out of Aeyangwon, then to Gwangju, and then to Busan. She had gone around the woods of Okjong-myeon Bukbang-ri and Aeyangwon in Yeosu in search of donations of food in the secret and brought them to the family. She had done her best to help this family which fell on hard times whenever possible. However, she could now not help but be shocked to hear that they were thinking about being dispersed. She was sure that the grownups, including Dong-In and Dong-Sin, would find work somewhere and support themselves somehow. But three younger children would most definitely become beggars. So she asked, "Mrs. Son, so have you make the decision to disperse?"

"Yes," replied Mrs. Son.

"How are you going to do it?" asked Ms. Hwang.

"Well, we haven't talked about that yet," answered Mrs. Son.

Ms. Hwang said, "Oh, I thought you have already come up with something..."

After a long discussion, the decision was reached to first send Dong-Hee and Dong-Jang to an orphanage in Gupo. Dong-In, Mrs. Son, and Dong-Su, the infant, would go into the woods of Namhae. But Dong-Sin did not have anywhere to go. He was too old to go to an orphanage. He could not follow his mother because the group would be too big in number.

"Me? Should I stay here and continue to work at the factory?" asked Dong-Sin.

"Well, that's an idea, but I do not want to leave you here alone. You should go somewhere else..." replied Mrs. Son.

After thinking again, Dong-Sin said, "What if I go to Bukbang-ri? Just like my older brother?" It sounded like a spontaneous outburst. Bukbang-ri was where Dong-In had spent a month in the past.

"Bukbang-ri?" wondered Ms. Hwang. It was because only lepers lived in that place. But she changed her mind and said, "Well, if you get there, at least you can hide well from the authorities..."

Though this was a passing comment, since there was no viable alternative, it was decided that Dong-Sin would go to Bukbang-ri. All the family members made this final decision together in a solemn state of mind.

A long silence persisted. Is that sound of people crying, "Light can be seen from a far away," the sound of *Keibodanin*?

They left the residence papers alone but ripped the rice ration tickets. Could it be a sign of repentance after having committed a sin?

Repentance

Tears of repentance are sweet raindrops of the Holy Spirit.
The sigh of contrition is the spring wind of the Holy Spirit.
The prayer of the born again is the work of the Holy Spirit.

Repent, for the kingdom of heaven is near.
These were the first words of John the Baptist in the wilderness.
This was the first impassioned sermon by the born-again Peter.

Faith without repentance is of an abominable heart.
Hope that hasn't repented is the Tower of Babel that will shortly fall.
Love that cannot repent is self-deceiving hypocrisy.

Heaven without repentance is hell disguised as a paradise.

Packs of shepherds that haven't repented are wolves disguised as sheep.

Flocks of sheep that cannot repent are Roman soldiers disguised as the church.

Seminaries without repentance are the factories of heretical doctrines.

Doctors in theology that haven't repented are the secret agents of the devil's world.

Organizational management that cannot repent is the work of the devil.

Repent, oh the church of Korea, the kingdom of heaven is near.

John the Baptist was a man of the old, and

It has been long since the death of the apostle Peter.

Jesus Christ is alive even now.

You can surely hear his voice.

How come you have closed your eyes, covered your ears, and opened your mouth?

It is only faith, faith, faith, and faith.

Well, faith without repentance is of an abominable heart.

It is only hope, hope, hope, and hope.

Well, hope that hasn't repented is the Tower of Babel that will shortly fall.

It is only love, love, love, and love.

Well, love that cannot repent is self-deceiving hypocrisy.

Repent, oh the leaders of the Church of Korea, the kingdom of heaven is near.

Give up the games of the devil.

Wake up from the drugs of the devil.

Fix the training schools.

Prevent atheism.

Get rid of the secret agents.

Burn the heretical doctrines.

Bring down the mask of the church.

Take off the mask of sheep.

Break the mask of hell.

Open your spiritual eyes and holy ears.

Be mute, if anything, as you
Cry your tears,
Let out your sighs,
And lift up your prayers.

If you cannot still understand,
Go to the back room.
Go to Arabia.
Go deep into the woods.

Repent, the kingdom of heaven is near.
The Holy Spirit of the Lord cannot be deceived.

Dong-Sin and Ms. Hwang got off the train at Jinju Station. Now they had to walk all the way to the woods of Okjong-myeon, Bukbang-ri, Hadong-gun, which was about forty *li* in distance from the station. Not only was there no easy way to travel, but to go far into the woods to find the only house where lepers lived was a difficult proposition in and of itself. The sun had already set and the trees in the mountain that were visible all around were fast becoming one big blur. They had to fight off the desire to take a break every time they climbed over a hill and persevered as they kept on walking. Dong-Sin was sure that he would receive a warm reception once he got there. But the fearful thought of how to greet them weighed heavily on his mind. After walking silently for some time on the path dimly lit by the clear stars in the night sky, they stopped and sat down on the side of the road. They thought that they had probably arrived about half-way to their destination, and decided to rest awhile. They had already eaten the lunch that they packed in the morning. They also ate dinner as they continued their journey on foot.

"Auntie, what time do you think it is now?" asked Dong-Sin. The children of the Son family called her "auntie."

"Maybe it is 9 p.m."

"One hour and a half, then we are there?"

"No, it will be less than that."

Ms. Hwang felt sorry for Dong-Sin, who was only fifteen years old. He was only a child. Not only had he left his father, mother, and siblings in order to protect the fidelity of his faith, but he was also on his way to go and live as the beggar of all beggars, the beggar who was not really a beggar, the leper who was not really a leper, a servant of lepers. She desperately wanted to comfort him in some way.

"Auntie, they do not know that I am coming, right?"

"Of course not. They must think that I came here to visit, but you? I don't think they would believe in their wildest dreams that you are here to stay."

"Then, do they all know me?"

"Of course they do. They all come from Aeyangwon. Why wouldn't they know you? And I am sure that you would recognize them when you meet them," said Ms. Hwang as she went through the names of the lepers. Dong-Sin recognized a few names, but others were a mystery to him. Anyhow, he thought that he must meet them. Not only meeting them, but he also needed to make sure that he should live with them here. When he first discussed the possibility of coming to this place with his mother, Ms. Hwang, and Dong-In, he thought he should now begin to serve in his father's place. But as that possibility was about to become a reality very soon, he felt a little apprehensive about the whole thing.

"Auntie, what will be my work once I get there?" asked Dong-Sin.

"There's nothing for you to do. Just making fire and chopping up some wood...," answered Ms. Hwang readily.

"Should I go out and beg for food with a bucket from time to time?" asked Dong-Sin again after a long pause.

"No, you don't have to do it and there's no need for you to do that," answered Ms. Hwang strongly.

"That's it?" asked Dong-Sin.

"That's it."

Dong-Sin felt relieved because he thought he could have time to pray and read the Bible. He thought to himself, "The best thing that I can do now is to pray to God for my father who is in prison, my mother, older brother, and Dong-Su who are in the woods of Namhae, and finally Dong-Hee and Dong-Jang who are in an orphanage in Gupo." From afar, he could hear the whistle of a train. He knew that it was the last train from Jinju to Masan, which leaves Jinju at 9 p.m. It must be 9:30 p.m. now, he thought.

As Ms. Hwang stood up saying, "Let's go now," Dong-Sin stood up as well.

The members of the household were waiting for Ms. Hwang who came to visit them from time to time. Thinking that she was not coming, they had already finished praying so that they could go to bed. Now that they were done with prayer and there was no rule forcing them to go to sleep right away, some were sleeping or lounging around liberally. Others were spending the night reading the Bible under the flickering lamp light. Though it is in the routine of the human life to work during the day and sleep during the night, there was no such routine for these people. Whatever they wanted to do, they did it. They would freely choose to read the Bible all night or pray through the night. There was neither restriction nor prohibition for them. For them, night was just as the same as day and vice versa.

"Are you all sleeping?"

The person who came out to greet the owner of the voice was Deacon Gil, who was the youngest of them and whose condition was the least severe. She also shared the room with Ms. Hwang whenever she came to visit.

"Who is this? Why, it's you!" said Deacon Gil as he greeted Dong-Sin.

Ms. Hwang said, "It is our Dong-Sin."

"Our Dong-Sin?" Everyone was shocked and got up, even those who were sleeping at the time.

"How come he is here?" The person who asked this question was Elder Sin.

"He came to visit you all," said Ms. Hwang as she entered the house. Dong-Sin followed her in and sat down. All of them had a moment of silent prayer. It was not that anyone told them to pray. Even a couple of them were praying in tears. Dong-Sin could not help but cry, too. It had already been five years since they had left Aeyangwon. It was good for them to see how Dong-Sin had grown, since it was when he was eight or nine years old that they last saw him. The resemblance between Dong-Sin and Rev. Son reminded them of their beloved pastor and made them feel like they were meeting their pastor in person. That was the reason for their tears.

They teared up whenever they thought about their pastor. For six years now, he had been suffering in prison due to his protest of Shinto worship and his resolution to keep faith. His family was scattered all over the place and going through a living hell in his absence. Even they were expelled from Aeyangwon because they did not want to observe the pledge to the emperor and Shinto worship in order to keep the purity of faith. They thought about what they had become, beggars. And still there was no recourse for all these things except praying to God. That was why they were crying.

After the prayer, Dong-Sin received a warm welcome. Though he was grateful to be welcomed in such a manner, he felt a sense of uneasiness as he canvassed their faces and hands, which looked far from normal.

"Is your mother doing well?"

"Yes!"

"Is Dong-In all right?"

"Yes."

"Yes..."

"You have grown so much. You look like a grown up now," exclaimed Elder Sin.

Ms. Hwang replied, "It must be tough for you."

"What you mean 'tough'? You are the one who is doing all the work," said Elder Shin as he comforted Ms. Hwang.

"How come he is here?" asked Deacon Kim again.

"He came because he heard that you are going through a difficult time. He came to support you in his father's place," briskly answered Ms. Hwang.

However, they could not take Ms. Hwang's answer for granted. It was because they clearly knew who they were. They were the disabled. Moreover, they were disabled and abandoned by others due to the illness of leprosy. They knew that Rev. Son was committed to caring for them for his unending loyalty to the Lord rather than for his personal devotion to them like a blood-related sibling or parent. However, Dong-Sin was still a child. They could not believe that he was there to care for them. Regardless, they understood that Dong-Sin came to them for a reason. While they were discussing the matter with one another, Dong-Sin began to fall asleep. He went to the room where Ms. Hwang usually stayed whenever she came to visit and went to sleep there along with Ms. Hwang.

When Ms. Hwang woke up, she did not realize what time it was. She was more startled to find that Dong-Sin was not in the room. Ms. Hwang got up in haste and went out of the room. It was still dark outside. Bright stars decorated the night sky. Wondering where he might be, Ms. Hwang went to the kitchen. He was not there. She went around to the back of the house. He was not there either. Remembering that there was a trail in the back of the house that leads to the mountain, Ms. Hwang began hiking up the trail. As she continued on, she called out quietly, "Dong-Sin, Dong-Sin..." There was no answer. She went further along the trail. Suddenly, she could hear a sound of somebody praying.

"Oh, I see that he went to pray." She still could not believe that Dong-Sin would go deep into the wood fearlessly all by himself. And he had never been here before. She tip-toed stealthily to the place the sound was coming from. She could not clearly hear all that was being said. However, she heard, "Father, if it is the cross given me, I will gladly carry it. These are the people that my father used to serve. They toil for you, Lord. I am sure that it brings you joy to see me work with them. It is all right with me that I become a servant of lepers. It is all right with me even if it means that I become a leper myself. Cleanse my heart of all the ugliness and help me to serve in joy..."

Ms. Hwang overheard these words in tears.

"I hear Japan is now surrendered."

"Really?"

"Yeah, they say Japan is now devastated."

"Is that true?"

"Joseon will now be liberated!"

"Is that really going to happen?"

On August 15, the bell of independence rang and the trumpet sound of freedom was raised throughout the Korean peninsula. Who among those that gave much of themselves and fought all kinds of hardship for the liberation of Korea had not cried? Who among those that groaned under the foreign rule for thirty six years had not jumped up and down? Yet, it must have been the so-called the ideological dissidents who had thought that they would spend the rest of their lives inside the prison and the imprisoned believers that cried the tears of joy and jumped in excitement at the thought of being reunited with their families who were scattered for the Lord and the freedom of faith upon learning of the liberation of Korea.

History flows; it flows like a stream. History changes; it changes like clouds. History repeats as it flows and changes. Time passed and history moved on; Already six years have passed and liberation has now come.

Dong-Su, just a year old then, was now six years old. Dong-Jang, who was five years old then, had now become ten years old. Dong-Hee was now beginning to look like a young student. Dong-In was now looking like a grown up.

The past six years have been deeply moving.
Though they were six years of oppression,
they were still six years of growth.
Though they were six years of suffering,
they were still six years of triumph.

This is the night of April 13, 1946.
Dong-Hee and Dong-Jang have returned from the orphanage in Gupo,
Dong-Sin has returned from the woods of Okjong-myeon Bukbang-ri,
Dong-In and the mother have returned from the woods of Namhae,
And our father has returned from the Cheongju Penitentiary, alive.
Dr. Wilson, who had left Korea in tears before the war, has returned.
The disabled warriors driven out by Director Ando have returned.

Though it had been nine months since all the family members and friends who were scattered while fighting for their faith had now returned to their respective homes and hometowns, Elder Son, the grandfather who used to pray for and write letters of encouragement to his imprisoned son faithfully at the old age of ninety-five was the only one who could not come home. He died while he was in Harbin, ten thousand miles away.

It was April 13, 1945, right before the good news of liberation to ring out. It was the night of memorial, one year anniversary.

All things come alive again in the spring.
The buds are sprouting on the old pine tree in the front yard.
The sparrows that migrated to the south of the river are coming back
    to their old nests.
But our grandfather does not seem to be returning home again.

The flower garden in the backyard and the hen coop in the front yard were grandfather's responsibility. The place right below the pine tree in the hill in the rear of the house and the desk in the room were the places where he used to pray. People gathered to remember the grandfather. They looked at the photos of him in that town, that house, and that room. There was even a picture of him sitting in front of that desk after getting his hair trimmed. Under the light of gasoline lamp, only half of those seated around could be seen.

Besides the family members, there were a few others who had come to participate in this service of remembrance.

Dong-In recited the spiritual chronology of his grandfather:

"The date that he cut off the traditional topknot of his hair was April 13 of 1909. He became a believer on May 2 of 1909. He finished his catechism on January 10, 1910. He was baptized on December 17, 1910. On that day, he was nominated as a deacon of his church. He was recognized as a *youngsu* (leader of the church) on March 18, 1914. He was nominated as an elder of his church on January 5, 1919. He started attending early-dawn prayer meetings on February 20, 1925. He had not missed a single prayer meeting since then...etc."

One thing that stood out from his chronology was that today was exactly the thirty-seventh anniversary of his cutting off the topknot of his hair. Since then, he had set apart himself from the world for thirty six years, until he went home to God.

"According to Dong-In who went to retrieve the elder's ashes in Manchuria, he went about his business on that day he died. He did not have any particular pain in his body. After lunch, he stayed in the sun for awhile with his grandchildren. As he went to bed in the evening, he said, 'I am going to pray now. Please put in some more heat in the room.' Then he went into his room and prayed, holding on to the rope tied to the ceiling. He passed away while praying in that posture," eulogized Ms. Hwang. It was only fitting that Ms. Hwang gave the eulogy. She had devoted herself to caring for Rev. Son's family through the time of war and in that way, she was just like a family member to them. But not only that, she had also carried out the duties of a daughter for Elder Son as if he were her real father, starting from when he moved around with his suffering children in an elderly body from from Aeyangwon to Gwangju and from Gwangju to Pyeongyang and from Pyeongyang to Busan and from Busan to Harbin in Manchuria. It was apparent to others that Elder Son also cherished her and she was given the forum to eulogize him on the basis of this connection.

"I would like to share with you a few of Elder Son's numerous stories of faith as I recollect them," said Ms. Hwang. Her eyes spoke of quiet confidence as she began to speak.

First, Elder Son began attending the church because of an article that was published in the *Christian Newspaper*, something that had been designed as an evangelism tract. As he reflected on the article that stated, "Jesus is the only begotten son of God," for one year, he became curious that God could have a son just like mortals. In order to dig deeper and find answers for that question, he began attending the church. At that time, he was thirty-eight years old. After his conversion to Christianity, he took a thorough and exhaustive approach to faith and chose to walk in a completely different path of life. This change brought him much ridicule and persecution from his family, relatives, and neighbors. Words cannot describe how much he suffered. However, he persevered till the end and eventually earned an understanding from his family and kinsmen. Because of this background of his conversion and spiritual fortitude, his daily life exhibited a faith that was thorough and complete.

To give you a real-life example, prior to his conversion, his life embodied the extreme form of familial piety. He abided by the Confucius teaching that since one's body in its entirety is given by one's parents, cherishing one's body is the beginning of revering one's parents. However, upon conversion, he began a new course of life: first, by cutting off the topknot of his hair (which was a symbol of pride for the noble class); second, burning all the utensils and items reserved for the use of ancestor worship when his wife, who opposed believing in Christianity prior to her conversion, was absent for awhile; third, by relocating his brother's grave which was originally in an inconvenient location for visitation without the proper procedure of discerning an appropriate day. For this, he was beaten up by his relatives and had to be put on bed rest for more than a month. But he did not hold a grudge for all that he suffered. He readily gave all that he had as offerings. Regarding his offerings, there was this incident. It was the spring of 1923 when there was the infamous quake in Tokyo, Japan. Chilwoneup Church, of which Elder Son was an elder once, had a series of revival meetings with famous Rev. Gil Seon-Ju. The purpose of the revival meetings was to mobilize the church for the construction of its sanctuary. People were to make pledges for the building fund at the end of the week-long revival meetings. Since the church was situated in a town that had only four or five hundred households and the church membership was only at about seventy or eighty, the amount of pledges were not expected to be significant. Elder Son was a little bit better off than most of the church members, who were considerably poor. When putting down the pledges, Elder Son got up and said, "I will donate to the church the three of the five rice paddies I have." Then after a few others had put down their pledges, Elder Son's wife got up and said, "I will give the remaining two rice paddies, which my husband and I had accumulated through our efforts since I married into this family, to the church.

Following this, you can imagine what kind of reception he got from his unbelieving relatives and even from his own church members. There happened to be many more people who criticized Elder Son's family for giving all they got in offering than those who marveled at their faith. Some even said that he was running his family to the ground. But in response, Elder Son said, "There are many ways for a person to be ruined in life. Fire or flood can happen any time. Many are ruined by robbery. Others fall due to failure in business. Some exhaust their life savings by spending them on prostitutes. But if I become a pauper by contributing to the construction of the church building, how precious and worthwhile would my ruin be? Even if I am ruined, would not the sanctuary of God remain?" In this way, he comforted himself. But the truth was, his family's difficult situation only grew worse each passing day.

Then, when the summer of that year passed and the autumn came, a tragedy struck in the form of an earthquake in Tokyo, Japan. The Japanese blamed the tragedy on Koreans and committed a massacre of innocent Koreans in Japan. At the time, Mr. Son Mun-Jun, a younger brother of Rev. Son, was in Tokyo to study. When the family of Elder Son received the news of the massacre in Tokyo, they were not only shocked, but also anxious to find out about the well-being of Mr. Son. The villagers said that a tragedy had deservedly befallen on the Sons. The family of Elder Son could not do anything but continue to pray for the safety of Mr. Son day and night. Thankfully, after a long time since that time, a letter arrived from Mr. Son along with a check. The letter said that not only was Mr. Son safe, but he was also able to help out with the recovery and relief effort in the wake of the earthquake and was paid for that work. Mr. Son gave the money to his father, Elder Son, for household expenses. It so happened that the amount of the money given was more than enough to buy eight rice paddies, more than enough to pay for the five rice paddy fields that the couple gave in offering and three more paddy fields.

"There are many other poignant anecdotes about Elder Son such as these. But since I cannot tell them all, I am just going to tell you just two more stories during the time of war," said Ms. Hwang. Then, she seemed to be thinking about something. Even Dong-Su, who would have been sleeping if it was another ordinary day, was attentively listening just like all the adults who were gathered there were doing. For Dong-In and Dong-Sin, the occasion allowed them to feel so proud to have such a grandfather and experience once again the love that their grandfather had showed them in the past.

Ms. Hwang began to speak again. "This letter was one of many letters that Elder Son sent to his son in prison. Elder Son never stopped praying for his son and constantly sent letters of encouragement to him. This letter was dated August 3, 1944 and written while Elder Son was in Busan. Allow me to read it to you."

As I read welcomely the precious letter from you on this day which is the first of the month, I can tell that, though you are imprisoned, your writing is better than that of a poet that has mastered the *Four Books* and the *Three Classics*. Forgive me for spending my years wastefully and not being a good parent to you. You are my truly dutiful son, Yang-Won. I cannot but confess that I have not been a good example to you both in body and spirit. Please understand my inability to write anything helpful to you. For whatever food and clothing are worth, the mind of a human being changes by day and night. But God's grace always brings answers to my prayers for the necessities of the family, your younger siblings, and your father... etc.

"Isn't this a spiritual and a humble letter? How amazing is the word given by a father to his son? The next letter was dated April 1, 1945 and was sent from Harbin, Manchuria. It seems this is the last letter written by Elder Son. I will read this one as well," said Ms. Hwang.

A son is his father's glory. A grandson is his grandfather's crown. These sayings fit you perfectly, my son, Yang-Won. I cannot imagine how you are living through the cold with your fragile body. I also want to know how you're doing with your eye infection. For the last two months, I have been suffering

from and taking medication for my asthma. I could not breathe due to much
mucus and heavy coughing. For a long time, I could even move on my own to
the point that my urine and stool had to be taken care of inside the room. But
now, I am so much better. I reckon that it is an answer to my prayer. That's
why I am writing so late. Please forgive me... etc.

Upon finishing the letter, it looked like Ms. Hwang had closed her
eyes. The group knew that these two letters of Elder Son showed
something unique that was evinced by the whole life of Elder Son
and all the members of the family. Could it be this character that
exhibited the strength of an eagle and the gentleness of a dove? It was
the boldness with which he sought after the freedom of faith and did
not fear any challenge. But at the same time, it was the humility that
allowed a father to apologize for his shortcomings to his son.

At that moment, Dong-In and Dong-Sin recalled how routinely their
grandfather would report his going and coming to them. He would say,
"Dong-Sin, I am going to Deacon Park's house," and "Dong-Sin, I have
returned."

"Finally, I just want to say one more thing," said Ms. Hwang as she
continued.

It was when Rev. Son was in the Gwangju Prison. It was when Rev.
Son's sentence was near its completion. One day, the director of the
prison called Rev. Son into his office. When Rev. Son came to see him,
the director told him, "Your father sent a letter. It said that you should
not be so stubborn and return home as soon as possible to restore
the family. What do you think?" Rev. Son asked him in return, "Who
said that?" "Your father," replied the director. Then Rev. Son said
quite confidently, "It cannot be. My father would never do that." The
director then said, "Is your father in Manchuria?" "Yes, that is true,"
said Rev. Son. The director said, "No, that must not be your father."
"What do you mean?" replied Rev. Son. "What? Is it better to come
out of the prison dead than alive, because life apart from faith is dead?

Sonna bakana oyajiga dokoni aruka (What kind of a father would say something so terrible)?" said the director angrily. That's when Rev. Son realized that it was not his father who wrote the letter. He thought to himself, "Of course, it was not he. There is no way that my father could say something so immoral!"

Later when Rev. Son was released from the prison, he heard from Rev. Park Sang-Geon in Seoul about what had actually happened. Rev. Park was at the time the pastor of Harbin Joseon Church and had even hosted the funeral ceremony for Elder Son later on. Since Rev. Son's remained unchanged as the completion of his prison sentence neared, the director of the Gwangju Prison had sent a letter to Elder Son asking him to tell his son to give into Shinto worship so that he could be released and restore his scattered family. Upon receiving this letter, Elder Son showed it to Rev. Park before writing a letter telling his son to do exactly the opposite. That's why the director was angry and cursing at him. "Like father, like son. Like Elder, like Pastor. Isn't it? How can the son be weak when his father is so strong?" said Ms. Hwang.

Of all the people present there, Dong-In, Dong-Sin, and Dong-Hee who were matured enough realized how happy they were to have had such a grandfather. Everyone was deeply moved as well. The light of the lamp seemed brighter and the quietness of the night felt holy.

"Everyone, as it said before, the grandfather passed away in Harbin, Manchuria. He always said that he wanted to return home to die. However, he ended up dying in a foreign land. I want to describe the death of Elder Son as martyrdom, too. Why? Because he died in a foreign land fighting for his faith, ten thousand miles away from home. He died while fighting for the Lord. I am sure if Elder Son were imprisoned, he would have entered prison laughing and dancing,"

Ms. Hwang said animatedly. Everyone was in agreement with what Ms. Hwang said.

"Friends, though we are here to remember Elder Son because he had gone away from us, we believe that he is with Jesus who is seated right next to our God, and that he prays for us. All of us should live our Christian lives well so that one day we would be there to meet him. Of all the things that I remember him saying, this comes to my mind." "He once said, 'I seek to give faith as the inheritance to my descendants more than the rice paddies that I have.'" "So, I ask you, Dong-In, and all your four siblings to uphold Elder Son's will by becoming great men and women of faith," said Ms. Hwang in closing.

When Ms. Hwang's eulogy ended, all those in attendance began to sing:

There's a land that is fairer than day.
And by faith we can see it afar;
For the Father waits over the way,
To prepare us a dwelling place there.
In the sweet by and by,
We shall meet on that beautiful shore,
In the sweet by and by,
We shall meet on that beautiful shore.

After singing the hymn followed by a prayer, Rev. Son gave a short address. He said the following:

"I am very grateful for your attendance here tonight to pay tribute to my father. It was the night that I was taken into the police custody. I went into my father's room and bowed to him saying, 'Father, I will go for a visit and return shortly.' Since there were detectives with me, my father did not say much except, 'Remember Luke 9:62 and Matthew 10:37–39.' As he was praying prostrated on the floor, I was taken away from him. I believe that that was the last time that I saw him at home."

As he finished speaking, he teared up. Everyone was moved by his words. Dong-Hee quickly opened her Bible to read the mentioned Scriptural passages.

Jesus said to him, "No one who puts his hand to the plow and looks back is fit for service in the kingdom of God." (Luke 9:62)

Whoever loves father or mother more than me is not worthy of me; and whoever loves son or daughter more than me is not worthy of me; and whoever does not take up the cross and follow me is not worthy of me. Those who find their life will lose it, and those who lose their life for my sake will find it. (Matthew 10:37–39)

Was it the father's gift to his son, one being taken into custody? Who knew that this would be the last words between the father and his son!

Old Middle School Students

Chapter 9

A s Dong-Hee, having come home early from school, was preparing
dinner, a drunken man came into the house.

"Oh, I am drunk! Hey, Dong-Hee! Has your oldest brother,
Dong-In, come home yet? I am getting drunk here!" yelled the man
as he opened the gate and came into the house to slouch down on the
wooden floor.

"Mister, where have you gotten yourself drunk again? Did you come
here to stop my brothers from studying with your drunken rant?"
Dong-Hee said firmly.

"Okay, okay, I won't do that. I won't do that, all right? Today, Mr.
Cheon, Cheon's daughter got married. He implored me to drink. Do you
know what? His youngest one looked very pretty in her makeup. I am
sure you will be pretty too on your wedding day, Dong-Hee, don't you
agree?" said the man.

"I don't want to hear it. It looks like my study's gone down the drain
now that you're here!" Dong-Hee said to herself. The man got up and
began to walk with a wobble toward the gate.

"Mister, where do you think you are going? You should stay here
and get some sleep," said Dong-Hee as she tried to dissuade him from
leaving. The puppy that was underneath the wooden flooring began to
bite on the man's shoe.

"Okay, but how can I always get drunk off of someone else's liquor?
I should pay it back somehow. What is this, a dog?" said the man as
he tried to push the puppy away and get to the door. In that moment,

Dong-In came through the door. He looked as tall as a college student in the hat with the patch of Suncheon Training School.

"Oh! It is you, Dong-In. I feel drunk! Can you give me some money? I feel drunk! Today, Mr. Cheon's daughter is getting married. I feel drunk! I went there and ate well. So, how can I stay here and do nothing? Heh, heh, give me some money. I feel drunk! Five hundred *won* should do it," said the man as he sat down on the wooden floor again.

"Mister, just go to sleep now. How could you go out again and get even more liquored up? Now, go in and sleep," said Dong-In.

"Are you going to give me money or not?" screamed the man. Upon hearing the commotion, Dong-Hee came out of the kitchen.

The man said to her, "Dong-Hee, bring out some of your brother's money."

She said, "I don't know anything about it."

"Oh, I see! You 'don't know' and your brother refuses to give me money. Then, should I wait for Dong-Sin? I feel drunk!" said the man as he collapsed on the edge of the floor and became silent. He surely was drunk. Dong-In, keeping his gaze on the man, went inside the room to get changed. When he came out, he had a blanket in his hand. Then he placed the man on the blanket and pulled the man into the room.

He thought about his father, who taught people that they should fear the power of sin and seek to be forgiven of their sins if they were to live a true Christian life. He wondered about the irony between his father going around and preaching the way of the cross and this man who used all his money to get drunken whenever possible. Then he got to think more about alcohol: 'What on earth is alcohol? People don't eat rice because they have no time; they don't eat rice cake because it sticks on the inside of the mouth; they don't eat porridge because it is too watery. But people say that they drink because alcohol goes down the throat smoothly. Does it really go down that smoothly? It is said that one just drinks alcohol in the beginning. Then it becomes that it is alcohol in the person that does the drinking. Then the alcohol in him drinks him up. He sells his house, rice paddies, wife, friends, and even himself in order to keep the habit. Alcohol is indeed magical. People drink when they are happy, when they are sad, when things are bad, when things turn miserable, when it gets cold, and when it gets hot. When did the existence of alcohol begin? Where in the hierarchy of things does alcohol fit? I do not know. But I cannot count the numerous evils in the world that came into being through alcohol. Perhaps, the serpent that tricked Eve into sinning designed it as a strategy of enticing people. Anyhow, alcohol should be forbidden.'

When he thought about the relationship between the mister and alcohol, relationship between alcohol and sin, and relationship between sin and determination, Dong-In felt fortunate to have not tried drinking it himself.

"Dear brother, what are you thinking about so deeply?" asked Dong-Hee. Dong-In was suddenly reminded–"Oh right, I am making dinner tonight!" He stepped down from the wooden floor, then exclaimed, "Oh, no, we don't have any firewood!" He went inside the room to get the money and then went on his way to buy some firewood. After a little while, though it was unclear how they met up with each other, Dong-Su, Dong-Jang, and Dong-In came into the house with firewood in their arms together. They pulled out an axe from the underneath of the wooden flooring and began chopping the wood.

"What's going on with Dong-Sin? Why hasn't he come home?" asked Mrs. Son.

"I don't know. What could be up with him? He has probably gone over to Jae-Min's house or something," answered the children.

It was nighttime and Dong-Sin still had not returned. The family waited until thirty minutes past their usual dinner time. But since he still had not come home, they had to start dinner without him. Ten minutes into dinner, Dong-Sin finally appeared.

"Why are you so late?" asked his mother.

"I am sorry I'm late. Since I just found out that there is an English test tomorrow, I went over to Jae-Min's house to do the makeup work for those three days that I'd missed a while ago," said Dong-Sin.

"You see, I was right!" said Dong-Hee.

"But where is the mister?"

"He is sleeping in the other room."

"He is drunk again!"

The family had a prayer time before going to bed. After he had finished the daily routine of reading three chapters of the Bible, Dong-Sin dove into studying for the test that he had the next day. Dong-Sin had a minimal level of schooling. He might have studied up to the second grade level, but even that was not consistent. From then on, he had received instruction in Chinese characters from his grandfather. During the time he was on the move to Gwangju and then to Busan with his family, his education was put on hold. When things settled down, he enrolled at Suncheon Middle School as an eighth grader with the recommendation of Rev. Nah Deok-Hwan, a relative of his father, Rev. Son. Dong-Sin had to work hard to catch up with his peers in the same grade. He had never gone to bed before midnight and he had never lied down until five o'clock in the morning. At times, he stayed up the whole night praying in the church. According to Nah Jae-Min, the son of Rev. Nah, Dong-Sin seemed unassuming when he first showed up at Seongju Church with a backpack. But seeing Dong-Sin pray and work hard at his studies really moved him. Immediately, they became the best of friends. Dong-Sin in his first year back in school barely made the cutoff line by being the 92nd in the class of 112 students. The following year, he ranked 77 in the class of 103 students. But his grades kept improving and he was working hard to be ranked about in the middle in his class. In order to close the gap, he had to work twice as hard as the other students. He would wake himself up with a cold shower whenever he found himself falling asleep at night. At times, he was so tired that he had a nosebleed. He also struggled tremendously whenever he felt any dizziness. When I, the narrator, went to Suncheon Middle School in order to do some research, Dong-Sin's student profile had read, "He is overall a sincere and diligent student who works twice as hard as the other students at his studies." At the same time, Dong-Sin also continued to keep up with the Christian duties of reading the Bible, praying, and attending Sunday worship.

Dong-In woke up startled and turned to his brother, who was still studying under the light of the lamp. "What time is it now?" he asked.

"It is four thirty in the morning."

"Is that so? I should get up now. Did you get some sleep?"

"Yes, I did, a little."

Dong-In replied, "Hey, be careful. You are going to get sick."

Dong-Sin wanted to say, "I worry about you getting sick, too" but was able to keep it to himself.

It was the same for Dong-In, too. Not only was he older than Dong-Sin, he was enrolled in the fourth year of the teacher training school which did not make it any easy for him. Dong-In was determined not to lose to Dong-Sin in terms of his studies. Moreover, he was planning to go over to America to study and he was busy learning English. His work in the subjects such as physical education, foreign language, and music was far better than in his other subjects.

Dong-In wrote the following letter in January of that year to Jung Gyu-Hwan who was in Busan:

My dear brother, Jung!

God's love is being unfolded before me in an orderly manner and without interruption. It seems like yesterday that I was suffering from the hot summer days in Busan, but it is already a blisteringly cold winter now. Time flew by fleetingly before we know it and half a year has already passed. It has been already half a year. I am sorry for being lazy and not being able to find the time to write you out of my seemingly busy schedule.

However, brother, I got your letter just in time as I was getting anxious to hear how things were at the First Middle School of Busan. I was so glad to read it and I must have laughed and cried at the same time. The middle schools in this region put out the slogans such as "Power comes from knowing" and "You are not a human being if you are uneducated." It shows how committed students are here to their studies and they are so passionate about their education that they light the torch of learning by sacrificing sleep and food. However, when I heard that the First Middle School, where I spent half a year studying, was on strike continually, I could do nothing but cry because of the great grief in my heart. As I think about the future of the young people of Joseon, I feel torn and I cannot stop the hot tears from welling up within me. If we neglect learning like this, Korea, already several decades behind others, would fall even further behind. What would become of the fate of thirty million Koreans with their history of five thousand years?

Brother! I cannot stop praying because I do not know what would become of our nation. I heard that Sodom and Gomorrah of the old were destroyed because there were not even ten righteous men. Then, how many righteous persons are on the face of the earth today? The human heart is becoming colder than the blood of a snake each day and it seems that the number of people that love the Lord is also slowly declining. The church that was expected to be thriving today has a cold wind blowing in it. It still harbors the sin of which it must repent. Since its condition warrants a heavy lashing from God, what are we to do about it?

In the wake of our independence, I thought that, since the people of Korea had suffered so much under the Japanese rule, they would return to God. But our society is without dispute corrupt to the point of persecuting the believers. The condition of Korea is such that brothers are out to kill brothers. And there is not much difference among the plight of the Korean society and its academy and the supposedly holy church. How can I not bemoan by beating my chest? How can I not cry over this tragic situation?

It is only right for a parent to give a lashing and discipline his or her child for disobedience. Then, what would become of a nation that willfully disobeys the commands and words of God? It is so sad! When I survey the people of this land including myself, I cannot but feel that God's discipline and lashing are inevitable!

But my brother, let us not be discouraged. There is success to come in failure. There is a rain after a drought. The wind blows and then it stops. There will be light after darkness. There is a saying that light will eventually reach a hole of a mouse some day. Trust that there will be light over our nation, our church, and our academy in not too distant future and pray for this.

Dear brother whom I love! You asked me to tell you about my school life here. But I do not know what to say about it. In fact, there is nothing special to write about. However, since you implore me, let me try to say a few things. As I told you about Suncheon on a numerous occasions, it is a small city with the population of approximately thirty thousand people. But since it is a cultural center conducive to poetic imagination, people here are enlightened. There are five middle schools in this small city alone and there is a plan to establish a technical school this year. It is a city well known throughout South Korea for its keen sense of culture and education. What is the reason for all these? I want to say that the driving force is the high level of interest in learning and education among students in the upper grades. This is not a boasting.

At night, you can hardly see a middle school student around the city. They all retreat to study. Furthermore, the educational authorities in this place command much respect and put in place a regular schedule for their students. The students here also seem to respect their teachers' words. Generally, the students are gentle. Because of this, this place has an aura of innocence and beauty, and as such, it is a better place to for students than a large and busy city. I had initially applied to Suncheon Middle School, but was rejected on the basis that there was no open spot. That was the reason why I enrolled at the Suncheon Training School, which was established this year. However, since my current school does not offer many subjects that I need to take in order to advance to the next level of education when compared to Suncheon Middle School, I think that I will need to transfer to the middle school eventually.

Brother! Brother! Brother! Brother! Please have great hope. And work with diligence upon diligence. Go at it persistently. If God gives us an opportunity, let us hold hands and work together to bring about the kingdom of God.

The students here criticize the school that is on strike and consider it to be foolish. Dear brother, what is happening to the Christian student fellowship at the Busan Middle School? Do they invite a pastor on a consistent basis? Please let them know that I have returned home safely. I heard that Brother Wu-Jin is attending either Busan Middle School or Dong-Rae Middle School. Is this true? You will get paid for the bag the next time either my mother or I go down to Busan. I am so sorry that you are burdened for this. The school here is in session for six hours a day. I am sure that the members of the guitar club, especially you, Brother Jung, and Brother Bae, have drastically improved their playing. Please give my regards to them all. And take care of yourself in this cold weather.

January 9, 1947
Dong-In from Yeosu

Dong-Hee: "Sun-Geum, where did your father go?"

Sun-Geum: "Well, he went out with a visitor."

Dong- Hee: "Hey, we lost our puppy the day before yesterday."

Sun-Geum: "You mean that the one you'd adopted before?"

Dong- Hee: "Yes."

Sun-Geum: "How did that happen?"

The conversation was being taken place at the residence of Rev. Nah, the pastor of Seongju Church. As the two girls were talking, Dong-Hee brought up the matter of her puppy, which had gone missing two days ago. The puppy was the object of adoration of the Sons but it had suddenly gone missing last Saturday. One of the kids in the neighborhood said that his mother had taken it. When Dong-In went to ask for the puppy, a big kid from that family came out of the house and argued with him. Yelling that Dong-In should stop the crazy talk, he charged in rage as if he wanted to fight and even slapped Dong-In in the face. After getting slapped in the face, Dong-In said, "Hey, look. Did we see it going into your house? We came here to ask because the kid in your family said that the puppy was here. How can we not come here to look for it then? Let's forget about it. It's better for us to not find it than fight you over it, especially on a Sunday."

Then Dong-In implored him to shake hands in peace. But the other guy refused to do even that.

"My brother looked funny when he tried to shake the boy's hand," laughed Dong-Hee.

"That dog, I think the Mister..." what Sun-Geum was going to suggest, Dong-Hee immediately understood and replied, "No, I don't think so."

Then she brought up the story of him getting drunk on the wedding day of Mr. Cheon's youngest daughter.

"He said that I would be as pretty as her on my wedding day! Ha, ha, ha," laughed the girls.

"Dong-Hee, you are here," said Jae-Min as he entered.

"Yes, Jae-Min?" Dong- Hee greeted him.

"Hey, I heard an interesting story from Dong-Sin..." said Jae-Min as he put the books away and came toward Dong- Hee and Sun-Geum.

"What is?" asked Sun-Geum.

But Jae-Min, oblivious to Sun-Geum who was asking him a question, turned to Dong- Hee instead and said, "You better tell it."

"What?" said Dong- Hee.

"That your brother translated for the American Army soldier."

"Of course he did. When he and I went out to the market street," said Dong- Hee recalling the event.

"But it is so funny," said Jae-Min. He then implored Dong-Hee. "Dong-Hee, since you know it better, why don't you tell the story to Sun-Geum?" So Dong-Hee began to tell the story. It happened when Dong-In and Dong-Hee happened to pass by the fabric shop, and saw that a crowd had gathered in front of the shop. When they stole a casual look, they found a young U.S. soldier in the middle with the owner of the shop. It seemed like they were arguing about something.

Dong-In wanted to find out what the whole commotion was about, so he pushed through the crowd. The soldier had accidentally broken a rare and expensive glass. The soldier wanted to compensate for the broken glass, but did not have enough money on him to take care of it on the spot. He wanted to tell the owner of the shop that he would come back later to pay for it. Because the owner of the shop could not understand what the soldier was saying, she thought that the soldier wanted to take her with him to the barracks. She feared what would happen to her if she went with him. So, she was demanding that he should bring the money back to the shop. This misunderstanding was at the root of their argument.

Dong-In translated and explained what the soldier was trying to say to the shop owner. The soldier then went to his barracks and came back in fifteen minutes to pay for the broken glass. Not only that, he brought two packs of candy and gave them to Dong-In. He said, "I am sorry if I acted rudely in your country." So the whole place broke out in laughter.

That encounter became the occasion for further engagement between Dong-In and the soldier. They would come together time to time and greet each other and carry on conversations in English. Dong-In took this opportunity to practice long conversations in English.

Dong-In had once suggested in his English class, "Let's only speak in English." His suggestion ended up being ridiculed by his classmates that did not like him to begin with. They jeered him, "Arrogant bastard! And he wants to go to America?"

Dong-In had kept in touch with his aunt who lived in Hawaii, and he dreamed of going to America to study. The time that he spent conversing in English with the soldier was far more productive than learning English at school.

Once the soldier asked Dong-In, "What school do you go to?"

"I attend the Suncheon Normal School," said Dong-In.

"What grade are you in?" asked the soldier.

"Middle school level."

"And how old are you?" asked the soldier curiously.

"I am twenty two," said Dong-In.

The soldier was surprised to hear it. "And you are still a middle school student?"

Almost spontaneously, Dong-In replied, "Yes, I am an old middle school student."

Old middle school students!

It was not because he did not have money. It was not because there was no opportunity for education. It was not because he did not want to go to school. Despite the opportunities and his desire to study, it happened because of something so abominable. Due to his refusal to observe Shinto worship, he had been kicked out of school. When his father was incarcerated for the same thing, it was he who needed to take care of the family. However, more than the demands that were placed on him, it was because of his faith that he could not stay in school. Even if his family had been well to do, he would have refused to attend school just the same. That was the main reason for falling behind in his schooling. Indeed, they were old middle school students. Not only were Dong-In and Dong-Sin way behind in their education, but Dong-Hee was also beginning to find herself in a similar situation.

Theology and Ph.D. are useful. However, theology and academic degrees cannot offer anything of a true value to the kingdom of God and his righteousness if they were far away from genuine faith. As old middle school students were true students as in the case of Dong-In and Dong-Sin, old seminarians, old scholars, and old doctors may benefit this nation more and old pastors and old elders may be what the church of this country truly needs.

The soldier explained to Dong-In why he called him an "old middle student" before calling him by his real name. He meant it as a way of showing his respect for all that he endured. In fact, the soldier was also a Christian. Therefore, the nickname of an "old middle school student" became stuck on Dong-In as the other U.S. soldiers got to know him better as well. Later, this nickname would forever be associated with the arrest of Dong-In for being pro-American.

To Students

Do not trust America;
Do not be tricked by Russia;
Japan shall rise;

Joseon, be careful.

Dear students in learning and fair ladies in reading,
What are you going to do with the land of this nation?
Which is surrounded by boundless seas in all three sides,
Which serves a gateway to the solid Asian continent,
Which has its history of five thousand years packed into the peak of Mount Baekdu?

Before calling America the country of beauty (美國),
Don't you want to turn this beautiful country into the country of courteous
people in the East once again, so that it would be known as a nation of dignity
in the world?
Before calling Russia 'my motherland,'
Don't you want to encourage and decorate this land as the Korean nation
under revival and modernization, so that it would become a nation that infuses
life into the world?

Rather than despising Japan for its past,
Do not reduce this land to be like Japan.
Don' you want to turn Korea into a nation that catapults peace to the world
over the 38th Parallel and over Yalu River?

In this way, we should open our eyes to the great continent before us,
And turn our ears to the great ocean in our rear,
And put our best foot forward toward the world,
And allow our blood and chest pump in passion.

Because you are the budding sprouts of Korea,
You should know that you are the workers of the world,
The warriors of Korea, The heroes of the world,
The crisis of Korea, The history of the world,
The scholars of Korea, The academics of the world,
The inventors of Korea, The explorers of the world,
The politicians of Korea, The artists of the world,
The entrepreneurs of Korea, And the businessmen of the world.

Why is that you cherish America more than you cherish your country?

Why do you love Russia more than you love your nation?

Instead, Korea boasts itself before the fallen Japan when it should come to its senses.

Dear students in learning and fair ladies in reading

Why is that you are lazy in educating yourselves and busy in fooling around?

Why is that you are into drinking on a daily basis and perming your hair and doing manicure?

Why is that you get dressed up and frequent movie theaters?

Why is that you are preoccupied with beating and fighting?

How could this be?

Why do you want to give this land back to Japan?

Why do you want it to become a slave of Russia?

Why do you want it to be an errand boy for America?

God surely does not want it.

Needless to say, spring had passed. Fall was almost over as well. All kinds of grain and fruit in the fields of the Suncheon suburbs were fully ripe and the harvest was near its end.

"Where did you get that from?" said Dong-Hee as she greeted Dong-In walking in with two persimmons on the vine.

"I got them from the residence of Rev. Kim, the pastor of Jungang Church. Do you like them?"

"Yes, they look ripe. But they would taste bitter, wouldn't they?"

"Of course," answered Dong-In as he handed the fruits to Dong-Hee. "Hang them under the picture of Jesus on the wall."

Dong-Hee walked into the room gingerly so as to not drop them.

Dong-In asked, "Is Dong-Sin here yet?"

"No, not yet," answered Dong-Hee from inside the room.

"Did he go over to Jae-Min's again?" said Dong-In as he sat on the edge of the wooden floor.

"Well, he seemed to be busy with the preparation for the fall in-school athletic competitions these days."

"Athletics are fine, but what good is it when he does not even have enough time to study?"

"But I heard that he is the fastest runner for the 100 meter sprint."

"Yes, I heard that too..."

While they were talking, their mother entered with something on her head and Dong-Ryun on her back.

"Oh, my, mother, you are here," said Dong-In as he ran to her and helped her unload what was on her head. Dong-Hee followed him out of the room and took Dong-Ryun off her back. Dong-Ryun was startled and woke up when Dong-Hee took her into her arms. But she did not cry and instead put on a smile. She looked so cute. Their mother went inside the kitchen to take something out of the basket that Dong-In took off her hand a moment ago and Dong-Hee took Dong-Ryun into the room.

"Aren't these so pretty? They look like your cheeks!" exclaimed Dong-Hee as she stole a glance at the persimmons hanging on the wall and as she rubbed her cheek against Dong-Ryun's.

"Mother! Where has father gone recently?" asked Dong-In.

"He went to conduct the revival meetings in Busan. He should be back the day after tomorrow," answered Mrs. Son.

"What is it that you have brought home?" Dong-Hee asked her mother from the room.

Mrs. Son thought to herself, "She must be a girl to be asking about it." "I got some rice, some red beans, and salted fish that I got from Yeosu the other day," Mrs. Son told her daughter in detail.

"By the way, Mother, would you sleep here tonight?" asked Dong-Hee as she held Dong-Ryun in her arms.

"Shall I spend Sunday here and leave in the morning of the following day?" said Mrs. Son.

"Mother, please do that. Brother is preaching at Seongju Church tomorrow evening," implored Dong-Hee. Her real motive for asking her mother to stay was so that she would not have to cook in the kitchen. They liked to have their mother around also for the reason that she would make nice meals for the children with the new varieties of food that she would bring and beef that she would buy. She also would bring clean clothes and take all the dirty laundry with her. Since the children stayed in Suncheon so that they could attend school there, their mother would visit them once or twice a month. Whenever she visited, the mood of all the children became festive as if it was one of their birthdays. At the least, it was a small feast for them.

The Seongju Church had a monthly worship service particularly for young adults. On that day, Dong-In was one of the scheduled preachers. When the first two student preachers finished their turns, Dong-In who was the third in line went up to preach. Mrs. Son was anxious to see his son preach, as could be seen by her sweaty palms. She was naturally excited to see her son preach. On one hand, she was grateful that Dong-In had come a long way in his development. He became competent enough to preach despite the circumstances during the war that kept him from going to school and forced him to work for a living. On the other hand, she was nervous and kept praying as she waited. Dong-Sin and Dong-Hee were also nervous. As for Dong-Jang and Dong-Su, they were just happy to be there. Did their excitement come from thinking that their brother had already become a preacher? Dong-Ryun was in her mother's arms, oblivious to all that was going on. Dong-In read Psalm 91:1 and began preaching the following sermon after taking a glimpse around the room.

"Judging from our experiences during the war, we have seen that there's nothing more important refuge to us than Jesus. The Japanese sought shelter from air raids by staying in bunkers, and the rich sought refuge in the remote places such as those deep in the mountains...But they could not find a true sanctuary. We have only in Jesus a true refuge for our souls," said Dong-In with confidence. His speech was oratorical.

After saying, "I would like to delineate a few reasons for seeking refuge in Jesus," he listed the following:

1. In order to seek freedom from the evils of the world
2. In order to avoid the guilt of conscience
3. In order to be free from sin
4. In order to avoid the punishment of hell at the judgment seat

After quoting these reasons, he said in conclusion, "As we need to take a ship in order to travel across the Pacific, we need to ride in Jesus, who is our refuge, in order to get to our destination." "I will tell you the story of a person who boarded the ship called 'Jesus'," said Dong-In as he continued with the story.

A young woman was arrested for her Christian faith, at the time when Regent Daewon (1820–1898) was persecuting Christians. The soldier taking her into custody implored her by saying, "Young woman, what is up with you? Please do not be stupid. Even now, if you just say that you are going to denounce Jesus, I will let you go. Why don't you just say this one phrase?" But the young woman without any hesitation said, "I can never say that." Because the soldier saw that she was fair in appearance and thought it would be a terrible thing to have her killed, he implored her again. "My superior has commanded us to kill anyone who believes in Jesus. Please, denounce him just once." However, the young woman shook her head in refusal. At that moment, the soldier put a gun to her chest and said, "Are you still going to believe in him?" Shockingly, the young woman put a smile on her face and said, "Even if I die now, the heaven where I will live eternally is waiting for me. Do as you wish."

Dong-In's voice became quiet as he put his right hand on his chest and canvassed the brightly lit light bulbs hanging high up in the ceiling. His mother and Dong-Sin were amazed by the young woman's faith and thought to themselves, "How amazing her faith is! Had all the pastors in Korea possessed such faith, they would never have given into Shinto worship!"

Dong-In continued to speak. "She said to the soldier, 'Therefore, you also need to put your trust in Jesus and go to heaven.' Though the soldier was astounded by her words and lamented that she did not change her mind, he could not help but follow his order and execute her. In that way, she became a martyr. But my friends..." Dong-In raised his voice and put forth his clenched fist.

Through her testimony and martyrdom, the soldier came to faith and a church was built on the spot where she died. A memorial was built in the honor of her martyrdom which stands to this day. That church is located in Suyeong. That church has had a lot of young women throughout history and is known as 'Virgin Church.' The church has produced a lot of female Christian workers and many churches have been reaping the benefit of their labor.

In this way, Dong-In emphasized that martyrdom is never vain but always produces good fruit. He said, "Like this young woman, we must possess this true refuge that keeps us from harm."

With the end of his sermon, all the items in the program for the night concluded. The story of the young woman who became a martyr had made a lasting impression in the minds of those who were there to listen to it that night. It was Dong-In's mother that had the greatest measure of pride that night. She knew now that Dong-In could succeed his father as a man of substantial faith.

"Brother Dong-In was the best of them all, right?" said Jae-Min.

"Well, others also did better than expected," complimented Dong-Sin.

"No, really. He was the best!" exclaimed Kim Seong-Ho.

"Really," echoed Kim Gyeong-Su.

These guys who were in the guest room of Rev. Nah, the pastor of Seongju Church were good friends in faith.

"By the way, according to Dong-Hee, Brother Dong-In once drank the water with which the reverend washed his feet. Is that true?" Jae-Min asked Dong-Sin in a voice expressed both his laughter and disbelief.

"Yes, that's true," laughed Dong-Sin before he could finish the sentence. Then he began dishing out the details. When Rev. Son returns home exhausted from an evangelism tour, it is customary for him to wash his feet in a basin. On that day, Rev. Son did not fail to honor this routine. Since he did not have a basin available on hand, he poured water into a bowl and washed his feet in it. He placed that bowl in the kitchen. Then he came into his room for a second to do something else. When Dong-In came into the kitchen looking for water to drink to quench his thirst, he mistook the water in the bowl as water from the left-over rice porridge and drank it down. He felt the water tasted different and came into the room to tell his father about it.

"What? That's the water I washed my feet with. Did you really drink it?" said Rev. Son anxiously.

"No wonder it tasted really good. It was the water that washed your feet," said Dong-In trying to mask his nauseous reaction.

Shocked by the unexpected response of Dong-In in the story, Jae-Min and others who were laughing to their hearts' content just a second ago became silent. As they recollected various events and experiences of the past, Dong-Sin brought up another story that captivated them once again.

While they were in Busan, they used to go deep into the woods and gather children in one place for worship. Once, there was an incident like the following. About ten children were present. The children told Dong-Sin to close his eyes and try to hear the sound of the rocks fighting with each other. Dong-Sin closed his eyes as told but opened his eyes because he did not hear anything. One of them told Dong-Sin to try one more time and keep his eyes closed. He pressed down on Dong-Sin's eyes with his hands. Dong-Sin allowed it for the moment. Then, they asked him if he could hear anything. Dong-Sin replied that he did not hear anything. The children said, "Never mind if you cannot hear anything." But they were heartily laughing at him at the same time. The boy that covered Dong-Sin's eyes did not say anything as if he was sorry and just laughed out loud. They told the clueless Dong-Sin to go look himself in the water at a nearby stream. Dong-Sin did not know what the whole matter was and touched his eyes with his hands. He saw that his fingertips were blackened with charcoal. At once, the children who were in that place also broke out in laughter. Since he did not have water, Dong-Sin tried to clean his face with a handkerchief. What was funnier was that when Dong-Sin returned home, his mother asked him if he had been to a charcoal factory. It was because those that helped him clean up intentionally left some smudges on his face. Those that passed him on his way home must have thought that he was a charcoal seller.

Again, the group broke out in laughter. It might have been merely a funny story to others. But for Dong-Sin, it was a precious memory from the time when he kept himself pure from Shinto worship and worked as a young evangelist. Though he roamed the streets with a blackened face!

The Country Where the Azalea Flowers Blossom

1. The blue country that winds along the side of Jangbaek Mountain,
   The abode of brotherly love for thirty million people,
   The land of freedom, the land of the Azalea that grows on the soil soaked
   with the blood of soldiers.

2. I will give my youth, my love, and my whole life for this nation and its
   citizens that have been harassed and afflicted for so long.

3. Turn this land where the Azalea flowers bloom every year into a pretty
   dreamland of mothers and sisters.

4. You are the land of the new moved by the strength of young people; Let your
   song ring throughout the world.

Dong-Hee was reading this poem. "Brother! You wrote this, didn't you?" She asked her brother, Dong-In, who was doing something in the room next door.

"What are you talking about?" He said.

"The one titled 'The Country Where the Azalea Flowers Blossom,' answered Dong-Hee.

"No, but do you think that it's well written?" asked Dong-In.

"Yes, it is very well written. I am going to memorize it," said Dong-Hee.

"You should study first and memorize that later when you have time," answered Dong-In.

"I am going to memorize it now," said Dong-Hee. Then, she went on to recite it two or three times.

At that moment, "What poetry?" asked Dong-Sin and his friends, Jae-Min and Gyung-Su. Then they listened to Dong-Hee recite 'The Country Where the Azalea Flowers Blossom.'

"The land of freedom, the land of the Azalea that grows on the soil soaked with the blood of soldiers," read Dong-Hee.

"That's a great line," said Jae-Min as he stepped into the room. Dong-Sin and Gyung-Su also came in and sat down in the room. Dong-Hee stopped what she was doing and greeted them.

"I wish that thanksgiving for the church of our country would come sooner than it is," Jae-Min said as he fixed his gaze on the red persimmons.

"Why?"

"Thanksgiving that we observe comes a little too late when we take into account the circumstances surrounding Korea. By the time it arrives, the excitement over the harvest is already gone."

"That makes sense. But isn't it better to keep Thanksgiving the way it is, since that's when it is celebrated in America?" said Dong-Sin.

"I always think that it is somehow more meaningful and impressionable to observe it a little after Chuseok," said Jae-Min.

Gyung-Su countered, "But since the end of harvest usually comes during the first ten days of November, isn't it better to do it near that time?"

"I agree. When the busy harvest season ends, people can relax and enjoy the Thanksgiving Day more. So, it wouldn't be so bad for the church to observe it now. It would also help to dispel the church's Thanksgiving as an imported holiday. Even if we do it now, it would still be earlier than Thanksgiving in America," Dong-Sin suggested.

"Well, that's true, too," said Jae-Min. He sounded as if he had changed his mind.

Dong-Sin said, "The harvest is full. But the workers are few." He seemed to have something else on his mind as he intently gazed at the photograph of some Christians celebrating their freedom upon being released from prison.

It had been already three years since the liberation of Korea. Rather than being stabilized, the country seemed more to be in turmoil. The ideological conflict due to the economic inequality in the society has been growing, leading to intermittent tragedies not only in the general public, but also in academic institutions. Students were aligned against teachers. The conflicts spilled over to students versus teachers, the left against the right, North Korea versus South Korea, and peasants versus government officials. This literally is utter division.

It is not particularly unusual for the general public to experience such upheavals. But what about the church that needs to cry out for justice and insists on love? Pastors and elders exhibited the appearance of faith, but actually betrayed the essence of it. As they had done before the independence, with an exception of a few, they sought to improve their lot by seeking the positions of power through skillful maneuvering and oratory. Though it is not clear whether they were skilled or lucky, those with abilities found their way up to better statuses or positions. Those that were left behind in the competition of power held on to their parishes, though reluctantly and jealous of others. They mumbled through their meaningless preaching. Some took advantage of those who died as martyrs for righteousness, truth, and the Lord by usurping their legacy. And others went as far as to criminalize and vilify the saints as legalists and hypocrites precisely for living through imprisonment and exile trusting in the providence of God. They seemed to be dead set on burying the saints alive in the ground. Some others tricked and cheated missionaries for their own gain. They, through their best and final act of atrocity, pushed the innocent flocks that were following them aboard the train bound for hell. Could this be what the righteous and the followers of the Lord desire? If anyone were to witness the wretched condition of the land and the pitifulness of the nation, it would be enough to make that person lament and cry loudly. How could patriots remain indifferent to this predicament?

"What are you thinking about?" asked Jae-Min.

"I just thought that, looking at the photograph, we should be as determined as they were in fighting for the Lord," answered Dong-Sin.

The photograph was of Rev. Son and other comrades in faith in the wake of their release from prison after the liberation of Korea. They were Hwang Cheol-Do, Lee In-Jae, Son Myeong-Bok, Kim Du-Seok, Ju Nam-Seon, Rev. Son, and others.

"Were they all released from prison?"

"No, a few of them were not," said Dong-Sin.

"Were there any more besides these people?" Gyung-Su said and he flipped through the pages of a book.

"There were several as far as I know...Rev. Han Sang-Dong, Choi Deok-Ji, An Rhi-Suk, Park In-Sun, and..." he continued to think.

"There were many who died as martyrs, right?"

"Of course, there were at least fifty known martyrs. I am sure that there are many others that people do not know about," said Dong-Sin confidently.

"How do you know so much?" asked Gyung-Su.

"I heard it from my father," said Dong-Sin. For a brief second, he wanted to say either that he had an interest in the subject or that he also possessed the faith of a martyr.

"You should study hard so that you can go to America to study and come back to work for the people of this country. I am compelled by the reality of this country to think like that," said Jae-Min.

"Yes, we must. I don't think that I must go to America to study for me to do that. Though my brother and I plan on going abroad to study, I am ready to give my body to the cause even if I somehow fail to go to America." Dong-Sin felt as if his faith was now beginning to control him.

Dong-Sin continued, "For example, let's say I am all prepared to go to America. But if there is oppression or a persecution in Korea and I have to fight for the Lord, I think that I should forget about studying abroad and give my all for the struggle... I think my brother would do the same. Since we are grown up somewhat, we can actively fight against any evil way more than during the time of oppression of Shinto worship."

As Dong-Sin spoke, the memories of being expelled from school due to his refusal to observe Shinto worship, following his mother to Gwangju, relocating to Busan due to poverty, working at the factory, having his mother stay with him due to the refusal of installing a shrine at home, going deep into the woods to do the work of evangelism, having his family dispersed in order to keep his brother, Dong-In, from being conscripted into the Japanese Army, living with lepers, and other events passed through his mind like a revolving lantern. Dong-Sin closed his eyes without knowing. Who knew that these words of Dong-Sin would come true!

The clock chimed to announce it was five in the afternoon.

"Guys, let's stop talking and get back to tomorrow's homework," Dong-Sin suggested as he loosened the cloth-wrapper that held his books together. Dong-In was in the next room. He came home from school after having a discussion that escalated to a shouting match with the leftist students. He must have heard what Dong-Sin and his friends talked about with a great interest.

The Worker of Korea

The whole land of Korea, the peninsula, the land of beauty;
the hill that God gave us.
The whole land of Korea, the peninsula, the land of beauty;
the hill that God gave us.
God calls workers to this hill from many different directions,
For there is a lot of work to be done.
Who will respond to the call today?
Let us go to work. Let us go.
We received God's call for the whole land of Korea.
Let us go to work in the peninsula, the land of beauty.

The whole land of Korea, the peninsula, the land of beauty;
the hill that God gave us.
The whole land of Korea, the peninsula, the land of beauty;
the hill that God gave us.
God calls workers to this hill from many different directions,
For there is a lot of work to be done.
When spring returns and it is time to plow the field,
Who will respond to the call today?
Let us go to work. Let us go.
We received God's call for the whole land of Korea.
Let us go to work in the peninsula, the land of beauty.

The whole land of Korea, the peninsula, the land of beauty;
the hill that God gave us.
The whole land of Korea, the peninsula, the land of beauty;
the hill that God gave us.
God calls workers to this hill from many different directions,
For there is a lot of work to be done.
Since it is the time for harvest,
Who will respond to the call today?
Let us go to work. Let us go.
We received God's call for the whole land of Korea.
Let us go to work in the peninsula, the land of beauty.

Stephen is Shot with a Gun
Chapter 11

"Dong-Jang, why are you here?"

"My older brother told me to come because he thought that our parents must be worrying. The rebels tried to stop me, but I insisted on coming home."

"Are your brothers and Dong-Su okay?"

"Yes, they are. But they were worrying about something all night long. After the morning service, they rubbed my head and told me to study hard and obey our parents. They said that they would see me when they go to heaven. Also, they said that their food supply has run out."

It was October 19 of 1948. With the sound of the gunshot by the rebel forces, some of those that began an uprising in Yeosu took the train and swarmed into the city of Suncheon. The police force of Suncheon received the telegram about the incoming rebels and fought against them valiantly. However, they were badly outnumbered and all perished in the fight. In this way, Suncheon was overrun by the rebellion and the leftist students joined the rebel forces. Then, they carried out the second phase of their offensive by indiscriminately killing political figures, political party associates, and rich people. The whole of Suncheon was filled with the sound of gunshots and was turned into a scene of carnage. The streets were filled with corpses and blood flowed as a stream in the city. Wailing reached the sky.

At the time, Yeosu Aeyangwon located in Sinpung-ri was having a revival meeting with the *Jeondosa* Lee In-Jae, who was a graduate of Korea Theological Seminary and who used to fight for the Lord while imprisoned during the latter days of the Japanese occupation. The revival was held from October 12 through 20. On the 19th, Dong-Hee did not know what was happening and came to the house with her uncle to fetch some food. But the safety of her four siblings was unknown. The Son household was busy feeding the rebels who were now the new occupiers of the village. It was around the noon of the 21st. Because there was a barrage of bullets flying, Dong-Jang, twelve years old at the time, had to take the barricaded road to reach home. Upon seeing Dong-Jang, Rev. Son was overwhelmed with joy and cried. Not giving him a chance to go inside, Rev. Son was asking Dong-Jang about a few things in talking with Dong-Jang in front of the house.

Rev. Son told Dong-Jang, "Go in and greet your mother" and he made haste toward Aeyangwon.

"Who are you?" A soldier yelled as he got out of the truck that flanked the flag of Korea and came running with his rifle pointed at the person. It was part of the impenetrable line of defense set up by the Korean government forces.

"Sir, my name is Hong Sun-Bok and I live at Yeosu Aeyangwon. I received the news that the son of my pastor at Aeyangwon Church was killed by the rebels in Suncheon. I am on the way to verify the truthfulness of the news. If he was indeed killed, I have to at least retrieve the body," the person said cordially. It was Hong Sun-Bok, one of the teachers at Seongsan Primary School, the charter school of Yeosu Aeyangwon.

"What kind of place is Aeyangwon?" It was a loud shout.

"Sir, it is a group treatment center for lepers," answered Mr. Hong.

The soldier believed what he said because of his strange appearance more than his tattered clothes. He then lowered his voice and asked him, "What do you have with you?"

"Sir? I do not carry anything with me, except my Bible," said Mr.

Hong as he showed him the Bible.

The soldier relaxed at the sight of the Bible, changed the tone of his voice and said, "It is dangerous here. Get out of here fast."

On the 22nd, there was a buzz going around that Dong-In and Dong-Sin were killed by the rebels. Hearing this, the members of Aeyangwon had become worried as much as the family of Rev. Son.

Rev. Son was resigned to say, "It is well for us either way. If they have died, they have gone to heaven. If they are alive, then they will be able to continue the work of God. So, there is nothing to worry about." It was his way of comforting his wife and the church members.

Then they had not heard anything about them until the 24th. Besides Dong-In and Dong-Sin, there was also no word from Dong-Hee and her uncle who had left for Suncheon with some food to find out about their whereabouts. Mrs. Son kept on insisting that she should go. Mr. Hong, one of the young adults at Aeyangwon could not help but volunteer to go and find out about the status of Rev. Son's children.

"Pastor, I will go to Suncheon to check on the children and come back," volunteered Mr. Hong. What he proposed was easier said than done. To leave in that moment was an act of risking his very life. However, because Mr. Hong implored him on, Rev. Son had to say in reply, "I thank you for your offer, Mr. Hong. But you and I know that the way is blocked. And you would not be able to pass through the barricade. Mr. Hong, if they are dead, then they are in heaven. If they are alive, then they will be doing God's work. Please forget it. Life and death is up to God, so let us forget it. What is the use of knowing? What if I do not know?"

"But Pastor, shouldn't we at least try to find out what has happened to them? Since I am a leper, I will be fine. I will put tar on my face and put on raggedy clothes. I will look like a beggar. There's nothing to worry about. Nothing will happen," implored Mr. Hong.

Finally, Rev. Son reluctantly gave in to Mr. Hong's plea and said,

"Then, take a Bible with you. You might need it along the way."

It indeed worked. The Bible helped him with getting through the first obstacle safely.

"The sky is high. People say that even horses get fat during the autumn. Now, the autumn is almost gone. People finished harvesting all kinds of staple grains and packing them in their barns. People in the village are busy making Kimchi for the winter. There is not even a speck of cloud in the sky that is so high. Evergreens far and near are as green as ever. Tree sparrows are as busy as ever in the field picking up leftover grains." As Mr. Hong thought about all the things that change, he felt sick to his stomach realizing that the world had become changed so much that he could not even walk down the road feeling safe. He felt hatred toward the mankind. "The world is far more dangerous than the disease that I possess." As his mind entertained all kinds of thoughts, he came across numerous trucks, trolleys, field-artillery corps, and others. Every time, he was checked and searched. And every time he was interrogated, he gave the same answer. And every time he gave the same answer, he was allowed to pass safely. Every time he would pass a checkpoint, Mr. Hong recalled with gratitude what Rev. Son said about taking the Bible with him.

He walked the distance of about forty *li* in haste. It seemed more like hundreds of *li*. The intermittent sound of gunshots and artillery coming from the other side of the mountain never failed to shake him to the core.

"Mrs. Son, Mr. Hong is back." Mrs. Cha who lived in the same neighborhood yelled as she entered the house as if she was being chased by something.

"What?" Mrs. Son said as she ran even before Mrs. Cha had a chance to pull open the gate.

"Over there. There." Mrs. Cha said as she ran ahead of Mrs. Son.

"Where? Where?" Mrs. Son followed her with the Bible that she was reading in her hand.

It was right after an autumn rain shower had passed by. The mud on the ground began sticking to the shoes of the two women. However, they ran as fast as they could without any regards to whether their shoes had slipped off their feet or not. Mr. Hong, however, was not in their view. Only two persons were coming toward them. They were Sim Wu-Yeong and Seong Jeom-Sun.

"Is Mr. Hong really coming this way?"

"Yes, but he is still far behind."

"Did you hear anything?"

"No, nothing. But the kids are coming with him." The women went ahead before another question could be asked.

From a far, she was able to see people approaching. It seemed like Dong-Hee and Dong-Su were approaching from the path near Guam-ri, the same path that they took two days ago.

Mrs. Son and Mrs. Cha switched places in silence.

"Hey, Dong-Hee! Dong-Su! Are your brothers coming, too?" Mrs. Son called out to them with a glimmer hope. But Dong-Hee and Dong-Su did not answer back. Mrs. Son thought that they could not hear her because they were still far away. So, she ran toward them.

"Dong-Hee! Your older brother is dead, isn't he?" Mrs. Son stood before Dong-Hee and desperately wanted to hear her say, "No." But Dong-Hee stood there motionless like a zombie. Dong-Su just continued to cry.

"Your oldest brother is dead, too?" Mrs. Son asked again. But still there was no answer.

"Dong-Hee, why aren't you answering me?" yelled Mrs. Son as if she was angry.

Instead of answering, Dong-Hee burst into crying, "Ah!"

"Oh, my God! Both of them are dead..." Mrs. Son fell instantly to the ground. "It was only several days ago that Dong-In came to Aeyangwon

Church to sing! It was only two weeks ago that Dong-Sin came home to change into new clothes! How could they die without giving me a chance to give them some medicine?" Mrs. Son, who did not have even strength to cry, lost consciousness.

"Pastor, Mr. Hong is back," said someone. Rev. Son ran to the gate of Aeyangwon as fast as he could to meet him. Elder Park, *Jeondosa* Lee In-Jae, and other staff members of the church also ran to the gate. Mr. Hong barely avoided running into Mrs. Son. Now, he was outside the gate of Aeyangwon, but he did not have the courage to enter. Mr. Hong, surrounded by those that came out to meet him first, stood there silently.

At that moment, someone broke the silence by saying, "There comes the pastor." Mr. Hong was startled by those words. When he looked up, he found Rev. Son standing in front of the gate and saw *Jeondosa* Lee and a few other elders in a hot pursuit. Mr. Hong felt so sorry to be there and wanted to hide in a rabbit hole. He could not move his feet to step forward. "How come I had to be the one to give this news?" He regretted going to Suncheon in the first place.

"Mr. Hong, have you been safe in your trip?" Rev. Son spoke rather in a surprisingly cold tone of voice to Mr. Hong, who hesitated a little in speaking.

"Our Dong-In and Dong-Sin are really dead, aren't they?" Rev. Son had already guessed that much. But he still somehow longed to hear, "No."

"Yes... Sun..." Mr. Hong could not even finish a sentence. He began crying without being able to speak another word.

After having his worst fear confirmed, Rev. Son proceeded to say, "Let us pray."

"Our Father in heaven..." Rev. Son could not continue.

He continued after a pause, "Thank you for giving me, a wretched sinner, this great privilege!"

After a pause, the prayer continued.

"First, give us faith," said Rev. Son tearfully. "Woo, woo," A person among the gathered began to cry out loud.

"Lord, thank you for the martyrs," said Rev. Son chokingly.

"I don't know who it is, but have mercy on the person that killed my sons." Rev. Son could not continue on. The whole place broke out in a wave of lamentation. At the sound of grown-ups and children crying, the villagers all came out. Nobody knew when they had come out. Nearly all of the members of Aeyangwon were there. They kept crying. There was no need to speak. Not only human beings, but also the green trees of this land seemed to be sharing in this grief. The clouds that skirt the mountain in front of them seemed to be soaked with tears. The leaves of fall foliage seemed to be crying with tears mixed with blood!

"Father! Give us your love. Give us your love that can make us forgive them. Forgive my sins, too. In Jesus' name, we pray."

In this way, the long prayer finally concluded. However, no one was able to raise his or her head. Everyone was still sobbing. Even the cawing of crows that flew by sounded like crying.

Someone whispered to Elder Park, "Mrs. Son has fainted."

"Pastor! Why don't you go and get some rest." Elder Park implored Rev. Son.

"No, let's go to the church," answered Rev. Son.

"No, you shouldn't. You should go home and get some rest," insisted Elder Park.

"No, the church is my resting place," said Rev. Son as he began walking. They could not possibly tell him that Mrs. Son had fainted. Everyone followed him. It was like a funeral procession. They had grief in their hearts and heaviness in their steps. Only *Jeondosa* Lee ran over to Rev. Son's house.

No bell was rung. It was not a time for a worship service. But the members of Aeyangwon began to gather in silence. They began praying and singing hymns. They believed that the only way to comfort themselves and Rev. Son was through praying and singing hymns. They did not know how many hymns that they sang or how long they prayed. Finally, Elder Park asked Mr. Hong to give the gathered a more detailed account of what happened, since people were anxious to know. Mr. Hong hesitated not knowing whether he should or not. But because he thought that it would give God the glory, he decided to give his report as exactly as he had heard and dragged his heavy body to the pulpit.

"Now, there will be a detailed report from Mr. Hong." Elder Park's words prompted people to raise their heads. Mr. Hong's face was still swollen due to crying and his facial expression exhibited sadness. Mr. Hong began to speak:

"Yesterday morning, I departed from this place. On the way there, I ran into many army checkpoints and was questioned by the soldiers every time I was stopped. But when I showed them the Bible and what my business was all about, they allowed me to pass and I was able to arrive in Suncheon safely. I was still able to hear the sound of gunshots coming from different parts of the city. It seemed like the battle was still going on. Then, I met a transit police officer who claimed to have come from Manchuria. When I asked him, he said that the city was under control. I expected the situation would continue to get better and went to the vicinity of the Suncheon Station. What I saw there was beyond my imagination. The streets were filled with mounds of corpses everywhere. Though the stench of corpses was something unbearable, it was nothing compared to what I saw. There was a swollen and yellowish corpse, tattered with bullets. There was a corpse halfway burnt with gasoline. The naked body of a dead woman, the body of a police officer tied around the telephone pole and executed... I cannot tell you everything. Whenever I came upon the people in desperate search of the corpses of their loved ones, I could not help but cry because I could see myself in them. At first, I was rattled by what I saw. But soon, I got used to the scene of carnage because it was everywhere. At once, I went to the house where Dong-In and Dong-Sin used to live. When I got there, I was surprised to find the gate of the house firmly locked. I thought there was no one inside and decided to go over to Seongju Church. Then I changed my mind and called in a loud voice several times, "Is anybody home? I came from Aeyangwon." That's when the owner of the house came out and opened the door for me. When I called out Dong-Hee's name, Dong-Hee and Dong-Su came out with Mr. Yang, the owner. The siblings' eyes were swollen from crying. She could not say much except, "My brothers are dead." Though I had already assumed that much, upon hearing the news, I felt all of sudden dizzy and everything became dark. When I was able to finally get my sense back, I asked where the bodies were. The woman told me to calm down because she had already found the bodies. I asked them about what in the world had happened. They told me the following story."

Mr. Hong stopped talking to let out a sigh. Everyone was quiet and was anxiously waiting to hear what he would say next. Mr. Hong teared up just thinking about it.

"In the morning of the 20th, everyone went to school. However, somehow Dong-In returned home early. When asked, he said that when he went to the Suncheon Station to bid farewell to someone from the church, he did not see civilians in the train from Yeosu, but only soldiers on board. Then he witnessed groups of people moving here and there as security forces and police officers began to fire gunshots at each other. When Dong-Sin did not come home, Dong-In became greatly concerned. In the meantime, the sound of gunshots was getting louder by the minute and they thought that the violence was spilling into the city. The owner said that he and Dong-In went out to the streets to find out what was happening. That's when they realized the rebels began an uprising. They heard the rebels yell that 38th Parallel was breached by the North Korean Army. The owner said that he also heard them say that the North Korean Army had already taken the entire Korea including Seoul, Daegu, and Busan. Now, they said that Yeosu and Suncheon were the last of the cities to be felled. When they returned home, they went down to the basement of a neighbor's house and hid there. When it was almost evening, Dong-Sin came home. According to Dong-Sin, the rebels had laid a siege over Suncheon Middle School, too. Later, when the siege was lifted, that's when he was able to come home. On the way home, he got to think about what was happening and shared with his friend, Jae-Min, "Since it is a conflict between the righteous and the wicked as well as the believer and the non-believer, we should fight hard." When the whole family gathered, Deacon Yang suggested that they should flee because everyone else was fleeing. But Dong-In said, "The only refuge we have is the Lord." Then he refused to go on the road."

Mr. Hong's eyes seemed to be feeling something supernatural. After a long pause, Mr. Hong resumed speaking:

"The next morning on the 21st, all the children got up very early. They usually stayed up late studying and woke up early to study. The fact that they were up early in the morning was not strange in and of itself. Dong-In must have stayed up all night or otherwise gotten only a couple of hours of sleep. On that day, Dong-Hee and their uncle were not there because they went to Aeyangwon on the 19th. It seemed that the siblings had fixed their own breakfast. What the owner remembered in particular was that Dong-In told him out of the blue, "Deacon Yang, I had a weird dream last night." Deacon Yang told him to tell him the dream at once, but he mumbled and stopped speaking. After the morning prayer, Dong-Sin told Dong-Jang to leave for Aeyangwon right away. Then Dong-Sin went to the well in the back and took a bath there. Afterwards, he got dressed in all new clothes. Then the brothers went inside to pray. When they came out of the room, their faces seemed to cry melancholy. Deacon Yang and his wife became concerned and implored them to talk about the dream by telling them that dreams are sometimes turn out for the good depending on the interpretation. But the brothers continued to be silent. When the wife of the wonder of the neighboring house in which they had hid the day before came and implored the brothers to hide out in the house, they refused to listen to her words. When Deacon Yang implored them to flee to Aeyangwon, they told him that it was better for them to face what was coming to them at home rather than getting caught on the way to Aeyangwon and suffering the embarrassment of being ordered to pick up a rifle for the rebels' cause. After managing to finish breakfast, Deacon Yang went over to Deacon Jung's house in the same neighborhood for a short while. Perhaps, it was about ten in the morning. A mob of students surrounded the house where Dong-In and Dong-Sin lived. By the time Deacon Yang had returned home despite his fear, Dong-In was getting beat up by a mob of students.

Dong-In cried out, "I do not know why you guys are beating me up, but I did not do anything wrong."

"You did not do anything wrong? If you are not a pro-American bastard, what are you? You wanted to go to America for study?"

"Listen, you people! I am not a pro-American activist. I only serve God. Why would I depend on a foreign country for the things that are of this country?" answered Dong-In.

"Shut up! You *still* can't stop talking about that Jesus ideology, huh?" They kept on beating him.

Then, Dong-In seemed to have decided on something and began speaking up, "Look, you people! What are you talking about? What is bad about the ideology and mentality that believes in Jesus? You might be able to pull my head off my body, but you could never pull my faith off me."

Somebody yelled, "Beat him up" As they beat him up, they picked up the small pieces of wood with nails in them that were lying around nearby and began beating him up some more.

Then, they turned their attention to Deacon Yang who was in the room next door and said, "Who are you?" They turned their hostility toward Deacon Yang.

"I am a carpenter."

"What is your relationship to these bastards?"

"Nothing, we just live in this room." When Deacon Yang denied of their association with the brothers, the wife of Deacon Yang showed the carpenter's tools to reinforce their claim.

Then the mob resumed beating Dong-In. Dong-Sin, who tried to intervene, was also struck down by the mob. Blood began to flow from their heads and there were red blood spots all over their body due to the beating they took. Someone yelled, "Let's take these bastards with us." Another echoed, "Let's do that." Then the mob tied Dong-In with a rope that they had and ordered Dong-Sin to raise his hands. Then they ordered them out. Several students entered and began searching the room saying that they were looking for evidences. Then, they came out of the room with a bagful of things. All the while, Dong-Su kept on crying. But his crying did not matter to the mob at all.

Mr. Hong wanted to say more, but he found himself unable to continue. It was because what he needed to say next was, "Deacon Yang did not follow them, but stayed inside his house because he was fearful." After a pause, Mr. Hong began to speak again:

"Since no one followed the mob, there was no information available regarding the brothers except that they were taken to the headquarters of the rebellion which was located above the office of taxation. Since the brothers did not come back even when the day turned to night, they assumed the worst for them but there was no way to verify that fear. When the full day of fear passed and the Korean Army moved into Suncheon and took it over, Deacon Yang and his wife went outside to find out what had happened to the brothers. The news they encountered was that they were shot to death. Still, they continued to search with the hope of finding the bodies. Because there were so many corpses everywhere, they split up to look for the bodies of the brothers. Deacon Yang went to the police station and his wife went over the Jangdae Bridge and went as far as the main road that led to Byeolgyo. When Deacon Yang reached the police station, the Korean army soldiers were already shipping all the corpses out to the outer fields. It was Mrs. Yang who found the body of Dong-Sin with unexpected ease. She was able to identify the body by the tag of the new clothes that he had been wearing. Soon thereafter, she found the body of Dong-In, too. The strange thing was that, whereas all other corpses had much disfiguration in their bodies including their faces, the corpses of Dong-In and Dong-Sin had not sustained much damage. Then, Mrs. Yang and Deacon Jung, along with three other persons, brought the empty sacks that were used for rice in order to retrieve the bodies. They were about to send the word about the brothers' deaths to Aeyangwon, when the uncle of Dong-In arrived. He was more devastated and paralyzed by the news to do anything. Then, I happened to arrive there. When I told them that I had come from Aeyangwon, they began asking me about what to do."

Until this point in story, Mr. Hong was speaking about what transpired prior to his arrival. Now that he was about to pick up the story from where he entered the picture, he seemed to feel a little awkward.

"So, I took Dong-Hee and Dong-Su with me to go and see their corpses. After that, I went to visit the church to discuss about having a temporary funeral for the brothers, but there was no one there. After discussing the matter with Deacon Yang again, I decided to bury the bodies temporarily at the bottom of the mountain nearby at night. Then, I received surprising news. The wife of Mr. Jung, who owned a

photography business in Suncheon-eup, went around the city looking
her husband upon hearing that many Christians were taken away by
the rebels in the direction of the police station. As she was going over
to the police station to see if her husband who supposedly fled for a
refuge had been arrested or not, she happened to come upon a mob
of students that was taking a couple of young men somewhere. One
of the young men was trying to witness to others even though he was
being punched, kicked, and hit by sticks and rifles. Though there was
blood flowing down his face, he kept on witnessing to them. Though
it was hard to hear everything that was being said, she heard him say,
"You should not do this. You should instead believe in Jesus. Let us not
commit the sin of killing each other for we both belong to Korea. Our
nation would be blessed if we live with faith in Jesus…" She testified
that this scene, though wretched that one could not witness it without
tears, was sacred. She said, "When I heard the words of the young men,
I could not help but remember the road to Calvary that our Lord Jesus
walked on.""

Mr. Hong tried to wipe away his tears with his fists. Everyone was
sobbing, too.

"Then, another story began to emerge. It was witnessed by a student
named Yun Sun-Eung, who was about fourteen or fifteen years old.
He saw that the mob had Dong-In standing in front of a huge mound
of corpses in the backyard of the Suncheon Police Station. The mob
said, "You bastard! You *still* can't get rid of your Jesus ideology? If you
denounce your Jesus ideology and Jesus mentality and join us, we will
forgive you. So, what's it going to be? Look at Goh Myung-Shin (an
alias)." They pointed at a student that had recanted his declaration of
faith."

But Dong-In declared, "You can pull my head off, but you can never
pull my faith off of me. Do not commit wickedness, but believe in
Jesus." At that moment, someone yelled, "It's impossible. Shoot him."

When Dong-Sin heard this, he went over to where Dong-In was and shouted to the mob, "Guys! My brother is the eldest son in our family. Since he is the eldest son, doesn't he have to support his parents? I will die in his place, so please let my brother go." Then, Dong-Sin stepped in front of Dong-In in order to shield him. Seeing this, Dong-In screamed in chains, "Dong-Sin, stop this madness! They are not trying to kill you, so why don't you go home and serve our parents in my place?" Then the mob pulled Dong-Sin away by force and one of them covered Dong-In's eyes. Dong-In, realizing that his end was near, yelled, "You! Repent and believe in Jesus. When I die, I go to heaven. But are you willing to receive the fearful judgment of hell?" Incensed by Dong-In's words, the violent mob grinded their teeth and clenched their fists in rage. They called out, "Shoot, one, two, three..." Before the countdown was finished, Dong-In cried, "Father! Receive my spirit. Forgive their sin..." Then, the gunshots were fired and without being able to finish what he was saying, Dong-In bounced and fell to the ground.

The audience turned into a sea of wailers. Mr. Hong continued speaking:

Dong-Sin, who had witnessed what happened, wrestled himself free from his holders and ran to where Dong-In lay in a pool of blood. He held his older brother in his arms and cried out, "Brother! Brother. You are in heaven now. I will follow you there." He turned to the rebels and the students yelling, "Why do you spill the blood of the innocent? How are you going to atone for the sin of spilling the blood of this innocent man? Now, repent and believe in Jesus."

"Let's kill that one, too." The mob chanted. Others echoed, "Let's do that. Let's do that."

Mr. Hong could not go on speaking. He was just standing there. Everyone was sobbing.

Dong-Sin, hearing the mob chanting, said, "I am going to follow my brother to heaven. My faith is just the same as my brother's." Then, he raised his hands saying, "I am going to pose just like the way my Lord Jesus hung on the cross. Go ahead, shoot me now. I am ready."

The mob yelled, "Wow, this one is worse than his brother. We should not leave him alone. Let's shoot him to death."

Dong-Sin raised his arms, thereby making the shape of a cross. He began to pray, "Father, forgive the sins of these people. Make them repent. Receive my spirit. And may my father and mother..." At that moment, multiple shots were fired at him. Dong-Sin fell to the ground right next to his brother, Dong-In.

"I thought that the deaths of the brothers helped recall the memory of Stephen, the martyr of old. I thought that their deaths were indeed the deaths of martyrs. On the spot, I believed the testimony about what happened to them to be credible. Since I knew how they lived their lives on a daily basis and what their faith was like, I knew that the brothers would be more than willing to give their lives as martyrs..." Mr. Hong could not go on. He just sat down where he was.

It was not clear whether he heard the report up to this point or not. But Rev. Son who had not moved at all but remained prostrated behind the pulpit, stood up immediately when the report of Mr. Hong was finished. He wiped away his tears and runny nose at the same time before standing in front of all the church members. No one told him to do so. No one could prevent him from doing so.

"My beloved parents and brothers in Christ! I heard most of what Mr. Hong said just now. I most definitely believe that my two sons, Dong-In and Dong-Sin, have gone to heaven. I am also certain that, as in the words of Dong-In, those who killed my two sons will end up in hell. As a father, how can I let that happen! I go around places and evangelize because I fear that people would go to hell because of their unbelief. How can I neglect those who killed my sons and remain impenitent?"

The church members began bawling loudly.

Rev. Son spoke again. "If they were foreigners, we would also have the responsibility of saving them. But they are our brethren, aren't they? Killing and being killed by fellow Koreans are this race's wretchedness and this nation's great tragedy. There will be the violence of vengeance. Who would be left if people begin killing their fellow countrymen for this and that? Therefore, send the message to Suncheon and tell Rev. Nah Deok-Hwan of Seongju Church that, while I don't care about others, however, if the individuals responsible for the murder of my sons get arrested, they should never be executed or even beaten up. Tell him to inform the authorities that I will take it upon myself to share the gospel with them, make them repent, and adopt them as my son. When they were alive, my two sons told me that they would go to a seminary, become ministers and come back to serve Aeyangwon Church in my place. Do not bury my two sons in Suncheon. But please bury them in the hill of Aeyangwon. Those two things are my requests to you all and God." Then Rev. Son sat down quietly.

The sun set and evening came. But no one went home to cook dinner. They must have thought, "What if we skip a meal? There are people who died as martyrs. Rev. Son just had lost his two sons…"

At that moment, somebody began singing, "When all my labours and trials are o'er…" Everyone started to sing along.

The Flower of Martyrdom

Someone said, "The blood of martyrdom is the seed of the church?"

It is the blood that succeeds the blood of atonement spilled on the cross.
It is the blood that seeps deep into the ground underneath a pile of rocks.
It is the blood of the apostles who fell by the beating at the hands of the jailers.

Blood! Blood! The blood was succeeded.
The blood spilled in the holy place;
The blood spilled at the mountain of the savage;
The blood spilled in the field;

The blood spilled in the streets;
The blood spilled on land;
The blood spilled in the sea;
The blood spilled at home;
The blood spilled at the pulpit;
The blood spilled by the tip of a spear and the blade of a sword;
The blood spilled during the daytime;
The blood spilled in the middle of the night;
The blood spilled in the east;
The blood spilled in the west;
The blood spilled in the south;
The blood spilled in the north;
The blood spilled in public;
The blood spilled in private.

The blood has been spilling for two thousand years without stopping.
This blood and that blood were overlapped and accumulated.
Your blood and my blood became tangled and mixed.
White blood and red blood were collected and collected again.
The church is the blood of righteousness and the blood of love budding and
    blossoming as a flower.
The blood of martyrdom that the Lord allowed would never be wiped away
    from the face of the earth by humans.
The living martyrs who were kept alive by the will of the Lord could never be
    buried in the ground by the devil.

The Church of Korea!
God has given you a unique opportunity according to God's great will and
    great love, but South Korea...
How come you mumble and do not know how to repent?
Why do you incur the new wrath of God just like Sodom and Gomorrah?
Kneel before the spirits of those that felled in Daegu.
Bow before the spirits that perished in Jeju Island.
Bury together the spirits that melted during the Yeosu and Suncheon incidents.
Close your eyes to the spirits that had been buried around the 38th Parallel.
Since it is the wage of sin, why don't you find out whose wage that is?

The Aftermath of the Tragedy
The family that lost its home,
The orphaned that lost their parents,
The elderly that lost their children and spouses,
The homeless that lost their families,
Go before them and beg.
Go and beg the police officers who fight against the cold and stay up through the night.
Go and beg the prisoners and the staff of the prison that is filled to its maximum capacity.
Go and beg the soldiers who hunt for communist guerrillas.
Go and beg the fellow countrymen who suffer in a remote and secluded place among the mountains.
Go and beg the bandits who are not altogether sane.

Go in front of the omnipresent God and beg, tearing your clothes, beating your chest, putting ash on your head, wailing, and confessing.
All these things happened because you did not repent.
They are the first calamity of God's wrath.

Those that had forgotten to repent, their first requirement,
Those that had glossed over God's kingdom and righteousness which they should have sought first,
They are now promoted to the positions of
Pastors who have gone fishing to the sea,
Elders who serve the churches that took over enemy properties,
And deacons who are really profiteering scoundrels under the guise of sheep and who publicly display their indulgence of pleasure up in their high places.
Do they think that they can deceive God?
Do they not know that the wage of their sin is the reality of this nation now?

Before you put forth the authority of the General Assembly,
Before you initiate diverse memorial projects,
Before you create this and that organizations, thereby causing divisions,
Before you build the church which is your place employment,
Before you set up the altar of Baal,
Before you call for the church breakup,

Before you introduce Dr. Mackay or market the scholars of Brunner,

Before you argue and fight insisting that you are orthodox or rice cooker (the
    words for "orthodox" and "rice cooker" rhyme – *jeong-tong* and *bap-tong*),

Before you enter diverse conferences for world heroes,

Before you brag about a church that you believe is the best in the east,

Before you talk arrogantly about your church members that are of high status
    and prestige,

Don't you know that you have already forgotten what you have to do first?

Repent for the heaven is near.

If you hesitate, there will be another calamity.

The Lord sent ten plagues in the past.

The saints in prison, come to Akihabara,

Like Peter who was on his way to Rome.

You that need to repent, go to your humble place of residence.

Like Jonah who was on his way to Nineveh.

You, who fled to South Korea, go back to North Korea,

If you hear the cry of the abandoned flock.

Rise up, you, young men of faith,

If you love the Lord truly and more than you love your church, your countrymen,
    and your country, and your land.

The blood of martyrdom shall be the seed of the church!

Be the flower of martyrdom.

God is waiting for the fruit.

The Sea of Tears

Chapter 12

"**B**ok-Sun, is my dress ready?"

"Not yet. I still have a little ways to go. I will make sure that you wear it tomorrow."

"I am not worried. I am just asking."

Mak-Dal needed her white shirt to wear for tomorrow's funeral. But since she had bent fingers, she could not sew it herself. So, she had asked Bok-Sun to do it for her.

"Did you go out before?"

"Yes, most definitely. But I could not bear to watch the sight of Mrs. Son begging them to open the coffins so that she could have a look."

"Don't you think that you would do the same? She lost not one but two sons. If we were in her shoes, we would have fainted and died." Bok-Sun stopped sewing and picked up her handkerchief to wipe away her tears.

"Yes, we would have. Even our kids were dumb, ugly, faithless, and spoiled through the latter days of the Japanese rule..." Mak-Dal wiped her tears away with her bent fingers.

"Besides, look at Rev. Son who sang hymns as he followed the coffins to the graves. He is not human!"

"I know! Didn't you see what he did the day before yesterday?"

"I know. He made us so nervous..."

It was the day after the uprising in Yeosu. They might have been on the run being pushed out of Suncheon by the government forces. A remnant of the rebels, thugs and student agitators came all the way to the village saying that they would kill off Rev. Son and Aeyangwon.

Then, an elder told them, "Come if you wish to come. I cannot protect you from contracting leprosy, though." The mob could not enter, but fired several shots from outside the gate. They threatened to come back the next day. Since the people of Aeyangwon cherished Rev. Son more than their own lives, they implored him to go and hide in a safe place. Instead, Rev. Son went to the church and sat down behind the pulpit. He sang hymns and prayed there. The church members opened up the church flooring so that he could hide there.

But Rev. Son refused by saying, "I am thankful for what you are trying to do. But there is no safer place than in the arms of God." The members of Aeyangwon felt powerless. Much later, people would have marveled at his faith saying, "There is none like him." But at the time, they could not stand what they perceived to be irrational stubbornness. So, people could not go to sleep without worrying about him.

"He will be called a saint!"

"Mother, I saw it, too. Mrs. Son is still there..." said the young daughter of Bok-Sun as she entered the room.

Upon receiving the news of tragedy from Mr. Hong Sun-Bok on October 25, the staff of Aeyangwon Church and external employees decided to borrow a freight truck and go find the bodies that Mr. Hong and Deacon Yang had temporarily buried in the public cemetery.

It was in order to carry out Rev. Son's request that the martyrs be buried in the hill of Aeyangwon. It was the 26th, the day after 25th, when the government forces retreated a little bit from their offensive into Yeosu against the rebels. Because they were getting ready for the next offensive onslaught, the security was very tight.

Hundreds of cars, tanks, and artilleries were heading to Yeosu. The Aeyangwon truck was the only on going towards Suncheon and it was constantly stopped at checkpoints.

Anyhow, the round trip should have taken only a couple of hours under normal circumstances. However, by the time they retrieved the bodies and returned to Aeyangwon, it was already evening. While in transit, they had already placed the bodies in the coffins. It was intentional for two reasons. Besides the bodies had been decomposing for several days, they did not want Mrs. Son to take a look at them. But to no avail, Mrs. Son kept on insisting opening the coffins so that she could see the bodies. On the other hand, when the bodies arrived, Rev. Son began singing, "When all my labours and trials are o'er..." as he followed the coffins. The sight of both Mrs. Son demanding to see the bodies and Rev. Son singing the hymn brought the tears and bewilderment to people.

In this way, all the one thousand and one hundred members of Aeyangwon whether they were adults or children with the exception of shut-ins watched the procession of the coffins with tears and conversed with each other tearfully about what they witnessed upon returning home. The whole Aeyangwon turned into a household in mourning as it took measures to prepare for the funeral.

"Ms. Bok-Sun, please give me the thing that I need to write their names on as we talked about before." The voice belonged to Elder Park.

"This should be good enough," said Bok-Sun as she pulled out of her work basket a white silk fabric that was about ten feet long. Then she showed it Mak-Dal before giving it to Elder Park by saying, "I have only this one." Elder Park already had a hempen hood on his head.

"This is great. I will write on it and bring it back to you tomorrow morning. Please have a stick ready." Elder Park left without listening to what she had to say.

"Yes," answered Bok-Sun. But when she thought about it, she realized how hard it would be for her to go and find a long stick somewhere. So, she whispered, "They should use a laundry pole." And then she went back to sewing.

"I should go and give it out," said Mak-Dal as she left.

Jeondosa Lee In-Jae tried to comfort Mrs. Son by saying, "Mrs. Son, it is an earth-shattering glory to produce one martyr. But how amazing and glorious it is to have two martyrs?" But when he realized that his words did not have the intended effect on Mrs. Son who kept on crying sorrowfully, he did not know what to do. Mrs. Son, who fainted for a little while on the previous day, had been weeping hysterically ever since she had regained her consciousness. Though it had been a full day now, she was in the same state of mind. Knowing that a car was being sent out to bring back the bodies would only compound her condition.

From what he heard yesterday, Rev. Son decided to forgive the killer that murdered his two sons and adopt him as his own. Not only that, he asked people to bury Dong-In and Dong-Sin at Aeyangwon. Also, Mr. Hong testified that Rev. Son's prayer was one of faith. But he thought, "They seemed to be coming apart emotionally. They have been like this all through the night and they are still like that now."

From Rev. Son's words, "My sins are so grave that I am suffering what others cannot even imagine even after all that I have been through," *Jeondosa* Lee was able to take a glimpse into the abyss of his heart.

They were told that breakfast was ready. Though he was not in the mood to eat anything, he knew that, if he refused, Rev. Son who did not eat anything the night before would not eat again. So, he decided to have breakfast and implored Rev. Son to do the same.

"Lee *Jeondosa*, please say grace." Rev. Son bowed his head. *Jeondosa* Lee bowed his head, but did not know what to say in thanksgiving. After a pause, he began speaking, "God, thank you for your infinite love." Then, unexpectedly, the following words flowed from his lips. "We thank you because your grace allows everything to work for the good of us. You have not received the sacrifice that we have been trying to offer you. But now you have received the sacrifice of two lives that were pure and not corrupted by the world. We do not know why you did this, but we trust that your will was done. Now, reveal that will to us. Help us to take the food that you have prepared and live the life of obeying your will..."

When the prayer was finished, the eyes of Rev. Son glistened. He laughed, "Huh, huh, huh" and said, "Lee *Jeondosa-nim*, I am truly thankful." Then he proceeded to having his breakfast.

From this point and on, Rev. Son was able to be thankful in all things. He must have realized that God indeed had taken not the sacrifice of his own life but instead the sacrifice of his sons' two lives. And he must have thought that the reason for this was that he still had things left to accomplish here on earth!

To Rev. Son, the deaths of his two sons as the sacrifice of martyrdom ultimately signified the triumph of faith over the world. Within this framework of meaning, his actions of receiving the bodies of his sons as if he was greeting a general on his return from a triumphant war and trailing the coffins singing the hymn, "When all my labours and trials are o'er..." need to be understood. To others, these actions of Rev. Son made them more heartbroken than his tears could ever do and, at the same time, gave them a sense of remarkable comfort.

"This is enough, right? Elder?"

"You dug well. It is wide and deep."

"When I was digging yesterday, I did not know how soft the ground was."

"Does water seep in at all?"

"No. I was worried about that when I was digging it yesterday, since it is near the beach. But I was glad when there was no water as I kept on digging. This must be an ideal spot. The blue dragon in the west and the white tiger in the east... Ha, ha, ha," said Bang Dae-Sik. He burst into laughter when he had a mental block and was not able to finish quoting the ancient Chinese saying. He was trying to explain the suitability of the chosen gravesite. He was known as a good-natured young man at Aeyangwon.

"You did very well, digging not one but two graves."

"You make it sound like I did it all by myself," said Bang with a smile. He was surely good-natured.

This site received more sunlight than any other place in Aeyangwon. To its front lay the open sea. It was called Dong-Do [Island of the East].

The beach of breaking waves was at the steep end of the golden slope of the grass field that extended all the way from the top of the hill.

It was on the grass field where the young adults of Aeyangwon Church had dug the graves under the supervision of Kim Won-Tae. Fitting for the graves dug by young men, they were spaciously wide and deep. Elder Sin, with a hempen hood on his head and a traditional top coat around him, came to check on the progress of the graves prior to the funeral service.

"And do you have the sods ready?"

"I have about four pieces of sod ready. I might need more though, since there are two graves."

"If we happen to need more of it, we will get it later. By the way, where is everybody?"

"They went to have breakfast and get changed."

"I see. Well, I trust in your work." Then, Elder Sin began heading back to Aeyangwon. The wind almost knocked the hempen hood off his head. Elder Sin instinctively grabbed the hempen hood and turned around to look at Bang Dae-Sik with a grin. It was not clear whether Dae-Sin Bang saw Elder Sin. He was looking down intently on the graves with a shovel in his hand.

The Morning of October 27

The staff of Aeyangwon Church and their families, having stayed up all night, did not wish for the daylight to come. But how could they stop a new day from dawning?

Several patches of cloud decorate the lofty and clear sky.

The wind blowing through fall leaves give a tinge of cold.

The ocean spreads out its expanse far under the sky as ever.

Unsympathetic seagulls draw a cross on the horizon.

Is that Jordan River beyond what can be seen far away from here?

Who laments the falling leaves blown off by a chilly wind?

Who would call a flower that was picked without fully blooming for its very first spring fresh?

We know that they had gone away to the place the Lord prepared for them.

Since we know how a misfortune struck them, how can we not shed tears?

More than three hundred flags of tribute were blowing in the wind. About a thousand Aeyangwon members were gathered dressed in the white garb that they had spent the whole night to make. They stood solemnly in front of the two coffins like a company of saints surrounded by a host of angels.

In this way, the funeral service started with the bereaved family in presence.

Elder Park, the presider, announced, "Now, Lee *Jeondosa-nim* will give us the message." The hempen hood on his head seemed to be small for him and almost fell off a couple of times.

"There's a land that is fairer than day, and by faith we can see it afar..." sang the gathered in tears. There was a tearful opening prayer given by Elder Park Chun-Gap followed by the reading of the Scripture and singing of another hymn. Now, it was *Jeondosa* Lee's turn to give his sermon.

Lee read Revelation 11:1–11. A strained look on his blushed face made it look especially red right below the hempen hood. He said, "I regard it glorious for me to be able to attend this funeral service of the two saints who were martyred. I always experienced a dose of jealousy whenever I read the chronicles of Christian martyrs either at school or at my study. Now, that we are able to witness the bodies of the martyrs with our own eyes and bury them with our own hands, what can be more glorious? With what words can we describe this honor?" The gist of his message was as follows:

"This event that happened before us was not an accident. I believe it to be the fulfillment of what I just read in the Scripture. Chapters 11, 12, and 13 of Revelation present a prophetic imagery of the battle between the church and the anti-Christ, the beast, in the end days. The two witnesses that appear dressed in thick hemp clothes in Chapter 11 symbolize the church of the end time that preaches the gospel of the Lord. The church should not only lament the sins of people in the world, but also carry out the work of testifying to Jesus with boldness and authority as Moses and Elijah had done."

"Chapter 11 verse 7 says that the beast that came up from the Hades fought against the church and even killed it. What does it predict? Isn't what we face today the partial fulfillment of this prophecy? Truly, the beast had risen from the Hades. What else would the hearts of his fellow students that shot these martyrs to death represent if they don't represent the heart of the beast? The reality of the martyrdom points to the literal fulfillment of what is prophesied here."

"I heard that the bodies of the two martyrs were abandoned for three days and a half in the streets and not buried. It says in the Scripture that the number of the martyrs is two and their bodies were abandoned and not buried. Though it is strange, but because this part of the prophecy came true, I believe that the part of the prophecy that talks about the resurrection in three and a half days would also come true."

"What do you suppose three days and a half could mean? Since it speaks of the fulfillment of all biblical prophecies, it must symbolize the three years and a half of the beast's active commission here on earth. After that period of time expires, the Lord would come again. And the servants who gave themselves as martyrs for the Lord would resurrect first. Oh, how glorious would the first resurrection be! Oh, my beloved, today we bury these martyrs. But we need to wait only three years and a half for them."

Jeondosa Lee gave all he had in preaching the sermon passionately. All the members of Aeyangwon along with the bereaved family seemed to have been comforted by the message. They remained silent. It seemed as if, besides those in attendance, the trees colored with fall foliage, the houses in the rear, and the mountains far away, and the open sea to the front were all listening to the sermon quietly.

It was as if all the creation that did not want to submit to the things futile was waiting for the return of the sons of God. The sound of individuals sobbing in the crowd seemed to give credence to the belief that all things work together for the good of those who love God and who are called according to God's will. Only the intermittent sound of weeping broke the silence. The sermon continued.

"People, Dong-In and Dong-Sin surely admonished their fellow students to believe in Jesus even as they were being dragged to the place of execution. They also cried out to the crowd telling them twice to put their trust in Jesus, thereby sharing the gospel to the end. Furthermore, they both volunteered to die in the place of each other for the sake of their parents. Even as they were shot, they testified to Christ by crying out "My Lord, please receive my spirit.""

His tone of voice now became tearful. "May we now emulate their faith and faithfulness. May we testify to our Lord till the end and have the privilege of seeing each other in his presence." *Jeondosa* Lee came down from the pulpit with tears filling his eyes.

It was followed by the heartbreaking brief chronology of the two brothers. There was also a condolatory address as well as a hymn beseeching God. It was now Rev. Son to give his address in reply.

When he went up to the pulpit, his short height was instantly increased by the yellowish hempen hood. Rev. Son in his hempen topcoat seemed as chilly as the autumn wind. He seemed as weighty as a volcano waiting to erupt.

He began to speak, "Ladies and Gentlemen, how can I possibly make a long reply? Instead, I would like replace my address with a list of several gracious items of thanksgiving that I recognized as I came to terms with the deaths of my sons."

His voice was coarse from either crying or praying. The gathered became silent. He opened a piece of paper and began to read from it:

"First, I thank the Lord for producing sons of martyrdom from the blood of a sinner like me. Second, I thank the Lord for giving me a privilege to take care of these beautiful treasures in the company of many believers. Third, I thank the Lord for his blessing in taking the most beautiful sacrifices of the first and the second sons among my children of three boys and three girls."

His voice became tearful. Along the ears with which they had been listening to the address, the audience now opened their eyes that were filled with tears. They wondered if Rev. Son was saying these things because he truly meant them or because he felt like he had to say them. Rev. Son continued:

"Fourth, they say it is precious to have a son who is martyred. Still more, I thank the Lord for giving me not one but two martyrs."

His voice got louder. His hands that were holding the note began to shake a little. He continued on:

"Fifth, they say it is a great blessing to die on one's own bed with faith in Jesus. Still more, I thank the Lord for letting my sons be shot to death while carrying out the work of evangelism. Sixth, my sons were preparing to study abroad in the U.S. However, I thank the Lord because my heart is relieved to know that they went to a better place than America–that is, heaven. Seventh, I thank the Lord for giving me a loving heart with which to embrace the enemy who killed my two sons and willingness to work hard in order to help him repent and make him my son."

As the audience bawled loudly, they were astounded one more time. People thought it was insane for Rev. Son to say such things, except those who knew that Rev. Son had already commissioned a person to go to Suncheon to carry out his decision.

"Eighth, I thank the Lord for giving me the conviction that there will be numerous sons in heaven as the result of the martyrdom of my two sons."

The audience now understood from where Rev. Son's deep gratitude was from. This made them cry all the more.

"Ninth, I give thanks upon thanks to the Lord for revealing the above eight truths to me, giving me joyfulness in my heart and strengthening my faith in a time of adversity such as this."

He seemed to be smiling now. In conclusion, he said:

"Lastly, oh my Lord, I thank you for giving me this blessing that is far greater than anything that I deserve. This is the culmination of what my father and my mother had been praying tearfully to you in the early hours of morning for thirty five, thirty six years. I take this to be the fruit of the prayers that my brothers and sisters with Hansen's disease have been for my family and me for the last twenty three years. I love them dearly, Lord. I am truly thankful to you, my beloved."

The funeral was transformed into a valley of tears through Rev. Son's address in reply.

Two Hours after the Funeral

In that first day of autumn, all the members remained where they were. Without even going home and changing their clothes, everyone who came to the funeral followed the procession of the coffins out of the sanctuary. The young men of Aeyangwon and the staff of Aeyangwon Church carried the coffins around the sanctuary once and headed out for the ceremony of lowering the coffins into the graves. The members of the church stood around the twin graves that were dug the day before. The believers dressed in white cried as they sang hymns along with the bereaved family. They cried listening to the sermon. They cried some more as they heard the chronology of the deceased and the condolatory address. They cried as they listened to the surprising words of Rev. Son's address. They cried as they watched and followed the procession of the coffins. But as they were about to lower the coffins into the graves and as they thought about not being able to see even their bodies that could not talk anymore and as they thought about their bodies being turned into a handful of dust, they were overwhelmed with profound grief.

Their tears were like the sea breeze

That blows over the southernmost island.

Their tears were like the waves in the oceans that envelope the earth.

Their sighs and tears did not stop.

"Rock of ages, cleft for me, let me hide my self to thee…"

They could not even sing the hymn #73 well. The words of 1 Thessalonians 4:13–18 roamed around their ears without being registered. What *Jeondosa* Lee was saying in a tearful prayer could not even alleviate the deep sadness, tears, tears, grief, tears, tears, and grief.

"Father, you should witness only to grown ups. I will witness to the children." Dong-In, your father is here, but where have you gone? Who will carry out evangelism in this land?

Dong-Sin! You used to build the altar of prayer in the deep woods of Okjongsan Bukbang-ri and pray earnestly for your father, mother, and your siblings. Your parents, your siblings are all alive. But where have you gone? Who will pray that prayer now?

Dong-In! You used to send home twenty *won* out of your monthly salary of twenty three *won*. Here is your mother and here are your siblings. But where have you gone!

Dong-Sin! You used to chop woods in the mountain behind the house. You were so hungry that you fell on the way down. Where have you gone? Who will chop the woods that are needed to warm this land?

Dong-In! You said, "I will go and study and return to you so that I can serve you in my father's place." We are still here. But where have you gone?

Dong-In and Dong-Sin! You said, "When I grow up, I will live with Ms. Hwang." Ms. Hwang is here, but where have you gone?

Dong-Sin! You used to comfort the middle aged women here at Aeyangwon by saying, "Let us live together with the pine trees on our backs, with sifters on our heads, and with shaved eyebrows in the future." Where have you gone? With whom are we going to live in this lonely world?

Dear brothers, you used to earnestly teach and guide us in our studies so that we would not disgrace our parents. We are standing here, but where have you gone?

Dear brothers, you used to wage in a campaign against Shinto worship. The war is over, but where have you gone? Have you gone to where our grandfather is? Have you gone to where our grandmother is? To who have you entrusted the things that you always wanted to achieve in this world? Why aren't you answering?

This is the Island of Dong-Do where you used to come and play time to time. Please sing the hymn "The Bright, Heavenly Way" one more time! Sing us the song "Rock of Ages, Cleft for Me" one more time! Why aren't you saying anything? Why aren't you answering?

In this way, the lives of the two brothers flashed through the minds of people in different ways like a revolving lantern.

Tears are flowing like a wave. They are not stopping.

Sighs are blowing like a wind. They are not stopping.
People, cry. Cry as much as you want.
Sadness is more beautiful than laughter.
It is more innocent than producing a worried look.
The mind of the ignorant belongs to his home.
The mind of the wise belongs to a house in mourning.
Cry in the direction of the wide open sea.
Shout in the direction of the wide open sky.
Is that the sea of the bitter world?
Is that the sea of tears?
Calm sky, why are you silent?
Triumphant sea, why are you silent?

The Atomic Bomb of Love
Chapter 13

R ev. Nah was suffering from exhaustion and stress that came not only from living through the ordeal of the uprising mindlessly, but also from working determinedly to extricate many individuals, several members of Seongju Church or their kinsmen, who were arrested and being prosecuted by the government authorities. His mind would go blank intermittently and suffer from the images of carnage. He could neither eat nor sleep well. He was feeling weighty and feverish, perhaps due to a cold. So, he was resting his body since the morning hours.

At that moment, he heard the words, "Father, Mother, Dong-Hee is here."

He was startled to hear the name "Dong-Hee." Fortunately, none of his five children was hurt from the incident. However, the two sons of Rev. Son Yang-Won, his dear friend, who were entrusted to him while they were in Suncheon for their studies, were ruthlessly gunned down. Though he was not personally culpable in any way, he still felt guilty from not being able to help them. He felt as if he had committed a terrible sin. In the midst of feeling torn over what happened day and night, he felt bad and did not want to face Dong-Hee. If it had been under different circumstances, he would have welcomed her joyfully. That explained his apprehension of meeting Dong-Hee. It felt to him like he was being confronted by Rev. Son himself.

Through their martyrdom, it was true that their end had been glorified. Furthermore, he had heard that the funeral at Aeyangwon was exemplary. However, the matter was personal between Rev. Son and himself and, as such, demanded a different avenue of resolution.

Though he got up instantly upon hearing that Dong-Hee had arrived, he did not know what he should do next. Being oblivious to Rev. Nah's predicament, his daughter, Sun-Geum, led Dong-Hee to where he was. "Come this way. My father is resting in this room."

The clock rang ten. But Dong-Hee was sporting an ambivalent look. It was not clear whether it was because she was worried or just apathetic.

Rev. Nah could not say anything because he thought that it was just a natural reaction on her part. Then, the wife of Rev. Nah who had been doing the dishes in the kitchen came in through the back door and asked outright, "Dong-Hee, how sad are your father and mother?"

"They are grieving hard. My mother even fainted and my father cried a lot, too. But he stated during the funeral service that he was thankful that they died decorously as martyrs. I don't know whether it was nine or ten things. He spoke of the things that he was thankful for at the funeral." Rev. Nah responded, "What was he thankful for?"

"I cannot recall everything. But he said something about our family producing not one but two great martyrs of faith. He said that it was not the end of it. He said, "How thankful it is to give two lives as the beginning of martyrdom." He also said, "How thankful it is that they did not beg to live, but died testifying to the gospel." He also mentioned that he was thankful that they went to heaven, a far better place than America..." Dong-Hee tried to recall more.

Though he did not get the full report, Rev. Nah could not help but be shocked. For him, it would have been better if had Dong-Hee said, "My father believes that my two brothers were killed because of your neglect and he blames you." It was, instead, very difficult for him to hear that Rev. Son was thankful for his two sons being the sacrifice of martyrdom." He thought, "Indeed, it is Rev. Son."

'Has it really been twenty three years? He was viewed as a foolish pastor for living with the Hansen's disease patients for all those years. He had spent six years in jails, prisons, and penitentiaries for his protests against Shinto worship. But how could he be thankful when his dearly loved two sons were killed? How could he say that he was thankful for their martyrdom when they were murdered? How can a human being think or say such a thing?'

As he listened to the story, tears flowed from his eyes. And he remembered that someone came to relay Rev. Son's message to him previously. He did not forget about it, but now he thought of it differently. The message was, "If the killer of my sons gets ever arrested, please do not allow him to get executed or even get a beating for the crime. Then, I will share the gospel to that person, turn him into a Christian, and adopt him as my own son."

Rev. Son had asked Rev. Nah's help in making this happen. At first, when he received the word from Rev. Son, he thought it was suitable. Then, he did not have the courage to follow it through, thinking that it should not be so. It was because Rev. Nah realized how hard it is to defend for someone who was falsely persecuted, let alone someone who is truly guilty. He thought that it would be crazy and unreasonable for him to open his mouth and ask clemency for a guilty party.

Now that Dong-Hee was here with the same entreaty, Rev. Nah found strength to probe further.

As he was about to ask, "Didn't he say anything else?" Dong-Hee said, "And he was thankful that God has given him love in his heart to want to help the murderer of my two brothers repent and adopt him as his son." Then she went on to say, "That's the reason why I came here hastily. The other day, my father sent Elder Park to convey his message to you. But he sent me to confirm that wish and ask you to actively support him in this endeavor. He said that he would be praying for this at Aeyangwon." He thought to himself:

'Are we witnessing a miracle in the twentieth century? It is the love of

God who sent his only begotten Son, Jesus, to this earth which is to be destroyed; it is the love of Jesus Christ who gave his blood on the cross in order to atone for our sins and save us who were destined to die!'

'The stories of all the martyrs and saints who tried to uphold the will of the Lord by dedicating their entire lives are remarkable. What kind of request is this to save the person responsible for the murder of his two sons and adopt him as his own, if it is not the wish of a saint who has truly tasted the love of God who gave his own Son and the faith of Abraham who tried to offer his only son in Isaac without any hesitation? Much more, this needs to take place in this world that is being corrupt by the advancement of extreme materialism of the twentieth century. Furthermore, it is cogent especially within the context of the church's hypocritical ideation of advocating justice and love on one hand and committing thievery on the other.'

'How can I be apathetic after being commissioned for this! If I remain quiet, this would not get done. Then I will be afraid of the judgment that will be upon me. The outcome of this work is up to God's will. Who knows if it indeed comes true?'

These thoughts brought on a renewed sense of strength to his weighty body and enabled him to get up from his seat.

At that moment, Jae-Min, Rev. Nah's son and a good friend of deceased Dong-Sin, came in to the room and said, "You are here, Dong-Hee." Then he proceeded to report, "Father, the student who killed Dong-In and Dong-Sin was caught. The student association is right now filing the charge and about to hand him over to the government forces."

It was not known whether it was a rumor or verified fact. But Jae-Min probably had what Rev. Son requested previously in his mind when he reported it.

For Rev. Nah, it was a God-given golden opportunity that he could not afford to waste. So, he told Dong-Hee that he would come back and hurried out the door with Jae-Min leading the way.

"Rev. Nah is back," said someone from the outside. Sun-Geum and Dong-Hee came out of the house to find out what happened. They wanted to ask about what happened, but they saw Rev. Nah and an old man who seemed to be listless and looked to be about sixty years of age walking into the sanctuary. Once they got to the front of the sanctuary near the pulpit, they prostrated themselves in order to pray. The girls waited for them to come out of the sanctuary thinking that the old man probably had had someone close to him arrested or executed for nothing, or he had come with a request for something else. But Rev. Nah and the old man did not come out for a long time. Mrs. Nah and other children snooped around the sanctuary, but they only found the two men praying tearfully. Mrs. Nah went inside the sanctuary in order to find out who the old man was. She had never seen him before. However, she listened attentively to the prayer that Rev. Nah was saying.

Rev. Nah was praying, "God who turned Saul into Paul through the martyrdom of Stephen, I ask you to fulfill Rev. Son's wishes not so much for having compassion on this old man's son but more for your glory, Lord. It is not possible with human power. You have to lavish your great power on me. You need to inspire me to speak boldly as well as others to be willing to listen to what I have to say. You need to work the miracle of the twentieth century so that this nation and these people and the humankind can live."

Then what was the story behind Rev. Nah bringing the old man to the church?

Rev. Nah, guided by Jae-Min, reached the office of the student association which was located in a large building right next to the Joseon Bank in order to get to the student that was caught. When he got there, he found the student lying on a bed apparently due to the injuries sustained from the beating that he took from others that were guarding him. There was an old lady who looked to be in her fifties holding the student in her arms. She seemed to be the mother of the student. She was crying and pleading for mercy.

However, the students that were gathered there were conducting the last part of the interrogation as if the investigation was almost finished.

"Yes, you bastard! If you did not shoot, then who pulled the trigger?" said the students angrily. They were ready to pounce on him again.

"Guys, please," said the student's mother as she tried to protect him.

"I shot at the corpses," said the student fearfully.

"I see. How hateful were you to shoot at him again after he was dead? Right, you shot him after he was dead, huh?"

"It was after Dong-Sin was dead," said the student in a shaking voice.

The students of the student association who were filling out the report based on their interrogation had their anger boiling inside them.

During those days, the government forces were occupying the region. However, since they were vastly limited in what they could do, they granted a special license to the young men's association and the police department to investigate and turn over to the military tribunal for trials anyone, regardless of age, gender and status, who had supported the uprising.

Of course, there were innocent people who were charged mistakenly. But in most cases, people were investigated only after some evidence had been obtained. Since it was a matter of life and death, they could not undertake the process carelessly.

It was a known fact that this particular young man had joined the leftist camp of students and was seen carrying around a rifle. More than anything, he was said to have participated in the shooting of Dong-In and Dong-Sin. Since he kept on denying his involvement, the other students were fed up with him and had beaten him profusely. His mother, however, whether she knew the full story or not, got in the way and begged them not to hurt him.

There was a young soldier standing nearby. He heard the details of what was confessed and tried to evaluate the suspect's situation.

After observing what was going on, Rev. Nah boldly interjected, "Guys, you are working hard here. But let me just say one thing."

A student that was next to him asked, "Who are you?"

"I am Rev. Nah of Seongju Church," answered Rev. Nah.

Another student said, "You must be the father of Jae-Min."

"Oh, is that true? What did you want to say?" The student in charge of the investigation asked.

Then Rev. Nah expressed his appreciation for the hard work that they put in and the hard work that they would continue to do. He also mentioned that he had been asked by Rev. Son to plead for the killer of his two sons to be exempted from execution irrespective of others. He conveyed Rev. Son's wish to adopt the murderer as his own son. Not only that, he shared that Rev. Son wanted to help him repent and save him from sins.

Upon hearing this from Rev. Nah, some students argued that this was not the right time to say things like that, that he could get into trouble for saying such things, and that it was not up to them to decide what needed to happen. At the same time, there were others who teared up and kept their silence. The young soldier might have thought that what Rev. Nah just said was nonsensical. After having sat silently for a while, he stole a look at Rev. Nah and tried to leave the place. When Rev. Nah got a hold of the soldier and tried to repeat his request again, the soldier did not take Rev. Nah seriously and rebuffed his plea by telling him not to go around making such idiotic statements. The one who sought to get clarification as to what was happening was the mother of the charged student rather than the student himself. With a desperate look on her face, she kept her gaze on Rev. Nah.

Without anything to show for, Rev. Nah went to the Suncheon

police station and conveyed his message to the station chief and his subordinates. But everyone tried to evade any responsibility by directing Rev. Nah to go and talk to the Korean Army.

Next, Rev. Nah went to visit a person who said to have some power in the citizens' council. However, the person, even without listening to what Rev. Nah had to say, told him that it would be politically dangerous to keep speaking of such ill-logically conceived notions. Now, there was no one left to talk to.

As Rev. Nah turned around and was about to pass by the police station, an old man came up to him and asked, "Aren't you Rev. Nah?"

When Rev. Nah nodded, he identified himself as the father of Jae-Seon. When Rev. Nah asked who Jae-Seon was, he referred to the student in custody as his son.

"I see—you are the father of that student who supposedly killed the two sons of Rev. Son?"

In tears, the old man said that the young man was indeed his son.

"What can I do for you?" asked Rev. Nah.

According to the old man, he had heard from his wife when he went to the student association about what Rev. Nah said in requesting forgiveness for their son. Since he was in a situation where he could not do anything and was glad to hear about that someone offering help, he came looking for Rev. Nah upon hearing that he went down to the police station. He thought that his son could not have done such the terrible act that he was charged with. Therefore, he sought Rev. Nah out to enlist his help in freeing his son.

The old man's plea added to the burden of what he was trying to do. Not knowing what to do, Rev. Nah brought the old man to the church so that they could pray together to the Lord. Also, Rev. Nah brought the old man, who hadn't seen a church building in his life, there to comfort him. As Rev. Nah talked about who Rev. Son was the old man seemed surprised to hear that he once was incarcerated at Gwangju Prison.

That was because he realized that Rev. Son was the famous pastor imprisoned at Gwangju Prison that he had heard about while he was serving his own sentence for a financial mishap.

Anyhow, as the conversation went on, they had come inside the sanctuary made out of stones. The interior of the sanctuary seemed strange to him, especially the big and long object hanging on the wall. Rev. Nah bowed his head and closed his eyes to plea to the divine power of the heaven and earth. The old man did not know what to say except to keep repeating, "Please save my son, please." Rev. Nah's prayer must have sounded like a shamanistic incantation to him.

While on the way to the church, Rev. Nah tried to witness Christ to him irrespective of what Jae-Seon's father would think. However, the father of Jae-Seon told him that he was already a believer. Not only that, he questioned how anybody could not know God. Even before Rev. Nah could ask him questions, the old man tried to come across as someone who already had the answers. It was understandably a ploy used by someone in desperate situation to cater to any kind of demand made by his helper. Regardless, he was a stout old man that exuded an aura of assurance. After praying at the sanctuary, Rev. Nah felt a bit more empowered by God.

Jae-Min who had broken the news initially followed them home.

"That student was taken to Palwang [Eight Kings] Café."

Confused, Rev. Nah asked him, "What kind of café is it?"

"The one where the government command center is situated."

Jae-Seon's father, who did not know what was happening, automatically presumed that his son was taken away for execution. He broke down in tears saying, "Oh my, this is no good. Now, what can we do?"

"Don't worry. I don't think it's final yet," said Rev. Nah in his apparent attempt to comfort the old man. Then, without an explanation to his wife, Dong-Hee, Sun-Geum, and Rev. Nah left for Palwang Café in haste as per Jae-Min's guidance.

As he left the church, he did not even have a chance to look back at Jae-Seon's father, who kept crying out to him, "Rev. Nah! Please keep my son alive." Now that he had arrived at Palwang Café with Jae-Min's help, he tried to slip through the entrance without asking for anybody's permission.

However, the soldier standing guard at the entrance yelled at him, "Hey! Who are you? What business do you have here?"

"Yes, my name is Nah Deok-Hwan and I am the pastor of Seongju Church." He seemed anxious to enter the building.

"What? A pastor? What you want?"

"I have something to discuss," he said as he quickly pulled out his business card.

"Sir, what is the business?" The guard changed his tone of voice.

"I need to discuss it inside. I want to have a word with the captain of the company."

As he peeked inside, he saw the same soldier that he had met at the student association earlier that day. He said, "I mean, I want to talk to that soldier." Then, as he had just done a moment ago, he again entered the building before the guard gave him permission to do so.

Dumbfounded by the action of Rev. Nah, the guard tried to follow him inside at first. Then, he turned around and went back outside.

"Who are you?" He saw Jae-Seon's father coming in and he tried to block him from entering.

"I am that boy's father," answered the old man.

Rev. Nah heard the words of the old man. However, he did not have the time to turn around and speak on behalf of him. He needed to find some way to speak to the soldier now. He found the mother of the student sitting next to him. She was crying and pleading for mercy for her son. The soldier was facing a dilemma. The investigative report had declared that he had killed the brothers. On the other hand, the student's statements disputed that. As he flipped through the pages of the report, his eyes caught Rev. Nah standing next to him. The look on the soldier's face expressed disdain and annoyance for what Rev. Nah might say.

Rev. Nah, then, asked for and received the permission from the soldier to ask a few things to Jae-Seon. "I am Rev. Nah, the pastor of Seongju Church. You should not hide anything from me and tell me everything. I represent Rev. Son, the father of two brothers that you have allegedly killed. Did you really join the rebel students? Were you also part of the mob that pursued the two students in question? Did you shoot them?"

Jae-Seon looked surprised to hear the questions. It was because, needless to say, Rev. Nah's approach to questioning had differed from those of the rightist students who arrested him and concluded him to be a guilty offender and the soldiers bent on condemning him.

Also, Rev. Nah's words differed from those of his mother in claiming the innocence of her son and pleading for clemency without really knowing the truth. His approach contrasted from that of the unconditional motherly love that demanded blindly for her child's survival.

"Pastor, I really did not kill them."

"Are you sure? You really did not kill them?"

"Yes, I am telling the truth."

"Then, I have nothing to do with you."

Those that were present, including Jae-Seon, his parents, Jae-Min and the soldiers, wondered, "What is he talking about?"

In a serious tone of voice, Rev. Nah said, "Not only did I come here to convey Rev. Son's words, but I am here also to make sure it happens. What I need to do is applicable only to the killer of his two sons. He did not request for anything other than clemency of the killer, instead of vengeance. He asked me to make this plea on his behalf." His tearful words differed from those of a professional preacher speaking at a prison, an institutionalized church, or a pulpit. His words carried an unexpected authority.

At that moment, Jae-Seon felt pain reverberating through his whole being. He grabbed tightly onto Rev. Nah who was trying to stand up and cried, "Pastor, please save me. I did join. I was on the witch hunt. I even shot them. Please save me. Please let me live."

Was what Jae-Seon said the same as "I killed them"? Or did it mean something else? Were those the words of a drowning person desperately trying to grab onto some loose straws? Was it a true confession? Who could discern the thoughts of Jae-Seon correctly? Only our omniscient God knows the truth! However, his words sounded a lot different from the forced confessions of others. They also represented a marked departure from his previous excuses that played on passive participation and mitigating factors as in the following statements: "When the rebels entered Suncheon, the leftist students came to enlist me. So, I could not help but join them"; "They forced me to carry a rifle, even though I did not want to"; "I just happened to follow the mob to the house of Dong-In and Dong-Sin"; "Since everyone else was beating him, I simply joined in"; "Because they dragged them out and tried them at the people's court and got them the sentence of death"; "Since five people got the order to shoot at the same time, I could not help but shoot them."

When asked again, "How did you kill them?" Jae-Seon replied, "I shot them. But since it was five of us shooting at them at the same time, I am not sure if my bullets hit them or not. But I shot two more times when Dong-Sin fell to the ground."

How shocking is this confession? It made sense coming from an amateur who had never worked with a rifle before.

Two of the students from the student association were surprised to see the changed attitude in Jae-Seon. No one would ever know if the

confession was genuine or mere posturing. Furthermore, whether the
shots that Jae-Seon fired had really hit Dong-In or Dong-Sin fatally
did not matter as much as the murderous intention of shooting at the
victims. It was clear from Jae-Seon's actions that he had the killer's
willingness to cut down anyone he deemed an enemy. Therefore,
irrespective of whether the victims were actually felled by Jae-Seon's
bullets or not, he was guilty as charged and would not be able to escape
the fate of a murderer.

"Really? If that's true, I will try my best. You did well to confess. Jesus
came to save sinners like you."

This statement of the truth of atonement, rather than being based
on a theoretical hypothesis or abstraction, was rooted in reality. God's
redemption of humankind through his only begotten son, Jesus Christ,
is applicable to anyone who confesses his or her sins and repents and
whose heart desires salvation.

Those who claim Shinto worship as a matter of conscience or those
that say that they have no need for repentance because they have
already repented exhibit the kind of abominable heart that does not
deserve the love of God. Let's say some have agreed to this travesty
because they were forced to do so. Is that behavior still fitting for
someone called to fear God or a leader? Can anyone really claim
orthodoxy by the length of time spent in studying or teaching the
word of God? Is orthodoxy determined by how long a person has been
preaching? That type of reasoning makes only as much sense as a rice
cooker (again, the writer is using the words "orthodoxy" and "rice
cooker" in a playful rhyme).

Let's say that those gave into the pressure of Shinto worship because
they felt that they did not have a choice. Then, how can they turn
around and condemn the true martyrs and the saints who suffered
imprisonment for being stubborn and hypocritical? How can they try
to exonerate themselves by mischaracterizing others as instigators of

divisiveness? Is that what you call the fruit of the Holy Spirit? That is the fruit of the devil that does not fear God! The leaders of the Church of Korea! You are far worse than Jae-Seon, who has at least confessed to his crime honestly. Go inside Palwang Café. Execution by shooting awaits the murderer. If you don't, it will come to you.

Do you still want to argue that you are not a killer? You are indeed a killer of God, an enemy of God, a murderer, a killer of sheep, a sinner worse than Jae-Seon. Your eloquence is speechless. Your tactic is complimentary. Do you believe that it was Judas Iscariot that pierced Jesus' side? He received nothing save thirty silver coins. You are not even Pontius Pilate. Not even Roman guards. You are truly the second coming of Judas Iscariot. Do you know that or not?

Being empowered by the confession of Jae-Seon, Rev. Nah went over to see the soldier with his head held high. There was an aura of holiness about him. He had the demeanor of a high priest.

"Sir, may I have a word with you? As you heard it from me back at the student association, I ask you to forgive this student," said Rev. Nah.

The solider in charge of the investigation must have thought that Rev. Nah was a cheeky fellow and not the dignified sort of pastor. Furthermore, the argument that the student should be forgiven now that he had confessed to the crime must have been baffling. The case for clemency or leniency on behalf of the student should have been better made on the basis of his denial, not his confession.

"Hey, I do not need to hear that from you. Hasn't he confessed to it already?"

"That's my point. Forgive him now that he has confessed. If he did not confess to it, I would not have asked you to forgive him," Rev. Nah emphasized.

"No, since he confessed, I cannot let him go," the soldier curtly refused.

"Please, you should do this since he confessed. This is the earnest request of Rev. Son, who has lost two sons—more than it is mine. Rather, it is what Jesus desires in whom we believe. It is also what God wants as well."

"Sir, I do not care about those things. I am too busy to be lectured. And by the way, what kind of logic is that? Forgive *because* he confessed?" the soldier said as he pulled out a cigarette and lit it. The smoke from the cigarette slowly rose like a stifling sigh.

"You! Stop this nonsense and go back home. I have nothing to say anymore. Anyway, it's already decided!" said the soldier.

'What does he mean by 'it's already decided? Who is this that has already tagged Jae-Seon for execution?' Rev. Nah thought in his mind. He was shocked to hear the soldier's words. He felt guilty thinking that he might have sealed Jae-Seon's fate by extracting the confession out of him.

He became anxious thinking, "Oh, no. Rev. Son told me to save him. Instead, I just pushed him to the brink of execution!"

"Sir, please hear me out. We appreciate the government soldiers for coming to this place of rebellion and working hard to restore stability, order, and peace for the nation without any regard to their own lives. Therefore, you need to save his life so that he would do great things for Korea," said Rev. Nah.

Upon hearing these words, the soldier slammed on the desk hard. "Hey, Rev. Nah! What kind of garbage is that? It violates the law of Korea to let him go. And we don't need this kind of ideology in this country. Rev. Nah, you mean that we do disservice to Korea by executing this guy?" The soldier who seemed to be about twenty five or twenty six years old rebutted forcefully.

"No, please do not misunderstand me. I don't mean that we cannot do great things for Korea if we don't have him. Rather, I am talking about the obligation that exists in Christianity that offers forgiveness to anyone who confesses and repents. If we offer that mercy, this student would be changed and be eventually turned into a fine individual and do great things in the future. I said this on the basis of Paul whom we have in the annals of Christianity. He once was a wretched man but became a great teacher of faith and did many great things after having repented and turning away from his old ways."

"I don't care about this... Paul guy or whatever his name is. I am bound by the law, so stop it already." The soldier seemed annoyed. At that moment, a Jeep arrived at Palwang Café with a lot of noise.

"If it concerns the law of the land, please give me a few days so that I can even appeal to Mr. President."

"I am saying that you can't."

At once, an officer entered the building. The soldier that was sitting down got up from his seat quickly and saluted the officer.

"Sir, there's nothing to report. The truck is on hand to go to the execution range," reported the soldier.

"I see. But that truck got a flat tire on its way here. It went back to get it fixed. It will be about half an hour before it gets back here," said the officer. And after seeing a whole lot of people that were inside, he questioned, "What are all these people doing here?"

"They are that student's family, sir..." said the soldier.

"Well, get them out of here. I will be back later." The officer then walked out of the building. After saluting to the officer again, the soldier sat down on his seat.

Rev. Nah tried to find a window of opportunity to talk to the officer because he came across as a person of reason compared to his subordinate. However, Rev. Nah was disappointed to see the officer go out the door before he could say a word.

Rev. Nah was now faced with the urgency of the situation. His eyes swelled with tears as he realized that in a matter of mere half an hour, Jae-Seon would be shipped out to be executed.

"Sir, Mr. Soldier, either give me few days or let him go," Rev. Nah said tearfully.

Then he said, "Let's say we do it by the law. But hear me out for a moment." And he made his case by saying the following:

"There was this missionary from the Presbyterian Church of Scotland named James Wylie. He came to Liaoyang to work as a missionary in 1888. During the first Sino-Japanese War in 1894, he was killed by the Chinese soldiers that were on retreat to Jilin. His father was a lawyer who lived in Hamilton of Scotland. Known as a man of uprightness and principle, he could have every right and evidence to sue for compensation for the death of his son. However, he gave up that right and instead wrote a letter to the authorities saying that he was satisfied with the fact that his son died while doing the work of the Lord. Along with the letter, he sent money in the amount of ten thousand pounds through his son's friend Mr. Douglas so that a memorial church could be built in the honor of his son's martyrdom and the gospel could be introduced to the people of the town where his son was killed. The government of England accepted this wish of the missionary's father and refrained from engaging in a diplomatic tug of war.

Likewise, Rev. Son's request for the clemency of this young man is not irrational. Because the young man has confessed to his crime, as the father of the two victims, he is asserting his right and wish for the clemency of the young man. If this wish ever gets conveyed to Mr. President or Mr. Prime Minister, they would not consider clemency to be inappropriate in this case."

Rev. Nah appealed his case tearfully.

However, the matter remained as a thorny annoyance to the soldier. He believed that refusal was the only appropriate response to the problem.

He said, "Look, if you keep pushing it, you will be misunderstood. I understand it, but others would charge you for protecting a supporter of the uprising or interfering with a matter of national security or obstructing official military business. Those supporters of the leftist rebels must be punished in order for the peace and stability of the nation to be established."

To hear the words "The supporter of the leftist rebellion, interferer of national security, obstructer of the official military business" put Rev. Nah in a further quandary. Not only did he enable Jae-Seon to be officially indicted for execution, but he also was about to put himself in the same predicament. What was happening could be compared to pushing a drowning person deeper into water and then being pulled into water by the same person. The thought of giving up had crossed his mind but he quickly erased it thinking of what would happen to the student as well as Rev. Son's request. He knew that he would eventually be cleared of any wrongdoing because of his status as a pastor. But he could not live with himself if he had failed to carry out Rev. Son's request. He would not also bear the burden of having the student killed. At that moment, he thought of something as the last resort.

"I understand what you are saying. But I think that should be the case. I have evidence to say otherwise," said Rev. Nah.

"What evidence? Why don't you tell me?" replied the soldier.

"It is not necessarily new evidence. But you can find out if what I am saying is true or not by speaking to Rev. Son's oldest daughter who came to visit me in my house."

"Then, bring her here," said the soldier. However, the real reason for agreeing to talk to the daughter of Rev. Son was not to verify the truth of Rev. Nah's claim, but to be free of the nagging until the truck returned.

But to Rev. Nah it was an opportunity that God provided and only chance to avert any danger.

"Jae-Min! Go and bring Dong-Hee, fast," ordered Rev. Nah.

"Yes!" Jae-Min answered and went out the door like lightning.

The waiting game had started for Rev. Nah and the soldier. It was a race between the truck and Dong-Hee. It was a race between execution and clemency.

It would be disastrous if Dong-Hee and Sun-Geum had gone out to play. It would be also disastrous if the truck would arrive sooner than Jae-Min.

To make a round trip between Palwang Café, the headquarters of Army, and Seongju Church, it would not even take ten minutes. However, it seemed like a year's time had passed and he has still not returned. What could have happened?

At that moment, Jae-Min and Dong-Hee came in panting, puffing, blowing, and gasping for breath. Dong-Hee, though short in height and small in her face, came across as one smart girl. She, however, sported a concerned look on her face. Dong-Hee, who came in breathing heavily from running, looked more like an angel who instantly brought in a breath of fresh air into the stuffy atmosphere of the place than a human being. Everyone received this girl with wonder and curiosity.

Rev. Nah hastily introduced Dong-Hee to the soldier that had fixed his gaze on her by saying, "This is the daughter of Rev. Son and the sister to the two students that were murdered."

"What is your name?" asked the soldier. Though she was very young, he could not talk down to her.

"It is Son Dong-Hee," answered Dong-Hee clearly and with a measure of disinterestedness.

Since her last name matched with Rev. Son and first name was Dong-Hee, it seemed to the solider that she was related to the two victims.

"How old are you?" asked the soldier.

"I am fourteen," answered Dong-Hee.

Everyone was taken aback by her answer.

"When did you arrive here in Suncheon?"

"I left home early in the morning today to travel to this place."

"Why did you come?"

Rev. Nah closed his eyes when he heard the question. He seemed to be praying, "God! Jesus!"

"My father told me concerning my brothers'..."

"Yes?"

"... my brothers' killer." She worked hard to control the tears that were swelling up within her. Then she continued tearfully, "... do not have him killed... or even have him beaten. If his life is spared, if his life is spared..." She could not continue but burst into tears.

Those who heard Dong-Hee's words also began to sob, including the parents of Jae-Seon.

Even the soldier was moved to tears! It was the same for Rev. Nah and Jae-Min.

It was made clear that every single word that what Rev. Nah had spoken was true. Furthermore, Dong-Hee's words were like an atomic bomb of love dropped into Palwang Café, and they ignited the explosion of an atomic bomb of peace, and an atomic bomb of truth. It instantly turned the whole place into a sea of tears.

The atomic bomb of love that was detonated by an angel of peace!

Palwang Café, which used to push young men and women into sin!

The place that was turned into the headquarters of the Army, which was bent on punishing the rebels!

The righteous judge of this den of crime, this atomic bomb of love that was received from the messenger of love and in turn detonated by the angel of peace in this place of judgment!

This was the place where a son denied his crime, where a mother pleaded without critically assessing what her son had done, where a father tried to defend his son, where a soldier argued for the letter of the law, where a tension of right and love transpired, and where humanity and law became intertwined like a mountain hemp.

Rev. Nah, who got in the face of the soldier while disregarding his own situation! Rev. Son, who pleaded for the life of the killer of his sons! Dong-Hee, who came on behalf of his father despite losing her brothers, had thrown this atomic bomb of sacrifice and love!

Would it explode only in a place such as Palwang Café and be done?

After regaining his composure at the sound of the truck, the soldier told Rev. Nah to accompany him back to the student association. Then, he deliberated the case with the people there. After the discussion, the soldier declared, "I hand over this case to Rev. Nah. I will report it as such to my superiors." The soldier then went out to the truck with another person destined for the execution range.

(Author's comment)

This story was once made into a production titled *Hyang* [Fragrance]. At the time, the Army Broadcasting Department reviewed the script and subsequently cleared the production along with this statement: "The suppression of communist guerrillas has not killing but rehabilitation as its goal." I believe that it is a fair and appropriate assessment by an inspector.

The Atomic Bomb of Love

The atomic bomb of love that was dropped from the airplane of righteousness!

If the atomic bombs that were dropped on Nagasaki and Hiroshima brought
down the citadel of the Japanese Empire and terminated the WWII, then
a rain of atomic bombs of love should be able to destroy the bulwark of the
sins of the murderous human society.
Rather than the outbreak of the WWIII or the maintenance of peace through
the possession of nuclear power, true peace and happiness should come
through the nuclear power of love!

The government officials that have lost their souls to bribes and corruption,
The society rotten by drunken orgies,
The nation that perpetuates the killing of the body and soul,
The human that dreams of military conquests,
The finale's gift is death!
The end's judgment is self-destruction!

It is not a famine due to the scarcity of food.
It is not a drought due to the shortage of water.
It is due to the lack of the word God who hates sin and therefore does not
    tolerate even a bit of it, who loves the humankind to the extent of giving his
    only begotten son...
Righteousness is the return of indestructibility!
Love is the eternal victory!

It is not the matter of whether one is a descendent of Dangun (the progenitor
    of the Korean race) or Abraham.
It is the matter of whether one is a child of sin or God.
It is not the matter of whether one's country is America or Russia.
It is the matter of whether your country and countrymen are righteous or
    unrighteous.

It is not the matter of the egotistical stubbornness of faith or the General
    Assembly's decision rendered by the majority.
It is the matter of true cleansing of the past or new beginning of the born-again
    heart.

Do you think that America of the present is based on resources and military might?
No!
Do you or don't you know that it is based on God, who blesses the sacrificial
    mission work of the missionaries that were sent by the descendents of
    Puritans that left their homeland in search of the religious freedom? Don't
    you know that it is because of the faith and spirit inherited from their pious
    forefathers?

If it is the resources and military might that makes a nation succeed, then why did Rome fail? Why then is Great Britain on the decline?

Great Britain had already collapsed when it persecuted Puritans.

The Japanese Empire along with its two cities, Nagasaki and Hiroshima, had already collapsed at the time of bombing of Pearl Harbor.

Do not regard the possession of atomic bombs as the pride of America.

Brag about its numerous apostles of love.

If anyone desires something more than this, then God's anger would be upon him or her.

Do you believe that Russia of the present is built on the ideologies of Marx and Lenin or their violent revolutions?

No!

They are the second coming of Ishmael's descendants born of Greek Orthodox Church becoming corrupt.

The wage of sin is death.

You red leader that perpetuate ruthless violence,

You should already know that you are an existence forsaken by God.

Disguise your subordinates, the spies you send out as spies, as the apostles of love.

Who would have known that your mind developed at the seminary would become a den of the devil!

You the red leader of "Kremlin Palace!"

You the white lead actor of "White House!"

Until when would you perform the trick of the devil?

Until you satisfy the needs of Satan?

Until the earth burns up in the brimstone?

Until the Lord comes again?

Don't you see that your greed is destroying so many Sodom and Gomorrah?

Don't you hear the screams of poor souls that are being burned up in the fire of hell as the consequence of your sins?

Would you be satisfied to see the culmination of self-destruction?

Do you suppose that several thousands of years of your ancestors' rise and fall to be constituted as the rightful history of the humankind?

Oh, if you truly desire world peace, you should go back to the seminary, you
　　red leader!
If you truly wish happiness for humankind, hear the sound of the bells of
　　Nagasaki, you white lead actor!

You who stand at the crossroads of the twentieth century,
You live mummies that serve as the slaves of the red and the errand boys of
　　the white!
Receive this atomic bomb of love that has fallen from righteousness.

The words of Jesus, "Love your enemies," are not the worn out latches of the
　　two-thousand-year-old papyrus documents.
The atomic bomb of love that was lobbed from Aeyangwon has fallen right in
　　front of the Eight Kings Café and is being dropped throughout the land of
　　Korea.
I hope that it falls in the world, too.

A Meeting between a Father and a Son

Chapter 14

It was November 14, 1948.

"Is Rev. Nah here?" asked Rev. Son as he entered Seongju Church.

"My, who do we have here?" Mrs. Nah greeted Rev. Son.

"Is Rev. Nah here?" asked Rev. Son again.

"He just went out with someone a minute ago." Mrs. Nah said as she waved him to come in.

"I see. Then why don't I wait for him here?" Rev. Son said as he sat down.

Mrs. Nah asked him, "Rev. Son, how difficult it must have been for you?"

Rev. Son looked pale. "Well, it is all in God's will, I must say. What can a mortal do?" His face betrayed a look of bleakness.

Upon reading his facial expression, Mrs. Nah's eyes welled up with tears. She said, "How painful it must be for your wife!" As they talked, the raucous sound of a group of young adults of the church practicing praise songs inside the sanctuary could be heard.

"Yes, it is. That's why she keeps lying down all the time." He sounded as if he was talking about someone other than his own wife.

"Of course, but it is still a testament to her strength and resilience. If it had been us, we would have died already." Mrs. Nah tried to add more sympathy upon sympathy.

She then asked, "Were you not questioned by the authorities on your way here?"

"I told them, 'I am Rev. Son,' when I passed by the station and near the make-shift bridge. Surprisingly, people bowed to me as if they recognized me and dealt kindly with me."

"I see. They must have heard the news." Mrs. Nah did not seem all that surprised to hear about people's reaction. "By the way, are you on your way somewhere?" asked Mrs. Nah.

"I am on my way to Busan Choryang Church to lead revival meetings there," replied Rev. Son.

"What kind of strength do you have to do all that? You should seriously rest some more. You have been through a great difficulty." Mrs. Nah responded half-surprisingly and half-worriedly.

"That event is that. This is this. Should I not honor what I promised previously?" Rev. Son was resolute in his attitude.

"How's Rev. Nah's health these days? I heard that he suffered from a fatigue after the uprising. And I must mention that he worked so tirelessly on my behalf."

"I don't know, but it was not really to his credit. If he had been a little late, he could not have honored your request. It all worked out because of God's help." Mrs. Nah recalled the things that she had heard about what happened.

"Well, where does that guy live?" asked Rev. Son.

Mrs. Nah was clueless about what Rev. Son was asking. "Yes? Who do you mean by 'that guy?'"

"I mean, Jae-Seon," replied Rev. Son.

"Why?" wondered Mrs. Nah.

"I want to go and visit him."

Mrs. Nah was surprised again by what Rev. Son said. It was not enough for Rev. Son to save the young man's life through Rev. Nah. Now, he had to go and visit the killer of his two sons, which seemed like a scary proposition to Mrs. Nah. She wondered if Rev. Son was a real human being after all. He seemed like a man of steel that was incapable of processing human emotions. That was why she kept staring at him with a blank look.

"Why don't you wait a little before you visit?" Mrs. Nah tried to stop him.

"What is there to wait? I need to meet him as soon as possible so that he can repent and be saved. Since I don't have much time to spare, I should meet him today since I have time today. And it is true that he and his family would not be relieved until they meet me, isn't it?"

Mrs. Nah could not stop him when she heard him say that it was for their relief that they should meet him right away. What could she say to a person who thinks of others' peace and comfort rather than his own?

The praise team's practice seemed to have been kicked up a notch.

"This is the house. Let me go in first." Mrs. Nah entered the house first ahead of Rev. Son. It was a house that had a shop built into it. There were all kinds of fish including salted ones. Since Rev. Nah had not returned and the curfew was set at six o'clock, Rev. Son and Mrs. Nah went to visit Jae-Seon's house by themselves.

Mrs. Nah came out again in a short while and waved to Rev. Son, who was waiting in front of the gate to follow her in. A portly woman came out to greet him also. But she could not raise her head.

Soon, other members of the family came out to greet Rev. Son. Their eyes expressed bewilderment upon bewilderment. They said, "Please come up this way."

Knowing that their son was saved from execution because of Rev. Son's words, they were intent on visiting him once the public transportation had been reestablished. They did not know how to receive this precious and surprising guest who came to visit them first. Therefore, they greeted him with a sense of fear and curiosity to which they could not put their words.

The family sat down inside the room. The father and mother did not know what to say, let alone their son.

After a short silent prayer, Miss. Nah broke the silence by saying, "That is him." She pointed to Jae-Seon.

After pointing at Jae-Seon by saying, "That boy is...," Mrs. Nah could not continue on.

Rev. Son told him, "Come here."

His father quickly commanded him, "Jae-Seon, bow to the pastor." His voice quivered a little. He was almost in his sixties, but he had never experienced something quite as stifling as this. He was at loss with his words as well as his spatial orientation.

Jae-Seon, at his father's words, barely managed get up, set his trembling arms on the floor and bowed to Rev. Son. His face still showed some wounds. From the pale look on his face, one could tell that he had been resting on the bed.

"Are you Jae-Seon?" After saying this, Rev. Son grabbed his hand tightly and looked intently at his face. Rev. Son seemed to be a little bit worked up inside.

"You can relax. I have already forgiven your mistake. And I also believe that God has already forgiven you."

Jae-Seon's parents began to cry to hear these words of Rev. Son. Understandably, Jae-Seon also burst into tears.

The words, "I have already forgiven your mistake. And I also believe that God has already forgiven you," seemed to echo what Apostle John had once done in trying to make one of his disciples who had fallen away from faith and become a thief repent. In the truest sense, Rev. Son's visitation of Jae-Seon's family was something that could only be accomplished by John, the apostle of love, if he were alive now. In another sense, this might even exceed Apostle John. Could it be that the words, "I have already forgiven you," were part of Rev. Son's daily routine?

Upon hearing Rev. Son's words, Jae-Seon's father tearfully said, "Rev. Son, you are next to the sun in our esteem. I really do not know what to say." His words expressed his deepest gratitude. For a village merchant, his words were of the highest extolment.

He then continued, "When I was imprisoned at Gwangju Prison for financial reasons, I heard of your name there. I wished to meet you someday. I just did not know that I would be meeting you under these circumstances. I am sorry for this, but at the same time, I am delighted to have you here." His disjointed words were the best praise that he could heap on Rev. Son.

He said, "By the way, I was set on going down to Sinpung and visiting you as soon as the transportation problem was resolved. Since you came to us, I don't know what to say. But if you allow me, I would like to say now what I was going to say later." His face looked tense. His head seemed to be shaking a little.

"Yes, what is that you want to say?" asked Rev. Son.

"It is that I have four sons. I would like to divide them into two pairs. I would like to ask you take in one pair of my sons and mentor them. What do you think?" He sounded serious.

"Oh, no! You should not say things like that." Rev. Son refused the request solemnly.

"That's a good idea. But that's not what I want. I just ask you to give me the opportunity to turn this son of yours into a great person. And I wish that all your family members believe in Jesus and be saved through revering God."

Rev. Son then turned toward Jae-Seon and said, "I am not going to even remember your past sins. I wish that you can repair your thinking by getting rid of wrong ideologies and become a great servant of the Lord."

After a short pause, he continued, "You need to do the work that my two dead sons were supposed to do. Please emulate their spirit and content of faith and become a precious servant for the Lord."

Rev. Son's earnest admonishment made Jae-Seon speechless and cry with his head down.

His mother replied in his place, "Yes, sir. Of course, he will do more than that." At the time, someone brought in a small table with a modest assortment of refreshments. However, when he realized that it was already five thirty, half an hour before the curfew, he tried to get up and leave after saying a short prayer.

Jae-Seon's father spoke again. "Rev. Son, I have another thing to tell you and you should really accommodate me on this one. I hear that you have a daughter who attends Maesan Girls Middle School. Please allow her to stay at our place and go to school from here. Can you? Our daughter also goes to that school." His tone of voice implied that he was not going to take no for an answer.

Rev. Son said, "Oh, no! Please, do not say such a thing. I do not wish to, in any way, materially or convenience-wise, be a burden to you. Now, I will see you all again." He tried to leave the second time.

Jae-Seon's father grabbed onto him and said, "Rev. Son. That's a misunderstanding. I did not mean anything like that. It is not that I want to have your daughter here as a way to pay you back for your grace in some way. Our family already attends a church. But now we feel ashamed to attend the church. If your daughter stays with us, she'd be helpful for my family of ten or more people to believe in Jesus. If your daughter stays with us, then you would frequent our house. If you frequent our house, then I believe that there will be more opportunities to hear the edifying words of God from you. In turn, that would go a great length to aid our family being saved. We are indebted to you greatly, but you should allow this for us." He forced the issue.

"I now understand what you are trying to say. But since I cannot make this decision on my own, let me ask my daughter and then get back to you with an answer," said Rev. Son. He began to walk out of the house.

"Please, you should make this happen for us. I will go to Rev. Nah's

house early tomorrow morning," said Jae-Seon's father. The whole
family followed him out the door. Mrs. Nah also stepped out the door.
Mrs. Nah kept quiet all throughout the conversation. It was because she
could not figure out whether it was right to agree or disagree with Dong-
Hee's coming to this household. Everyone seemed to be longing for a
longer conversation with Rev. Son and possibly about many different
things. This described a change in the mood from the beginning of the
encounter. Now, they were finally relieved to see for themselves the
beneficent motive of Rev. Son.

"Dong-Hee, Jae-Seon's father wants you to stay at his house. He has a
daughter that goes to the same school as you do and wants to keep you
with her. Would you like to do that?" asked Rev. Son.

"What do you mean? I could never do that. It just horrifies me. It
does not matter how much they insist." Dong-Hee was shocked by the
suggestion.

Rev. Son teared up recognizing the weight of the pain under which his
daughter was during this whole ordeal.

"Well, I understand it. I did not account for your feeling. I initially
refused the proposition because of something else though. But he
insisted that your presence in their household would help them believe
in Jesus better."

"Father, what kind of thinking is that? If they can't believe in Jesus
even after being granted that much grace, what difference would
it make even if I stay with them? Isn't it useless?" Dong-Hee was
perplexed.

"Dong-Hee, what you say makes sense. Even if you don't go, they
would still believe in Jesus. However, I am sure that the about ten-
member household would benefit from your presence. Because of you,
I would naturally visit you. In turn, they think that my frequent visits
would bring them much goodness. That's why they were insisting on

having you there." Rev. Son conveyed to her the explanation of Jae-Seon's father.

Dong-Hee was quiet for a while. Then she said, "Well, I do not want to go, but if my presence would help them to trust in Jesus and be saved..." She began to give it a serious thought.

"Well, is there any desire in you to go?" Rev. Son asked again.

"I will think about it," said Dong-Hee with her head down. Then she said, "I will pray about it."

"Do that. Pray about it. They would probably come to visit us tomorrow morning." In this way, Rev. Son delegated the decision to her.

This was how Dong-Hee got to move to Jae-Seon's house. Jae-Seon's family showed up the next day ready to take her belongings and lobbied rather forcefully for her move. But the truth was that Dong-Hee moved in with them because she thought, "Should I not suffer a little if it means that they become saved?"

Rev. Son was glad and thought, 'That is indeed my daughter, my true daughter.' Jae-Seon's family could not be any happier about her coming.

Fathers! Sons!

Brothers, countrymen, fellow human beings,
Fathers, sons,
Who are your fathers? Who are your sons?
Do you think that those formed through the love of fathers and the blood of
    mothers are only fathers and sons?
You drunken fathers that gave birth to your children that are like piglets, are you
    true fathers of those piglets?
Sons, you immature sons,
Are you true sons?
Aren't you like baby spiders?

My fellow countrymen, you keep concubines saying that you don't have children;
    do you think that you would do well as fathers?
You stand drunk before the table of ancestor worship; do you think that you
    fulfill your duty as sons by merely burning incense and bowing twice to your
    deceased parents?

Though Abraham was the father of faith, do you know what the consequence of
    sinfulness is today?
Though David was a righteous king, do you know what the consequence of his
    sins was for his nation?

Do you think that you can escape your judgment for bringing ruin to families
    and your country, you, concubines who indulge in pleasure?
Half of Great Britain had fallen to the charm of Simpson, the enchantress.

Do you think that you fulfilled your duty of fatherhood, you, fathers of faith,
    who gave yourselves up as concubines to idols and said this was the way to
    protect your child, the church?

Do you think that you fulfilled your duty as sons, you, so called 'sons of Abraham,'
    who still cannot repent after selling God over three meals a day?

Are all fathers true fathers just because they are fathers?
Only those who fulfill their duty as fathers are true fathers.
Are all sons true sons just because they are sons?
Only those that fulfill their duty as sons are true sons.

There are certain things you need to do if you have sons.
There are certain things you need to do if you don't have sons.
Why do you go over your boundary and commit the sin that God hates?

Aren't there many unfortunate sons that need to be cared for?
Aren't there many weak fathers that need to be supported?
Was Jesus suffered at the hands of others because he had sons?
How many sons and brothers did Paul have?
How many generations came after Confucius or the Buddha?

Which genealogies list the descendants of Socrates?
It is not a matter of being a father or a son.
It is rather a matter of being a father of Satan or a child of God.

Oh, you, the fathers of the world, do not waste your precious time trying to
    produce sons that you would name in your genealogy.
Oh, you, the sons of the world, do not fixate your gaze on your father from
    whom you would inherit rice paddies.

Sons, only look up to God, the father of righteousness.
Fathers, guide your sons only with true love.

L et us go back to January of 1947 and look back on the days of Dong-In's youth.

People were shocked and frowned at the news that, "There was an uprising in Yeosu and Suncheon."

Then, people were shocked in admiration at the news that, "Two innocent students were martyred."

Then, people were shocked in disbelief at the news that, "He adopted the killer of his two sons as his own."

Then, people were shocked in delight at the news that, "That young man has become an earnest Christian."

The peers of Dong-Sin shed tears as they remembered his life of daily reading of the Bible and prayer.

The friends of Dong-In sobbed as they remembered his beautiful singing voice and heroic conducts.

Those who knew their mother cried because they knew how she loved her two sons.

Those who knew their father teared up because they were almost able to touch the remarkable love Christ in his compassion.

Those who knew their grandfather marveled at his humility and life of prayer.

They all exclaimed, "Where else in the world could such a family of faith be found?"

As today was a dream, can tomorrow be another dream?

Death reminds the vanity of life that is born in a dream, lives in a dream and moves onto the dreamland upon dying!

Though no one has ever gone to heaven and come back, since the paradise that Jesus talked about is my destination, is not death the gate to eternal life?

Those that believe in this life will not die when they die.

To those that have died, if they had believed in this life, death will not be death!

These thoughts made a few women feel ambivalent about the past of their youth. They felt surprised, and at the same time, heartbroken; they felt refreshed and at the same time troubled; they felt like it was good, better to cry, fortunate to cry, and happy to cry. However, despite all, they felt that being disregarded and miserable were the essence of who they were. It did not matter whether they were virgins or mothers with children.

It causes one to imagine the woman in the poem "The Woman" by Han Ha-Wun, a poet with Hansen's disease.

A familiar woman passes me by with a man of broad shoulders and a baby.
The woman seems barely old enough to be twenty.
Her manner of walking seen from the rear,
Her figure...
Who should I say that she is?

She is a woman with a name that's on the tip of my tongue.
She is a blast from the past that I can almost see if I close my eyes.
Was she happy in the past regardless of her circumstances?
Truly, is she really happy in the present?
What is this sentiment what I am feeling now?

Dong-In was walking toward the pier at Busan. He was on his way to get on board the ship bound for Yeosu. He looked too big to be a ninth grader. Probably for that reason, he did not look too gallant. In contrast to his manly face and physique, however, his shoulders seemed droopy.

"Would I be here if I had known it? I don't know what to make of the whole thing. What is my father going to do? My mother even said that she had met all of them when she was here. I don't know where her parents are. Why was she so cold to me? It seemed like she was trying to avoid meeting me today. She seemed prettier than how I'd remembered her on a couple of occasions I'd seen in the past. Her face, hair, ears... the way she was dressed, and her voice, though I had not listen to her singing solo, I could hear whenever she sang hymns... I don't know if it is fortunate or unfortunate that I have interest in music, but perhaps with her..." While being lost in his thoughts, Dong-In ran into something.

"Why don't you look at where you're going!" said a voice.

"Ouch," said Dong-In as he turned around. He saw a lighted figure pulling away from him into darkness. It looked like a young man on a bicycle. He was holding a wooden container that restaurant delivery boys usually carry around.

"I was nearly..." His face turned red and his mind became alert by the thought of what could have happened.

"Why I..." He saw that it was now 6:30 from the clock that was on one of the stores near the pier.

He had some time before the ship was to arrive. The end of the year was near. Soon, New Year's Day would come and he would be one year older–for nothing.

It was the second New Year's Day since the independence. Perhaps, that was why it did not feel as exciting as the year before. He had made an intentional effort to come down here so that he could meet with a candidate for marriage. Another item on his itinerary was to pay a visit to those to whom he was indebted while he was in Busan during the days of war. Though he had done enough of visiting and greeting people, he was on his way home now after having a disappointing encounter with his date.

"Was it because she knew that I was behind in my schooling? Is it really my fault that I am behind? More than anything, it was because of the intrusive policy of Shinto worship and other things erected by the enemy, the Japanese. My schooling suffered because I had to work hard to preserve my reward before God by opposing Shinto worship rather than trying to appease men. Moreover, I had to work at Baekil Market and the tin-can factory trying to support my family financially after my father was imprisoned. Didn't I lose the opportunity to continue schooling when I had to move around in order to live a life based on faith?"

He remembered what his father wrote to him once. "... However, please do not ever forget that, while it is good to work at a factory for the time being, this is the stage of your life when you need to devote yourself to study. You can still earn money in the future. But it is so hard to pick up studying again once you lose that chance. For everything, it is crucial to not miss the timing."

"Well, what about money? Besides schooling, I do not have much in possession. If we had some wealth, much of it would have been spent just living through the war. It did not help that my father was a pastor. And it was God's grace that God fed and clothed us through many people during the war. It is just normal not to have had much wealth. We are still barely making it now in the wake of independence. Well, didn't I try my best in doing what I have to do living for God according to His commandments?" As these thoughts preoccupied him, he had already come to the waiting room of the shipping company. When he sat down inside the waiting room, the past came alive in his thoughts again. He thought of how he was talked into bowing to Shinto shrine by the chief of the broadcasting department at the Cheongju Penitentiary. He remembered how he lied to himself and God and how close he came to sinning greatly before God. He recalled the times when he'd cried, as well as other sufferings that he had to endure. The hardships of the moment seemed to be so insignificant compared to what he had gone through. He remembered how his family had to pay for the sin he committed when they were in Busan.

"What I am going through now is nothing compared to what I endured!" He comforted himself with the thought.

There were only a handful of people coming in and out of the door. Night deepened along with the coldness that began to settle down on the pier.

Dong-In dressed in an overcoat was ultimately resigned to the will of God prevailing in his life. In this way, his values were being seasoned by his deepening faith.

While living with the people at Aeyangwon that year, Dong-In began to keep a diary on his thoughts about his past and future aspirations. He began making brief entries in it starting that year.

Wednesday, January 1 (clear weather) 2 degrees Celsius, study–reading

The weather is very mild and the trees are calm. It feels peacefully festive–a fitting tribute to New Year's Day. Last night, mother went down to Busan. The winter break of the fourth year in the middle school was adorned white with snow and commenced on Christmas Eve on the school grounds. I spent Christmas Day strolling down the silvery streets and singing Christmas carols. Starting with the student fellowship meeting the night before, I did not rest my tired body until the afternoon on Christmas Day.

Thursday, January 2 (clear weather) 2 degrees Celsius, study–reading

The weather was good until 3:30 in the afternoon yesterday. Suddenly, the northerly wind began to beat down very hard and clouds began to gather from the west. This premonition of a wickedly cold weather came true with the freezing of the muddy ground, and a blistering wind blowing through the forest. I worried about the health of my mother, but I trust that God has protected and guided her safely to Busan. Today is as cold as yesterday and it seems that a cycle of three cold days and four warm days is upon us.

Friday, January 3 (clear weather) 2 degrees Celsius, study–reading

I made a resolution upon being rejected by her. Didn't I clench my fists and make the determination that I would become successful before her very eyes? On that day, I saw arrogance in her eyes. No, it was her arrogant attitude. Yes, it is true that I am behind in my schooling because of what I decided about faith. Yes, it is true that she has punched in more days at school than I did. Of course, even in my abilities, I am of a lesser standing. Presently, she is a middle school graduate and I am attending my fourth year in a mediocre middle school. She can look at the lack of money I have and laugh at my face. But come to think of it, it was the arrogance with which she looked at me that compelled me to be this determined. It was the rejection that compelled me to clench my fists and pursue after my one goal with an unwavering determination, wasn't it? From now on, I am not going to be discouraged but I will keep running after the final mark. I am sure that she did not mean to be arrogant in her heart. I would like to think that she could have smiled at me and treated me with kindness, but instead she chose to be cold to me because of my conviction in faith that I should live according to the Bible. After all, the Bible says that anyone who sees a woman and lusts after her in his heart commits the sin of adultery.

Saturday, January 4 (cloudy before it rained) 1 degree Celsius, study–reading

Today's weather is not so good. The northerly wind is beating down on us again and I can hear things very clearly, even from a distance. Rain seems to be on the way. At two in the afternoon, laborers from Aeyangwon came and planted garlic. To my liking, they cleaned up the manure in front of the pigpen and used it as the fertilizer for the garlic field. It is an efficient way to solve two needs at once. But why is my mind filled with Ms. B? Is it Ms. A or Ms. B? I am indeed torn inside!

Tuesday, January 7 (clear weather) minus 2 degrees Celsius, study–reading & music

Is this a good or a bad trait to have? If I try to study, I want to read a novel. If I try to read a novel, I want to play music. If I try to play music, I cannot stop thinking about my studies. What is happening? As I was looking at *Jisang* (perhaps a magazine title), I felt the desire to play the music that was percolating in my guts. Having overrun by this emotion, I threw away the novel and started toward Aeyangwon with a music book under my armpit. When I play the organ, many people walking and crouching because of the cold weather look at me. I am sure that they pass me and say, "Where does he get the energy to play the organ in the cold? Poor thing..."

Wednesday, January 8 (clear weather) minus 2 degrees Celsius, study–reading & music

Deacon Heo Yeong-Seo preached. In the morning, I organized the sheet music and I went to work at the church in the afternoon after doing some reading. After hearing Dong-Hee talk about her dream,

I went out to the street corner and waited for mother, who had gone to Busan. Then, it hit me. Why did I go out to wait for her? Whenever mother went on a trip, I usually did not pine for her return as much I am doing now. There seems to be a different connotation for my waiting for mother now. It is a different kind of loneliness and curiosity.

Sunday, January 24 (cloudy) minus 3 degrees Celsius

After breakfast, I went to visit Deacon Son. The first thing that Deacon Son said was that Ms. B and I should make a decision. I struggled because I did not know what to say. I cannot do it. How can the matter of choosing the mate with whom to spend a hundred years in the same embrace and share all kinds of affection be decided in such a short period of time? Sure enough, I gave some thought to many things about Ms. B, but my answer is difficult in coming.

June 19

For the first time, I submitted my writings to the in-school newsletter.

Spring, Why Are You Leaving?

Spring, why are you leaving?
The northerly wind on top of the snow is beating down the ears and the nose,
Vegetation is being stripped and thrashed by the wind and snow.
Who, then, is not yearning for you?
But Spring, why are you leaving so soon?

Spring, Spring, why are you leaving?
I had many complaints in my deep thoughts of waiting for you.
I wanted to sit down with you on the soft grass at the bottom of Mount Nam
    and place myself deep in your embrace.
But Spring, Oh Spring, why are you leaving so soon?
Spring, Spring, why are you leaving?
You only made me miss my mother in hometown, long ago,

Who used to turn up the wick of a dim lamp with a needle,
Who used to quilt a red vest, sounding tap-tap,
And used to tell stories of Jeong Mong-Ju and Lee Sun-Sin.
Then Spring, Oh Spring, why are you leaving so soon?

Spring, Spring, why are you leaving?
In between a distant mountain and sky, I see a haze in and out.
A skylark pitifully chirps as she goes up
To blossom a golden-bell tree by nipping out the haze.
Spring, how could you leave upon seeing this?

Spring, Spring, why are you leaving?
When can I ever see you again if you are leaving now?
Could I see you if I'd rowed a boat in the Pacific?
Or could I see you at the peak of Mount Hanra or Mount Baekdu?
No, I might only see you when I go to paradise.

Revenge
Chapter 16

It was May 30, 1949. The spring was nearly over and the barley crop was full in the field. It was the season of sparrows busily foraging for worms. There was an entourage of three individuals inside the coach full of merchants of an early morning train that left from Suncheon for Yeosu.

"Jae-Seon, do you think we will see Rev. Son when we get there?"

"Well, I don't know. I did not let him know ahead of time." The conversation was between a woman, who seemed to be in her fifties, and her son.

"It's likely that he is not there. That pastor is always going around places and doing evangelism." The man who spoke seemed to be about forty five or forty six.

"Since Rev. Nah is accompanying us, we can meet with Mrs. Son, even though Rev. Son is not there, right?"

"Of course, it's no problem," confidently answered this man named Rev. Nah.

The woman looked out the window as if she was relieved to hear those words.

"What can I say? What can I say that will bring comfort to her? And I..." thought Jae-Seon's mother. She remembered how pathetic she must have looked when she pleaded to Rev. Nah and the soldier for mercy for her son. In pleading her case, she cried and begged for forgiveness saying that her son must be innocent of the crime and even if he had done something wrong, it was probably due to his immaturity.

"I worried so anxiously about losing even one of my four children. How must it have been for her to experience the tragedy of losing her two sons to murder at the same time?" wondered Jae-Seon's mother.

At that moment, she imagined in her mind a woman with hair pulled down, attacking her in order to avenge her grievance. "Oh my, she probably wants to do the same thing to me." Jae-Seon's mother felt fearful all of a sudden at the thought of the possibility. She felt dizzy.

"Caramel candy, milk, and squid for sale!" The words of a vendor who wiggled through the passengers packed like bean sprouts brought her back to her senses.

Jae-Seon was thinking about the same thing. "How shall I address her? What shall I say?" He said to himself. He now thought that it would have been better to have contacted in advance and visited when Rev. Son was there.

Jae-Seon thought, "I should have brought Dong-Hee with me even if she had to miss her school." As the train was getting closer and closer to the Sinpung Station, he felt as if something was pulling him from behind. The only one who did not feel any sense of apprehension was Rev. Nah. This entourage was of Rev. Nah, An Jae-Seon, and his mother.

Jae-Seon and his mother felt sorry that only now they were able to go visit the family of Rev. Son after postponing day after day, and especially Mrs. Son, though it had been for a while that they wanted to pay a visit. It was not like visiting just a friend's house. It was not anything like visiting a relative. Though it was their own volition to go and visit, in one sense, it was not something they could afford not to carry out. On that day, after putting it off from day to day for about half a year, they were finally on their way to visit them. There were several young vendors making a commotion right next to them.

"Hey, Mister, do not step on my foot. Don't you have eyes?"

"Hey, Miss, did I do it intentionally? It just happened that there are so many people on board today. And it was your baggage that I tripped over."

"You, Mister, stop yapping. It is not like you've done something good here," said the woman argumentatively.

"It was not something good, but at the same time, I did not do anything wrong. I have never seen a woman as weird as you!" The argument was getting escalated. Everyone around them tried to intervene by saying, "Please, stop it, you two." But they refused to let it go and continued bickering.

The whole thing would have diffused had someone said, "It was my mistake." But since each of them claimed to be in the right, it was turning into a noisy confrontation. All those who were trying to intervene probably would act the same if they were the ones arguing.

However, Jae-Seon's mother thought that had it been Rev. Son, he would have apologized profusely already. In this way, she pictured in her mind the humble Rev. Son who came to visit her family time to time. Rev. Nah got up from his seat and pulled the arguing parties apart. The train was moving along oblivious to all the human drama it was carrying within it. Human existence is fraught with conflicts. Then which is better? Going through life fighting or acquiescing to its demands?

"Hey, Yang-Geun, would you watch over Dong-Ryun?" Having entrusted the care of Dong-Ryun to Yang-Geun temporarily who had been running errands at home, Mrs. Son thought hard about whether to work on the field or do the laundry. Then, she decided to do the laundry and she came to the usual spot for doing laundry with a container full of dirty clothes on her head. For some time, she immersed herself in washing the clothes. It was more difficult than usual for her to hand wash the load for she had been under the weather for the last several days. After beating on the laundry with the laundry bat for a while, she decided to take a breather. She was still holding the bat in her hand. Her view caught the train bound for Yeosu pulling into the Sinpung Station.

"Already lunchtime is over." These words took her back down the memory lane. She remembered how her two sons used to take the Suncheon train home.

She began to think, "The train that used to take you home never fails to arrive here. The friends you grew up with are still here." She also remembered how around this time last year, a deaconess of a certain church in Suncheon wanted to introduce a marriage candidate for her son, Dong-In, saying how he had, at the age of twenty four, already passed the suitable age for getting married. She had responded to her by saying that she would get back to her after asking her son. She wondered, "What if I had asked Dong-In to find a mate then?" Then, she almost immediately regretted entertaining a useless thought even if she was tired from doing the laundry. She regretted, "Had that happened, it would have been terrible. We would have turned a precious child of someone into a widow." She told herself, "Forget it, what is the use of thinking about such things now?" And she got back to doing the laundry. She must have thought, "What is the use of washing the dirty clothes? I should wash my mind, too."

It was a stream that was about 60 cm in width and ran idly in between a barley field and a grassy field. The water from this gently flowing stream was clear and made doing laundry exceptionally efficient. Behind the spot for doing laundry was a hill with a grassy field attached to it. It was a convenient setup for anyone doing laundry because clothes could be hung to be dried right over the field. Mrs. Son was busily alternating between washing and hanging the laundry when she saw Yang-Geun running toward her. Mrs. Son was surprised to see Yang-Geun approaching, so she kept her eyes on him. She worried that he came because Dong-Ryun was crying. Yang-Geun said as soon as he reached Mrs. Son, "Mother, a guest is here. Something's wrong though. Let's hurry home." Being perplexed by Yang-Geun's words, she took a deep breath to compose herself. It was her way of battling severe dizziness that got triggered by even a slightest distress. "Yang-Geun, what are you talking about?" said Mrs. Son dropping the laundry bat to the ground.

"Mother, Rev. Nah and a woman and a student has come from Suncheon. The thing is, when Uncle saw the student, he tried to attack him with a kitchen knife, saying that he would kill him. Rev. Nah is trying to intervene, but it is a big mess. You should go back." Yang-Geun still seemed distraught.

Mrs. Son was shocked by what she heard. It seemed like Rev. Nah had come to visit. She had already heard from Dong-Hee that her new brother, Jae-Seon, would come home to visit. It sounded as if that student was indeed Jae-Seon. It also seemed that Uncle was trying to harm him. As she tried to walk toward home, she suddenly felt dizzy and her mind turned blank. The world turned black in an instant. Then she saw two graves opening up and the angry Dong-In and Dong-Sin rising out of them. They began running toward Aeyangwon and then disappeared. She then saw Uncle running after Jae-Seon with a knife in his hand. He also faded away. Then, she saw her husband, Rev. Son, approaching her with a smile on his face. He faded away too. Then she saw the ear of Malchus, the servant of the high priest, being cut off by Uncle and rolling toward her. Judas Iscariot tried to take the knife away from him, but he failed. Jesus came down from the cross and picked up the ear. He began looking for Rev. Son so that he could have him put the ear back on Malchus. Saint Stephen was singing hymns on the top of the grave made out of a pile of rocks. The pile of rocks turned into a group of people. After the group had danced, they told her that they were going out to evangelize. Paul was coming toward Aeyangwon holding a piece of paper in his hand. He was beaten by the people of

Aeyangwon. Paul, having been beaten, called out to Stephen. Stephen came and rescued Paul from the angry mob. Instantly, Paul became a little child and began to beat on the laundry with the laundry bat. The laundry then turned into Dong-In and Dong-Sin dressed in white. They began walking toward her. All these things flashed through her mind in an instant.

"Dong-In, Dong-Sin..." cried Mrs. Son as she fell into the water.

"Mother" called out Yang-Geun. But his voice was as loud as the buzzing of a mosquito.

"Oh, no, why am I like this?" Mrs. Son bemoaned as she gained her consciousness again and sat down on the side of the stream.

"Why am I like this? I have already decided, haven't I? Haven't I already sworn before God? Hasn't Rev. Son been telling me that all the land of Korea as well as the whole world has been impressed by the great good of God that was achieved through the deaths of our two sons? Didn't he say that it was better to give glory to God through death than live for a long time in sin? Didn't he say that we should be grateful? Oh, but that was his reasoning, not mine. What about me? Didn't he say that Abraham had to offer Isaac as a sacrifice? But the Bible does not say that it was Sarah that offered Isaac, does it? On the other hand, the Bible also does not say that Sarah opposed it, does it? Did Sarah know about the whole thing or not? But it does not matter to me. That was then. This is now. This is about me. This concerns my own sons. Their long-suffering life, their exemplary faith, their strong bodies...these innocent sons of mine were executed, why? What did they do wrong? What is there for God's glory? God's glory? I mean, that is that, but it is about me! My sons are my sons! Then what should I do? I should avenge their deaths. Avenge their deaths. This is all useless. How could I ever tell Uncle to kill them with the knife? Or should I go crying, kicking, screaming, and rebuking him to bring my sons back? It is all pointless." It was a session of chaotic self-talk born out of desperation. "Should I just send Yang-Geun back and get him to tell them that I am nowhere? It's all pointless. Do they really think that things fell into place so fast for them to come to this house?" thought Mrs. Son as she came back to her senses again. The moment felt like a year.

Yang-Geun kept imploring her, "Mother, let's go." Though she tried to move, she found herself immobile. It was as if the sky was pushing down on her shoulders and the earth was pulling down from beneath her. Her body felt as if it was glued down to the ground. She did not even want to move her eyelids or a finger. She began praying, seated on the ground. Yang-Geun bowed his head to pray also.

"Father, why has my faith become so weak? Why am I in such agony? You gave your son Jesus..." As she prayed, the song 'Jesus Love' that Dong-Sin used to sing came to her mind. She pondered, "We have God who gave his only begotten son to us. Then what is so terrible about giving two sons, out of my many children, to God? Haven't you known about the life of Mary, the mother of Jesus? Don't you know what happened to Job at the end?" It was as if somebody was telling these things to her. Then she was told by a voice to read the words of Romans 12:19 through 22. It was a passage that she used to recite frequently.

"Beloved, never avenge yourselves, but leave room for the wrath of God; for it is written, 'Vengeance is mine, I will repay, says the Lord.' No, 'if your enemies are hungry, feed them; if they are thirsty, give them something to drink; for by doing this you will heap burning coals on their heads.' Do not be overcome by evil, but overcome evil with good."

"Why is she not coming? It has been about two hours, right?" Jae-Seon's mother asked nervously. Her voice seemed to be shaking a little.

"It has not been that long. Only an hour," said Rev. Nah. He turned to the child and said, "You are one gentle baby. You are not even crying though your mom is not here." He complimented Dong-Ryun.

"Who was that?" asked Jae-Seon's mother.

"Well, he is the uncle of Dong-In. He took care of them when they were in Suncheon."

"Now, I can understand his reaction." She talked to herself. She was anxious about what would happen next. The moment seemed like an eternity to her. It was because, when they set foot inside the house, a cousin of Rev. Son, who happened to be there, saw Jae-Seon and began yelling at him, "You are the murderer of my nephews. You bring my nephews back right now or you should kill yourself." "If you do neither of what I ask, I am going to kill you." Uncle cried as he tried to attack Jae-Seon all of sudden. Jae-Seon barely avoided getting hit and Rev. Nah intervened to calm him down. Then, Rev. Nah sent Yang-Geun to fetch Mrs. Son, who had gone to do laundry.

But Mrs. Son did not come back even after an hour. Yang-Geun had also not come back.

They sat down on the grass right in front of Rev. Son's house, which also had a pine tree on it, and waited for Mrs. Son. "Is Mrs. Son as gracious as Rev. Son? Or is she an aggressive person like the uncle we met? Is she going to yell at us? Or is she going to cry hysterically? I want to meet her not so much for satisfying my curiosity as relieving myself of this burden that I carried it here," thought Jae-Seon's mother. At that moment, they were able to see Yang-Geun and Mrs. Son with a washtub on her head. They were walking toward them on a small trail in-between the rice paddies over the main road. They were able to tell that she was coming back from doing the laundry by the look of her. However, it was unclear whether she went to do laundry or make laundry because she had a washtub on head but the bottom of her skirt seemed to be soaking wet. She had some dirt on her skirt as well.

Mrs. Son was only 30 m away from where they were. However, that distance seemed like 100 *li* to Jae-Seon's mother. Her chest began to beat fast. Jae-Seon's heart also began to palpitate hard in anticipation.

Mrs. Son also felt her heartbeat getting faster and louder. If someone was able to hear the sound of these hearts beating, he or she would say that it was louder than the sound of the pistons of a locomotive. The distance of thirty meters that seemed like 100 *li* began to collapse with sparks of wonder and suspicion flying everywhere.

Was it rain? Was it a thunderbolt from a clear sky?

"Mrs. Son, are you coming back from doing the laundry?" Rev. Nah said.

"Yes, let us go in," said the shaking voice. It was unclear to whom she was saying this, but it was definitely the voice of Mrs. Son.

As soon as she entered the room, though it was unclear who came in the room first and who came in second, she put down the laundry on the floor and went over to Jae-Seon. She grabbed his hand tightly and said, "You are here finally." With that greeting, she began to cry, "Rev. Nah, pray…"

Jae-Seon began to cry for he felt a heavy burden of a mysterious kind being placed on his shoulders, which he could not fully understand. Jae-Seon's mother began to cry at this unexpected gesture, recalling the pain of being mistreated by Rev. Son's cousin. The neighbors and children that surrounded them began to cry watching this unexpected encounter unfold right before their very own eyes. Rev. Nah began praying while trying to control the upwelling of emotion within him. But his prayer was more crying than anything else.

"God who is abundant in love…" Rev. Nah began crying like a little child, "Unng, unng."

"Why do you cry? Why? Just kill that bastard," yelled Uncle from the outside. Those that were trying to calm him down also were crying.

Mrs. Son tried to keep Uncle in check. She then made it comfortable enough for everyone so that they could share the rice cake that the visitors had brought. She also provided them with a lunch. Time and time again, she offered prayers of blessing for Jae-Seon. After turning the afternoon into a cheerful occasion, she sent the visitors home on the evening train out of Suncheon.

After seeing them off at Sinpung Station, Mrs. Son felt so relieved. It felt good as if she was cured from a disease that she had suffered for several years. At the same time, however, she felt a little disappointed for not being able to do more when they were with her. As she neared home, another thought began to come over her.

She wondered what Dong-In and Dong-Sin would have said if they knew about the encounter. "Would they say what I did was right?" or "Would they say that I was wrong to be kind?" She felt like she could hear them speak. At the same time, she felt like they were blocking her way. All the way home, she was torn whether to go into the house or not. She felt that her every step was as weighty and burdensome as that of a cow on its way to the slaughterhouse. It felt like the weight of the whole earth was pulling her legs down.

The distance between the gate of her house and the street was less than ten meters. However, it felt like she had been walking for several days. When she barely made it into the room, it was no longer her body but her head that could she could not lift.

She could not open her eyes to look around the room because she felt like Dong-In and Dong-Sin were sitting in front of the desk at the corner of the room.

When she had mustered up enough strength to lift her head, it felt like her sight was turning dark again. She felt the pain of her body tearing apart, the sensation of the floor giving out, and the throbbing of a spear at her chest. Tears kept flowing from her eyes.

After gaining her senses, she opened her mouth, "Dong-In, Dong-Sin..."

"I... your..." As she muttered a few words, she tried to restrain herself from crying hysterically.

She looked out the window. The pine tree that was standing tall under the evening sky became suddenly huge in her eyes before shrinking as small as a bean. The tree turned into Jae-Seon. He ran away several hundred feet. Then it turned into the figures of Dong-In and Dong-Sin and came right at her nose.

"Can you say that I avenged your deaths?" After a while, Mrs. Son spoke again, "Did I do you wrong? Please chastise your mother." It was a question that twisted her tongue and put her chest on fire. However, the tree in the form of the human figure did not answer her.

"Then did I do something good? Why don't you say something?" Mrs. Son rephrased her question. The question made her want to hop for ten or twenty *li*, laugh for one or two days straight, and run to the end of the earth. The tree still remained silent.

"Then, do you say that I supposedly did what I needed to, according to the Bible?" It was a tearful sigh more than anything. It was something that needed to be done, something that was necessary. Her heart belonged to the graves though her body remained in the room!

Mrs. Son became a stone sculpture.

Her tears were flowing like a water fall...

She wished that her husband was there with her...

The sound of lullaby that Dong-Su was singing to help Dong-Ryun go to sleep on his back!

> Baby, baby, our baby,
> Good baby, sleeping well.
> Hush a bye baby, Hush a bye baby
> Hush a bye baby, sleeping well.

Do the children know their mother's trouble?
With the sound of the lullaby, night has arrived.
Without any problems, the earth must have turned a few angles!

The stars that shone brightly on the night that Abraham had offered Isaac on the altar have come out again.

One, two, ten, hundred...

Shall I go to the beach to count the sands?

Revenge

Isn't there a saying,
"You cannot be with your enemy under the same sky?"
Do you know who came up with such a principle?

Should the rise and fall of a nation,
Should the success and failure of a republic,
Should the birth and death of the humankind be dependent on this ironclad rule?

If so, was Jesus a powerless man?
Were the apostles fools?
Were the martyrs ne'er-do-well's?

It is said, "For all they that take the sword shall perish with the sword."
How fearful is this saying which has been proven time and time again by the history of humankind!
It is said, "Seek first His kingdom and His righteousness."
How faithful is this saying which has been so clearly revealed by the history of believers!
It is said, "If your enemy is hungry, feed him; if your enemy is thirsty, give him a drink.
How amazing is this saying to which has been testified by numerous witnesses!

Greed grows and gives birth to sin;
Sin grows and gives birth to death.
Do you know its father?

Fists grow and give birth to weapons;
Arrows and bows give birth to spears and swords;

Spears and swords give birth to guns and cannons;
Guns and cannons give birth to poisonous gas;
Poisonous gas gives birth to atomic bomb;
Atomic bomb...;
Weapons grow and give birth to destruction;
Do you know whose trick this is that entices humankind?

You who claim that religion is the opium of the people,
Do you know what kind of opium you inject into your bodies?
You who claim that religion is a tool of capitalism,
Do you know whose tool you are?

You who perpetuate materialism,
Do you know what golden crown brings you?
You who dream of pleasure,
Do you know what that dream brings you?

Human beings,
Do not be deceived by yourselves.
Understand whose descendents you are.
Find out whose descendents that you should be.

It is not a matter of democracy or communism.
It is not a matter of nationalism or internationalism.
It is not a matter of materialism or spiritualism.
You are the descendents of the devil.
It is a matter of whether God is your father or not.
It is a matter of the communism of giving or the communism of exploitation.
It is a matter of the democracy of mutual benefit or the democracy of self-centeredness.
It is a matter of the internationalism for cooperation or the internationalism for imperialism.

Yes, if you really desire peace, happiness, and triumph,
You humans!
You should seek first the kingdom of God and his righteousness;

You should feed your enemy who is hungry and offer a drink to your enemy
   who is thirsty.
You should work hard to give rather than receive.

Give food to eat.
Give clothes to wear.
Give a place to live.
Give forgiveness.
Give care.
Give love.
Lift up the iron curtain.
Open up the door of the United Nations.
Then...

Paul to Arabia
Chapter 17

The way of the call, the way to salvation!
Noah was delivered from the flood of judgment.
Abraham was called out of the city of idols.
Lot was delivered from the fire of judgment on Gomorrah.
Jacob was called 'Israel' at the riverbank of Jabbok.
Joseph was given a way out of his brothers' jealousy.
Moses was delivered from the waters of Nile River.

All thirty nine books of the Old Testament speak of how the ancestors of faith have received God's call and deliverance.

All twenty seven books of the New Testament speak of how the history of the gospel has begun with a manger in a barn in Bethlehem of Judea.

The two-thousand-year history of martyrdom began with an open tomb.

Paul was captured on the way to Damascus.

Do not ask about the beginning, the method, or the conclusion to "those who love God, who have been called according to his purpose."

This is the providence of God.

Who can say the gospel movement of the twentieth century cannot emerge out of the carnage of the Yeosu Massacre?

Who can stop the world's salvation movement from reemerging in Korea, the peninsula of the Far East?

God is almighty and does not rest—night or day.

I (the author) do not want to write about the subjective experience of

An Jae-Seon as he moved from repentance to faith from my subjective vantage point. Instead, I seek to present a compilation of what I saw, what I heard, and what I felt about An Jae-Seon from an objective perspective.

At the time of the uprising in Yeosu and Suncheon, I was in the United States. But I made the decision to come back to Korea not only because my family lived in Yeosu and I was the only son to my elderly parents (though I have sisters), but also because my family's estate was taken away during the uprising. As I looked through my diary during those days in order to be honest in my report, I could glance at the following sentiment. Assuming that the uprising in Yeosu and Suncheon had its origin in both government officials and the populace neglecting their civic duties as well as being overrun by their greed, there must have been extortions and shameless acts of profiteering going on. Therefore, these circumstances made the uneducated and ignorant public to be susceptible to the instigation of the bad elements in the society to the point of uprising. The pitiful situation of Korea made me realize that it urgently needed the Christian gospel and education, and this ultimately led to my decision to return.

Even before having a chance to hear about the well-being of my family in Korea, I had heard about Rev. Son and how he went the extra mile to save the murderer of his two oldest sons from being executed for his crime, instead adopting him as his own (The truth was that it was Rev. Nah acting as Rev. Son's proxy. I was given misinformation at the time).

I could not but be moved to tears by Rev. Son's life of faith and found in him a true teaching that was powerfully relevant to contemporary Christians. That was the reason that I wanted to help Rev. Son in sharing this remarkable story with the world even as I was engaged in the process of returning to Korea. It was not about promoting Rev. Son's prestige or boasting about him. Rather, it was because I could not keep silent about the love of Jesus and the power of God that were at work in Rev. Son in this event.

Immediately following my arrival, I went to Yeosu Aeyangwon (concern for my family took a backseat) and worked actively to support Rev. Son. This relationship expectedly put me in contact with Jae-Seon, Rev. Son's son in faith. My first meeting with Jae-Seon was during a revival meeting at a church in Seoul of which Rev. Son was the speaker. Of Jae-Seon, I saw that he was reluctant to meet people. As I thought about what could have possibly made him act in such a way, a deep sense of pain gnawed at me. Was it because of his experience of nearly getting executed? Was it because of the fact that he committed murder? Was it a fear as the result of guilt from knowing that he had killed? This was an understandable reaction of someone who had committed murder as an indiscriminate act of violence while living immersed in sin. Then, how about those who, though not killers, are going around brazenly while carrying out a lifestyle that is far worse than that of a killer? In comparison, Jae-Seon seemed more human than many others in the world.

At the same time, whenever Rev. Son was invited by churches to give a testimony about the Yeosu tragedy, he would not fail to preface his speeches with the following. "I do not consider myself to have fulfilled the duty which God has entrusted me just by forgiving the young man. Rather, I have the responsibility to pray for and guide him so that he could become a great evangelist in the mold of the Apostle Paul and bring much glory to God. Therefore, I beseech you to pray for this young man." Furthermore, he never failed to include Jae-Seon in every one of his prayers. Jae-Seon was frequently in attendance to hear Rev. Son's sermons and prayers. He would usually sit all the way back in the sanctuary and pray.

Then in the spring of 1949, with the recommendation of Rev. Nah and the consent of Rev. Son, Jae-Seon enrolled at the Busan Goryo Bible School. Under the tutelage of caring teachers, Jae-Seon was able to progress not only in academics, but also in the life of faith. As he immersed himself in the Bible study, prayer, and work of evangelism, his faith became deepened as days passed. On the other hand, Rev. Son, having sent Jae-Seon away to a school, wrote to him many letters of encouragement. I obtained a letter that Jae-Seon wrote as a reply to one of Rev. Son's letters, in order to better gauge Jae-Seon's faith of those years. The letter is as follows:

Dear Father

I greet you and mother in the grace of the heavenly Father and wish for your health and wellbeing. Are my younger siblings and Dong-Hee's uncle well? Is everything fine with Aeyangwon and the church through the grace of the Lord? Your son is doing well in this foreign place, thanks to the power of God's truth. I am thankful that I am saved through believing in the merit of the blood of Jesus. It was due to your love, father (Rev. Son), that this sinner became born again. I repented of my sins before God and believed in the power of the blood of Jesus. Though born again, I cannot help but sin from time to time for I am a mortal. However, I am truly thankful that God never forsakes this sinner but continues to love me. It always brings me to repentance. I study here at the Busan Goryo Bible School, which has been built on the truths of the blood of the Lord, learning about the word of God along with many servants of the Lord. I cannot be grateful enough for this privilege given me by God's grace and love as I go about learning the lessons and truths of the twelve apostles. Having been born again, I am determined to give my body to God as a sacrifice. I insist that all the saints have the right to give themselves as martyrs. The one who observes and puts into action the Ten Commandments is a true saint and a born-again Christian. Now I understand that we do not believe because of the existence of heaven and hell, but because of God's love. When I was delivered from the place of death, I could finally come to understand the love of God and Jesus. We must glorify God to the point of death. I am thankful that I was delivered from a place of death. How can I lift up my head and claim the heaven above as mine? But when I look at my salvation, I become certain of the existence of heaven. Even if we do not want to go to heaven, God's hand takes hold of our hands and leads us forcibly to heaven. I do not wait for the cross. However, even if it hits me in my face, I am not going to relent it to someone else, but take it up and carry it and follow Jesus. The time of martyrdom is here. I will take up the cross of martyrdom. Prison is near. I will follow your footsteps and endure the life of imprisonment. Even if oppression, persecution, and trials come my way, I will not veer from the power of the blood of Jesus Christ. Please be assured that your son, Jae-Seon, makes the daily decision to uphold truth and to live as the solider of the cross. I also read, study, and copy the word of God as well as carrying out the works of praise and evangelism. I will be grateful if you pray for me frequently. All this is due to your and mother's prayers. Since I am born again by trusting in faith the power of the blood of the cross, I honor my status as your eldest son by not forgetting to pack the food of salvation. I am so joyful that anyone can receive the love of God. Father, please forgive me of everything. The love that you have shown me is the love that God has given me. I am taking baby steps in trying to follow the Apostle Paul. I pledge that I will follow the footsteps of my brothers.

September 15, 1949
The evening I have received and read your letter
Sincerely, Son Jae-Seon

What can we make of the life that was described in this letter? What can people make of the fact that he wrote his name as "Son Jae-Seon" and not "An Jae-Seon?" After commencing the project to author the book *The Atomic Bomb of Love*, I went on a journey to collect some data about Yeosu Aeyangwon and the event in Suncheon, as well as to verify the truthfulness about the life of faith of Rev. Son's family. I was able to gather much data on the two Sundays I spent on my trip. Once, there was this following event. I met a certain missionary who, after hearing about my intent for the work, said, "It is my opinion but I am not sure if Rev. Son did the right thing or not."

"What do you mean?" I asked.

"I am not sure whether that act of forgiveness was beneficial to the law of the country or not."

"Why?"

He said, "Those acts hinder the law of the land from being established. The judgment must be carried out."

I was startled by what I heard. I wondered if it was something that a missionary could possibly say. I wasn't sure if he had not given it sufficient thought. I said the following. "Of course, pastor, the judgment must be carried out. It must be. However, you are mistaken if you think that imprisonment and capital punishment are the only avenues of judgment for people's crimes. Judgments can include disasters, diseases, and even censure of conscience. There are many consequences of sins. I am sure that the young man would receive judgment in some form or fashion. His inability to go around freely would be another penalty. Furthermore, the predicament that our nation is in fact the judgment of God for the past sins of pastors and elders whom God called earlier. The law of the nation, in this sense, cannot be undermined by Rev. Son's act of forgiveness."

He then said, "I still do not know if that young man has truly repented or not."

"You are right. Whether he has repented or not, that's something that either you or I cannot say. Only God knows the answer to that and only through God's power, he will come to repentance. However, we still bear the responsibility of praying for him and doing due diligence in guiding him right. Who can say that he cannot come to true repentance and faith of trusting the power of the blood of Jesus? Since I was born into an unbelieving family, when I was living in Ganggyeong, I did not attend church until I went to the Jeonju Sinheung School through God's special providence. There, I received much love and guidance from the missionary William Alderman Linton, through whose assistance I went on to Kobe Central Seminary and then to study abroad in America. That's how I came to be a Christian. If I did not hear about the way of atonement of Jesus, I would never have been a Christian. What I can suggest is that, before demanding an evidence of repentance, we should discern his heart by looking into his daily life and keep on praying for and guiding him..." Then, the missionary and I continued to carry on the conversation about the matter.

Then this happened on that afternoon. I had visited Jae-Seon's house, because I had heard that he had been bedridden for a month due to an illness. When I entered the house, the family greeted me kindly. When I saw Jae-Seon, who also came out to greet me, I realized that he looked pale and his clothes looked rather big on him. From the color of his face, I could tell that he was not well.

Instinctively, I called out, "What happened to you?" His mother then tried to give many explanations. She said that it was indigestion or malaria and that he received a shot in the morning of that day in describing his condition. I intuitively recognized that his condition was more than just physical in nature. Immediately, I spoke up.

"Why do you keep him here? I am on my way to Yeosu, then Busan, then Seoul. You can send him on his way with me now or do it before I get to Seoul." To me, it was clear that Jae-Seon's ailment was that of his soul. His recent trouble and a meager lifestyle at dormitory (seminarians were given the monthly allowance of only three thousand and seven hundred *won* for food) together seemed to be keeping him bedridden.

Again, I said to him, "Why do you still doubt and worry needlessly?

There is no one who can judge you on the face of the earth now. As soon as Rev. Son has forgiven you, all the weight of your sin has been stripped away in the eyes of human rights and law. Then, why are you so fearful? You should only think about two things. First, God's commission to you, and second, depending on the Lord's will, to study for the next twenty years, walk life's path of faith and pursue academic research. Besides these, you should not worry about or fear anything. Only I hope that you receive righteousness as the work of sanctification that comes from faith. Also submit your future to God. Would God who has given you a great commission not clear the way for you?"

Then, I turned to his mother and said, "Don't you ever think about getting him married early. This child was dead once. Now that God's love brought him back to life, he should live only according to the will of God." Then, I spoke a few things about my journey of faith and encouraged him by saying that everything works for the good of those that love God and who have been called to according to God's will. Then, I told him to give some thought about going with me to Seoul the next day or coming up to Seoul shortly thereafter. After saying a prayer, I left Jae-Seon's house. I went back to Jae-Seon's house the next day. When I asked him what he wanted to do, he told me that he wanted to leave with me right away. However, his parents were trying to dissuade him from doing so because Jae-Seon had received a shot that day and they were concerned about how he would hold up physically. They demanded that Jae-Seon should stay for a while before leaving for Seoul. I agreed that it was better to follow the parents' advice. Then, I left their house. Jae-Seon walked with me all the way to the station. He also bought the train ticket for me and carried my luggage to the platform. Since I had some time until the train was to arrive, I told Jae-Seon to go back home. However, as he began walking away from me, someone called to him from the inside of the waiting room at the station. It was a young man named Seong-Bae. He was known as a half-crazed man who used to shuttle back and forth between Suncheon and Yeosu Aeyangwon. When he saw Jae-Seon, he hugged him like a mother hugging her baby and began shaking him. But Jae-Seon did not resist or push him away. Instead, he stayed motionless and allowed the nuisance to go on. When I saw what was happening, I called out to them and put a stop to it.

I yelled at Seong-Bae, "What are you doing to the person who just wants to go home?" Seong-Bae let go of Jae-Seon before grabbing his arm and pulling him in the direction where I was standing. Again, Jae-Seon did not resist. Can I say that he looked like a mouse in front of a cat? Or a frog in front of a snake?

"Why are you doing this?" I asked. Jae-Seon was silent and Seong-Bae tried to pull him to go somewhere with him.

"Why are you trying to take Jae-Seon along with you?" I asked. Then, he began to mutter something.

"Let him go. Do not do anything stupid. Why are you bothering him when he just wants to go home?" I screamed. Seong-Bae, then, finally let him go. Jae-Seon began walking away. The reason that Jae-Seon was helpless before Seong-Bae was because he knew about what had really happened around this time last year.

I could not help but cry. What could make a twenty-year-old so powerless? So incapacitated? How terrible is the cost of sin even if it was due to an accidental and momentary lapse in judgment? What I told the missionary the day before had really come true that day. The world is bent on burying the guilty. However, as Christians, we must offer the guilty the way of and opportunity for repentance. After that, we must pray for and guide the person in faith. If the guilty resists all such measures, then there is nothing that a person can do except leaving the guilty's fate in God's hand.

From his recent life, I discovered a certain truth that is at work in him. It is a necessary process for Jae-Seon to go through. Only thing we can do is to guide him so that the Lord can use him.

Though I initially planned to stop by Busan, I had to go straight to Seoul because of an unexpected event. Upon arriving in Seoul, I want over to the Andong Church in order to see Rev. Son who was there to lead the provincial revival meeting of Gyeonggi Presbytery. However, Rev. Son was not there on that day and I was pleasantly surprised to find Jae-Seon there instead. He had come up to see Rev. Son as well. I realized that what I intuited about him was right. I asked him to come to the place where I was staying so that he and I could talk further. He came to see me the next day.

I heard his earnest presentation of his past, present, and future. In return, I told him about the future that I thought was appropriate for him. The following was part of what he shared with me. Speaking of his life at Goryo Bible School, he said, "I would not have gotten to know God even if I read all the books in all the libraries in the world. But I am thankful that I found God at the Busan Goryo Bible School." He also said, "Though I was not qualified to teach at Sunday school, I went to where the Sunday school was being held and helped out by hitting the drums and gathering little children in one place." He also mentioned, "Every Sunday, I was part of an eight-member team that went out to Busan Station and markets to do street evangelism. From four to six in the afternoon, I passed gospel tracts out to people."

After listening to his stories, I asked him a question. "I am in the process of writing a book titled *The Atomic Bomb of Love* and I want to write about you truthfully. But when it comes to your name, I want to use an alias. What do you think about it?" Jae-Seon replied, "Use my real name. Even if you don't use it, people in the vicinity of Suncheon would know that it is I anyway. Even if you use it, people in other parts of Korea would not know it is I. Before God, there is no hiding."

I was as glad as if I had taken down a star from the sky. I pat him on his back as tears flowed from my eyes. After giving thanks to God, we talked some more until we parted.

The second Apostle Paul was on his way Arabia.

Arabia was a desert, geographically speaking. But spiritually speaking, it signified repentance.

For what did Paul go to Arabia? It must have been for self-reflection. It was to not only discover the true self, but also discover Jesus, God's son, who had once captured him on the way to Damascus.

Weren't the beginnings of Moses and Jacob the same as this?

I do not speak of the location. I do not speak of the rhythm of that time.

I only want to see the bud sprouting in the field of heart. One does not need to travel to Arabia. The desert of Midian might not be needed. The riverbank of Jabbok is your desk. It is the house in which you live. It is the church where you gather. I only wish for the fruit of repentance.

Recently, a letter was sent to me.

Dear Uncle

I hope that you are well in the gracc of God. Jae-Seon was so sick physically that he had to come down to Suncheon on the 21st without seeing you. I don't know whether I was fortunate or unfortunate to come down here, but I was hospitalized at a hospital in Suncheon on the 28th.

The diagnosis is that I have a bad stomach and my lungs are weak. They told me that I should be hospitalized for ten days. Uncle, don't worry about me. God has graciously given me this opportunity so that I could get healed. When I get better, I will get up there right away. To live is to live for the Lord. To die is to be with the Lord. Please pray for me, a lot...

God has given me a nephew of faith.

What is Christianity?

Christianity is not a religion of individuals,
Though individuals can obtain salvation through it;
Christianity is not an American religion,
Though America has been Christianized;
Christianity is not a religion of Europe,
Though Europe has been graced by it;
Christianity is not a religion of Judea,
Though Christianity has its origins in the land;

Christianity is not a religion of pastors or elders,
Though pastors and elders were called by it;
Christianity is not a religion of whites,
Though whites have derived morals out it;
Christianity is not a religion of Westerners,
Though westerners have been graced by it;
Christianity is not a religion of Jews,
Though Christianity rose out of the bosoms of Jews;

If it were a religion of pastors and elders,
They all go to heaven, wouldn't they?
There wouldn't be Judas Iscariot, would there?
There wouldn't be Ananias and Sapphira, would there?

If it were exclusively a religion of the descendants of Israel of Judea,
Why would they kill Jesus?
Why would Peter preach the gospel to Cornelius?
Why would Paul go to Rome?

If it were a religion of Europeans,
Why would there be a great persecution in Rome?
Why would Puritans leave Europe behind?
Why would there be numerous white martyrs?

If it were a religion of America,
Why would seventy percent of its population be atheists?
Why would it boast of its materialistic culture?
Why would it brag of its atomic bombs?

Therefore, Christianity is not a religion that belongs only to a certain individual, or nation, or race, or region, or class, or denomination, or country.

Therefore, Christianity leads individuals to faith while transcending individuals.
Christianity unifies nations while transcending nations.
Christianity preserves races while transcending races.
Christianity conserves regions while transcending regions.
Christianity submits to authorities while transcending authorities.
Christianity recognizes denominations while transcending denominations.
It is a religion that calls for cosmopolitanism while transcending cosmopolitanism.

Christianity is a religion that asks,
Are you righteous before God and others or unrighteous?
Do you believe in God or not?
Do you have hope in heaven or not?
Do you love Jesus or hate him?
Do you accept the spirit of the Lord or not?
Do you share the gospel with others or keep it for yourself?

Therefore, it destroyed the descendants of Abraham, Isaac, and Jacob when they committed unrighteousness and abandoned God.
The Bible clearly shows it.

If the European race hates Jesus, it will be ruined as well.
The Great Britain of the present shows it.
If America abandons the Holy Spirit, it will be destroyed without dispute.
One American missionary prophesied, "If America continues on the present course, I do not know if it will be there fifty years from now."

If Korea remains righteous, God will bless it.

If it upholds the faith of martyrs,
If it lives only for the Lord just like Puritans.

Questions such as, "How? In what way? When? Through whom?" are what
God has to look into and decide.
It is said, "Seek first the kingdom of God and His righteousness, and all these
things shall be added unto you."

Therefore, God will forsake those so called believers if they are unrighteous.
The Holy Spirit will depart from the so-called churches if they become sinful and evil.
God will give so called denominations away to the devil if they become corrupt.

If so, how much more for a pack of wolves disguised as sheep?
How much more for profiteers disguised with the mast of religion?
How much more for Roman soldiers disguised with the mast of the church?
How much more for secret agents disguised with the mask of theology?

Christianity is contained in a certain individual's words.
It does not exclusively cater to a certain organization.
It does not get swayed by hierarchy or class.
It does not become an enemy of a certain regional conflict.
It does not get influenced by scholarship or judiciary.

It is the religion that offers the way, the truth, and the life.

Therefore,
If we call individuals, people of a nation, races, regions, denominations, nations,
and the world "length,"
Then Christianity is a religion of "width."
The religion of "width" that springs into "length,"–it is a religion of the cross.
But it is not an androcentric but a theocentric religion.
The Bible says, "So then, no more boasting about men! All things are yours,
whether Paul or Apollos or Cephas or the world or life or death or the
present or the future–all are yours and you are of Christ, and Christ is of
God." (1 Cor. 3:21–23)

Therefore, if a killer repents and belongs to him, he will be saved.

Even if somebody has been living the life of a follower for many years but does not belong to God, it cannot be said that he is a Christian, according Christianity.

"**P**astor, the last time I went to Suncheon, I heard that there were five shooters at the time of Dong-In and Dong-Sin's deaths. Is that true?" I asked.

"Mr. An, did you just find that out?" Rev. Son smiled.

"Yes. How could I know when no one told me about it?"

"That's what I heard. For that reason, I went over to the Seoul Seodaemun Penitentiary and asked one of the inmates there if there was anyone else besides Jae-Seon that was involved in the shooting. The inmate said that he did not know about it.

"Would they tell you just because you ask them?"

"Well, it was up to that person to tell me or not. But I just want to find out."

"Why?"

"If I ever find the others, I would like to fully forgive them and share the gospel with them and turn them into second and third Jae-Seons." Rev. Son laughed.

"Would that be possible? I heard that Jae-Seon was dealing with a lot of hardship," I said.

"But for me, since I have seen Jae-Seon, I want to witness to others all the more," replied Rev. Son.

"Well, still, would that work out?" I said.

"If it does not work, then I am ready to give my life to save them." He sounded determined.

"That would be nice—if it could work."

"Let's forget about it. What is the point of continuing to talk about it? We can only do something about if they are found." He put an end to the conversation.

It was the early November of 1949 when I met and talked with Rev. Son, who had returned to Aeyangwon in Yeosu after leading a special revival meeting in Busan. This conversation was followed by Rev. Son's report about what he heard while he was away for four days. He showed me the following documents as he talked.

- June 23, 1949–Moderator of Gyeongnam Presbytery, Rev. Lee Yak-Sin's *Announcements*
- July, 1949–Founders of Korea Theological Seminary, Ju Nam-Seon and Han Sang-Dong's booklet titled *Daehan-Yesu-gyo-Jangroh-Hui-Sungdo-Deoul-Ahp-Aeh-Deoul-Lihm.*
- September, 1949–Missionary Rev. Han Bu-Sun's *A Petition and the Declaration of a Public Pledge.*
- October 15, 1949–The moderator of Gyeongnam Presbytery, Rev. Sim Mun-Tae's *Proclamation.*

As he showed me these documents, Rev. Son stated, "It seems like the Church of Korea is demanding more of the blood of justice and love to be shed." The following is the summary of what the documents contained.

The Notice

It was decided at the 35th General Assembly that Gyeongnam Presbytery should sever its ties with the missionary from the group of Rev. Han Bu-Seon and his cohorts, that the presbytery should not associate with Korea Theological Seminary or to maintain ties with it for it violates the decision made at the level of the General Assembly, and that all the matters should be entrusted to the plenary commission of five persons for review and discipline.

Plenary commission members are Kim Sae-Ryeol, Kim Jae-Seok, Song Ha-Yong, and Seo Jeong-Tae.

I, as a commission member, following the rules of the commission,

have reviewed the case with both parties in reference to the matter of Gyeongnam Presbytery. I subsequently decide and declare the following for the edification, peace, and progress of the church (The details of the resolution are listed).

The moderator of Gyeongnam Presbytery, Rev. Lee Yak-Sin, submitted a written protest against the resolution. The reason for the protest is as follows:

1. We do not trust the members of the plenary commission.
2. Until an opportune time in the future, we would continue to preserve the presbytery as it is as the rightful successor of the 51st Gyeongnam Presbytery.
3. We decide to disobey the plenary commission and the declaration of the resolution until they are unconditionally withdrawn.

The booklet titled *To the Saints of the Korean Presbyterian Church* also contained information about the founding of Korea Theological Seminary. It also contained a rebuttal of Rev. Han Bu-Seon's faith and a complaint regarding the conduct of the members of the plenary commission sanctioned by the 35th General Assembly.

The document *A Petition and the Declaration of a Public Pledge* listed the pledge of the person in charge of Korea Theological Seminary and the petition that was sent to the Korean Church.

Furthermore, Rev. Sim Mun-Tae's *Proclamation* listed the contributing factors and the immediate cause for Gyeongnam Presbytery's split.

The reasons for rejecting Kosin and the presbytery are:
1. They disobeyed the resolution of the General Assembly.

2. They carried on the business of the presbytery illegally.

3. They promoted divisiveness and caused church split.

The reasons for rejecting three Presbyteries are:

1. It is not compatible with the constitution and the principles of polity.

2. The organization is illegal and there is no official precedent.

3. The division is expanded due to the presbytery's actual circumstances.

He stated, "The following items are the points of our insistence."

1. We seek to turn neither to the right nor the left, but correct the faults. We seek to be focused on the goal of unification.

2. We seek to resolve divisions and chaos in the church through the gospel and peace.

3. We seek to follow the creeds of the Presbyterian Church and submit to the authority of the General Assembly.

4. We approve the above guidelines and welcome those individuals and organizations of the estranged brethren.

After having read the documents, I said, "Well, isn't everything cool?"

He replied, "All is good. However, what's not good is neither in the resolution nor the declaration, but in the hearts of these people." He then went on to say, "The most important matter is whether they would lead and govern the General Assembly, the presbytery or the church itself with their contrite hearts, earnestness, and love or they put a yoke around the neck of their opponent through the strategy of sugarcoating and the craftiness of the serpent. Furthermore, it is a matter of whether to maintain my stubbornness that prevents me from acknowledging the truthfulness of the other or not. Looking at the phenomenon that is sweeping the Korean nation and the church presently, I cannot say honestly that there is a movement of earnest repentance going on regarding the sins of the church. Only thing that I can do is to preach against those sins. Some object by questioning me about the authority with which I go around and lead revival meetings. But I cannot abandon the flocks in order to save my own skin. There are also those that encourage me to establish a different sort of church, but that is not my intention. That's why the church of this land is demanding the blood of justice and love, isn't it?"

I replied, "Why does the preaching against the sin require the shedding of blood?"

"Well, it is nothing other than the fact that when the servant of the age points out and preaches against the sin of the age, the people of that age do not want to hear what he has to say. Like the mob that stoned Stephen to death, people would ultimately kill the servant of the age. That's why I said that it requires the blood. Jesus said, 'Woe to you, Scribes and Pharisees, hypocrites! For you build the tombs of the prophets and decorate the graves of the righteous, and you say, "if we had lived in the days of our ancestors, we would not have taken part with them in shedding the blood of the prophets." you testify against yourselves that you are descendants of those who murdered the prophets. Fill up, then, the measure of your ancestors. You snakes, you brood of vipers! How can you escape being sentenced to hell?' (Matthew 23:29–33) didn't he?" His eyes swelled with tears. Then he said, "But eventually it is justice and love that win at the end."

At this moment, I recalled what I heard from a friend of mine when I went to attend the Gyeongnam Presbytery meeting in Masan last spring. It was the second year after the liberation of Korea. The matter of Shinto worship as it pertained to the church's accommodation in the past was brought up as a point of contention. A great argument arose between the progressives and the puritans (Kosin) regarding whether the problem of Shinto worship was a matter of conscience or not. As a plain example, some even compared the issue to being raped. As the issue began to divide the assembly, Rev. Son stood up and spoke.

"My fellow pastors, since many of you are my seniors and I felt that I am not well qualified to speak, I wanted to remain silent on the matter. However, I felt that it was truly unjust for me to hear all of you talking too much. Have you forgotten what you told me regarding the issue of Shinto worship at a meeting in Busan some time before I was taken into the police custody? Aren't you the ones that told me, "You think that you are the only one with an exceptional faith? Because of you, we have to suffer. Leave our meeting"? Who was it that treated me like a heretic?"

From the perspective of Japanese Christians, I might be a heretic. Anyhow, it was true that I was treated like a heretic by you. But this is not the time to argue about who said yes or no to Shinto worship. Rather, it is the time when true repentance is needed. Not in front of people, but in front of God. Those that have truly repented would be recognized by the conduct of their lives. For those whose spiritual eyes and godly ears become open as a result of their repentance, it is better for them to become mute and become witnesses through their actions. Instead of saying, "Why are you requiring me to repent again when I have repented?" it would be better to keep silent. Instead of giving an excuse in front of people, it would be better to plead to the Lord. I have to regard those who say that Shinto worship is a matter of conscience and therefore there is nothing to repent about as the children of the devil. Also, I ask you who boast about having repented to be quiet. It is wrong for people to not recognize your true repentance. However, there is no need to fight in order to earn that recognition. If people misunderstand you, it is a consequence of their sins in the past. And it would be better to wait until the Lord to make the evaluation. Just like the way that the righteousness of the martyrs who fought against Shinto worship became clear in the present age, if you truly have repented, soon the fruit of that repentance will be made clear to all. Don't we all know what kind of misunderstanding and trouble that Paul had to suffer for his past of voting for the killing of Stephen and trying to kill the saints of the Lord with an official order? However, who can condemn Paul as being anti-Christian? I hope that, as you carry on your lives of faith in earnest, you would not become the second coming of Balaam and the problem would be resolved in not such a distant future."

His admonishment was cogent to the point that a certain pastor tried to avoid him altogether and the presbytery muddled through its business. Despite his efforts of forging a sensible approach to the problem, the fact that the presbytery has become this chaotic again refers to the uncertain leadership of the General Assembly regarding the affairs of the presbytery. Instead, the General Assembly exhibited a hostile attitude toward the movement of repentance by utilizing the majority and the law. It seemed like Gyeongnam Presbytery was being swayed by that influence.

"Pastor, the problem of Gyeongnam Presbytery would not go away even if the presbytery resolves it on its own, right?"

"No, it won't go away. Until the leadership of the General Assembly comes around to resolve the problem, the problem of Gyeongnam Presbytery will not go away. Therefore, I understand the church's viability to be dependent on the success or failure of the movement of repentance. Any insistence on love without repentance or any effort of unification without repentance will be a vain attempt." As he spoke these words, his eyes seemed to sparkle.

On that night, I was able to attend the Son family's prayer meeting. I attempted to recollect and record the earnest prayer of Rev. Son as much as possible because I was so moved by what was said.

Lord, I am thankful that we were able to live another day of our lives in you. I thank you for that grace and I thank you for sending a special friend whom I love and esteem so that we can conduct this prayer meeting together.

We human beings must live a life of walking with, serving and following the guidance of the Lord. However, since we destroy ourselves and neglect this holy vocation, how can we expect to receive the blessings God gives in this life and the life hereafter?

Jesus, you prayed to the point of sweating blood on the hill of Gethsemane. Have mercy on this sinner who fails to pray for and teach this country, this people, this church, and this flock. This failure is the result of the sins of the past, the sins that are being committed daily, and the sins that are committed both knowingly and unknowingly. You must forgive this sinner first.

Jesus, you walked toward Golgotha with a thorny crown on your head and a cross on your shoulders. Have mercy on this sinner who fails to preach and lead the humankind of this world unto salvation in you. Rather than preaching against the ancestral sin that started with Adam and all the sins that we commit because we are mortals, I perpetuate sin in front of God. How can I ever point out the sins of others? Wash me again in the blood of the cross.

Jesus, you came to life again in three days and ascended to heaven. I am thankful and joyful that you have overcome the power of death. Bestow on me your power and empower me so as to triumph over the power of the devil.

Lord, help me to open my spiritual eyes and pray for the church of Aeyangwon that you have allowed me. Though this is an isolated community of a few, the devil also works around here, too. They say that the external diseases are fearful. However, sin that resides deep in our hearts is far more fearful. Therefore, protect and guide your children. Guide us to the green pastures beside still waters. Provide us the food for our bodies. And turn us into persons who can feed others with spiritual food.

I pray for the church of Korea. Because of your great providence, it has been almost a century since the gospel of the Lord came to this land and you have produced numerous servants out of us. But how come your servants and flocks are like this now? Jehovah, you desire our humble service to you more than oil that flows like water from thousands of rivers. You must give righteousness, mercy, and humility to these servants and flocks.

I pray for the people of Korea. After being oppressed by a foreign race as the judgment for our sins, it has been five years already since it was liberated through your grace. But not only has the 38 parallel been more solidified as times goes by, how can it be a coincidence that much trouble is brewing in all four corners of this land? It must be due to the failure of those who were called first in not carrying out the call faithfully. Lord, who used to answer the prayers of Abraham, have mercy on us. Make us not into Sodom and Gomorrah but the city of Nineveh. Compel us to repent as we wear hemp clothes and throw ashes on our heads. You must turn your wrath away from us.

I pray for the peace of this world. While human beings try to assert their will, assuming that it is what makes the world move, your word never changes. Didn't you tell us to repent for the kingdom of heaven is near, that those that take the sword would die by the sword, to seek first your kingdom and your righteousness, and feed and give drinks to our enemies?

Lord, Jehovah, Abba Father, you took James, who was in prison, back home to you; but you spared Peter's life, who was also in prison, according to your sovereign will. But they want to wash away from the face of the earth the blood of the martyrs whose lives you received according to your sovereign will, even before their tears are dried up and their wounded bodies are healed up.

They also want to flog the saints whose lives you spared from death while imprisoned according to your sovereign will even before their tears of prayers get dried and their broken bodies get mended. They want to turn them into living sacrifices.

They want to bury those whom you have preserved on earth according to your will alive in the ground even before their sighs fade away and their prayers come to an end and their Amens can be uttered.

Lord, Jehovah, Abba Father, let *me* give my body up to them—for the people of this nation are ignorant and the members of this church are evil. How could I not go up to the pulpit of the devil? How could I mind going to the streets of Satan? How could I refuse the valley of death when sin that is far more fearsome than a leper controls this world?

Send me to the hill of Gethsemane or lead me to the value of Golgotha or move me to hilltop of Calvary. I will stumble while I preach the repentance of sins. I will fall while I teach the gospel of the Lord.

Lord, Jehovah, Abba Father, since this people would still not comprehend, send me back to the Yeosu Police Station where I used to shiver and pray in the cold of the night. I was thankful for a spoonful of rice and a spoonful of soup. Send me back to Gwangju Prison where I used to read the Bible while being cursed at day and night. My life in the red uniform was a paradise for I was able to reflect on your word while awake or in sleep. Send me back to the Cheongju Penitentiary where I made a seat for myself in order for me to spend the rest of my life there until I died. I miss the time when I had forgotten about this world and been living my life with you. I would like to pray to you for all the days of my life in that seat.

Lord, Jehovah, Abba Father, extinguish this life of mine on earth for the people's hearts are hardened. I would be grateful for the interior of a stone tomb and I would appreciate a mound of firewood and I would not refuse a cave of beasts. Hasn't my blood that is less than three liters already been offered to you? Haven't my bones that are less than three hundred in number already been offered to you? Hasn't my flesh already been torn?

I hear that they insist that Shinto worship is a matter of individual conscience. They still bow to the flag. Did I remain stubborn because my body was immune to the beatings? Did I fight because my heart was wicked? Did I go to prison because I did not have anywhere to live? Though Shinto shrine had been removed, why is the idol still there behind the pulpit? Though the Japanese rule has been withdrawn, why is the campaign to Japanize in full swing? My kinsmen thrust the spear of jealousy and of the Japanese trickery, sharper than the thorny crown, deeper into my chest. The Pharisaic actions of unrepentant colleagues, rather than the persecution by Roman soldiers, flog, tear, and beat my body.

Lord, Jehovah, Abba Father, for this people would still not repent, take this body and soul of mine away. I would like to go up to the place where you have prepared for me, congregate with numerous saints that had already gone to be there, meet my parents of the flesh that are there already, call to me my two sons of flesh that are there already, and pray with you for the church of Korea and this world. I thank you and pray all these things in the name of Jesus, Amen.

I could not help but cry.

The deep stillness of the night kept the sound of this prayer in its heart.

Epilogue

As I put my pen down, I feel like my body will soon become ill from all the stress under which I have been. However, my real concern is about what is to come.

I fear that I have not done all I could. It is unfortunate that all these details of the living history were recorded by a poor writer like me. By all means, I wish that many other writers bring to life the stories of faith of the martyrs and the imprisoned saints and the hidden saints and share them with the world.

One of the things that I realized while authoring this book was that God has greatly blessed us in giving a martyr like Rev. Son Yang-Won and the remarkable persons of faith in his family unto our sinful nation. I thank the Lord that they were God's special gift to the Christian community and the Christian movement in the world.

I express my thanks to my brothers in faith, Jang Shi-Hwa of *Gidoggyo Shinmun* (Christian Newspaper) and Jeon Yeong-Chang of America who worked tirelessly to support this project financially, and Kim Jae-In whose assistance in reviewing the content of this book and editorial contribution has been invaluable. I would also like to thank Seoul Gonginsa for expediting the publication of this book to their best ability.

In conclusion, I would like to say that the most fearful thing in this world is neither leprosy nor communism nor rebellion nor weapons nor atomic bombs. It is the human heart that devises evil and refuses to acknowledge or seeks to betray God of righteous love, who does not tolerate even a sliver of sin. This seems to be particularly true as the human civilization advances. Therefore, rather than being afraid of the offensives of August, September, or October, we should be afraid of the offensives of betrayal, profiteering, social decay, and church corruption.

While writing this book, the scandal of a certain church in South Korea regarding its renovation fund of ten thousand dollars has rung in my ears and troubled my heart. I hope that the accusation is groundless but if it is true, then it is an example of an offensive church profiteering.

Through all, I wanted to expose to the world the individuals who remained unrepentant and shameless even after having committed the acts of Satan in the past. But I believe that it is too early to do so. Instead, I look forward to a future opportunity. Be forewarned, you who cannot come to enlightenment even after being bombarded with this atomic bomb of love. Be prepared to end up inside a fish in the Red Sea!

Part II

Elegy

I. Why has he gone away alone
Leaving behind the thirty million kinsmen
In this land that has so much work to be done
Due to the collapse of the 38 Parallel?

(Refrain)
He dreamed of being a sacrifice of martyrdom all his life.
He dreamed of being a sacrifice of martyrdom all his life.
He sent his two sons ahead of him.
Did he go away in pursuit of Jesus?

II. With twenty five years of caring for the sick,
With another six years of life in prison,
With the offering of his two sons,
Was he done with his mission?

III. He met the sword and rifle with gladness.
He met the beating and whipping with laughter.
He met his enemies with love.
Was he finished with journey?

IV. Over the hill of Gethsemane,
Across the valley of Golgotha,
To the top of Mount Calvary,
Did he go away in pursuit of Jesus?

(Sung to the tune of "I Can Hear My Savior Calling")

Preface

Rev. "Sandol" [living-stone] Son Yang-Won.

His life was a breath of prayer and fed on the Bible as its sustenance.

He was truly a possessor of the heaven and his life was a martyr's sacrifice.

For twenty five years, he was a parent, husband, and child to the leper.

For six years in prison, he lived as a member of God's perfect household.

During the Yeosu-Suncheon Incident, he spoke as a confessor of love.

In the age of the communist reign in Korea, he was content to be an heir to the cross.

His faith and life illustrated God who loved humanity to the extent of freely giving his only Son, embodied the grace of Jesus Christ who willingly bore the burden of sin unto dying on the cross, and personified the Holy Spirit who transcends time and space.

I would like to conclude the preface by quoting the ending of Rev. Park Hyung-Ryong's word of remembrance given during the memorial service held in Seoul. He said,

"We certainly do not know which one word to use in describing Rev. Son who was a devout man, evangelist, warrior of faith, friend of lepers, lover of enemy, and martyr. Perhaps, the title of saint needs to be used in relation to him. It is said that even the Japanese jailer at Gwangju Prison referred to Rev. Son as a saint upon being impressed by his words and actions. How much more should we, who know his words and actions in their diverse aspects, not hesitate to call him a saint

along with the world? If we think about it, there has not been a saint
like him in the annals of the history of the Korean church. It is also a
rare phenomenon in the history of the world Christianity. Though we
conferred sainthood on Saint Anthony for his life of devotion, there
does not seem to have been, in his life, the marks of an evangelist, a
warrior of faith, a friend to lepers, a lover of enemies, and a martyr.
Though we revere Saint Augustine and Saint Francis, they did not have
the honor of dying along with his family members as martyrs while
living out their life of godliness. Though Jan Hus and Wycliffe gave
their lives in martyrdom in order to protect the integrity of their faith,
they lacked the honor of being friends to the leper and lovers of their
enemies. This comparative examination clearly locates Rev. Son Yang-
Won as a rare saint in the annals of the world Christianity.

Oh! Does the world know that Rev. Son Yang-Won is the only saint
that the seventy-year history of the Korean Church has ever produced
and a rare find even in the history of the world Christianity? Dear the
devout sons and daughters of the Korean Church! Lament the passing
of the great saint in Rev. Son Yang-Won and sing a song of lamentation
for him. And let us truly, earnestly, and eternally memorialize his
great achievements. In that way, we can try to follow at least one of the
trails that he left behind. When that happens, all the believers in the
world might be able to imitate us in memorializing this great saint and
following his footsteps."

God has allowed us a saint like Rev. Son Yang-Won because God did
not want to forsake Korea.

And I heard a voice from heaven saying, "Write this: Blessed are the
dead who from now on die in the Lord." "Yes," says the Holy Spirit,
"they will rest from their labors, for their deeds follow them" (Revelation
14:13).

Christmas of 1951

Aeyangwon, Son Yang-Won
Chapter 1

It was probably three in the morning.

"Ha, ha, ha..."

"Ho, ho, ho..."

"You, too, Pastor, ha, ha, ha...," a sea of laughter broke out.

The window was kept open halfway in order to keep the pungent smell of food being cooked and the charcoal burner from filling the room. Kim Soo-Nam, Kim Bong-Rim, Lee Num-Jin, and few other deacons were sitting together and pan-frying breaded fish and beef.

Out of nowhere, a stray cat emerged and cried, "Meow."

"Shoo! You, stray cat!" Deacon Kim yelled startled.

"Meow," the cat cried again without running away.

The stray cat was in no way startled and Deacon Kim peered out the window while standing still. At that moment, a figure emerged crying, "Meow."

"I am a human cat," said Rev. Son. The sound made Deacon Kim who was trying to peer out the window startled and fall to the floor. Everyone instantly broke out in laughter at the sight. Rev. Son, pretending as if he did not know what the matter was, plainly said, "I appreciate all of you working hard without any sleep." The way he said it made them burst into laughter again. They were doing the preparation for tomorrow's Senior Day which was an annual event.

Senior Day.

Aeyangwon Senior Day.

Senior Day for Yeosu Aeyangwon, the group home for lepers. Senior

Day was an occasion of happiness for it gave all the young people of the community an opportunity to serve its elderly as if they were their actual biological parents. It was also a day of joy and tears for the seniors because of the parental role given them to play. In this way, Rev. Son stayed up all night without getting any sleep and walked around to make sure no little detail had been overlooked so as to prevent any mix-up for this special day.

"By the way, I can tell that you are cold-hearted from the way you pushed that cat away!"

"[Would you do the same to] a human cat?"

"Of course, if you are a stray cat, too, Pastor!"

"Pastor... a stray cat?... ha, ha, ha..."

"Ha, ha, ha..."

"Did Gyung-Sik went to bring Mr. Cheon?"

"Yes, he already went."

"Who was it that went?"

"I think, Deacon Jeong."

"Then, was an arrangement made to bring everyone over?"

"Yes. But who went to get Grandma Gap-Ju?"

"I sent Deacon Cho."

"Then, it seems that everything is in place."

This exchange about the seniors took place between Elder Park who functioned as the master of ceremony for that night's program and Kim Gyung-Sik, the chair of the religion committee of the association of young people, who was the usher for the day. Among the seniors, there were those who could not see well due to old age and those who were shut-ins due to weak legs. But even these seniors were brought out to a social function like this. After having given birth to and raised their children, seeing their children have children of their own, helping raise their grandchildren, and seeing their sixtieth and sixty first birthdays come and go, it was customary for the seniors to be treated as a burden by their children and relegated to the backrooms of the houses. How could they expect to be given even the backrooms by those that were not their own children? Furthermore, for those that had become bald, their fingers twisted, their noses fallen off, and their limbs disabled due to leprosy from which they could never extricate themselves as long as they live, how could they even expect to be given turns at the garbage cans on the side of the street or given space underneath a bridge somewhere, let alone living in the backrooms? They could not see themselves as being worthy to be accepted into a gang of beggars in this small world. But to be given a chance to be entertained and comforted by younger patients of the community on Senior Day was for these senior lepers to experience a fellowship of human beings that is even a rarity in the world of human beings.

This event was instituted by Rev. Son's insistence after he arrived in Aeyangwon. It was one of the most fun and joyous annual events of the church.

For this event, people would bring out the goods such as sweet rice or grains that were given to them on Thanksgiving Day the year before. Also, money was collected from church members that were younger than forty in age a week ago. Several relatively healthy people were chosen from the younger members and sent to the market in Yeosu or Suncheon to buy food for a joyous feast.

The excerpts from his letter to his father, Elder Son, while in prison and the letter to his wife regarding the anniversary of his mother's death show the spirit of filial piety that led Rev. Son to found Senior Day. During the six years of his incarceration, he sent a letter to his father that contained the following words.

When I met you, Father, for the first time in three years on January 4 this year, I was saddened by the whiteness of your hair. Though I wondered whether it was due to this sinful world or aging, I realized that it was all my fault and thus became contrite. You aged from having raised me with all your strength and praying for your son who is in prison to the point of your blood bring dried up...

In his letter to his wife titled 'My reminiscence on the anniversary of my mother's death,' Rev. Son penned the following sentiments.

As May 6, the anniversary of my mother's death, approaches, I cannot help but reminisce about her sacrificial love. Whenever I think of her great love with which she loved me, I cannot calm my troubled heart. The more I think of her love in giving birth to and raising me so delicately, the more I am filled with sadness. Whenever I think about the day that my mother died, I remember how red the persimmon flowers were in the garden of our house. I would also be reminded of her death whenever I come upon persimmon flowers.

Though sparrows that migrated to the south of river had come back this spring, it is lamentable that geese that had been gone to the northern country for some time may not be back to see the spring blossoms. Even as persimmon flowers are in bloom as it was back in the garden of my old house, there is no reason to think that my mother who had left for the paradise would return to this world.

My belief that the glory of heaven is better than the pleasures of this world finally brings my tears to stop. I ask you to comfort my father today.

[In the same letter, Rev. Son addressed filial piety to his sons.]

Now as I use my pen to beseech you, Dong-In, Dong-Sin, Dong-Hee, Dong-Jang, and Dong-Su, to offer the acts of great filial piety unto your grandfather, I first want to thank you. How can I not be thankful that you care for your grandfather wholeheartedly and earnestly to the best of your abilities? Right! This is the way, duty, and responsibility for you.

Of course, if I don't respect and revere my parents, who would cherish and care for them? Therefore, I should not serve my parents in order to be blessed or calculate the benefit and cost of doing so. Rather, it should be regarded as one's rightful duty. The greatest among three thousand sins is forsaking the duty of caring for one's parents and such a person becomes the chief of all sinners. You should live peacefully with your siblings and learn to repay your grandfather and mother with filial piety. This is only right. What you should remember is that blessings come upon those who fulfill their duties. If goodness and righteousness were sowed, why would blessings not sprout?... The reason why I say the things I say here is based on the words of a sage of old, "A tree wants to stay calm but wind blows incessantly, and a fool wants to care for his parents but they cannot wait for it." The fact that parents cannot wait for their child to care for them when they are several hundred years old regardless of how much he wants to care for them brings tears to my eyes and I cannot help but stop to put my pen down for I know I cannot fulfill the term of my life in the future. For this reason, I continue to beseech you not for the reason that I cannot trust you. I trust you wholeheartedly. Not only in my place, but also for my portion, double your efforts in serving your old grandfather who is in his eighties. In order to prevent any regret or bitterness in the future, I request this earnestly. There is a time for doing good and if this opportunity is lost, then having delayed only brings about remorse. If you happen to remember that you had not been faithful in serving your deceased grandmother, then do your best to not repeat it unto your grandfather who is still alive.

These excerpts clearly show Rev. Son's heartfelt devotion to his parents. Starting Senior Day for Rev. Son must have an attempt to repay his father's love for him, which was demonstrated by how his father died in a faraway place, in Harbin. He died while praying for Rev. Son, his son in prison and holding onto the rope that was hanging from the ceiling at the old age of seventy five.

Once there was an actual event described in the following:

There was an elderly patient who had his throat surgically removed after it became infected and to breath out of a hole in his neck. This elderly man, right before he passed away, insisted on seeing Rev. Son. Upon seeing Rev. Son in person, he asked him for a bottle of soda with a grin on his face. However, when Rev. Son returned with a bottle of soda to the intensive care unit where the patient was in, he received the news that the patient had died. Rev. Son cried and wondered about how refreshed the patient would have been had he been successful in giving the patient a bottle of soda in time. From that time on, the sight of a soda bottle would remind Rev. Son of that old man and frequently exhort others to do their best to do good unto the old and young whenever possible, since it is God who allows us to do good.

1. How gorgeous is the beautiful scenery of the mountain and water surrounding Aeyangwon!
Let us build on the foundation of the truths of God's word,
Make it into a precious garden like that of Eden,
Bring about the blessed land like that of Canaan.

2. We become one true body of one thousand and one hundred individuals
By driving out all sorts of evil from us.
May we enjoy thoroughly the company of each other
As one family in one abode.

3. Every early morning, we can worship
And eat breakfast together.
From there, we go about our days,
Fulfilling each duty given us.
Whenever time allows, Let us read the Bible.
In the evenings, let us gather in each room
And have a time of devotion.

4. Our Lord Jesus, Mr. Jesus, is the grapevine.
We are his bountiful branches.
May we receive his nutrients and blossom
And spread our fragrance throughout the land of Korea.

A long table with all kinds of dishes on it was placed out in the middle of the hall. It looked like its legs were about to fall off with all that food. Around it were seated the elderly, both men and women dressed neatly in white. There were also the young men and women who were the designated servers for the elderly. Though only forty or fifty persons were healthy enough to hit the low and high pitches of the song, all of those gathered were dishing out the Aeyangwon's version of the Song of Happiness including the elderly woman with a twisted mouth and swollen facial skin and the young man without any trace of facial hair whatsoever. Among was Rev. Son singing along in joy whose short stature was accentuated in the seated position.

This song was composed by Rev. Son and routinely sung before the start of banquets such as this one. Rather than excitement and elation, people would be filled with deep emotion of sadness from singing the song. Many elderly people cried and even the young people were moved to the brink of tears. In particular, an elderly man named Kim Myung-Soo broke out in a loud weeping.

He came from a not-so-small town in the countryside of the southern Jeolla province and he had been living in Aeyangwon for more than ten years now. He was sixty three years old, already three years past his 60th birthday. His family had clout and wealth comparable to the very rich in town. His father even reached the position of a town magistrate but gave it up due to the corruptions that he saw in the government prior to the annexation of Korea by Japan. He then relocated to where the family came to settle eventually wanting to spend the rest of his days submerged in books. His father belonged to the class of *Yangban* (the ruling class) of the Chungcheong province.

At the same time, his family was known for generosity in single-handedly providing hospitality to the visitors of the town. At the age of thirty five, however, he realized that his body was suffering from an unknown disease and tried all sorts of remedy for his condition including acupuncture and exotic medicines. Without any improvement to his condition, his body began to worsen and the symptoms began to appear even in his face. Believing that it was due to some kind of curse and feeling hopeless about his life, he certainly kept waiting for the day of his death. However, to him, the greater concern had to do with the welfare of his family and the future of his children. His two sons and three daughters were honor students at school and praised by both their teachers and elders of the town. In particular, his second son was known for his devotion to him.

Because he thought that his illness became a constant source of worry and shame for his family, he struggled to decide whether to die expeditiously or leave his family, neither of which was a viable option for him. After living with the disease for more than seventeen years, he ran away from his family one night when the moon was bright in an apparent attempt to rid his family of any more pain and bid his children success for their lives. According to his testimony, prior to running away, he tried to acquire arsenic poison in order to kill himself but failed to get his hands on it. Once, he tried drinking lye to kill himself only to damage the inside of his mouth and suffer from immense pain. On those occasions, his second son tried ever so hard to comfort his father and alleviate his anxiety by saying, "Dad, just continue living and do not worry about anything else." Despite his son's desperate plea, the elder Kim felt torn apart inside and ended up leaving a will behind and running away from home. For many days he wandered about as a beggar until he found his way to Aeyangwon.

Then, ten years passed and another year passed. At first, Kim wanted to hear about his family. But since he did not wish to give away information about his whereabouts, he even changed his name upon registering for the admission into Aeyangwon. Only after the fourth year, Kim inquired about his family and heard that his second son died of heartache in the wake of his elope. Thinking that it was he that killed his son of great filial piety, when Kim was reminded of his deceased son on an occasion like this, he would cry his heart out in mourning of his son.

He used to say to his peers, "I killed that boy. This wretched old man killed my son! I should have died at home a long time ago. For what shall I live! I cannot believe that he died!"

Also, there was the case of this young woman.

She was a deaconess and thirty five years of age. Her name was Kim Jeong-Hee. It had been about fifteen years since she came to Aeyangwon. She was married into a very rich family in a small city somewhere in the Jeolla province as the wife of the third son of the family.

Her rich husband was very talented and handsome that many matchmakers competed to find a wife for him. Finally, Deaconess Kim was the one to marry him and she was also without an equal in terms of intellect and beauty. Had she not contracted the disease, she would have gone to Japan with her husband to study abroad there.

At the time of her marriage, she was in the fourth year at a girls' school. The husband's grandfather's insistence to be able to receive a granddaughter-in-law into the family before he died led to the wedding being expedited. Ms. Kim's teachers at school and townspeople all lamented the fact that she was not able to finish her schooling with only a year left to go.

Because of this, her husband in an effort to soothe her promised that after getting married they would go to study abroad in Japan and continue their education together there. Furthermore, her father-in-law showed greater affection to her than to the first and second daughter-in-laws, though she was the third daughter-in-law in the household made up of four brothers. Soon, however, her sisters-in-laws came to suspect that she suffered from a mysterious illness. Though Ms. Kim was able to receive treatment for her condition away from other's view, since her condition worsened in time, she ended up moving back to her parents' house for a prolonged period of time. Because that living arrangement could not last either, she ended up moving into Aeyangwon.

When she first arrived in Aeyangwon, she used to receive letters and money from her husband time to time. Then, with the excuse that her husband was busy, her father-in-law sent her letters and money in her husband's place. Her father-in-law truly felt sorry about her situation and sent her enough money for her needs. In the fourth year at Aeyangwon, Deaconess Kim received the news that her husband married someone else. Of course, it was her own idea that he should forget about her and get remarried. But her husband seemed to reject her gesture initially. However, when the letter came from her father-in-law that contained the words of apology, she was overwhelmed by grief and emptiness that she cried for three days along with her daughter. Though she was able to write back with the words of blessing and relief through the strength of her faith, she nevertheless remained heartbroken for her daughter who had to live with her without an illness. She regretted for not having left her daughter with her husband from the very beginning of the separation period again and again. Thankfully, more than her real father ever did, her father-in-law continued to send her money and letters, but he also died a year ago.

Around that time, she went to visit with her in-laws and discuss the future of her daughter. However, from afar, she saw a great commotion surrounding her old house and when she inquired of it, she learned that it was due to the funeral arrangements being made for her father-in-law who had just died three days earlier.

She could neither go inside the house to mourn because of the way she looked nor go back to Aeyangwon pretending that nothing had happened. She then decided to wait for the funeral procession to leave for the funeral site and pay her tribute from afar. However, while she was watching the family and funeral procession move along, she fainted and fell to the side of the road.

People murmured, "Here is a leper lying on the ground."

"Well, she does not seem to be dead."

"How ominous it is!"

The voices rang in her ears faintly. Then, she regained her consciousness only to find herself covered over with a ragged blanket at the corner of the road. She managed to immediately return to

Aeyangwon. Today, she was crying thinking of her father-in-law and her daughter whose future remained a grave concern to her.

Also, it was not as if Rev. Son was without a personal story of pain himself. There was an elderly woman who was in her seventies and whose name was Choi Sung-Nyuh. She was known for praying day and night inside the chapel. She apparently took it upon herself to pray for Rev. Son because she regarded him as a son to her. Not only was her birthday the same as that of Rev. Son's deceased mother, but she also looked like her. Because of this, Rev. Son tried to visit her whenever he could in memory of his mother. The woman also thought fondly of Rev. Son like a son. Whenever in Rev. Son's presence, she made it a habit of telling him that she wanted to go to heaven right away. Though she looked forward to this Senior Day event, she died unfortunately with only two weeks left to go before the festivities. Rev. Son could not be there for her when she died because he was away for a revival meeting. It is said that she died crying unintelligibly, "Where is Rev. Son?... Where did he go?... When is he coming back?... How can I die without ever seeing him again?... I should not die without Rev. Son being here... Please, let someone go and bring him to me..." Since it was commonplace for the people of Aeyangwon on their deathbeds wanting to see Rev. Son for the last time, no extra effort was made in contacting Rev. Son about the woman's imminent death. But Rev. Son mourned her death greatly upon returning to Aeyangwon and receiving the news of her death. Rev. Son felt lamentable thinking that had she lived just three more weeks, she would have seen the festivities of Senior Day for herself.

In this way, many had reasons for having heavy hearts on this day including the aforementioned Mr. Kim, the woman, and Rev. Son. With the past and present intertwined, many stories and experiences of pain converged to give rise to the collective singing of this song of tears.

The following is a part of Rev. Son's sermon of encouragement:

"We are not people who live life by the ways of men. We live by the ways of heaven. Though we lost a few of our sons and daughters of the flesh, we gained many more of the spirit. Though we lost our parents of the flesh, we gained many more of the spirit. Though we do not have our parents and children of decayed sin, we are here in one place with our parents and children of eternity through the blood of Jesus Christ. Isn't it something for which we are greatly thankful? How can we not speak of the joy of being blessed in this life for we have been made one family in the name of Jesus Christ? Therefore, let us make sure that we would not regret later. If our parents or children of the flesh are still alive, let us share the gospel with them. If they had already died, let us pray for them..."

With these words, Rev. Son moved everyone's heart. Elder Park who was the master of ceremony for the event said, "This time, Rev. Son will say grace for everyone before we eat." The quietness inside the sanctuary of Aeyangwon Church became all the more silent. Only the chirping sound of birds was heard.

"Lord!" There was a long silence before the prayer continued on. The sound of someone sobbing with tears flowing from eyes and nose was heard. Rev. Son blurted out, "Lord!" in a tearful voice. Then he continued on:

"What kind of grace, what kind of love is this? Again, what kind of grace is this? What kind of love is this? What kind of grace is this that you loved us and offered this banquet of love to us who were once destined to die in sin, who were sinners more worthless than worms, dust, and dirt? Especially, we were separated from others by the society, ridiculed by our kinsmen, and driven out from our homes. We do not have anything to live for, let alone a sense of worth. We are nothing more than a nuisance. But you showered your blessings upon us and led us to believe in Jesus Christ and gave us this heart of compassion. What kind of grace, what kind of love is this? Lord, I ask you to keep us captive by your grace and love and turn us into the warriors of prayer and keepers of faith and practitioners of compassion. There are many in the world that desire to be the warriors of prayer, keepers of faith, and practitioners of compassion, but they cannot follow through with their decision and only lament of this inability due to the pressures of their life situations. However, since you gave us a blessing in the form of our illness and led us to this place on this occasion, help us bear fruit to your liking. Today, we shall take this food that you have prepared for us with joyful hearts. Help us not to take this food in order to satisfy our appetite or hunger or flesh. Instead, help us take this food so that we could have strength to pray even if we are shut-ins. Let this food give us strength so that we could better prepare ourselves for the heaven in this brief life we live. Bless those young people who worked hard to prepare this food, because I believe that they did so unto you. And bless all the elderly who take this food now as they understand that they are given it by your love. Lastly, I once again beseech you to bless those that led us to this place, whether be it our families of the flesh, the society, and the church, and allow your will be done on earth as it is in heaven. Help us to be vigilant so that we would not fall into sin in this hour. I thank and pray all this to you in the name of our Lord Jesus Christ. Amen."

Now the young servers removed the white sheets from the tables that had been covering the food and urged the elderly to start eating. Those who found it to be a challenge to eat on their own, such as the five seniors that were blind and three whose fingers were crooked, had to be fed by the servers.

"Wow, they really did a number on the food!"

"Wow, I can't believe it!"

"Why don't you eat, pastor?"

Even Rev. Son was lost in exclamation as everyone else was. Not only did he approach the table and eat joyfully with others the food that was prepared in earnestness, he could also be seen feeding personally those that were either blind or could not use their hands. Though it was an act that brought people to tears, it was nothing unusual for Rev. Son.

There was an incident like this immediately following the liberation of Korea. His knees began to ache all of a sudden. Upon hearing his complaint, the doctors of Aeyangwon wanted to examine him and do a blood test on him. Rev. Son said dispassionately, "Why are you all concerned? Isn't this a great thing? I finally have my wish come true. It means that I can live under the same roof..." When an examination was finally done due to people's persistent request, the result from the blood test came back negative and showed that his blood was still clean. Learning of the result, Rev. Son, "Is that so? Again, it's a disappointment." He spoke as if he was not at all affected by it. In fact, even leprosy did not pose any concern to him.

Day and night, with tears in my eyes,
I await my Lord's return.

My Lord, you said, as you were leaving, that you would come back.
When will it be that you return?

With a flickering lamplight
That brightens this lonely and solitary field,

I wonder if you are returning,
Whenever I see a parcel of strange cloud floating in the sky from a far.

On this night, I cannot fall asleep
due to my longing for you that plagues me as an illness.
My Lord, when will it be that you return?

With a golden crown raised up in my hand, I let out a hurrah.
This love is decorated with the seven treasures.
Erase it only after I am gone.

Ms. Kim sang this song of sad melody in order to comfort all the disabled elderly who were seated. Everyone was quiet, but people broke out in a round of applause when the song ended. Even those with crooked fingers clapped with their palms.

There is a story behind this song. There was a certain *Jeondosa* who defied the order of bowing to Shinto and was imprisoned for three years in Pyeongyang for that reason. Not only was his hardship great, but he worried about how difficult life must be for his family on the outside. He thought that he could better care for his family and others in prison by getting released. So, it led him to compromise his stance on Shinto worship and was released from prison upon giving his consent for Shinto worship. However, that became a cause for further apostasy and led even to his moral failures. But at the end, he repented deeply and turned his way around to live the life of a true Christian. During those days, he wrote this song and started wandering about like a beggar and ministered unto other beggars.

Somehow he found out about Aeyangwon and moved to Okjong-myun Bukbang-ri, a sanctuary for the persecuted Christian lepers who once fought the good fight of faith during the reign of Japanese rule. He then carried out the work of helping and comforting them and taught them this song. This song brought back the painful memory of their past. It brought them back to the time when they had to support Rev. Son's family members who were scattered to all different places in order to follow the example of Rev. Son's faith who was in prison. They did this while managing their own living. It meant that they often had to depend on other's generosity for food and went around begging for rice and barley. On some summer nights when an infinite number of stars quietly sparked across the night sky, they had to stay in empty fields. There were some nights in the autumn when they had to stay in the deep woods. On one snowy winter night, they had to sneak into a rice mill and brave the cold there. All this hardship, during the

Japanese rule, was due to the vigilance of many village leaders who reported to local police stations and provincial offices on people moving about from place to place. When arrested, many suffered a great deal of trouble because they were treated as spies. In such instances, people resorted to singing hymns such as "Nearer, my God, to Thee," "He leadeth me: O blessed thought," "Must Jesus bear the cross alone," and "I can hear my Savior calling." But the song that was most frequently sang was this song. A few of men and women in this place knew this song well and whenever they heard this song being sung, their memory of the past's hardship was renewed. In the same manner, they knew the importance that underlined this banquet for the seniors. However, it is not only the past that took them down the memory lane. Presently, they remain lonely in the wilderness of life with their broken bodies. It is easy to understand their belief and longing for the paradise, their desire to trust and meet their Lord, their excitement at seeing a strange cloud floating in the sky from afar thinking that it might signal the Lord's return, and their yearning to leave this place with their golden crowns in hand, shouting hurrahs, and decorated ornately. Should I say that it is like the inside of a shipwreck? Or should I say that it is like a cicada that has come out of the body of a larva with a full set of wings?

The master of ceremony introduced Rev. Son by saying, "Now the pastor will tell us a funny story." Rev. Son got up readily with a grin on his face saying, "It's about time..."

"Once upon a time, a long long time ago, there was a pair of brothers. The older brother's name was Yang-Won and he was dumb. The younger brother's name was Dong-Su and he was one smart cookie," said Rev. Son. The audience thought that he was referring to himself and Elder Park.

"These brothers lost their parents at an early age. Now the younger brother came of age and wanted to get married. Since his older brother needed to get married in order for this to happen, the younger brother,

Dong-Su, looked everywhere for a bride for his brother and finally he
was able to get his brother married. However, when the older brother's
in-laws found out that Yang-Won was dumb, they decided to ask him a
question to test him. They said to each other, "Let's ask him tomorrow
about the grain chest, what it was made of, what its name was, and how
much rice it can hold."

However, Yang-Won's wife overheard what her parents were
discussing and she told him about the test to avert embarrassment. She
told him, "My dear husband, when my father calls you and asks you, tell
him that it is made of paulownia wood, it is a grain chest and it holds
about 180 liters."

Yang-Won kept repeating what his wife told him, "It is made of
Paulownia wood, it is a grain chest and it holds about 180 liters." As
imagined, the next day, his mother-in-law called to him out of nowhere
and told him, "Hey, son, your father-in-law wants to see you suddenly."
"Yes," he said as he walked toward the guest room. As he walked, he
kept on repeating, "It is made of Paulownia wood, it is a grain chest and
it holds six sacks of rice." When he opened the door, he met his father-
in-law who actually called him in because he was having a stomach
ache. Yang-Won then got close to his father-in-law and hit his belly
with his fist saying, "It is made of Paulownia wood, it is a grain chest
and it holds six sacks of rice." Then, his father-in-law in obvious pain
called out, "Oh, he is killing me!" Yang-Won imitated his father-in-law
by rolling on the floor and yelling just as he did. The audience broke out
in a laughter. Then, the story continued.

Yang-Won's wife who realized that her husband failed the test
instructed him to say in such a case, "I cannot imagine how much
you are hurting. You would get better once you go buy and take the
medicine." Then, Yang-Won kept repeating it. One day, his father-in-
law returned home from market with a cow. He then called his son-in-
law to showcase the cow. Yang-Won proceeded to examine the cow by

saying, "I cannot imagine how much you are hurting. You would feel better once you go buy and take the medicine."

Once again, the audience broke out in a laughter. The laughing faces looked funny in and of themselves. The faces laughing with mouths twitching, the faces laughing with eyes jolting, and the faces laughing without moving a muscle.

Learning of her husband's second failure, she instructed to say the following words in such a situation, "It will chew well because it has many frontal teeth and it will give birth well because it's rear is big." Upon being instructed, Yang-Won kept repeating what he was told. The following day, he went to visit his ailing mother-in-law. As soon as he entered the room, he respectfully bowed and said, "It will chew well because it has many frontal teeth and it will give birth well because it's rear is big."

"Ha, ha, ha..."

"Ho, ho, ho..."

"Uh, uh..."

The place turned into a sea of laughter.

In this way, he came to be hated by his father-in-law and mother-in-law. As for their daughter, the parents felt that she was already given away and allowed her to get married to him.

Within the first ten days of the following year, the couple went to visit and pay respect to their in-laws. Despite their disappointment, since he was their son-in-law, they treated him to delicious dishes.

When he returned home, his friend and brother, Dong-Su, asked him if he was treated well. Yang-Won replied that he had the soup called, "Hush, don't say."

"Hush, don't say" soup was actually a dumpling soup. Not knowing what he was given to eat, he asked his wife about what it was. His wife, fearing that this would turn into another embarrassing moment, told him, "Hush." As he was eating the soup, the inside of the dumpling came out. So, he asked his wife about what it was. Then, for the same reason, she said, "Don't say." That's how he came to understand that the name of the soup was "Hush, don't say."

The audience burst into a loud laughter.

"Ha, ha, ha..."

"Ho, ho, ho..."

"Hee, hee, hee..."

Rev. Son pointed to the soup that he was having a few moments and said, "Therefore, the soup that all of you are having today is called 'Hush, don't say' soup." He seemed to be satisfied from having had everyone laugh out loud and seen their happy faces.

His singular agenda and assignment was to find out and deliver what could help them to lose themselves for a moment and enjoy the moment. That's the reason, whenever there was a special occasion, whether it is Easter Sunday, Christmas pageant, Flower Sunday, Mother's Day Sunday, a picnic, Summer Boating Day, Fall Festival, and a game of Yut in winter, he would find a way for people to have fun and enjoy themselves. It is said that Rev. Son was often heard saying, "Do not spend a lot of money to make your faces look like the devil, but make your face look like that of an angel without ever spending a penny." He meant for people to just smile.

Lord, Help Me Love Aeyangwon

1. Lord, give me true love with which to love Aeyangwon.
   Give me love with which you love these people.
   They have been abandoned by the world.
   They have been removed from the love of their parents and siblings.
   They have been shunned and hated by all the people of the world.
   Oh, Lord! But help me love them truly.

2. Oh, Lord! Though I love them, help me love them more than I love my

parents, siblings, wife, and children.

Help me to even love them more than I love my own body.

Even if my body falls to the same state in which they remain, I want to still
love them.

If I ever become like them, I want to live happily with them for the rest of
my life.

Lord, help me love them truly as you love and caress them.

3. Lord, even if they despise and betray me,

I want to faithfully and truly love them

And help me not abandon them till the end.

Even if I get exiled from here,

Give me the love that I need to pray for them for the remainder of my life,
even as I remain exiled for loving them.

4. Oh, Lord! Even if I say I love them,

Let my love not be the man-made kind of love, he humanistic kind of love.

Help me not love for the sake of love.

Help me love them for you.

But help me not love them more than I love you.

Since it is love that is from you and for you,

How can I love them more than I love you?

But help me love them more than I love my self, parents, wife, and children.

Let my love for Aeyangwon be a little less than my love for you.

5. Lord, help me not love on the basis of my desire for the worldly fame nor
on the basis of my ambitious love that seeks reward in the future.

Help me love with the love born out of the love of Christ

And simply out of compassion for these poor souls.

6. Oh, Lord! I do not know how many days that I have left in my life.

But help me love Aeyangwon from the center of my being, as I dedicated
this body and heart of mine to you.

(Rev. Son recorded this prayer on March 22, 1940 sometime before he was arrested and incarcerated for participating in the anti-Shinto-worship movement and when he was fired up in his faith due to the same reason)

* It is a mere coincidence that Aeyangwon and his name, Son, *Yang-Won*, are spelled the same. Though there is not an illustration of note revolving this commonality, Rev. Son thought highly of this match and whenever he wrote his name in Korean, he would always put them together. For this interesting reason, I titled Chapter 1, Aeyangwon, Son Yang-Won.

"Dumplings soft and warm, dumplings soft and warm…"
It was one wintry night, cold enough for the shadow of
the moon to be frozen in what was left of the snow. The
northerly was blowing down from Mount Inwang and Mount Bukak
and onto the main intersection of Anguk-dong. Fighting the bone-
shivering cold and hunger, a young man with the nickname "Sandol"
was yelling "Dumplings soft and warm!" and hopping through the main
intersection of Anguk-dong, moving away from the imperial Japanese
Governor-General's building and toward Changdeok Palace. He had
a winter cap on and was dressed in a suit. However, without winter
undergarments, he had no choice but to hop so as to fight off the cold
that kept his whole body shivering.

"Let me tell you about this student by the name of Sandol as much as
I know," said the teacher.

It was a warm spring day that had driven away almost all the
remaining traces of winter from the nature.

Standing in front of the gravestones of Dong-In and Dong-Sin in the
island of Dongdo was Mr. Kim, a teacher, who was about to tell the
story of Sandol to a group of students from Seongsan Primary School.

Sandol was born in the province of Gyeongsang. His family had been
poor even from the time around the birth of Sandol. When he was
born, some people in his family thought that the baby would die within

several days. I think it must be because they were so poor that it was even difficult for them to survive on a day to day basis due to lack of food and money. But Sandol somehow survived and grew to be seven years old. That's when his father began to believe in Jesus. Sandol followed his father to church and sometimes piggybacking on his father.

However, his father's newfound faith posed a grave concern to his relatives and family members. Even Sandol's mother opposed her husband being a Christian. Despite this opposition, once he made up his decision to believe in Jesus, he was going to be as committed as possible to it. He cut off the topknot which was a traditional symbol for grown men and cut his hair short just like all of us now. He also quit alcohol and smoking altogether along with ancestor worship that his family had practiced since a long time ago. One day, his wife came home to find their yard on fire. Sandol's father was burning all the utensils and plates used for ancestor worship. Sandol's mother cried, "Dear, what is all this? I heard that people who believe in Jesus go eventually out of their minds. Are you really crazy? How in the world could you throw all these things used for ancestor worship into fire?"

I am sure that Sandol watched all these things. However, about a year passed that incident, around the time his mother was about to give birth, she came down with several serious medical conditions and ended up turning to faith in Jesus. From this point and on, all six members of his family believed in Jesus. When this happened, observing early-dawn prayer meetings, family devotions in the morning and at night, giving tithes, and going to church on Sunday became instituted as family rule. Soon, his father became a deacon and a *youngsu* [spiritual leader] in his church. Sandol also attended well Sunday School and began reading the Bible and praying.

Then something happened when Sandol was in the third grade in primary school. The principal of the school held anti-Christian attitudes and made it miserable for Sandol and his sibling. One of the strategies the principal used was to call school assemblies on Sundays meeting so as to prevent Christians from going to church. Despite this, Sandol and his sibling did not show up for the assemblies because they did not want to miss church. They had never missed a school event on other days of the week except when absent due to sickness. Apart from defying the principal's orders on Sundays, the siblings complied with all other rules of the school and acted respectfully in all areas and conducted themselves exemplarily. Then, the principal devised a plan to sabotage the faith of the siblings. He commanded the bow-to-the-emperor to be observed by all students. This observance required people to bow in the direction of the east saying that the Japanese emperor resides there. It was a show of allegiance to the Japanese monarchy.

However, during that time, no other primary school was enforcing this imperial bow except Sandol's school. During the morning assembly every day, the school enforced this bow on the students, but nevertheless, Sandol and his sibling did not comply at all. One day, when they were brought into the principal's office, a conversation took place between the principal and the brothers in the following manner.

Principal: Why, being the citizens of the Japanese empire, do you stand stiff and not bow, whenever it is the time to pay respect in the direction of the east where the emperor resides?

Sandol: If the emperor is here right in front of me, I would do the best bow to him that I could possibly do. But merely bowing in the direction of the east where there is only empty space is vain and violates the second of the Ten Commandments. Therefore, I cannot comply.

Principal: Wouldn't it be a crime for a Christian to disobey the law of the nation?

Sandol: Even if bowing in the direction of the east is mandated by the law of the land, I cannot observe such a law.

Principal: That is indeed a serious offense. If you break the law of the land or oppose the emperor in this way, you are committing an offense of contempt. Instead, stop all this by not believing in Jesus. You know what the church says about heaven and hell? That's a lie designed to deceive the uncivilized or the ignorant. It is a foolish thing for a person who is receiving all this schooling to adhere to such superstition. Do not fall victim to all that superstition.

Sandol: I know that this phenomenon of believing in Jesus is not only restricted to Korea. In fact, it occurs in the western world and I heard that it has followers among famous doctors and scholars of both the west and the east. Do you suppose that people believe this superstition because all of them are uncivilized and ignorant?

Upon hearing this, the principal became enraged and beat the Sandol brothers mercilessly. Sandol's face became bruised and his eyes sustained blood marks and he bled from his nose greatly. As an insult to injury, he was threatened with the prospect of being expelled from school. At the end, it was the principal who got transferred to another school.

The principle who threatened to kick Sandol out but got himself kicked out!

Sandol who was determined to obey God's commandment even if it meant being expelled from school!

All the students who were listening to the words of their teacher, "Though he was young, he gained the final victory," felt a sense of gratification. At the same time, they came to remember what happened when they were little. They remembered how the adults fought against the order to observe Shinto worship within the walls of Aeyangwon. They remembered when Rev. Son was arrested and taken away for defying Shinto worship and how Rev. Son's family was expelled from

Aeyangwon before the Japanese director came on board. Mr. Kim's story continued at once.

In the wake of the independence movement on March 1, 1919, Sandol's father was identified as one of the conspirators and given the prison sentence of one year. Trying to insure his future success, though he could not live apart from his family, Sandol moved to Seoul and barely made it into Jung-Dong School. Since there was no support available for his tuition, he could not help but sell dumplings at night and go to school during the day. That was the reason that he was going around on that wintry night, trying to sell dumplings. He cried, "Dumplings soft and warm!" But the truth was that he was not able to sell many on that night. On a night like that, I bet that he thought all the more longingly for his father who was in prison and for his mother and siblings who were down in his hometown."

He must have thought, "How cold he must be in his prison cell? I am cold just going around like this!" He also thought, "How hungry my mother and siblings must be?" In those moments, he was tormented by the thought, "Should I just give up school if it is this hard and go back home to help my mother and siblings?" In addition, there was another source of hardship. He was ridiculed by his boss or other young men whenever he could not sell enough merchandise. They made fun of him by saying, "How come you have to sell dumplings when you believe in Jesus? Doesn't Jesus give you money miraculously?" On the days when selling was stagnant, he was ridiculed, "Why has God kept you from selling your merchandise?" Though Sundays were better than other days for selling things, Sandol would rather go to church for worship and also refuse to work on Sunday afternoons. It was understandable that his sales figures were terrible compared to his peers. Apparently for this reason, his boss initially did not take liking to Sandol. However, when the owner of the dumpling house saw Sandol getting up early in the morning to clean the house and carrying on honestly in all things, he allowed him to stick around and continue working for him. Once, he told Sandol, "There's nothing bad about you except the fact that you believe in Jesus."

The students who were intently looking at their teacher and listening to his words wondered how nice it also would be for others to say the same thing about them, "There's nothing bad about you except the fact that you believe in Jesus." Then, Mr. Kim continued on.

"It was the winter of that year. Now, New Year's Day passed according to the western calendar and it was about the last day of December according to the lunar calendar. It was a busy time for the dumpling store that all the student workers had to work around the clock except when they had classes at school. Even in this situation, Sandol did not work on Sunday that week and attended church without failing. Furthermore, in addition to Sunday worship, he went out to do evangelism with his church peers and returned home only after the night worship service. The owner of the business then, without even asking where he had been, told Sandol to pack his bag and get out of the house."

"Why? Since it was a very busy time for the business, the owner probably thought that Sandol could miss at least one Sunday. To his anger, however, Sandol went out early that morning after having breakfast and returned home only after spending the whole day outside."

"But for Sandol, there was nothing more urgent or important to him than serving God. For this reason, he could not plead for an understanding by telling his boss that he was in the wrong or he would not do it ever again. Thinking that the boss would not understand him even if he tried to explain himself, Sandol said that he would get out of the house but he needed a few days. But the owner insisted that he should get out immediately and Sandol was kicked out by the next day."

"It was very cold during those days. On that day, it snowed and the whole city of Seoul was turned into a silvery city. Though it looked clean to the eyes, Seoul was a cold-hearted place in the eyes of Sandol. He was able to stay just one more day by pleading his case to his boss who wanted him out right away. Now, he could not stay any longer and was out in the streets."

"At first, he went to a classmate's house. However, his classmate's family members who were not Christians, upon hearing Sandol's case, rather than showing compassion, told him that he was foolish to have done what he did and he should go back to the boss by pleading for his mercy. In addition, they told him that no business would offer him work if he kept thinking about doing the same thing while he tried to put himself through school. Unless he did the work of delivering newspapers or milk jugs, there would not be any work for him."

"For a few days, he went around staying with a classmate here and another classmate there. When he had used up all his money doing so, he went without food for three days. Facing a dead end and praying to God about his pitiful circumstances, he entered and cut through the pine grove of Namsan. As he prayed, he kept on thinking about the remaining ten *won* that he had. However, that was the money he had already given to God as his tithe and he promised himself that he would never use it up regardless of how hungry he got."

"But God was not about to abandon Sandol who was kicked out of where he had been staying for not violating the Lord's Day and who went hungry for refused to use up his tithing money. And God worked through his family and sent him the telegram and money stating that he should urgently return home."

"What happened was that his mother heard about his difficult situation and had to call him back home. On his way back home, Sandol stopped by Anguk-dong Church where he used to attend and tithed the remaining seven *jeon* there. In fact, there was a person in Seoul who pitied Sandol and wanted to look after him. However, though he had the financial wherewithal, he was a non-believer and had a concubine. For this reason, Sandol refused his help."

The teacher praised Sandol profusely by saying, "How do you think God blessed Sandol who strove to do right before God in both small and big things?"

His words reminded the students who began living out their Christian faith from very early by observing their parents and living in Aeyangwon about the harsh world where it is so difficult to keep Sunday holy and be faithful in doing tithing. The teacher began to speak again.

"Sandol went back home and stayed there for a while until an opportunity opened up to study abroad in Japan and he went to Tokyo, Japan, to complete his study there. He enrolled in the night class at Sugamo Middle School and put himself through school by delivering newspapers. On Sundays, however, he did not work and asked one of his peers to take the shift instead. Though his income was lower than what it could have been for this reason, it was, according to him, enough for him to get by and finish his schooling. Not only that, while he was studying in Japan, he began attending a holiness church in Tokyo and became swayed by the passionate evangelism ministry of the church. Whenever he could, he made time to go out to the streets with a drum over his shoulder and carried out the work of street evangelism. At night, he would find a quiet place such as a public cemetery and pray in earnest."

In this way, Sandol became passionate about prayer and reading the Bible and eventually returned to Korea having given up the goal of moving onto the next level of his education. Instead, he returned home having decided to become an evangelist for the urgent work of sharing the gospel throughout the land of Korea. This was how Sandol became a precious servant of God who carried out a great work of contributing to the kingdom of God.

When Mr. Kim finished speaking, he looked far out to the sea. The sea to the front of the island of Dongdo boasted infinitely its golden and silvery water as reflected by the light of the warm spring sun. A sailing ship was painted gently gliding over the sea.

Six Years of Imprisonment
Chapter 3

"**R**ev. Son, do you understand the situation?"

It was deep into the night. It was nearing almost one o'clock in the morning. The chief detective of the intelligence unit was conducting a brief session of interrogation of Rev. Son of Yeosu Aeyangwon who had been brought in. To him, Rev. Son was a pro-American sympathizer running wild who did not understand the times in which he was living.

"Being aware of the times? Of course, I do. Right now, it is the time when the Mukden Incident is about to enter a systematic phase. It is the time that the Japanese-German-Italian axis is negotiating an anticommunist pact. It is the time for Japanese people to start believing in Jesus and praying to God so that this national crisis could be averted," explained Rev. Son.

The detective posed a perplexed look on his face as he kept gazing at Rev. Son. He then blurted out sneeringly, "Now that I got to hear of your knowledge of the times we are in, I know that why you frequent police stations."

As if he knew what the matter, he said, "If it concerns Shinto worship, you should say it regards the problem of Shinto worship. Since you said it regards the awareness of the time, I spoke about the time. You are saying all this to ask me if I would do Shinto worship. That can never be allowed by true Christianity." He was short but exhibited a forceful demeanor.

"So you say. But what are you going to do when all other believers and pastors including the moderators of presbytery and General Assembly regard Shinto worship as a civic ceremony? Is the god that you believe in any different from others?" asked the detective. Surely, he exhibited a condescending attitude.

"Don't ask me. Go ahead and answer yourself," said Rev. Son defiantly.

The detective remained silent and just kept gazing at Rev. Son. Rev. Son tried to explain again, "Hey, detective. Listen to me. I am sure that you already know commonsensically that Christianity is a monotheistic religion."

"Whether it is a monotheistic religion or whatever, why do you alone insist on opposing Shinto worship to which other pastors, professors, and doctors of theology had already consented?" asked detective.

"Well, you can make a case in that way. But Christianity is not a religion of knowledge, but a religion of faith. It is not a religion of feelings, but a religion of experience. Therefore, there can be truths in it that scholars cannot understand, but at the same time ignorant old people might understand them. In the same way, there can be things that cannot be understood by scholars and doctors that are known through experience by little children and ignorant women. There are points of convergence between the worlds of knowledge and faith. But there are also points of divergence between these two worlds. That's why people say that Christianity is the religion of the supernatural," said Rev. Son as if he was preaching or lecturing at an academic conference.

"Hey, stop it already. This is a police station. It is not a church or a school," said the detective annoyingly. "Anyhow, don't think that you would get to see the outside world until you consent to and observe Shinto worship," said the detective. In this way, Rev. Son's life in prison had started.

Ten months later, a written report of five hundred pages was filed against Rev. Son. Even then, Rev. Son insisted that the testimony he had given was solely based on the word of God and not of his personal opinions and refused to give his consent.

This angered the interrogating detective, Keinabe, who was the state police chief, greatly and he lashed out at Rev. Son. He brought him a Bible as he often did whenever it was requested by Rev. Son and said, "Now, say more." "You say that it is the word of God, but didn't Matthew, Mark, Luke, John, Peter, James, and others write it?" The detective thought that he had asked him the perfect question and stared at him right in the eye.

"You are right. They indeed wrote it, but they did not write down their own opinions but what God inspired them to do. In short, the Holy Spirit moved them to write these down. There is nothing written in it that was of their own," explained Rev. Son.

"I do not understand what you mean. They wrote it, but they didn't?" said the detective with a perplexed expression on his face.

"To say that it is not the word of God just because it was written by human hands is the same thing as to say a letter was penned by the postal worker just because he was the one who delivered it. Does that make sense? Just as the post worker is just a deliverer and there is someone else who wrote the letter, though the Bible was written by human authors, the Bible is not the product of human minds, but it is truly the word of God. I mean that, since everything in the report is what I quoted of the Bible, it is not my words," preached Rev. Son.

"That's tricky... I guess, then the Bible should be altered," said the detective as if he was saying something profound.

"What did you say? Change the Bible? Well, that's up to you, but you would not be able to do that anyhow," said Rev. Son.

"What you mean that I cannot do it. It just needs to be changed," said the detective unpleasantly.

"Since the Bible has been translated into about seven hundred and seventy seven languages, you would not be able to achieve anything by altering the Japanese or Korean Bibles. You would have to change all seven hundred and seventy seven languages and the rest of the world would not follow suit just because you and your country ask them to do. Well, let's say the world would listen to you and make changes to the Bible as you wish. Then, it becomes no longer the word of God but your word and we could not call it the Bible. The Bible is only Bible because it was inspired by the Holy Spirit. If you change even a little, then wouldn't it become your own word? Not one iota of the word of God could be deleted from it," Rev. Son gave a long explanation and tried to make it an opportunity for sharing the gospel.

"Well, it does not matter. Whether it is your word or God's word, since it all came out of your mouth, put your thumbprint here," insisted the detective. In this way, Rev. Son was forced to sign off on the police report.

Around this time, Rev. Son's health plummeted and his life was in jeopardy. In fact, the detective, out of pity, reported Rev. Son's case to and consulted with the justice department. In response, Gwangju Attorney General's Office sent a district attorney named Yoda Katsumi to Yeosu Police Station. His intention was to interview Rev. Son in person and examine his beliefs. In fact, he was ready to release Rev. Son on probation if the only problem was that of Shinto worship which really did not have any legal basis for punishment. Because Rev. Son did not even have the strength to walk on his own, he was carried to the meeting with the district attorney on a stretcher. After barely sitting up on a chair, he was asked about the basic information such as address, name, profession, and health condition.

Then, the district attorney proceeded to ask him, "Hey, Rev. Son, our venerable Japanese Empire is deemed a divine nation and our emperor is a divine-human being. What is your thought on that?"

Rev. Son curtly shot down the attorney's claim by saying, "I do not think that is true."

"How do you know that?" said the attorney.

"There is no divine-human being except Jesus Christ who is the Son of God. Therefore, no one else could fulfill the same qualifications of being the Son of God as Jesus did," said Rev. Son calmly.

Intently gazing at Rev. Son, the district attorney said, "Well, I know that the emperor is truly a divine-human being. Not just me. One hundred million citizens believe that."

"Since you say that a hundred million people believe it, then please do explain it to me how the emperor could be a divine-human being that only the Son of God could possibly claim? Then, I would explain to you how Jesus Christ is indeed the Son of God, therefore a divine-human being."

"No, before I explain, why don't you go first? What claim are you making here?" asked the district attorney.

"All right, I will go first, but you have to listen to me to the end. The first qualification for Jesus is that his birth was prophesied four thousand years ago and he indeed was born as the fulfillment of that prophesy. On the other hand, had the emperor's birth ever been prophesied? The second qualification is that Jesus was conceived by the Spirit of God and born of the virgin. This is a special condition. Thirdly, while Jesus lived on earth for thirty three years, he performed many wonders and miracles. On the contrary, I have never heard of wonders or miracles that the emperor performed. Fourthly, Jesus was crucified in order to save the sins of people, but I have never heard an emperor dying for the sins of others. Fifthly, Jesus rose to life again after three days of his death. Who of all the emperors of the past did ever come back to life? Lastly, after his resurrection, Jesus lived the period of forty days with his disciples and ascended to heaven eventually. The six great facts of the fulfillment of the prophecy about his birth, being born of a virgin, wonders and miracles, atonement of the sins of the world, his resurrection, and his ascension point to the reality of Jesus as the only Son of God. Then, what are the qualifications does the emperor bring to his claim?," confidently stated Rev. Son.

"Stop that nonsense," the district attorney stopped short of giving a response to a sermon-like speech of Rev. Son.

"You might think what I said is nonsense. However, I only explained the truths that are in the Bible to you," said Rev. Son solemnly. This is how, the district attorney who initially came to meet with Rev. Son with compassion could not do help him but returned to his office without having achieved anything.

Approximately ten days from that incident, Rev. Son's case and report were handed over to the Gwangju Provincial Court.

There was another incident like the following.

Eight or nine months in prison had weakened Rev. Son's body to the limit. In addition, he caught a cold and ran a fever and had a terrible headache to the point that he could not sense his hunger. When Rev. Son gained consciousness, he found himself not in his own cell, but in the room right next to the room of overnight staffers which was being used also as an infirmary. Now alert, Rev. Son was still feeling cold, shivering, and suffering from a massive headache, and he began to cry profusely. However, when he thought of the suffering that the Lord endured for him, he felt that what he was going through was nothing and he should not be crying like this in that room. He began singing.

> Nearer, my God, to Thee, nearer to Thee!
> E'en though it be a cross that raiseth me;
> Still all my song shall be nearer, my God, to Thee,
> Nearer, my God, to Thee, nearer to Thee!

Then, the person who was on the bed beside him cried out angrily, "Stop it. I don't want to hear a song coming from a patient." He did not even stop singing when jailors told him to stop. Now, he was not going to stop singing just because another patient demands. So, Rev. Son sang the song to the end albeit in his tears.

In Gwangju, he was placed on trial and received the sentence of one year in prison. However, since he had served one year in prison already, the judge pitied Rev. Son and felt that he could place him on probation and release him. Therefore, prior to sentencing, he called Rev. Son in quietly and wanted to hear his thoughts about it.

"It has been more than a year since you left home, I cannot imagine how much you must be missing your parents, siblings, wife, and children. I assume that you want to go back home so badly. I believe that you had enough time to think through the matter. How about dropping the stubbornness that made you oppose bowing to the emperor in the direction of the east and Shinto worship and do a roundabout?" asked the judge in a gentle and compassionate tone of voice.

"I have no desire to reverse my position. On the opposite, my faith has been getting only stronger," replied Rev. Son readily.

"What is your reason for opposing it so much?" asked the judge.

"Yes! I have three reasons for my position. First, bowing in the direction of the east, silent prayer at noon, and Shinto worship all violate the commandment of God. Therefore, I cannot subscribe to it. It's not right to disobey the command of the emperor of a nation. How much more should the command of God who rules all the nations of the world be obeyed? Secondly, those who bow down to idols cannot be saved. The reason that we believe in Jesus is to gain salvation. How could then we violate the great commandment of God and expect to be saved? Lastly, I cannot do so because of my civic duty as a citizen," said Rev. Son.

The prosecutor who did not care too much about other words was surprised by what he heard. "What you mean because of your civic duty as a citizen? Isn't it your duty as a citizen to do these things?" The judge insisted on the reverse logic and stomped his feet.

"You don't have to get so angry. Am I not saying that it is my civic duty to oppose it? Please speak after I am done explaining myself. The reason that I say that it is my civic duty is that, when you look at the Bible, the history of Christianity, and the world history, there has not been a nation that did not come to ruin by bowing down to idols. On the other hand, there has not been a nation that was not blessed by believing in Jesus. Knowing this, how can I go out to the Shinto temple and bow down in the empty air? Therefore, it is my civic duty to oppose it," said Rev. Son.

"That's a well-crafted excuse!" said the judge. He could not help but hand out the sentence. The official record of sentence read as below.

The Record of Judgment No. 35.

The Judgment

Birthplace: South Gyeongsang Province, Haman-gun,
Chilwon-myeon, Gujeong-ri, No. 685.
Residence: Jeollanamdo(South Jeolla Province), Yeosu-gun, Yulchon-myeon,
Sinpung-ri, No. 231.
The pastor of Aeyangwon Church, Yulchon
Name: Son, Yang-Won
Age: 40

Upon carefully reviewing the case brought in by the district attorney, Yoda Katsumi, of Joseon General-Governer's Office, this court issues the judgment regarding the defendant's failure to comply with the peace preservation law.

Sentence
The defendant is hereby sentenced to one year and six months in prison.

Manuscripts 2 rolls (Exhibit No. 1 and No. 2) are confiscated.

Reason

The defendant inherited faith in Christianity from his father, Son Jong-Il, who was a member of Joseon Presbyterian Church. Shortly thereafter, he studied abroad in Japan and upon returning to Korea, he began serving as a Presbyterian pastor-in-training under the auspices of Presbyterian Church in the province of South Gyeongsang Province. In April of 1936, he enrolled in Pyeongyang Seminary and graduated in March of 1939. Upon graduation, he obtained the minister's license. Through the invitation of the American missionary, Rev. J. Kelly Unger, in charge of Aeyangwon Church within Aeyangwon, the residential Hansen's disease treatment center located in Jeollanamdo(South Jeolla Province), Yeosu-gun, Yulchon-myeon, Sinpung-ri and run by the American missionary, Dr. Wilson, belonging to Suncheon Presbytery of Joseon Presbyterian Church, he was called and installed as the senior pastor of the aforementioned church. He ministered to more than seven hundred and tens of patients with Hansen's disease who lived in that community.

To speak of his beliefs, he adheres to the Bible as the only and supreme source of doctrine on the face of the earth and believes it to contain the word of God and as such nothing should be deleted from it, not even one letter or one line. He also espouses the delusion that the will of God expressed in the Bible would absolutely and completely come to pass in the future. He worships this God, Yahweh, who created and sustains everything, who rules over all things in the cosmos as the only rightful and almighty God, and who exists eternally. All gods are under the rule of this God, Yahweh, and even the long line of emperors who claim to be in under the protection of 8 million gods beginning with Amaterasu has actually been allowed by God's command to rule over their lands. Therefore, the right to rule has been given by God, Yahweh, to the emperor. In this sense, the emperor also received the authority to rule Korea by proxy from God, and it means that this authority could also be taken away according to God's will. He believes that the rise and fall of our nation depends on the will of God. Furthermore, he implies that the power structures in our nation as well as other nations are presently being controlled by the forces of anti-Christian orientation and are being served as the devil's instruments in wreaking the war in Europe, the Mukden Incident, natural disasters, droughts, and epidemics. All the human in the world are being harassed by this devil and they are losing their lives and wealth to it.

In addition, he believes that all gods except God, Yahweh, are virtually idols and the practice of worshipping them as in Shinto worship in our country violates the biblical doctrines that forbade idolatry. Those who practice idol worship cannot be saved. Therefore, the imposition of idol worship on the Christian church in Joseon is the manifestation of the end times as described in Gospel of Matthew 24 and the precursor for the second coming of Christ.

God will surely send his son, Jesus Christ, to the world in not too distant future and destroy all nations under the rule of the devil including our own, Japan, through him. When Jesus Christ comes again in the clouds, all the resurrected saints with Jesus Christ will attend the heavenly wedding party in the air for seven years. The period of these seven years is called the age of great tribulation and will see Armageddon, the great battle between the good and evil, occur at the end of which Jesus Christ comes down to the earth from the clouds and all the principalities and powers of the nations that had been under the rule of the devil are annihilated by Jesus Christ. And the new kingdom with Jesus Christ as the head and Christianity as the proper base of rule will be established on the earth and reign for one thousand years. This paradise of absolute peace then will be ruled by Christ as the Lord of all nations and the faithful will be installed as the princes whereas the weak and the unbelieving will either become its subjects or imprisoned or humiliated.

The defendant espouses the biblical view of spiritual eschatology that bases the destruction of the nations presently in existence and the need for the establishment of the millennial kingdom. This ideology of the defendant causes him to disturb our nationalist consciousness. He has actively working towards altering the national consciousness and infusing chaos into the order of things and ultimately fomenting the downfall of the present power structures through the war of Armageddon, thereby reforming the power structures of each nation in the world including ours. In this way, he seeks the creation of and the construction of the millennial kingdom through propagating the teachings of his lord for the purpose of global transformation.

The exhibit No. 1 is the copy of his sermon manuscript titled "The minister that the church of the present needs" and dated one day in mid-October around 7 p.m. in 1940. The sermon was preached at Aeyangwon Church to Kim Gyeong-Ho, a patient and seven hundred others. It reads as follows.

"Currently, our Joseon church is facing a time of great emergency and tribulation. Presently, each nation in the world is embroiled in war and many disasters such as droughts, floods, and epidemics have been on the rise. Right now in Joseon, Christians are being persecuted because of the imposition of Shinto worship. This is a sure sign of the end times and signals the imminent return of Jesus Christ for which we have been longing as well as the final judgment. Since true faith is only gained after trials and tribulations, we cannot but overcome this hardship and become firm in our faith. In a time like this, the church needs ministers who would serve the faithful with love, wisdom and courage. All of us, the ministers of Joseon Church, must commit ourselves to the work of evangelism with the spirit of martyrdom as found in the martyr, Rev. Han Gyung-Hee. For the return of Jesus Christ has come near, Japan and other nations under the reign of the devil will surely fall and the paradise on earth, in other words, new heaven and God's kingdom, which is ruled by Jesus Christ, will be established. The church of Joseon, in order to actualize the new heaven and earth, requires the best of the ministers and must work hard to expedite this vision."

The defendant used a sermon like this to incite the audience to be mobilized for his own agenda.

The exhibit No. 2 is dated sometime in mid-April, 1941. Again at Aeyangwon Church, he preached the sermon titled "The return of the Lord and our longing" to the audience of seven hundred patients including aforementioned Kim Gyeong-Ho at three o'clock in that afternoon.
"The fall of all the unbelieving nations which represent the devil has come near. The time has come for the unbeliever to be punished and the righteous

to be rewarded. Jesus Christ will return with the sovereignty of the king of all kings and destroy the modern nations including Japan and rule the world. When this time comes, all disasters including wars, diseases, famines, and hunger will disappear, the lepers will be cured of their leprosy and the earthly heaven or at least the kingdom of God of eternal peace and happiness will be established. Therefore, let us put our hearts together and long for the speedy coming of the Lord." The defendant preached a sermon of this intent and instigated others for the achievement of this goal. The defendant's act is based on the continuation of this criminal intent.

[Omitted]

The defendant's judgment is based on the statute No. 54, the Peace Preservation Act, of 1942, and the criminal code No. 5, statute No. 55. The defendant's crime at the time violated the statute No. 46 of 1940, the 3-year-long emergency royal decree under the statute No. 129, the Peace Preservation Law (called Old Peace Preservation Law) and the equivalent in the criminal code No. 3, statute 55. Given consideration under the present Peace Preservation Law, item 2, the criminal code No. 3, the lighter sentence of termed incarceration under the Peace Preservation Law is chosen. The defendant is hereby sentenced to one year and six months in prison and the two sets of sermon manuscripts (Exhibits No. 1 & No. 2) are hereby confiscated as evidence for the crime in this case according to the criminal code No. 19, item 1, No. 2. The judgment is issued as above.

November 4, 1942
Gwangju Provincial Court Justice Department

Presiding Judge of Governor-General of Joseon
Justice Watanabe Yami (渡邊彌美)
Presiding Judge of Governor-General of Joseon
Justice Koda Teruji (幸田輝治)
Presiding Judge of Governor-General of Joseon
Justice Kawada Kenjo (河田兼三)

"You are being called out, Prisoner No. 99," a voice shouted. Rev. Son was startled by the call. It was because it meant something not so good to be called by jailers when unexpected.

"Come out quickly," said the jailer. As he walked out of his jail cell, Rev. Son began to think that he was being called out regarding the issue of Shinto worship or bowing in the direction of the east. Then, another prisoner was also called out. As Rev. Son followed the jailer, he realized that he was being led into the room of the Japanese chaplain. The Japanese chaplain was a monk and he greeted the two prisons kindly.

"Do you know what today is?" asked the monk. The prisoners did not understand what he meant and could not give a ready answer.

"Today is June 3," quickly answered the monk.

"So, now do you know what kind of day it is to you?" the monk asked again.

"I don't know about him, but I think it is my birthday," Rev. Son remembered and said.

"That's right. Today is the birthday for you two and I called you because there was something for me to do for you. So, please follow me," said the monk kindly.

Rev. Son figured that something was up and said, "Well, following you is not that hard, but what's that something that you want to do for us?"

"It's nothing really. I wanted to say a blessing for both of you in front of the Buddha," explained the monk.

"Well, I thank you for your kindness, but I cannot receive that blessing," Rev. Son refused curtly.

"I know that you are a Christian and a pastor for that matter. I don't mean that you should be a follower of Buddhism for bowing down at the altar of the Buddha. I just wanted to follow the prison regulation that requires me to carry this out for the prisoners. So, let's just follow the rule," the monk explained and demanded it as if he was embarrassed and upset about it.

"No, I cannot. Though it is the rule of the prison, I cannot follow it. Though my body is in chains inside the prison, my mind is not chained or my faith cannot be chained. I was not brought here because I committed thievery, murder, arson, or fraud which violates the laws of the encyclopedia of law. I am a person that makes it his own life's goal and duty to believe in God, Yahweh, and His son, Jesus Christ. But they made laws for things that are not crimes and imprisoned me as a criminal in this prison for not obeying the law of Japan. If I am going to follow the rules of the prison, I would have observed the bow to the emperor or Shinto worship while I was outside, wouldn't I? Furthermore, since I am a Christian, wouldn't I want to follow the Christian ritual of blessing and be blessed before my God? I cannot be blessed following the Buddhist ritual," said Rev. Son.

"You are pitiful. I am not asking you to bless me. All you have to do is to stand there," said the monk.

"If you want to say a blessing for me, do it in front of God, Yahweh. I was born through the grace of God and continue to live through the grace of God. So, I will say a blessing in front of God. I was not born through the grace of Buddha or live through the grace of Buddha, so I do not want to be blessed before Buddha. Everyone likes and wants to receive blessings. I also want to be blessed. However, would there be a reason why I say that I don't want to be blessed? Is there a need for a blessing to be said for a person who refuses?" Rev. Son refused again after giving a long explanation.

From afar, a jailer came running toward them saying, "Hey, what?" He slapped Rev. Son and grabbed him from behind so as to drag him on. Rev. Son just sat on the ground like an immovable object. Then, the monk could not do anything but take the other prisoner to the chapel alone.

The monk came to the administrator of the prison to report this and discuss about how to punish Rev. Son. Surprisingly, the administrator said, "You have done something wrong. Rev. Son is different from other prisoners. He is here because he opposed Shinto worship. We cannot punish him because he refuses Buddhist blessings. Even if we did, he would be willing to endure greater punishments. So, do not bother him and just leave him alone." For this reason, Rev. Son was not punished and was able to get through the ordeal.

In this way, Rev. Son was able to spend his sentence of one year and six months in Gwangju Prison. However, the greatest challenge to him came when he was first sentenced for a year and a half. He feared, "While I was in jail without a formal sentence for a year and two months, I had to suffer gravely every time I refused to observe the bow to the emperor and Shinto worship. How can I live through the sentence of a year and a half in the prison where there are prison rules for sentenced prisoners? I know that they will try to enforce the bow to the emperor, being silent at noon, and Shinto worship on a daily basis. If I am going to refuse these, I will surely put through hellish torture. How in the world am I going to withstand it?" Since he had one week before being placed in the prison, he prayed earnestly to God for the strength to endure the great hardship that was to come and on the last day of the week, he gained a boost of strength.

He prayed, "For suffering in the name of the Lord is an inevitable reality for those who live for the Lord, I will have done my work if I spilled the three units of blood and have all of my 200 and some bones of my body be broken for the Lord. It is not my business to know what my concerns and pains will be. I will just obey as you lead me..." After this prayer, he was renewed in strength and was able to go to prison in joy.

In this way, he was able to resolve all the problems that came his way from the perspective of his faith and fight to overcome them. In the beginning, he was beaten and cajoled so as to break down the integrity of his faith. He could not speak of how he struggled and anguished trying hard not to be deceived but remain steadfast. Because he would try to proselytize others when placed in a group cell, he was put into solitary confinement and given work to do. Even then, he would sing hymns and pray and observe Sunday worship alone. He also refused to work on Sundays, and for this, he was dragged away to jailors and had his food withheld from him. Whenever that happened, though he was weakened in his flesh, he experienced being renewed more and more daily in his inward being. Once, his body was so weakened due to having his food withheld from him and he caught flu and he came so close to dying. Once, he wrote a poem to comfort himself.

I feel lonely being in this empty room alone.
(獨守空房 孤寂感)
But because the Trinity is with me, it becomes a family of four.
(三位同居 四食口)
Come, all ye come, all kinds of hardship.
(多種苦難 皆來)
I shall experience all the truths in the middle of my suffering.
(高中眞理 皆體得)

"Prisoner No. 99, receive the statement of resolution to your case," said the jailer as he handed the letter to Rev. Son. The jailor who usually treated prisoners rudely sported a look of feeling somewhat sorry for Rev. Son. Upon hearing his number being called, Rev. Son who had become as weakened as he could possibly be got up from his bed immediately and said, "Thank you," as he received the letter. In that moment, his heart was filled with an indescribable sense of excitement and joy. Dressed in his black outfit, his pale face showed that tears were ready to flow from his two eyes and a deep sigh filled his mouth. "What does it say?" Rev. Son thought to himself as he opened the envelope with the title, "The statement of resolution."

1944, No. 1

Decision

Birthplace: South Gyeongsang Province, Haman-gun, Chilwon-myeon,
Gujeong-ri, No. 685
Residence: Busan, Beomiljeong, No. 1474
Status: Incarcerated at Gwangju Prison
Pastor: Daechon Yang-Won
Age: 42

The hearing requested by the defendant in protest of the order of preemptive incarceration issued by Gwangju District Court, the case No. 2 in the year of 1944, is to be ruled by the council after hearing and considering the opinion of the district attorney, Kondo Haruyoshi, of Governor-General of Joseon.

The text of a judgment
Rejection of this appeal.

Reason

After a review of the case records, it is stated that the complainant is a minister of the Christian church and, as such, subscribes to the Christian worldview that God, Yahweh, created all things in existence and controls the world as the only supreme deity and so gratefully even Amaterasu is under his authority. He defies Shinto worship on the reason that it constitutes idolatry against this God. He also believes falsely that all the power structures and entities in the present world including our sovereign nation will ultimately come to ruin and the eternal utopia of the kingdom with Jesus who will return as its lord will be actualized. He worked to facilitate the coming of that utopian kingdom by propagating a subversive ideology to many church members. Because he worked to paralyze the patriotic consciousness of our citizens and attempted to bring about a systemic structural change in this society, he was sentenced to one year of imprisonment on November 4, 1942 by Gwangju District Court for violating the Peace Preservation Act. Though his sentence will be completed on May 16, 1944, since he has not come to accept the profound importance of our national structure of governance and continues to obstinately insist on and refuse to give up the anti-patriotic and subversive Christian ideology, he is deemed likely to reviolate the first item of the Peace Preservation Act upon being released for the completion of his sentence. For this reason, it is deemed appropriate to incarcerate the complainant preemptively according to the No. 39 of the Peace Preservation Act. Therefore, it is necessary to dismiss the complaint as unnecessary and the legal opinion is hereby entered as in the advisement based on the No. 1 item of the criminal litigation code No. 166.

September 16, 1944
Daegu Appeals Court Criminal Division 1

Presiding Judge of General-Governor of Joseon
Justice Takashima Koetsuro (高島幸悦郎)
Presiding Judge of General-Governor of Joseon
Justice Arihigashi Masayuki (有東政行)
Presiding Judge of General-Governor of Joseon
Justice Jikuhara Moto (軸原素雄)

Uto Motoya (右膳本也)
September 20, 1944

Daegu Appeals Court Criminal Division
Trials Division of General-Governor of Joseon
Arida Kei (有田計)

Lost deep in reading the letter, tears did not stop flowing from his eyes. He prayed, "Oh, Lord, thank you so much. Because you have kept this life like that of a worm alive, it was possible for good news like this to reach me today." The story behind receiving this letter of resolution was like the following.

May 17 was the day that the sentence of a year and a half mandated

at Gwangju Prison was to expire. Everyone including Rev. Son himself
and his friends and his beloved members of Aeyangwon Church looked
forward to this date. For this reason, according to his letter to the
members of Okjongsan Church dated February 15, Rev. Son asked them
to wait until May 17 to come to meet him at Gwangju Prison instead
of coming to see him at the prison sometime in the month of April.
Especially for his father, Elder Son, and his wife and Ms. Hwang and
his two sons, Doing-In and Dong-Sin, this day of Rev. Son's anticipated
release could not come any earlier.

However, despite having been imprisoned for a year, Rev. Son's faith
did not change, but only grew solidified. This development posed a
great problem for the justice department. For this reason, the justice
department sent Prosecutor Yoshida to assess Rev. Son's position
once again. (Refer to the chapter 4 of the prequel) The result of that
inquiry came in the form of a court order for extended incarceration
at a detention center on May 20. In response, Rev. Son submitted a
complaint to Daegu Appeals Court and he did this in order to acquire
an opportunity to share the gospel to high-ranking officials.

This is clear from his letter to his father dated June 8, 1943. He wrote,
"...How worried were you on May 17 to which you looked forward so
anxiously by counting each passing day? What words could I, your
disobedient son, use to comfort you? I cannot make it up to you, but
I can only plead that you should be comforted and blessed in the
faith like that of Abraham and Job. On May 20, I was sentenced to
imprisonment at a detention center. The reason was that I professed my
faith in accordance with the Bible. On June 2, I filed my complaint with
the court. It was not in order to express my dissatisfaction or somehow
evade the enforcement of my sentence. Rather, my motive was to
preach the gospel. Perhaps on the twentieth of this month or before the
last day of the month, I will be moved to Daegu, and I believe that this
would be over by the month of August upon which I shall be moved to

Gyeongseong Jail..."

However, deducing from how it took several months for his complaint to be heard, it can be assumed that his case was not an easy one to handle for the court. On September 16, it was dismissed altogether. It was decided that he would be sent to Gyeongseong Jail based the Peace Preservation Act No. 39, Item No. 1. Rev. Son could not be any happier about the decision. It can be deduced from his letter to his father dated September 25.

"... Dear father, today is September 25. Four years ago on this day at 9 pm, I was forced to leave my home and taken into custody by police and brought in to Yeosu Jail. The time was 12:45 am. From that day on till today, I had been a prisoner. Now, I received an order to be sent to a detention center and I will be leaving to Gwangju in coming days. I wish you well in the Lord."

> As I am inside the prison far away from home, (遠離本家人獄中)
> I am faced with the depth of the night, the prison cell, and grief in my heart.
> (夜深獄深愁深)
> Despite the depth of the night, the prison cell, and grief in my heart,
> (夜深獄深人愁深)
> I am filled with joy always because the Lord is with me. (居主同居恒喜滿)
> Four years of life inside the prison walls is a long time, (獄苦四年多多日)
> but it seems like a day because the Lord is with me. (興王同樂如一日)
> I trust that the Lord will protect me (過去四年安保主)
> As he has protected and kept me in peace for the past four years.
> (未來確信亦然主)

"God who was with Joseph and Paul in the past is with me today. I also believe that God who protects me is with you and my wife and my children. With that faith, I am on my way to Gyeongseong."

He also wrote the following poem as a way of comforting himself in faith.

> The crows of the autumn and other birds fly in for the season,

And sparrows that came on March 3 fly back to their homeland to the south of
the river,
The way home for the guest in the jail cell who left his hometown is still
obscure.

The cold autumn wind brings me news day and night,
The autumn weather is excellent,
And the breeze is getting chilly,
And the falling leaves return to the earth,
Three years since I left home,
The way home is still obscure.

Everything in the universe and all the signs point to the autumn of life,
The sinfulness of billions of people call for the Lord of judgment,
I am not prepared
And the way home in the heaven is still obscure.

September 9.

"Hey, Rev. Son, stop being so stubborn and think about how you can
find your way to freedom," said a man named Yokoda.

But Rev. Son replied, "Well, thank you very much. But I have a greater
problem at hand than getting released from prison." He changed the
topic of conversation to something altogether nonsensical.

"A greater problem? What problem?" replied Yokoda not knowing
what Rev. Son meant.

Rev. Son said, "Japan will surely fall in the future. When that
happens, you should bear the blame. The problem lies not in getting
released but in bearing the responsibility."

Yokoda was startled by what he heard. He was more surprised than
angered by hearing that Japan would most surely fall and he should
bear that responsibility.

"What kind of disrespectful thing to say! To say that Japan will fall is
in and of itself disrespectful. And by the way, how can the blame be on

me?" asked Yokoda seriously.

Rev. said forcefully, "I say this because I heard that you studied theology and you are an elder of the church of Japan."

Realizing that Rev. Son's reasoning did not make much sense, he replied, "What has it got to do with the fact that I studied theology or an elder?" This conversation took place inside the administrative office of Gyeongseong Jail. Rev. Son who was transferred from Gwangju to Gyeongseong Jail was called into the administrative office time to time and interviewed.

There were Sixty-three prisoners charged with dissident ideologies that were transferred from Gwangju to Gyeongseong Jail. Two of them were nationalists, sixty persons were communists, and one Christian, Rev. Son. The administrators of the jail tried all kinds of method in efforts to rehabilitate Rev. Son's faith-based ideology.

At times, they would bring in other Christian pastors to convince him. Other times, they would bring the ministers of other religions to convince him that Shinto worship is a civic ceremony and not a religious one. Initially, Yokoda, the administrator, boasted that he would turn Rev. Son around within one month. For this reason, Yokoda enlisted all kinds of knowledge in defense of his view. On this day, he once again called Rev. Son in to conduct another session of lecture.

Rev. Son challenged him, "At least regarding Christian doctrines, you should be well-versed in them. From the Bible and the church history and the history of the world, we can see that the nations that committed idolatry surely came to ruin whereas the nations that worshipped God prospered. Therefore, the argument that Shinto worship is a civic ceremony, which I know is idolatry, could be used to convince an unbeliever. You, on the other hand, are a believer and already know that it goes against the will of God. By permitting this idolatry to go on, you are contributing to the decline of Japan. Therefore, if the blame does not lie on you, on whom should it lie?"

"I know that sinning leads to destruction, but it also includes other sins besides idolatry," said Yokoda trying to make an excuse.

"Other sins are not fundamental to a nation's destruction. However, idolatry is fundamental to a nation's destruction. Other sins accompany this sin of idolatry. Don't you know Romans Chapter 1? It talks about the idolatry of gentiles and how all kinds of sin emanate from the sin of idolatry, doesn't it? The people of Japan show an exemplary spirit of national pride and unity. But they also have more than eight million idols. Therefore, there is no way that Japan could be saved from coming to ruin and you should remember that. I know that you would blame Christians for this, but it is truly your fault for imposing Shinto worship on people. If you remember this, there will come a day in the future that my prediction was the truth."

In this way, admonition did not work but instead produced the opposite effect of encouraging him on, the administrator decided not to do the work of convincing himself and brought in a wise teacher to mount a defense of the issue. One day, with the warden, the chief inspector, and the intelligence officer in attendance, they brought in a renowned Japanese monk named Ohara in order to defend their position. Ohara thought Christianity was an inferior religion and there was some immaturity to his questions.

He asked, "Have you seen your God?"

Rev. Son replied, "You cannot see God with the eyes of the flesh." He added, "It is truly difficult to meet a king of any nation in person. How can then a person see God with the eyes of the flesh?"

Getting aggravated at Rev. Son's calm and immovable demeanor, Ohara said, "I cannot accept either your position or faith until you show me the god of Christians."

To this, Rev. Son replied, "First, show me the god of Buddhism, then I will show you the god of Christians."

At this, Ohara got up instantaneously and began to slap and kick him three or four times saying, "This is the god of Buddhism." Having lost the argument, he wanted to triumph over him through violence.

Rev. Son did not move an inch but received the beating sitting down. He sneered in his mind, "You say that you believe in the Buddha who is greatly merciful and compassionate. But you don't mind beating up a lonely prisoner mercilessly. I know that you are trying to prove your case through violence now that you have lost. In truth, it is you that lost."

Those who saw what was happening were shocked and tried to stop Ohara. From this point on, the bi-monthly lecture by Ohara became discontinued.

"Rev. Son, how much you be suffering? If a pastor like to get holed up in a place like this after abandoning his flock in a time of tribulation for the church of Joseon, it is the same as Peter trying to leave Rome because of the Christian persecution by Emperor Nero."

After Rev. Son was transferred in to Cheongju Jail, the chief warden of the jail and a few of his subordinates invited the representatives of an organization which specialized in ideological rehabilitation of dissidents. They set up a panel as an attempt at redoctrinating Rev. Son. Among them was an individual who graduated from a Christian school in Japan and used to believe in Jesus but later rejected Christianity. These words of propaganda belonged to him.

Rev. Son appalled by what he heard said, "You are right about this being a time of great tribulation for the church of Joseon. It is because you cannot preach the truth as the truth and are forced to preach the non-truth as the truth. Rather than preaching the non-truth as the truth thereby massacring the innocent flock, it is better for the shepherd to sit inside a jail cell and keep silent. It will be a great sermon of silence."

"It is not that government is opposing your Christian faith. It is only asking you to believe it not in the manner that people do in America or

Joseon. As long as you believe it as the people of Japan do, you would receive a wide breadth of protection from the government."

"I know that Christianity cannot be categorized as Japanese or American. There can exist Christianized Japan or Christianized America. But the reverse can never be. You can reform America to be more Christianized, but you can never promote Christianity that is American. It is the same with Japan. If you do Christianity that is Japanese, then it ceases to be Christianity. Isn't it more right to reform the nation of Japan so that it conforms to the truth of God who is almighty, instead of trying to modify Christianity to fit the Japanese political structure?"

"Japan is a nation that creates, modifies, and perfects religions. Don't you know that? Look at the example of Buddhism. Though the Buddha was born in India, Buddhism remained as imperfect there. It is when Buddhism came into Japan, it became perfected here. Look at Confucianism. Though Confucius was born in China, it remained as an imperfect religion there. But when it was imported into Japan, it was turned into a perfect Japanese version of Confucianism. In the same way, Christianity has to be modified. The religion of Christianity as in Europe and America has many imperfections. Now that it has been imported into Japan, it must be modified to fit Japan. Soon you will get to see that perfection." As such, he laid out his heretical viewpoint.

Unmoved by what he heard, Rev. Son answered him, "Religion have different origins and there are unique characteristics to them. You say that Japan modified Buddhism and perfected Confucianism. However, following the spirit of the Buddha is the right principle. It is only right to propagate the original teachings of Confucius. Isn't it? If you neglect the original spirit and modify the religion to fit the spirit of Japan, then the product would not be true Buddhism or Confucianism. Even if we say that you can modify Buddhism and Confucianism along the

Japanese attitudes, you can never do the same with Christianity. Since Confucianism is based on humanism, you can change it to your liking. However, Christianity is not human-centered, but God-centered. Changing Christianity is inconceivable. I know that what the Japanese are trying to do is a dangerous thing, since they are trying to subjugate God, Yahweh, the creator of all things, under the auspices of the god of Japan which is so minor. You can put a plate inside a pot. But you can never place pot inside a plate. Isn't it? The saying, "Those who oppose the heaven are sure to come to ruin and those who obey the heaven are sure to prosper," is golden and true."

"The nation comes before the religion. Without the nation, the religion of that nation can never progress constructively. Didn't you see what happened to the nation of Israel? After the ruin of Israel, what happened to Christianity?" He mounted a strong rebuttal.

"That's precisely what I point out to be wrong. To think that one's nation triumphs one's religion is wrong. I can admit that principle might apply to other religions. But Christianity cannot be placed under that principle. God existed before the establishment of nations. Nations did not come into being prior to God, did they? God existed before the nation of Japan was established. Japan did not come into being first. You used the example of Israel. However, Israel was a laboratory for Christianity. Therefore, it is wrong to view the destruction of Israel as the destruction of Christianity. Rather, from the perspective of Christianity, the destruction of Israel was the destruction of fulfillment."

"What? What you mean by the destruction of fulfillment?" His face bore a strange frown.

"There are three reasons for saying that it is the destruction of fulfillment," said Rev. Son.

"First, the destruction of Israel referred to the destruction of the temple in Jerusalem. According to the faith of Israel, God, Yahweh, is the only God of its people. They believed God to be exclusively the god of Israelites. They believed that God, Yahweh, loved only Israelites and would save Israelites. They believed that this God only existed within the temple in Jerusalem and thought that they could only worship God at the temple in Jerusalem. However, with the dawn of Jesus Christ, God, Yahweh, revealed himself to be the god for all nations and the god of the cosmos. The destruction of the Jerusalem temple which meant the destruction of Israel was brought about in order to fulfill the new concept of space. Secondly, the destruction of Israel referred to the law-oriented faith being shattered. With the incarnation of Jesus, the life-giving gospel appeared and the law-oriented faith with only its shell remaining was to be shattered. However, when this faith remained stubbornly, God brought Israel to ruin. In this sense, the destruction was for the fulfillment of the life-giving gospel. Thirdly, since many Jews were made Christians, God destroyed the nation of Israel for it was inevitable that Israel was to be destroyed by Christians. Being aware of what is happening, we cannot say that the destruction of Israel is the destruction of Christianity. Though Israel was the birthplace of Christianity, it is not subjugated to it. Therefore, we cannot see Christianity from the same perspective with which we see Confucianism or Buddhism. The principle that religion comes only after one's nation might apply to Confucianism or Buddhism, but it cannot be applied to Christianity. The Bible says, "The one who falls upon this rock will be shattered and if this rock falls on a person, it will turn that person into ashes that will scatter all over the place." In some ways, Christianity seems to be injured. But when this rock of God's judgment falls on you people, you will all turn into ashes. Please remember that." This was how Rev. Son finished his argument.

Then, the individual sneered, "Well, then you believe what you will. You are pitiful."

Perhaps, this happened after an episode like this. They made him read books about Shinto religion and forced him to write a reflection.

The following is that reflection Rev. Son penned.

The Monotheistic Religion

How can there be two suns in the sky and two kings in one kingdom?
How can two owners of the universe and there be another salvation besides
the way of the cross?
There are many lords and gods, but to me there is no other god except God,
Yahweh.
The Buddha is famous and Confucius is a great star, but how can there be
another redeemer besides Jesus? How can I serve two gods and can there be
another redeemer besides Jesus?
What shall I spare for this God? Where can I go after abandoning him?

Autumn Chrysanthemums as a Model for Saints

1. Hundred flowers are withered and grasses dried up, but Chrysanthemums
   are in full bloom. Beautiful Chrysanthemums on an otherwise flowerless
   autumn hill.

2. Fall foliage look splendid as the autumn matures. The blood-thirsty oligarch
   becomes enraged. Fragrant Chrysanthemums on an otherwise flowerless
   autumn hill.

3. It is very different from Sakura that falls off in the late autumn. The
   firmambition that never breaks in even if it gets bended a hundred times. It
   stands alone against the cold autumn wind. Victorious Chrysanthemums.

4. I believe that autumn Chrysanthemums are a model for saints. Undivided
   loyalty for the Lord along with beauty, fragrance, and victory. I wonder if
   we can truly become autumn Chrysanthemums if we become blossomed in
   name alone.

This was also a reflection that Rev. Son wrote after a session of forced
reading. He wrote it examining the autumn Chrysanthemums that were

in bloom in the field of the jail. After reading this poem, the authorities had never forced Rev. Son to write another reflective piece ever again.

(Rev. Son was ordained after the 8.15 Independence. But when dealing with Rev. Son, police or prosecutors or judges called him a minister and that's the reason for using the term here)

"**P**astor, why don't you stay here one more day? You can send a telegram..."

"No, I should go today," said Rev. Son in haste.

"You say that you need to go, but you have fever and did not have dinner yesterday..."

"Well, I must go the way that I must take," said Rev. Son. And he began picking up and wearing his clothes. But Rev. Lee Ki-Hyuk and several members of Incheon First Church who were sitting around him tried their best to keep him from leaving.

It was some time in the second half of October in 1949. He was there as the speaker for the revival meeting at Incheon First Church. For some unknown cause, on the last day of the revival meeting, he began running a high fever all over his body. Not only was he unable to have dinner that evening, when he went up to the pulpit to preach, he could deliver only a short sermon. Upon returning to where he was staying, he suffered through the whole night. The next morning, however, he was insisting to depart for Daegu Suhnam Church to honor the speaking engagement at their revival meeting.

That was the reason why those in presence tried to stall him.

"Well, by going the way that you should go, what if your condition gets worse and you end up not being able to lead the revival meeting?"

"To get sick is God's will and to get better is also God's will. Therefore, shouldn't I do the work that I promised to do? Even if I collapse while preaching at the pulpit, I must go." Sweat began to flow profusely down his a bit famished face. He thought that even if he was hungry, become famished to the point that his face shows it, and sweats a lot, he could not afford to not go to the revival meeting that he promised to preach the gospel of the Lord.

In the year before, after the funeral of Dong-In and Dong-Sin when they were martyred, he traveled to Busan Choryang Church despite the difficulty in arranging the transportation to get there. He could care less about his own health when doing ministry. However, it was a different story for those who were about his wellbeing and did not know what to do about it. But at the end, he went his way. While those who sent him away did so in tears, Rev. Son did not treat it any differently. Upon arriving at the Daegu train station, a church member, though it was unclear how he found out, was there waiting for him with medication. He drank the medication and when he went up to the pulpit to lead the revival meeting on that night, his fever dissipated. And God blessed them greatly.

"Pastor, I know that you are busy. So, I am sorry to ask you. But can you tell me how to find a way to meet the president? I really want to meet him concerning the issue of the allegiance to the flag." It was some time in the second half of the month of March in 1950. Rev. Son was visiting a man who used to be pastor in the past but was now a prominent figure in politics and brought up the top almost apologetically.

"I know very well what you mean. But in my opinion, even if you go and meet with President Lee, you will not be able to resolve the issue. As you know, for it is the time of democracy and things are done literally in a democratic manner, even if Doctor Lee wants to change it, he may not be able to do it alone. The way to resolve the issue is to first have a change in the secretary of education. Second, there has to be an increase in the number of Christians among government officials who attend the cabinet meetings. Third, there has to be an increase in the number of Christians among the legislators. Then, finally, they can address not only the issue of the flag, but also all kinds of issues from the Christian perspective." The person answered logically.

However, Rev. Son thought that the man exhibited a lukewarm kind of faith in his answer. Isn't it true that right now, from all over the place, the children of Christians were being expelled and ministers were being beaten or imprison? In fact, during the month of May in 1949, all the denominations with the General Assembly of Presbyterian Church as its leader produced a position statement regarding the allegiance to the flag and visited the highest ranking officials under the president to give a detailed explanation. However, the secretary of the education unilaterally and forcefully carried out the enforcement. The consequence was that it made a huge [negative] impact [on Christians]. [Rev. Son thought], "How can we wait until there is a change in the secretary of education or an increase in the number of Christians among cabinet members or legislators?" According to the rumor, when the issue of the allegiance to the flag was first discussed, it became a problem during the cabinet meeting. When people inquired about it of a high ranking official within the state department who was supposedly a Christian, they did not get a clear answer. Then, they were rebuked by the secretary of education and any opposition to the allegiance to the flag had become an act of disloyalty to the country. For this reason, Rev. Son felt that more it was delayed; there would be greater impact on the populace and the Christian community. That's why he canceled his revival meeting engagements in Shintaein and Gwangju though he never canceled them even if he was gravely sick. And that's how much he wanted to meet the president and plead his case. He thought that there would be five to six avenues through which to meet the president and he waited for an opportunity while conducting revival meetings in Seoul until April 17. For some unknown reason, however, things did not work out. The following is the letter of request that he wanted to submit to the president.

Dear Mr. President

On this day after forty years of all kinds of tribulation, on this morning when the hope of the East brightly shines, I pray in all earnestness that God's hand of blessing be upon your head for you have risen as the leader of three million people. You have received the divine command and do your best to insure the survival and prosperity of this nation as well as seeking after the peace and happiness of all the people in the world.

During the Japanese rule of forty years, we cannot even name the numerous instances of persecution, suffering, and loss at the hands of the occupiers. Especially, Christians and the church were greatly oppressed by so called the policies of reengineering imperial citizenry. Now that we regained the sovereignty of our country along with their destruction, I cannot help but say that it was God's special grace. Therefore, it is time for us, the military, the government, the citizenry, to earnestly work together to support and nurture that which God desires.

However, Korea is still divided along the 38 parallel and its ideology is confused. The acts of violence against fellow Koreans do not seem to end and the corruption of individualism leaves its marks everywhere, the harmony between the government and the church has been lost and it has become commonplace that police, school, and youth organizations among others beat, imprison, and lynch Christian ministers and Christians alike. Furthermore, there are ominous signs that a great dispensation of unrighteousness would occur. So, I along with one million Christians beseech you to be forewarned and act wisely to exhort the Korean people to proclaim, "God bless the Korean nation," and worship God that Dangun used to worship so that they could enjoy freedom and happiness through many generations.

Though the Roman empire of the old persecuted Christians for three hundred years, it later enjoyed great prosperity as a Christian kingdom. Germany and Italy came to ruin after persecuting Christians and trying to effect fascism on the face of the earth. When the Japanese imposed the policies of reengineering imperial citizenry such as Shinto worship, bowing to the emperor, and pledging allegiance to the national flag on Christians, fifty Christians were condemned to death and two thousand believers were put in prison while protesting against these things. In due time, Japan ultimately received God's judgment of righteousness.

Pitifully, some pockets of our country also defy God's solemn truths and copy the Japanese's misguided ideologies and policies and impose restrictive programs on the people of Korea. They impose Dangun Altar Worship in the place of Shinto worship, bowing to the holy mountain in the place of bowing to the emperor, and the allegiance to the Korean flag in the place of that of the Japanese flag. These programs will inevitably turn into oppressive nationalism and push Korea off the map of democratic nations.

True patriots are those who illumine the path to prosperity from the path to ruin. Who at the time of Dongjo and Hitler pointed them out as disloyal? Those who help their countries prosper are true patriots. If atheists cause a great deal of trouble for a nation, then those policies that oppose the will of God would surely bring it to ruin.

If Christian pastors and believers are being beaten and imprisoned, if students are being expelled, then isn't it a violation of the religious freedom that democratic nations are to uphold? Though the capital of the country does not see the great effect of this, however, many unfortunate events due to pledging allegiance to the flag from various parts of the country are being reported on the pages of the newspaper.

If the world hears about it, not only would the reputation of Korea be greatly tarnished, but I do not know what other kinds of negative consequences would arise. I can only ask you, the founding president of the republic of Korea, to build the foundation of the nation on the rock of ages and lead this nation in the manner worthy of President Washington who still receive praise from the people of all nations so that the people of Korea would receive God's blessings.

Psalm 33:12–17

The Proposal

1. Issue the executive order to prohibit the persecution of Christians
2. Suspend civic events on Sundays

March, 1950 A.D.

Rev. Son Yang-Won, the Presbyterian Church of Korea

Though he was not able to submit this petition to the president, while he was staying in Seoul and conducting meetings at three different churches, he continued to pray for this issue. Finally, when he was in attendance at the 36th General Assembly, the news on Joseon Daily dated April 27 about the allegiance to the flag being altered. "... You are to gaze at the flag while standing straight up and place your right hand on your right chest..."

Like this, he was fully invested in preaching the gospel or the matters of faith to the point of neglecting himself. And he was so busy doing this work that he was never in one place long enough to be comfortable. From 8.15 Independence Day through right up to the moment of his martyrdom, he conducted 93 revival meetings and his sermons numbered more than 2,000. These figures do not even include the regular worship services that he conducted at Aeyangwon Church. I hereby would like to introduce to the readers the excerpts from the diary of Rev. Son dated 1949 that records his life devoted to reviving so many souls through these countless revival meetings. First, I will introduce the writings that Rev. Son used to utilize at and publish for his revival meetings.

To Read before Leading a Revival Service

James 3:1–18

1. Depend on God's knowledge and not to trust my own intellect (knowledge of rituals)
2. Be careful that I, the Lord, and not myself is revealed
3. Make sure I do not make false statements based on my knowledge because of my ignorance about the principles that the Bible teaches
4. Make sure not to exaggerate my testimony and turn it into a lie
5. Do not burden someone with something I myself can't even do
6. Remember that each word I speak bears responsibility to the congregation's eternal life so as to be careful with my words and give all my passion and give my best in faithfulness; To remember that it may save someone up from going to hell but also it may send someone down there.
7. Be careful with food and material things–
   1) Since I am being treated to a [feast] in place of the Lord, ponder if I am worthy to receive it in the first place
   2) Do not eat for the stomach or the taste, but so that I may work
   3) Do not care about material things or the gifts at all

(Conclusion) Oh Lord, please help me not to sin before you in this hour, and help me not to return without having given any blessings to the people, like a cloud that does not bring rain. Also, let the sixty six books of the Bible to be the only guidebook for this hour and the intelligence of my teaching be only a prayer. Amen.

Beginning Words at a Revival Meeting

1) Cancel everything and be wholly united for one week. I came here after dropping everything. Let us do this for our life and death depends on it.

(1) Let us receive God's blessing for believing in Jesus.

(2) We must prepare ourselves for it is the end of times.

(3) Since we can take care of our business in the flesh throughout the year, now is the time to resolve the problem of our souls (Make sure to publicize that we would pray for leprosy patients).

2) Come to the early-dawn prayer meetings for this is the most important thing. Make sure people go to sleep early (the illustration about the evil spirit of slumber).

3) Do you want the revival of the Pentecost happen to you? (Storytelling) One week (Remember the experiences of imprisonment or being healed). *Make sure to announce the exact time... Tell them to work with me in carrying this out.

Sunday, May 8, Clear (April 11, Lunar Calendar)

I start my diary today. My life should be that of a diary. I should live just today.

Today is my day. Only today is my day. Yesterday is past and no longer concerns me. Tomorrow has not arrived yet. I do not know what will happen to me tonight. Therefore, only today is my own. Whether I do good or commit sin, only today is that day. The matters of good and evil as in my going to heaven or hell depends on my actions today. Whether to make tens of thousands to keep alive or die, it all depends on my actions today. Today is the day to reflect on and learn from my past. Today is also the day to prepare for tomorrow. Therefore, I should treasure today. In such a way, my daily life is so important.

Uchimura Kanzo said, "Each day constitutes a life. As there is a good life, there is a good day. As there is a life of misfortune, there is a day of misfortune. Regard each day as a short lifetime so as not to take the life of each day for granted."

I have been leading a revival meeting since the 6th. It is the holiness church located in Seoul, Mapo-gu, Shinsu-dong and pastored by Rev. Yang Seok-Bong. It makes me feel heavy to see the pastor living a difficult life as he ministers to people at this church which has about two hundred people in membership. It is so true that the servants of the Lord bear the cross on this earth in the same manner the saints of the old did. The suffering of a saint is the same now as it was in the past and evinces only the rightful relationship between the Lord and his disciples.

Mr. Cha Jong-Suk and An Yong-Jun came and attended the morning service. I was overjoyed to hear that the food ration for the patients of Aeyangwon which had been cut in half was restored to the four *hoppe* (a unit of weight).

In the afternoon, I was invited to be present at the organizing ceremony of the young men's association of Korea of this town, Shinsu-dong. There, I gave a speech titled 'the one who loves the kinsmen' which spoke about the uprising in Yeosu-Suncheon Incident. I located the origin of the tragedy in veering off from the traditional Korean ethos as embodied in Dangun's spirit. In short, the blame lies in the irreverent actions of atheists who forsook the spirit of reverence for God and love for humanity.

I cannot help but pray. Since I decided to write my diary starting today, I pray that I could live my life in the manner that I am not ashamed to write all my actions down and honestly record my good and bad as is.

Tuesday, May 10, Cloudy (April 13, Lunar Calendar)

I am still doing the revival meeting at Shinsu-dong Holiness Church. Even to this morning, only about fifty people came to the early-dawn prayer meeting. The pastor of this church has been blaming the congregation by saying that they usually do not congregate well, they do not pray much, and they have not been spiritually fervent. But I took it as an opportunity to look within myself. I realize that the atmosphere has been lukewarm because I have not been praying much and spiritually fervent. If the great fire of the Holy Spirit is upon me, if I am filled with the Holy Spirit just like Peter on the day of Pentecost, why would not there be a crowd of three or four thousand people with the Holy Spirit's great fire on them? I can only fault my own shortcomings. Only if I had been aflame the fire [of God], people would have come even when told not to come or pray. No one could have prevented it. Oh, Lord, give me the rod of Moses, the robe of Elijah, and the Holy Spirit that Peter had!

Today is May 10 and it is the one-year anniversary of the 5–10 election. It is truly the joyful day for all the fellow citizens of Korea.

Wednesday, May 11, Cloudy (April 14, Lunar Calendar)

Today is the last day of my revival meeting at Shinsu-dong Holiness Church in Mapo-gu.

At 4 p.m. this afternoon, I met President Lee. Nine of us in total, Rev. Choi Jae-Hwa, the moderator of the General Assembly, six other Presbyterian pastors, one representative from Methodist Church, a Christian Newspaper reporter, and I, attended the meeting. The reason for this meeting was to present the president with the proposal of scrapping the ceremony of bowing down to the national flag which I originally submitted to the General Assembly. It was to petition the government to adopt the same resolution of discontinuance the General Assembly ratified. When we sat down with the high ranking officials from the premier to the minister of education on the 6th and 7th, we were deeply hurt to find them not being able to understand our position. I am greatly grateful that President Lee was able to understand us.

Thursday, May 12, Rain in the Morning (April 14, Lunar Calendar)

After finishing the revival meeting at Shinsu-dong Holiness Church in Mapo, I headed to the church in Yongsan-gu, Bogwang-dong. On the last day of Gyeonggi Presbytery Meeting, Rev. Choi, the moderator of the General Assembly, Rev. Lee Dae-Young, and I went to meet with the minister of transportation. We celebrated because our position regarding the ceremony of bowing to the national flag was well received by him.

Revival meeting at the church in Chuncheon, Daewun-dong from the evening of June 2. Revival meeting starts at the church in Bogwang-dong on Friday evening, June 10. (Study on Laodicea Church)

Tuesday, May 17, Rain (April 20, Lunar Calendar)

May 17! May 17, it is the day I would never forget in my life. Taken into police custody at Yeosu Police Department on September 25, I received the sentence of ten month detention in prison. Today is the anniversary of taking off my red prison garb and changing into my blue clothes upon the completion of my one-year-and-a-half life in prison. May 17 was the day of my release and union with his son to which my father anxiously counted down. May 17 was the day that my wife waited for me at the gate of Gwangju Prison with a set of new clothes. That day is today. More than these, however, today is the anniversary of the day that I experienced freedom from all my sins with which I wrestled in my life, the day that I found freedom and peace in my soul.

1. The sentence of heavy suffering expired as I disrobed the red

uniform of evil.

2. I was united with my Father in heaven when I longed for and waited being united with my father and children.

3. I was clothed in glorious white linen as I put on the white clothes that my wife brought.

In this way, the shiny fine linen has become the white linen of holiness in my private life and the robe of authority and power in the pulpit.

May the staff of my Lord, my Shepherd, which has guided me to this day become the staff of authority that guides the people of this land and protects the sheep. Amen. Hallelujah.

At 1 p.m. this afternoon, I lectured at the YMCA of Transportation Department with the title 'Love for Kinsmen.'

Saturday, May 21, Clear (April 24, Lunar Calendar)

There were many prayers of confession being said during the early-dawn prayer meeting at the church in Gunsan, Gaebok-dong. I heard that, in the afternoon, the women's mission group decided to repent of the sin of bowing down to the national flag since it clearly constitutes a sin according to Christian faith and does harm to the nation. The group is moving toward publishing its resolution on the newspaper.

Monday, May 23, Clear (April 26, Lunar Calendar)

God's great grace continues to bless people during the Gunsan Provincial Revival Meeting. While praying in the morning, I realized that not only in the moments of weakness do people commit mistakes and sin, but also in the moments of strength if one is not humble but arrogant. The devil seeks to discourage us through our deficits as well as entice us to sin through our strengths. Regardless who it is, people should be careful about both their strengths and weakness lest they sin through their pride over their strengths and become discouraged through their despondence over their deficits. In life, both carelessness and despair are to be avoided. Only we are to look up to Jesus who strengthens and perfects our faith.

Today, Rev. Kim Hyun-Jeong along with four others leaves for Gyeongnam Goryo (Korea) Seminary in order to investigate the veracity of its faith and doctrines. I am deeply concerned.

Tuesday, May 24, Clear (April 27, Lunar Calendar)

While I was at the church in Gaebok-dong to lead a revival meeting there, I was able to speak at a jail at three o'clock in the afternoon. I met Mr. Hwang Yong-Wun (formerly the assistant warden at Gunsan Jail) who is an executive officer at Cheongju Prison and accepted his invitation to speak. I was mindful and thankful of how he helped me while I was in prison in the past. I wanted to repay my debt through leading him to Christ.

I was overwhelmed by what Mr. Kim Ji-Ho preached to the women prisoners. He said, "Go and do not sin again."

Friday, June 3, Clear (May 7, Lunar Calendar)

Tonight was the last day of the revival meetings focused on the faith of young men and women in the region of Busan and there was a great crowd in attendance.

It is said that this event was Busan's very first witness of great work being done. Nearly forty thousand households were witnessed to and there was the harvest of five hundred converts. What was greater than the crowd of three thousand people in attendance was the great blessing of the Holy Spirit present. I have no words to express how great an awe I was in to see God working through a sinner like me. I give thanks to God for I know that this was the fruit of all the prayers lifted up by my wife, the congregations of Aeyangwon Church, and the teachers and students of Busan Goryo (Korea) Seminary.

Thursday, June 7, Cloudy (May 13, Lunar Calendar)

1. Upon finishing the revival in Daegu, I spent one night in Seoul before boarding the train headed to Chuncheon in Gangwon Province at Cheongyang-ri Station. It is my very first time visiting Gangwon Province and I was at loss for words about the beautiful scenery I saw. People say that they like the mountain or the water. The border between Han River and its adjoining region featured both beautiful mountains and clear water. It is truly impossible to describe in words. Cars meander through the valley with thick forests on both sides. Han River is draped in beautiful fields of grains and white beach all the up to Chuncheon. Literally, Gangwon Province is the origin of rivers and the lines of trees decorate the city streets. It is forever springtime in Chuncheon. Clear water and white sand become my heart washed anew with the precious blood. Splendid evergreens become the fidelity of my faith. In this way, I shall give all my devotion to God the creator of the beautiful nature. If the corrupted nature is this beautiful, how much more beautiful would the world of the thousand years where there is no sin and precious fragrant plants bloom on the bank of the river of life?

2. The source of Han River is blessed and the backbone range of Korea is still connected, why is the 38 parallel blocked? Mount Geumgang still stands in its grandeur, but it is my anguish for not being able to go and see it even when I see it with my eyes. Seen from the top of the mountain, they are still the people of Korea, but I cannot proclaim so verbally. It is the fault of the 38 parallel. Is this water of the river flowing from the north the tears of my northern kinsmen? As my tears fall into the water of this river, I will plead to my Lord. My work as an evangelist in this land divided by the 38 parallel is of great and solemn duty, but my sighs of ignorance and powerlessness frighten me all of sudden. Fellow citizens of Korea, please do not complain or be bitter. Who can you blame for the 38 parallel? It is not a geographical problem or that of American politics. Do not even blame Kim Il-Sung. It

is more the reflection of our sinfulness rather than that of Russia. Only resolve the problem of sin that stands between God and you. Only work on the problem of the 38 parallel. Do not consider it as the wage of sin of Korean people from afar. Rather than saying, "It is your fault or my fault," it demands of us the kind of repentance that springs from deep self-reflection. Do not look far to size up the land of Korea. The land on which you stand is that land and the census of thirty million people begins with one individual. If each of us confesses sins and works compassionately with each other to promote mutual aid, then the peak of Mount Baekwoon will shine brightly tomorrow morning as it has done always.

3. The task of this meeting is great. Let us destroy the 38 parallel through the mighty work of the Holy Spirit. Even before I came, a great number of people wanted to see my picture in the newspaper. The revival meeting at the church in Chuncheon, Gangwon Province to which many have been looking forward with so much anticipation started at 8:30 p.m. on May 13. The number of people in attendance reached about one thousand. I came all the way from the southernmost region of Yeosu, a site of past uprising, to this area of the northernmost border with a solemn task. May the great fire of the Holy Spirit that came upon the meeting in Busan descend on this border of the 38 parallel. God, Yahweh, you are the same God who destroyed the fortress of Jericho and brought down Babel Tower. Lord, I pray that you pour out the double measure of the fire on this meeting as you did in Busan. In this manner, I praised, prayed, and worshipped on the border of the 38 parallel with the group. Counting this church, the number of the revival meetings that I conducted after Korea's independence was sixty. I have been to every place in South Korea except Gangwon Province. For this reason, I am greatly thankful to God for giving me this chance to preach the gospel in Gangwon Province.

Not only is there yet to be a presbytery in Gangwon Province, only two churches were established here merely ten years ago. Upon the liberation of Korea, it is said that all the denominations entered this province. However, there are only three pastors and they live exclusively in the city. There are only 13 elders, 3 male *Jeondosa*, and 1 female *Jeondosa*. Methodist Church which came in about fifty years ago has six churches, Holiness Church has three churches, and Presbyterian Church has ten congregations in the entire province.

Friday, June 10 (May 14, Lunar Calendar)

I told people during today's early-dawn prayer meeting that our revival meeting should be the one to destroy the 38 parallel.

In my prayer, God said, "You need to be the watchman that protects this hill." Today, there are many bent on destruction and they are actively working to cause chaos in Korea. It was an angel's spiritual message that not only are communists these destroyers but also those within the church that actively betray the truth and that I should be God's watchman.

First, there are people destroying worship. Second, there are people destroying piety. Third, there are people destroying the Church . Lastly, there are people destroying fidelity. The devil has been actively working through all these people to shatter the peace of the Lord within the church. Because the devil, the destroyer of all righteousness, love, truth, and peace, is actively working through those who subvert the integrity of faith of individual believers, those who destroy the peace within families, those who work against the harmony of the church, the presbytery, the General Assembly, and the nation, God is telling me to become a keeper of truth so as to protect all these people and institutions.

I truly want to be the watchman that protects the church of this land. I desired to keep true to the three principles that I saw written on the walls of Rev. John Park's room, the pastor of the church in the south Jeolla province, Hampyeong-gun, Gungsan a long time ago. One, be a truthful follower of the Bible. Two, be a firm protector of the church. Three, be honorable and loyal. I wanted them to be the principles of my life as a pastor.

Saturday, June 11, Clear (May 15, Lunar Calendar)

Today's early-dawn prayer meeting was so blessed. Through the testimony that Mr. Seong gave this afternoon, I realized that I am a great sinner and shook and cried in fear. I have experienced two wonders in my life.

First, I have been well-clothed and well-fed by God despite the fact that I deserve to be stripped naked and go hungry because of my sinful deeds.

Second, I do not know why God has chosen a sinner like me to carry out the works of the Holy Spirit and been using me as an evangelist of Korea.

St. Francis of the old answered the following questions.

1. So many people follow you. What do you think about that?

(answer) I am the chief of all sinners. I know that I am the worst of all.

2. Do not be so modest. There are so many people who committed greater sins. Isn't it useless thing to say?

(answer) Had God given them the same grace that He gave me, they would have done greater things.

3. Then, how come God did not choose others to do greater things but chose a person like you?

(answer) Yes, you are right. God chooses the wretched and the weak and the sinner to reveal his wisdom and power through them.

I decide, therefore, not to concern myself with things such as my right or wrong, the reward or punishment in the future and the matter of my survival. Rather, I am only overwhelmed by God-given grace and strive to be faithful in my life as God gives me strength as a way of paying back for the debt of grace given for the forgiveness of my sins.

Tuesday, June 14, Clear (May 18, Lunar Calendar)

While I was praying in the morning today, I looked within myself if I am truly worthy to be a child of God, a bride of Jesus, and a temple of the Holy Spirit. Help me, Lord, not to seek any other glory for myself than for being a son of God, the temple of the Holy Spirit, the glory of being the bride, and the sake of our glorious Lord. Help me to be able to truly sacrifice everything for the glory of my Lord.

For my household, my Aeyangwon Church, Christianity in Korea and the glory of God, help my being to be melted, rotten, humbled, and ultimately dead as a sacrifice.

1. I want to be a person of love that willingly sacrifices his one body for his family.

2. I want to be a person of love that willingly sacrifices his one body and his one family for the church.

3. I want to be a person of love that willingly sacrifices his one body, his one family, and his one church for the nation.

4. I want to be a person of love that willingly sacrifices his one body, his one family, his one church, his one nation, and everything for my Lord and God of all people and nations.

At 3 o'clock in the afternoon, the director of social services, administrators, and fifteen pastors and elders visited and worshipped at Aesungwon and were deeply moved. I told them that the Spirit of God locates great resources among leprosy patients and shared my vision for them. I encouraged them that they are great workers of prayer for our nation. I exhorted them to be a factory of prayer.

Wednesday, June 15, Cloudy (May 19, Lunar Calendar)

Tonight was the last day of the revival meetings at the church in

Chuncheon. I have asked God to lead me to the green pasture and beside still waters as in Psalm 23. Indeed, isn't Chuncheon literally the green pasture (Chun:春野) and still waters (Cheon:川)? Truly, God set me free in my soul as a calf without a yoke runs around on green pasture. These revival meetings have been good to me that I grew as a tree planted on the bank of a stream that flows with living water grows according to the seasons. The Chuncheon revival meetings will surely impact me as a person as well the entire nation so that a major revival will take place in this place situated adjacent to the 38 parallel and reach out to all thirty million people of Korea.

At 1 o'clock in the afternoon, I hiked up to the top of a peak that oversees the 38 parallel. The land below the mountain was a blessed land.

Thursday, June 16, Clear (May 20, Lunar Calendar)

I left Chuncheon and came to the residence of Ms. Kim, a sister in Christ, which is located in Seoul, Seongdong-gu, Sindang-dong and was able to rest comfortably. From the old and to this day, a woman's faith is indeed God's special grace given to her. Devotion, as it seems, is a privilege that God has given to women exclusively. As Judas Iscariot could not understand the faith of Maria who rubbed oil on the feet of Jesus, ordinary men still cannot understand the faith of Christian female saints and even women who are without faith cannot understand the devotion of Christian women.

Though Eve was a corrupted woman without faith, as it is said in the New Testament that where there is sin there also is grace, the grace that Christian women possess is thus more abundant. One sister in Christ gave me a piece of paper and asked me to write down when my birthday was and what my address was on it. I assumed that she was going to send me a gift on my birthday. So, I wrote my reply on the paper, "My address is the heart of my Lord and my birthday is the day that I was saved and I do not remember the date. Therefore, my life here on the earth is as provisional as the life in a tent and I shall have the joyous feast of my birthday on the day that I enter heaven."

Sunday, June 20, Clear (May 24, Lunar Calendar)

In the afternoon today, I made the visit to Second Army Hospital with the choir and thirty other people. There were two hundred of the three hundred patients in attendance and the arrangement was made for the patients to be able to hear through the speakers in their own rooms. There was truly a blessing of God. Particularly, I told real stories of martyrdom because they pleaded with me to do so. It seemed to have had the effect of making people regard my deeds as noble and put me on a pedestal and regard me as some kind of saint. I truly wish that people do not force me to tell these stories. Someone even took a picture of my two sons and me and sold it to others saying that I was a saint of martyrdom. In this way, they promote my name. For this, I am truly hurt inside and in much anguish.

I know that I am truly a great sinner. Even if my littlest good deed was magnified, truly it is something that my Lord did. I had never overcome even one small sin on my own. It is agonizing for me, a powerless and evil person, to be treated [like a saint] and brings me tears. For this reason, whenever I speak, I try to be careful so as to not exaggerate the measure of my faith and refrain from speaking pompously.

Oh, Lord, hold my tongue and restrain my image so that I do not commit excess. Help me to desire your glory and be a blessing to the listener. Hide me completely and hide even my sins in your embrace.

Friday, June 24, Clear (May 28, Lunar Calendar)

I was frustrated because I was not able to pray well in the early morning. After praying together with Rev. Kim Chang-Geun, I was able to feel blessed in my prayer. Twenty seven years ago from today,

I started to pray in Tokyo, Japan, to receive the blessing of holiness. Since then, I have been praying for this gift. I prayed because I was concerned about why it is that I am the only one out of whom the nature of sinfulness has not gone. According to the words of Rev. Kim Chang-Geun, John Wesley, the originator of the doctrine of holiness, said that it is likely that there is more sin after a person has been sanctified than before he was sanctified. Being holy is only through action from a human perspective and therefore perfect holiness is not possible. From the perspective of God, it is only that God regards me as a righteous person. Therefore, righteousness is only possible from God and not from a human being. Only through the faith that God regards me as righteous, I believe that I am a righteous man.

To this day, I have been seeking the perfection of holiness in my body and soul, but [I realize that] the Lord of perfect holiness is in my heart through God's grace. I have been striving to be a person of complete faith and devotion, but [I realize that] my Lord who in essence is what I have been seeking has already come within me. I have been praying for wisdom and power and the Holy Spirit has come within me. I am thankful. Hallelujah, thank you Lord.

From now on, there is a reason for me to not be discouraged. I am not seeking, finding, and knocking alone. Rather, there are many who intercede for me. A thousand people of Aeyangwon are praying for me day and night. There are four thousand in Sorok Island, seven hundred at Aerakwon, eight hundred at Sangaewon, and four hundred at Bakaewon who pray for me. Besides them, twenty somewhat organizations for leprosy patients are praying for me. In addition to the teachers and students at Korea Theological Seminary, there are more than tens of thousands of students and believers in Korea who pray for me. Therefore, since I have the sighs and prayers of the Holy Spirit as well as the prayers of my Lord of five wounds at the altar of heaven, I shall not be discouraged. If I fail, whose failure would it be? Hallelujah, thank you Lord. Therefore, I am not discouraged.

From now on, whether my Lord pulls the nature of sinfulness out of me or not, whether I am given an opportunity to do evil or not, whether heaven or hell, I shall not concern myself with these things. I shall only long for the cross and the Lord and forget every worldly and fleshly thing and. Instead, I shall long for the things of heaven.

In the afternoon, I visited and sat down with the provincial governor and the director of social services and told them about the situation of leprosy patients. There are no compassionate people. It is as if people are helping others for themselves and the betterment of the society.

Friday, July 1, Clear (June 6, Lunar Calendar)

I arose at four this morning and went directly before the Lord and gave thanks for his granting even this sinner the grace of prayer. I finished my prayers and opened my Bible to the day's scripture readings. I was comforted and emboldened when I read Jeremiah 31, which turned out to be a grace appropriate to my circumstances.

This year, in particular, is my silver anniversary—the 25th year since my marriage, and the tenth year since I moved to the Aeyangwon. So I traveled with the family to Suncheon to take a family photo and a photo with my wife. Also, Pastor Won, returning to Korea from the States today, brought to me a suit, shoes, and socks sent as a gift by someone.

I am full of thanks for this good gift, a sign that I will now put on new clothes and walk a new road.

Glory to the Lord.

Friday, July 5, Rainy (June 10, Lunar Calendar)

Today is the funeral for Mr. Kim Koo. It is said that he will be given a public funeral and I believe that this public idolatry of Mr. Kim does him harm. It is really not for him that they do this but for them only. Instead of saying that it is an abomination that they are ritualizing his death to which he was opposed while he was alive, I would say that it is more of harassment. I also hear that An who killed Mr. Kim used to be a student under him. He had received the words 'Even in the face of death, his righteous spirit soared up to the heavens and his magnificent blood filled the earth' (雖死 義氣衝天 壯血滿地) from Mr. Kim.

In the evening, the emergency Gyeongnam Presbytery meeting took place.

Thursday, July 7, Clear (June 12, Lunar Calendar)

I got to preach again. I could not oppose it. Rev. Lee Yak-Shin implored me to preach saying that I was the only one capable of doing it for the blessing of others. In fact, I came in a shirt without a necktie in order to prevent such scenario. Since I always get to preach and don't have an opportunity to hear someone else speak, I came resolved to have the blessing of hearing someone else's sermon. That's why I came without a tie. But still, I could not keep myself from being asked again.

Oh, Lord, I do not know why you choose to use a sinner like me. There are plenty of intellectual, powerful, healthy, and righteous people. Of them all, how come are you entrusting your work to a sinful and ignorant person like me? I truly do not know.

After the presbytery meeting, I slept at Rev. Han Dae-Sik's residence in Jinju.

Tuesday, July 26, Clear (July 1, Lunar Calendar)

Hallelujah, Amen. Oh, Triune God, you are my God and my Father. Though I continued to sin ever since I was young, though I am unrighteous and disobedient, I trust that there is forgiveness from you for the chief of all sinners like me and give you thanks and glory. To me who toiled in my sense of powerlessness, discouragement, despondence, and despair till last night, you led me to surrender to you and read Ezekiel 16 in my daily reflection of the Bible. At the end, you spoke to me through Ezekiel 16:59–60, "For thus says the Lord God, 'I will also do with you as you have done, you who have despised the oath by breaking the covenant. Nevertheless, I will remember My covenant (the blood of Christ, predestination, blessing to me) with you in the days of your youth, and I will establish an everlasting covenant (Old Testament, rainbow, salvation, unchangeable, eternal life) with you.'"

Hallelujah, Amen. Truly, Yahweh is the rock of my salvation, glorious Lord. You parted Red Sea and River Jordan and made a way. You are my God who made a sprout appear on Aaron's staff and brought skulls come to life. You create both misfortune and fortune. You are my Father and my God. Oh, Lord, I am alive.

I shall live in your grace forever. I cannot give enough glory to you, Lord, for revealing to me the things in my daily life in a manner that fits so adequately and appropriately with my circumstances. I shall sing of you forever and Yahweh shall by my shepherd forever. Hallelujah, Amen.

Workers for the Harvest

The harvest is plenty but the workers are few.

Souls stir up winds and clouds and become busy trying to settle down.
Heroes stir up waves and try to foment their future.

The nation tries to expand its territory and guard it forever.
People plan things to give them eternal luster.

History flows silently and subverts these undertakings.
Ages change vainly and fade away by erasing their tracks.

The wind of history blows endlessly.
The waves of ages come crashing limitlessly.

You know though you don't seem to know.
You have though you don't seem to have.
You are wise though you seem to be a fool.
That's the life.

You might find something happen.
You might be able to see some place.
You might hear someone call.
That's the journey.

If the springtime of planting seeds is the beginning of faith,
If the summer of growth is the street of hope,
If the winter of storage is the resting place of love,
Then, the autumn of harvest is the workplace of judgment.

The spring morning of everything blooming is fragrant.
The summer day of everything growing is precious.
The winter night of eternal rest is priceless.
Then, the autumn evening that flows
With the golden waves of fertile field is all the more precious and priceless.
Abraham became the father of faith on Mount Moriah.
Joseph became the premier of Egypt through his life as a slave.
Moses became the leader of Israel in front of Pharaoh.
David became the righteous king under Saul.
Elijah became the warrior of Yahweh in front of idols.
Daniel became the witness of God in a lion's den.
John the Baptist became the pioneer of the gospel on the top of a plate.
Stephen became the inheritor of the cross under a pile of stones.
Peter became the rock of the church in front of Nero.
Paul became the apostle of letters in prison.
All the martyrs became the possessors of heaven through capital punishment.

When is the time of harvest?
Where is the place of harvest?
What is the work of harvest that needs to be done?
But do not ask who the workers for harvest are.

God says that there is much to harvest but so a few workers.
How much more workers are needed in the 20th Century world
Where atomic weapons have become God in the world affairs?
Where ruthless fighting is considered that of peace,
How much more in the 20th Century Korea
Where illegal powers are legalized,
Where deceitful propaganda are standardized,
Where frauds and embezzlements have become a way of life,
Where profiteers and bookkeepers are enriched,
Where the love of alcohol and women is a life of paradise,
Where lewd stories and gossips are being made into gospels,
Where a bloodthirsty man is idolized,
Where idolatry is worshipped,
Where corrupted officials are justified,
Where the workplace of military police is praised.

How much more in the 20th Century church
Where the works of men are being masqueraded as the work of the Holy Spirit,
Where the descendents of Balaam are accepted as righteous,
Where the heretical doctrines are accepted as orthodox,
Where the church has turned into just another place of employment,
Where an abominable heart has been made into one of faith,
Where the declining Tower of Babel has been made into a hope,
Where incompetent ministry is made into a ministry of love,
Where the watchmen of truth are being anathematized,
Where true pastors are criticized as being self-righteous,
Where three thousand and some altars of the Lord are being desecrated.

Now, hear those who have ears to hear.
Now, see those who have eyes to see.
Now, speak those who have mouths to speak.
Now, rise up those who have a reason to rise up.

There might be other people's works that Rev. Son copied and are mistakenly included here. Since I do not know if any such work is contained here, so I decided to publish them as belonging to Rev. Son. If you find something that is not justifiably of Rev. Son's original work, please contact me.

Not titled, No. 3

The leader of ten million people should be a person who possess a heart in the size of a vast ocean so that he or she could be able to accommodate all different dispositions of ten million people. Learn the tolerance and humility of the great leader, Moses.

In all things, do not complain about or hold a grudge against the disjointedness of things.
See everything as being my fault and the result of my mistakes.

August 26, 1950

Hold poverty close to you like your loving wife,
Regard your suffering as your teacher,
Turn your humble situation into your castle,
And make nature your friend.

Faith

Oh, Lord!
Even if you have to take away from me my parents, my siblings, my
   wife, my children, my basic necessities in life, and everything else
   for that matter, do not take away my faith with which I trust you.

Even if I lose everything, as long as my faith remains,
I would be richer than anyone who possesses everything.
Even if I have everything in abundance but have not faith,
   then I am a man already in ruin.
The flowers of the Japanese apricot tree call for spring, then my much
   more my actions.

January 29, 1933

The Love of God Shown Me

1. How cruel is my suffering that beats on me.
   Beat me as hard as you can with your might
   Then I shall taste the truth of the love of God
   That is concealed within cruel suffering.

2. How cruel is destitution!
   (Here is the missing part)

3. But, I do not want to rise out of my feeble condition in which my
   Father who works through his fervent and profound love. However,
   as Peter did not want to leave the hill of transfiguration, if God's will
   is done through my joyous suffering, then God will be pleased with
   it.

The Joy of the Lord's Supper

Oh, Lord!
My cup of thanksgiving is running over.
You are the greatest of all saints.
I am the greatest of all sinners.
How is that you come to me bending your back
And give your flesh and blood for me to eat and drink
And bring about this spiritual union?

Oh, Lord!
Without any way to repay you,
I only cry the tears of thanksgiving.

September 2, 1932

I am a Christian

To live is to trust that God's will is being done.
To live is to obey only God's will.
Therefore, I am more content to be a failure if it is God's will than a
    rich man according to my wish.
As a person who adjusted his view on life in this way,
I have learned to be content in life by being the Lord's possession
Whether I die or live.

September 28, 1932

I do not Want to Speak of Others' Weaknesses

Because I am a human being,
Because there is no one who does not have the fleshly nature,
Because I still have a long way ahead of me,

Because I do not know what will happen to me in the future,
I want to be a man of faith and character by being silent and godly.
Therefore, I do not wish to gain compliments or attention from others.
I only want to gain the glory of God.

January 16, 1932

My Prayer

Oh, Lord! I have been lied to by my own resolve and courage.
I am a man of failure.
The ten million decisions that I made in the past all point to one thing
　　and one interest.
Oh, Lord! Please come in person and take hold of me and guide me,
So that I would not stand ashamed before God and men
And help me to live a life of courageous faith.
Amen.

The Christian Faith

Enthusiasm as if it is on fire, this too not faith.
Conviction strong enough to move the mountain, this too is not faith.
Intoxicating emotion, this too is not faith.
Patience that ignores hardship, this too is not faith.
Hope that minimizes the present and sees the imminent glory of the
　　future,
This too is not faith.
Faith consists of truth.
Faith of truth is true faith.
Truth is the will of everlasting God.
It is calm, certain, orderly, eternal, unchangeable, and does not waver
　　depending on the place.

The grand universe is its expression.

The orderly nature is its law.

The truth of true faith is like that of the universe and nature.

God created the universe with truth.

And God made faith out of truth.

Faith is not humanistic but the creation of God.

For God has placed himself in it,

It is mysterious, eternal, and life.

It is the life of eternity.

The life that lives by truth is a tower of truth that is being built up infinitely.

Glory shines from it and namely, it is the glory of the Creator and the glory of a person's faith.

My Concise Testimony of Christian Faith

It has been already twenty five years since I first believed in Jesus. For a long time, I have been confused by all kinds of forms of faith. I was lost in a myriad of views of faith that came from all different perspectives. I also endured many doubts and much agony in my interior life. Then in the 30th year of my life, I seem to have finally become an orthodox Christian. Though I have been a Christian in the past, I experienced doubts and dissatisfaction about my faith because it contained many strands of paganism within it. This continued until the age of thirty when the life of a true Christian began to take hold. Now, I have become all the surer. From now on, I decide not to seek anything that is extraordinary. I will not open my eyes to or heed multifarious doctrines in the world, mystical teachings of each religion, or strange traditions of Christian faith.

1. Only I came to regard the death of Jesus as my own and accept the fact of his resurrection as the fact of my own, thereby receiving the

person of Jesus himself and believing that the life of Jesus has become my life in the present and growing in my faith of him in the place of my ordinary life.

2. Only I came to commune with Jesus without ceasing, hope in him, measure my growth against the perfection of Jesus Christ, experience the resurrection of Jesus as the hope of my present life of faith by receiving the living seed of his resurrection.

3. Only the heart of Jesus Christ that became the perfect faith and the energy for the perfect hope helped bring about this real life of fervent love.

Therefore, faith to me was this life of prayer that sought to discern the truth of things and obey the will of God day by day.

1. To have faith is to have the life of receiving the entirety of the person of Jesus into my present life of faith.

2. To have hope is to hope for the growth of my life in accordance to the measure of faith of my object of worship.

3. To love is to have the dynamic power of righteousness and to be transformed by being united with Christ in love and the perfect living. I will not seek anything else but to belong the work of trusting and loving the Lord and living my life of love in an ordinary fashion.

(This is my prayer offered during an early-dawn prayer meeting in Namchang.)

September 28, 1933

The Simplification of Christianity

My view of Christianity has become simplified.

That is... to pray, to live a life of truth. Prayer is the soul's breathing. The life of truth is to discern the true nation of things and deal with them accordingly. I pray without ceasing to give life to my soul and strive to do the will of the spirit and not flesh in regards to things that I encounter in life. This makes me a person who lives the life of the Christian faith.

My Christianity, therefore, does not entail the in-depth study of knowledge, the study of the Bible, the admiration of Paul's Christianity as a great sage of knowledge, or being captivated by John's Christianity. It only entails the work of praying and striving to live a genuine life of truth as guided by the Bible. This is a person who possesses Christianity and practices the life of Christianity.

The life of prayer and truth, my Christianity has become simplified.

November 9, 1937

Early-dawn Prayer

Therefore consider the members of your earthly body as dead (Colossians 3:5)

You have not yet resisted to the point of shedding blood in your striving against sin (Hebrews 12:4)

By your endurance you will gain your lives (Luke 21:19)

Ley's say that you are dying because you could not overcome the sin or if you are dying because you have overcome the sin. If you are dying either way, which would you choose to be the reason for your death?

It is the embodiment of the pinnacle of faith to choose the death of godliness than the life of sinfulness.

Oh, Lord!

I desire the life of sinlessness even if I live for one day.

I desire the life of sinlessness even if I have to endure one hundred years of suffering.

For I want it and want it all the more,

Help me with your bloodied hands.

I do not have the appetite to sin and live on the earth.

Rather, I ask you to take this body of mine away.

Be Joyful Always and Give Thanks in All Things

Do not grieve that spring is passing.
Do not be reluctant that the days of hot summer are coming.
Do not lament that the autumn moon is setting.
Do not be scared that white snow is falling.
Do not be sad that flowers are dying.
Do not be overly concerned over sad tears.
Do not brag about the pleasure of youth.
Do not sigh at white hair below your ears.
Do not sing the praise of your fortune too much.
Do not neglect the lesson of your misfortune.
It is God's sovereign will to give and take away.
Who in the world could block or hide from him?
One should discover and learn the lesson given.
One should give thanks in all things when pressed from all four sides.
The praise of thanksgiving becomes a melody of joy before the Lord.
The tears of repentance become a melody of sadness.
The joyous melody of praise and the sad melody of tears become
mixed to give rise to the truth in the life of a Christian.

(1 Thessalonians 5:16–17)

As I am Faced with the Dilemma of My Sinful Nature

From now on, why don't you trust the power of the Holy Spirit and
embrace the patience of do-or-die spirit and work hard to be disciplined
in the habits of righteousness?

Even if you have to cut off your hand and pluck your eye out,
work had to live a life that subdues your flesh (tense Christian life–

preservation of soul through patience).

Why do you trick yourself into one thing? Do you want to avoid the cross? Isn't Christianity an active religion? Do not retreat, but charge ahead. (Those who do not follow Jesus with their crosses are not acceptable)

Even if I fall seven times, I shall rise again and receive salvation by looking up to the cross.

Therefore, from now on, I will never criticize others, be prideful, brag that I am standing tall, depend on my own strength, trust my resolve, or make loud noise. Instead, I will be completely humble, carry my own cross, and be a practitioner of faith that looks up to the cross.

God is Love

God is love. God's essence is love. Everything that God does is based on love.

God governs the universe and everything in it with love. God is my Father who controls everything that appears to me from all sides through his love. Though you do everything out of love for me, how is it that my eyes are blind and prevent me from finding all the traces of your love?

How is it that I am so insensitive and cannot praise my Lord of love? God is love. All the universe was created through love. I should trust that my Father still moves in love.

Everything given me is love. Tears are of love. Suffering is of love. Leaving me in my flesh is of love. Allowing me to be in the world a little more is of love. God is love great that even death is scripted in the content of God's love.

God's essence is love. God's feet of love traverse the universe and everything in it. I shall sing of this love.

Oh, Lord, help me to find all the traces of your love and turn them into a melody of praise and sing of you.

The Self-reproachment about My Life, I am a Christian

The life of a Christian needs to incorporate the life of Jesus Christ into the very fabric of his living. Most importantly, it must translate into concrete life.

Christianity is the actual practice of living. One could doubt anything that a person says received if it does not manifest itself in life. There can be actions of men that are difficult to understand. But whatever he knows comes to change his life and he would become bold in the core of his being as result.

Without saying, Christianity is not a religion of words, instruction, philosophy, discussion, or knowledge. It is a practical and religion of power.

It is not all about prayer. It is incomplete by teaching others well. It is the power, reality, and life of a Christian to put into practice whatever one receives.

My ignorance thus is not a problem. The fact that I am not born well is not a problem. The fact that I am not satisfied with my family is not a problem. The fact that I am not treated well, that my name and honor are not recognized, and that my mind and body are weak does not pose a problem. The problem is that I do not possess the abundant life of a true Christian, that my living is powerless, and that the life of Christ has not manifested within me since I have not become a good believer before being a good pastor.

Even despite all this, how is it that my mind is preoccupied with so much stuff. What am I seeking and thinking so hard about day and night? What is up with the attitude of my life?

Am I the practitioner of life that glories God and the keeper of salt and light that benefits others? Has my life been like that? Haven't I sought the favor of men instead of the glory of God? Haven't I impacted others harmfully rather than beneficially? It seems like that it has become the age of Carmel. It is an age where people make clear demarcations saying, "Your faith, my faith, your religion, my religion, your God, my God." It is an age where authenticity is clearly defined and judged.

Though I speak of extraordinary things, but there is no extraordinary power in me. Though I say that I am working to bring the end time to reality, there is no preparation. Am I not sighing uselessly?

How am I as a Christian?

1. Since what is destined would come to pass for all people, a person does not become a Christian by carrying out the duty of a believer.

2. A Christian is not someone who fears the burning fire of hell in the afterlife because of his eternal sins.

3. A Christian is not someone who tries to repay Jesus for his grace of being crucified in his place.

A person becomes a Christian by being saved born again through the life of Jesus Christ who has become the Spirit and living the life of a Christian in the Spirit.

(January 1, 1933, morning reflection)

The Steps of My Christian Living on the 25th Anniversary

1. In my primary school years, I was a person of blind faith.

2. Up till my middle school years, I believed in the end time without certainty and in the preparation stage in my faith.

3. Later, I tried to practice the life of a Christian because I feared the punishment of hell and longed for the pleasure of heaven.

4. Then I lived my life as a Christian less for avoiding the punishment of hell and wanting the bliss of heaven but more for the reason that I

could not abandon the great love of God showered on me by Jesus and did not want to disappoint him.

5. Lastly, after the age of thirty, I came to live my life as a spiritual Christian by receiving the spiritual life of Jesus Christ and allowing Christ to move within me.

The Need for Faith and Learning

1. The heretical Gnostics who tried to turn Christianity into a Hellenistic philosophy ended up failing. Particularly in attesting to the way, academic studies were used to refute misguided philosophical numerations of Christianity. For this reason, People like Justin the great apologist, Clement of Alexandrian School, Origen the theologian, and Tertullian and Augustine the scholars of Latin School based in Carthage rose up to attest to the way.

In the years of Protestantism, Wycliffe, Luther, Zwingli, and Calvin were the greatest scholars. We, too, cannot afford to not promote scholarly subjects needed for Christian apologetics. It has been two hundred years since Catholicism came into Joseon. And it has been sixty years since Protestantism came in. Modern knowledge is needed for the people of the modern age, particularly in this phase of founding the nation. Korean and Eastern knowledge is needed for Koreans.

2. The knowledge of right truths is needed for believing in Jesus and receiving salvation. Isn't educated faith better than uneducated faith? It is not right to meddle with everything in trying to pick up the treasure. Then, don't we need the apparatus with which to pick it up?

The Will of the Lord and My Will

Oh, Lord, let my chosen will be the same as your will. I discover your will and my chosen will are vastly different. Lord, see your hidden truth within a single grain of wheat, but my thoughts about a grain of wheat concern only eating it to satisfy my hunger. You look at a flower and sing about it, but I am only driven by the curiosity to pick it. You look at a sinner and have compassion to save that person, but I abhor and try to avoid him. You look at a prostitute and have compassion on her soul, but I only see her as an object of fear and hatred. Lord, help me to have your mercy.

Lord, you demand the truth of all things. But I am only attracted to the materialistic nature of all things. You seek truth from all people, but I encounter people with the desires of flesh. Lord, open my eyes and help me to see the truth of all things. Lord, help me to live in the world of truth where you live.

Lord, what is it that I scheme and attempt to do from morning till night?

Oh, Lord, save me.

Money and Heart

Which is evil, money or the heart of a person? Which is pure, money of the heart of a person? Money can turn a heart evil and an evil heart can use money in evil ways. Money can make a person good. A good heart can use money wisely. Money can make a person evil. An evil heart can turn money evil. Perhaps, money is good but a heart is evil. Perhaps, the heart is good, but money is evil. It is true that money can be used according to what the heart desires. It is also true that people can be used according to what money seeks. Therefore, it is hard to distinguish between money and a heart.

Money can compel a person to drive. The heart of a person can drive the money. However, I do not consider this a problem. A true person should not be swayed by whether money could turn a person into a new person or one could use money wisely with a good heart. A person should attach no connection between money and his heart. Christians are people who could care less about these things. Only Christians are not ensnared by these things. If there is a person who has not resolved this problem within the sanctuary of a church, then that person can hardly be said to be a Christian.

Money cannot turn a person good or evil. Also, it is hard to control money in one's heart. Even if someone who can use money well with the heart that is influenced by money is said to exist, I wouldn't know if it is true or not. Christianity neither requires the kind of money that can be used well by the heart of a person nor the kind of person that money can use well. In addition, I do not want to be that kind of commendable person.

In short, just know that Christianity is a religion that places no connection between money and the heart of a person. I only think that money is a useful servant who helps us to conduct daily life while on the earth. It is only true that money goes and comes.

November 4, 1933

For Whom Do You Work?

Am I not a person predestined before the ages to be born and die for the kingdom of God? But when I look inside my interior life as a Christian and minister, I look like a person who is living for himself. When I examine the things that are important to me in my daily life and activities, it seems like I am working hard for:

1. My stomach
2. My fame
3. My ideas

I realize that it is the Lord that works things out for me in order for me to do his work and care for his sheep, but

1. I shear the wool of the sheep to make my own clothes

2. I milk the sheep to fill my hunger

3. I run around as the leader of the sheep but I do not give my earnest and best effort for them. Woe is I for this reason.

My Soliloquy

I shall be an addict of Jesus.

1. An addict of alcohol lives and dies through alcohol.

2. An addict of opium lives and dies through opium.

3. Let us be addicted Jesus and live and die through Jesus.

When we live in a manner that our living and lives are wholly devoted to Jesus, then we shall resurrect just like Jesus did. Since we are the Lord's servants, let us be people who work only for the Lord and not for ourselves.

I Exhort My Beloved Friend to Pray

–I exhort my younger brother to pray–

I want you to be a person of prayer. Jesus Christ was a person of prayer. From the hair on his head to the sole of his feet, he was a person of prayer. From the manger to the top of the cross, he was a person of prayer. From the time of his resurrection till today, Jesus Christ is a person who prays without an end.

Therefore, Christianity is the religion of prayer, Christians are people of prayer. Trust that you have become a person of prayer and you are a person who needs to pray.

The life and prayer of a Christian cannot be separated from each other. The entire life of truth for a Christian becomes his prayer.

Therefore, there is not one prayer of a Christian that goes unanswered. A Christian's prayer is not for the fulfillment of his greed. It is fundamentally different from the prayer of the worldly people in wishing for their dreams to come true or the selfish prayer of people that seek the satiation of their greed without any regards to which is good or bad, or true or false, or right or wrong.

The Christian prayer is the kind of prayer that is perfected in heaven rather than that which springs up from the earth. In this sense, there is not one single prayer of a Christian that goes unanswered.

Now, the time has come to pray. When the disciples came to Jesus and said, "Lord, teach us how to pray," Jesus said, "Therefore, pray like this." The content of how one should pray according to Jesus has become the greatest prayer. This prayer was his voice shouting out loud. As his shout rang out through the world, the prayers of the worldly people, the legalistic prayers of the Old Testament, the ritualistic prayers, the prayers of human earnestness, and others came to crash and disappear altogether. As stars fade away as the sun, the origin of light, rises, when the prayer of Jesus appeared, the prayers of the world people came to a halt and the curtain fell for the prayer of the John the Baptist here.

For this reason, Eui-Won, trust that you have been reborn as a person of prayer. And pray without ceasing, give thanks always, and pray earnestly. I saw some Christians worry needlessly without praying. Others speak of the life in truth but they believe that the life in truth and prayer are two different things. On too many occasions, I met fools who did not understand that dealing with everything in faith is the same as prayer and that the life in truth is the same as prayer. Please understand all the more this truth and become a person of prayer. I want you to be a person who prays about everything, prays without ceasing, and prays in earnestness. Pray to overcome the flesh and experience that the strength to overcome sin lies in prayer. Recognize that prayer is the power to accomplish everything and put prayer above all things. Then, you will be able to verify all the content and truthfulness of our religion through prayer. Experience the true worth of Christianity through prayer.

December 10, 1933

To My Beloved Friend in Faith

Dear brother who lives daily and takes each step in the garden of God's heaven and earth, how deep an experience of the Spirit have you gained in the meantime? I rejoice and am glad for I know that your life has increased as much as it could in that place where you encounter God in your countless mornings and evenings.

You received that free life of greatness for which you were chosen and given the unchanging covenant from the beginning of all things. Your life now consists of walking around on that land while singing high and low melodies of praise and enjoying the surroundings. Your life of calmly walking on the stormy waves of this world is indeed mysterious and profound. How many would know this mystery? How many could receive this calling to walk on the earth while singing this song of praise in joy and satisfaction? Only those who understand this truth and live accordingly are truly blessed. Oh, it is a grand life and holy truth. The waves of a great sea crashing endlessly with a loud notice! The blood of Christ that flows in the vein of the universe creates the sound of harmony. There is no reproach or fight, there is no difference between rich and poor and there is no separation between day and night to us who live the life of praise in accordance to the tune of this melody.

How could time and space control and prevent the truth that which even the force of the universe could not subdue? His blood that became the spirit devours my flesh with the rotten stink and his flesh that became life hovers over the grave of our skeletons. My flesh and blood are singing in the heaven of resurrection and our life forces united with the universe are dancing in the glorious paradise. There is nothing to lament about even if my body is torn apart and death and the Hades surrender before us.

Oh, death, where is your triumph? Oh, Hades, where is your devouring force? The logos of salvation devours this land. The universe has become the holy of holies of life and every created thing is dancing within it. His blood and flesh are giving life even to the heap of skulls where death had been dealt. His life which collided with my soul can more than enough blaze. If one knows happiness through receiving God's love, he would deceive himself. When God's love collides with a human being, it turns into sighs, tears, and even death. This is truly mysterious and profound. Who among those in flesh can understand this limitless and profound love of God? No one except those whose spiritual eyes have been opened could not understand this.

Oh, this is a surprising and profound truth of love. Through death, I shall experience a grace that is greater than being on the side of death. I shall eat the great love of God that comes through tears and exists in the tears of God. Without going through all the hardship and suffering, I cannot taste the truth and love that are hidden in them.

Therefore, I give thanks in all things and rejoice always. To us who came to understand this truth, it comes to us as contentment and satisfaction. Therefore, we shall complete the heaven with the law of faith and wear the crown of glory through faith. Before those who have such faith, all people will bow down in worship and the nature will clap hands and sing. In this way, this life which shines eternally as the glory of faith itself will shine infinitely.

For from Him and through Him and to Him are all things. To Him [be] the glory forever. Amen. (Romans 11:36)

"Pastor, you are here."

"Yes, I arrived yesterday."

"Are you having a good time?"

"Well, yes. I am thankful, but I could not get to Busan which was my final destination."

"Why?"

"The war broke out and transportation was affected by it."

"Pastor, have you heard anything of note?"

"No, I did not. Have you heard anything?"

"Nothing this morning, but I heard something last night over the radio."

"What was it? Last night?"

"It said that Suwon was overtaken by the enemy and our forces are on a strategic retreat. But the American airplane B29s were launched from the far east and the American government is looking at the Korean crisis optimistically," explained the man.

Rev. Son mumbled, "B29s... American government..." as he teared up in his eyes. In this way, he dropped a couple of ambiguous words and it was unclear whether it was a reply or a question.

It was July 7, 1950. This conversation took place between Deacon Lee and Rev. Son at the gate of Aeyangwon. Rev. Son had just returned from a revival meeting the night before. Deacon Lee seemed to paint the picture of an imminent resolution to the crisis when he spoke of B29s and the American government. However, in Rev. Son's mind, this crisis was just the beginning of a major tragedy for the Korean nation and would not be resolved easily until the nation and the church came to repent genuinely.

The 25th of June marked the day of great tragedy not only for Korea's present but also Korea's distant future. When Seoul, the capital of South Korea, fell to the communist invaders, the government of South Korea evacuated out of it. Both those civilians fleeing the war and those who remained behind in the enemy-occupied regions were suffered all kinds of hardships and difficulties. When Rev. Son thought of their distress in hastily evacuating as well as the state of affairs for his nation turmoil, he literally felt his body burning up and shrieking in pain.

Initially, the people of Aeyangwon heard about the news of invasion on the radio just like people in other countries would. As they heard the news coming out of General McArthur's command center and the government's publicity department, people believed that the allied forces would take back Seoul immediately, cross over the 38 parallel, and even conquer North Korea. But the state of the war painted a different picture. When they thought the communist army could not reach Suwon after taking the capital, Suwon was immediately overrun by the enemy and the crisis threatened to grow into a full-blown war. Though Rev. Son left for a week to conduct a revival meeting at Busan Seobu Church on June 26, he was stopped at Samcheonpo as traveling by the sea to Busan became implausible. Therefore, he changed his plan and went to lead revival meetings at Samcheonpo Church and Hadong Central Church and Hadong-eup Church on his way back to Aeyangwon. He got back to Aeyangwon on July 6.

In fact, he could have gone to Busan if he really tried. However, because he could not prognosticate the outcome of the war, he became concerned about Aeyangwon and decided to return to Aeyangwon as soon as he could. According to Bae Sam-Sul who was in attendance at the revival meeting at Hadong Church, the following conversation took place.

After breakfast, Deacon Kim said, "Rev. Son, I think it is best for you to evacuate."

Rev. Son replied, "Do not worry about me. All of you must evacuate and I suggest that you evacuate to Namhae Island." In this way, he refused to talk about the safety of himself.

"Since it is true that you are more valuable than all of us put together, you should evacuate. The reason that I did not go down to Jeju right away but came here instead was because of Rev. Park's request. As Rev. Park was moving down to Jeju, he told me that you are also in great danger and you should also evacuate to Jeju or Busan."

"Like I said, do not be worrying about me. If I decide to flee, then I can do so very easily. But you all need to evacuate. I will take whichever the course of action after praying some more. I only ask that you pray for me." Rev. Son did not seem to be in any hurry.

I think that it was July 24. After Seoul and Suwon fell to the enemy forces, many thought that they would never invade Daejeon. But Daejeon also was soon overtaken by the enemy forces despite a great loss of lives. The provinces of southern Chungcheong and northern Jeolla were invaded shortly thereafter and it was a matter of time that the invading force would move into Suncheon or Yeosu.

Deacon Kim Heung-Bok who was summoned by Rev. Park Jae-Bong to come and visit Rev. Son made a heartfelt plea to him. However, before his visit, there were others from Seoul, Jeonju, Suncheon, and other places that came to plead with Rev. Son to evacuate as soon as possible as they themselves were on their evacuation trail. Rev. Son still did not heed to their warnings.

It might have been July 21. When Rev. Na Deok-Hwan pleaded with him, Rev. Son said, "I will pray and do as God instructs me. I will make sure that it is not a man-made decision." On July 22, he said, "How glorious would it be to die in the name of the Lord? I was already dead in prison. I am just thankful that I did not die before the 8.15

independence. There is no way for me to ever repay my Lord's love for me even if my eyes are plucked out, my nose is pierced, my mouth is torn apart, my hands are cut off, my feet are fallen off, all of my blood is shed due to my narrow neck being cut open, and my bones are grounded into powder. How could I ever flee to save my life?"

Again, Deacon Kim pleaded by saying, "Though you say to wait for you, timing is everything. You should really be fleeing by now. We would stay here if it means that you would evacuate. Please, do not be stubborn and come with us. It is urgent." Rev. Son solemnly replied, "Hey, Deacon Kim, I am thankful. But what is the most urgent thing in this time of great tribulation? Isn't it an urgent thing for a shepherd to care for his flock of sheep so that they are not harmed by predators such as wolves? Is it truly an urgent thing to evacuate in order to preserve one life or that of one household? If there is a place to which all of the Aeyangwon members can evacuate, then I might go with them. But since there is no such a place available, if I still evacuate, how is it any different from allowing eleven hundred sheep to be slaughtered? What good is it for me to live after leading this flock of mine to self-destruction?" His attitude foreshadowed his readiness to defend Aeyangwon Church to death. After organizing and leading a non-stop series of special meetings such as fasting prayer services and overnight prayer services for one whole month as an effort to prepare the faith community of Aeyangwon so that they would not fail in their faith just, Rev. Son no longer sported that appearance of freshness and instead looked very much languished.

Prior to Deacon Kim's visit and upon hearing that the pastors from Seoul fled to the south as refugees, Rev. Son was heard saying, "Oh, no, this is a catastrophe. Now that God has raised the whip of judgment on this nation in response to the sinfulness of our people, how is it that all the prophets who should preach and embody repentance in Seoul and die as sacrifices came down? In their place, I should go up to Seoul."

In fact, he inquired about the ways to travel to Seoul. But he could not go as the people of Aeyangwon worked hard to hold him back and no viable way to Seoul presented itself. Being reminded of these stories, Deacon Kim thought, "Of course, Rev. Son is indeed special. Didn't Lord say that a good shepherd gives up his life for his sheep? Rev. Son is a true shepherd." This made Deacon Kim all the more aggressive in trying to convince him to evacuate and he pleaded his case as having greater implications.

"Pastor, I know what you are saying. But isn't the future of the church of Korea and the salvation of the Korean nation just as important as or even more important than this Aeyangwon Church? You need to be evacuating for this work of yours." Deacon Kim thought that he made a convincing and powerful case.

"Deacon Kim, that's it. One of the Korean churches is Aeyangwon Church. And the Aeyangwon family constitutes a part of the Korean nation. I cannot neglect the flock of this church and then treat the Korean church and the Korean nation importantly. To discount a local church or an individual believer is to discount the Korean church and the Korean nation as a whole. To care for the church of Korea and the nation of Korea is to care for a local church and an individual soul. The very reason that presbyteries cannot unite as one and the General Assembly turns into a place of conflict more often than not has to do with this. This also is the wage of our unrepentant hearts. The Korean nation being divided into the north and the south regions as well as the killing that is currently taking place is the fault of the church leaders who are not repentant. Think about it, Deacon Kim. How grateful should we have been? God is the god of grace and God has given us the bloodless 8.15 independence for the cost of the lives of fifty somewhat martyred who died while protesting Shinto worship. However, no one thinks of this price of all the blood that was shed. No one does not understand because of whom this gift of liberation came about and remains repentant. Because of this, God temporarily rang the warning bells through the incidents in Yeosu-Suncheon, Jeju, and Daegu. Since the people of Korea became more hardened in their hearts, God allowed the capital, Seoul, to be attacked and all that has transpired so far. Look, even then, the repentant church leaders who pretended to care for their sheep in good times have abandoned their flocks and are now on the run trying to insure their own safety only. If things continue on like this, very soon the entire land of Korea will meet the same fate as Sodom and Gomorrah. If we do nothing, God's greater wrath will come upon us and it is very likely that the day will come when the Korean nation would be wiped off the face of the earth." Deacon Kim's hair on his head stiffened up as he heard these words. It was because Rev. Son's words echoed like a terrifying prophecy.

Rev. Son continued on. "Therefore, we must offer God the blood and sweats of the righteous again. Though I am greatly unrighteous and inadequate, I have been clothed with the righteousness of our Lord Jesus. Therefore, as long as Lord permits it, I would very much like to be an offering of sacrifice." The orderliness of his logic and seriousness of his attitude carried the weight of the universe and likened the enormity of a mountain. There was nothing left for Deacon Kim to say. With what words could he plead for Rev. Son's evacuation more?

"But pastor, wouldn't you need to keep alive in order to work?" said Deacon Kim.

"Listen, Deacon Kim, I am saying that your thoughts and your words are wrong. To say that I need to keep alive is wrong to start with. Our Christianity is not for people to live well. Christianity is a religion that calls for people to die well for God's kingdom and righteousness. Now that the time has come for God to receive glory through the church of Korea, to where should we flee?" Once again, Rev. Son refused the idea of evacuation forcefully.

Thinking that it is merely futile to go on, Deacon Kim concluded his words with a smile on his face and saying, "I should go to Busan immediately and send a plane to this place to bring you out by force."

"Well, unless the Lord allows it... but I am sure that it is not in his will," said Rev. Son as he put it to rest.

"How did you get here?" Rev. Son was surprised.

"Well, I thought I would better come to tell you that I want to take my mother, father, and siblings to Busan with me."

Rev. Son was surprised and grateful to hear these words. He became tearful in his eyes. He thought, "He came to save our family." But he was not in any condition to give him an answer.

"From where have you come?" Rev. Son changed the subject.

"I came from Sinseongpo."

"Are your mother and father with you?"

"Yes."

"How about your older siblings?"

"Only the household of my oldest brother went down. My second-oldest and third-oldest brothers were in Seoul, but I have not heard from them."

Some of the guests who came down from Seoul overheard the conversation and became perplexed. The person addressed Rev. Son himself as father when he said that he came down to take his mother and father with him. But interestingly, Rev. Son asked him, "Are your mother and father with you?" The visitor was none other than An Jae-Seon who became an adopted son to Rev. Son through faith and love. Around the noon of July 24, Jae-Seon came to visit Rev. Son. Jae-Seon used to go to school in Jeonju but at the time he was resting his fatigued body at the house of his family of origin in Suncheon. However, because it made him uneasy to remain in Suncheon, he decided to evacuate to Sinseongpo after discussing it with his biological parents. On this day, he walked the distance of about 30 *li* to get to Aeyangwon in order to ask Rev. Son and all his family to evacuate along with him to Busan. Though he explained this reason to Rev. Son, Rev. Son did not give him an answer but only asked him about the wellness of his biological family.

When Jae-Seon was about to press his case, Rev. Son asked him, "Have you seen Rev. Nah recently?"

"Yes, I saw him out on the street earlier today. But, father, what will you do?" asked Jae-Seon again.

Rev. Son seemed torn about how to reply to Jae-Seon's request the second time around. After a long pause, he said, "Well, I am thankful for your words. But why don't you ask your mother?" He decided to not answer it directly and instead take on a deliberately evasive posture. If it was Dong-In and Dong-Sin that asked, it would have been easier for him to cut them off right away. However, it seemed more difficult for him to curtly refuse Jae-Seon's appeal. That was the reason that Rev. Son told him to go and ask his wife instead.

So, Jae-Seon entered the room and asked his mother. She refused to evacuate by saying, "Where is the refuge? Our only refuge is in the embrace of our Lord. Where can we go especially now that the second coming of the Lord is imminent?" Then, Jae-Seon asked them if he could at least take Dong-Jang with him. This was also rejected by Rev. Son. Coming to his wit's end, Jae-Seon decided to go and consult Rev. Nah about it.

Rev. Nah said, "Rev. Son will never flee." And he added, "Why don't you come with me to Namhae Island?" However, Jae-Seon did not go with him saying that he would not flee, too, if Rev. Son does not flee.

> God be with you till we meet again,
> By His counsels guide, up hold you,
> With His sheep securely for you:
> God be with you till we meet again.
> Till we meet, till we meet, till we meet at Jesus' feet;
> Till we meet, till we meet, God be with you till we meet again.

In the afternoon of that day, they sent away the refugees from Seoul or Jeonju to Namhae Island by the boat, Aeyangho, from the dock on the beach of Aeyangwon. They sang this hymn of farewell as they were about to send the rest of the refugees. But the feeling was different from other occasions of farewell when they sang this song. Furthermore, when they were singing the second stanza, "Neath His wings securely hid you," it embodied the desperate concern on the part of those who were staying behind and the rightful worry on the part of those that were moving away. Those that were evacuating could not help but cry when thinking about for how long they would have to endure this difficult situation now that they have abandoned their houses and clothes in fleeing just like how the family of Lot did in the old. Those that were staying behind could not help but sigh when thinking that they would very likely die at the hands of the enemy soldiers who don't mind killing healthy civilians like flies and who would most readily treat lepers as the easy targets of their submachine guns and bamboo spears.

Then the next line, "When life's perils thick confound you," was their collective plea to God to take care of Rev. Son who was in grave danger because he refused to flee and at the same time Rev. Son's plea to God to take care of those who were fleeing for they were in a tenuous situation. Though in that moment of that day they were praying together, they knew that they might become food for fish or evaporate like dew before submachine guns in the very next moment. The last line of the hymn, "Receive me, Lord, when I depart from this world," expressed their yearning that they would become the possessors of faith that the Lord accepts in his presence. In this way, the overwhelming emotion and sense of blessing they experienced went beyond anything that they experienced during a revival meeting.

The cross on the top of the bell tower of Aeyangwon Church overlooked the wide open land below the blue sky dotted with white clouds. The cross seemed to look to the sky and want something so yearningly. When they sang the chorus of the hymn, "Till we meet, till we meet, till we meet at Jesus' feet," there was no one who did not taste the happiness that was only possible through persevering through sorrow.

Whether it knew what was happening or not, the boat was rocked gently by the waves. Whether it knew what was happening or not, the waves were blown by the wind. Whether it knew what was happening or not, the wind nudged the clouds on. Isn't life is like a floating cloud? What is the rise in prosperity or fall in decay but a life in the bitter human world that is divided by a screen? Rev. Son sent them away and cared for the remnant with fervent prayers.

The face soaked in tears felt the cool of the ocean breeze.

"Grrrrrrrr..." the sound of airplanes,
"crack, crack, crack, crack..." the sound of machine guns.
"pow, pow, pow..." the sound of long range cannons.
"Grrr, Grrr, Grrr..." the sound of tanks,
"click, click, click, click..." the sound of submachine guns
"tick, tick, tick..." the sound of M1 rifles.

The cacophony from a battle field which at times sounded near and other times far finally came to a stop. City by city, village by village, the flag of North Korea dotted the landscape and people shouted the praises of the communist north. It became a world of farmers and laborers who celebrated day and night ecstatically that their time had come. Those who fled to either to the north or Mount Jiri after the incident in Yeosu-Suncheon came back to their hometowns and paraded themselves as patriots. The rumors of the arrest of a son of a chief of a township, the murder of police officers that were hiding out in a village, the martyrdom of a pastor who was on his way down from Seoul, and the execution of a father and a son tandem upon being tried at a People's Court were flying in by the end of the month of July.

Already, Yeosu was completely overrun on July 27. Since Aeyangwon was also a community of people, all kinds of stories were being exchanged. Thinking that the situation called for some kind of response, the manager of Aeyangwon and Administrator Cha called for a meeting of six departmental heads, the church staff, the school staff, and forty prominent members of the town and wanted to decide on a common approach to the crisis.

The facilitator put forth the agenda after the opening prayer by saying, "Now, we are going to talk about whether we will welcome the communist forces or not." However, silence ensued because no one wanted to volunteer his or her opinion. Though it was a legitimate concern that demanded attention, it could never be an issue for Aeyangwon.

After the fall of Seoul, Rev. Son, whenever in personal conversations or in preaching publicly, called for his audience to suffer in the name of Jesus since they had been treated well in the name of Jesus in the past. "So called the people of the world can never be the sacrifice of martyrdom because of their parents, siblings, spouses, children, possessions, and status. But we are truly free since we do not have parents, siblings, possessions, status, and any other thing. Therefore, let us who are about one thousand and a couple of hundred in number hold hands and die in martyrdom for thirty million Koreans. How could people who are awaiting an opportunity for martyrdom ever welcome the communist forces? To welcome the enemy soldiers implied a way out of facing martyrdom."

But one person said, "In my opinion, the communist soldiers are not strangers but our kinsmen. Since the politics have changed, don't we have any other option than welcome them?"

"That's wrong," replied Rev. Son.

"I am saying this because I cannot commit the sin and at the same time I cannot look the other way while you commit the sin. You are right in that they are fellow Koreans, but they are also atheists, materialists, and people against God. Therefore, the communist soldiers are not mere soldiers that are ideologically or volitionally free but the forces of God's enemies. In other words, they are the forces of Satan that opposes God. Since we know that they wage war not only to massacre their own kinsmen but also oppose God, we can never welcome them," said Rev. Son as he looked around to his left and right.

"If we take such a position and do not welcome them, we do not know when they would come and kill at least those of us who are in the management. Isn't that true?" It was a plea more than a question.

"Even then, we can never do it. Even if we die, we can never do it. Since we received much grace in the name of Jesus, we can never betray him even if all of us die." Rev. Son maintained a resolute position.

"But, Pastor, who among us would go out to meet them when they come and look for us?" said someone.

"I will face them as the representative. Do not worry about it. I will take it upon myself. If I get sacrificed while confronting them, then you can decide whatever you want to do after that." Rev. Son exhibited coldness.

"As long as your arrest leads to peace for people here, it would not matter. But what if Aeyangwon is harmed even after you are taken away? Then what?"

"What do you mean, 'Then what?' Just die for God!" No one dared to speak anymore as Rev. Son replied in a low and dispassionate voice.

It was unclear if the sound coming from a distance was that of trucks or airplanes.

"Then, Pastor, let's forget about welcoming them. But how about hoisting the flag of North Korea?" said someone.

"That cannot be done either. To hoist the flag is to welcome them. For this reason, we cannot do it," Rev. Son rejected the suggestion forcefully.

"Pastor, what's so wrong about hoisting a flag? What does the Bible have to say about it?" a dissident voice asked.

"There's nothing wrong with a flag in and of itself. We did hoist the Japanese flag during the days of the Japanese rule. We also did the same with the national flag of Korea as well as the American flag. However, the flag of North Korea, as I said earlier, represents the blasphemers of God. Therefore, how can we hoist it up? We did not bow to the Japanese flag. We could not bow to the flag of South Korea either. You know how much I went around teaching people about the flag of our nation, don't you? In any case, we were once deceived by what people said about the times during the Japanese rule. Let us not be deceived by it again." Now, there was no one asking about this issue anymore. Rev. Son was the only one giving an answer. Ultimately, everyone thought they could not help but abide by what Rev. Son said.

"The next item to talk about is the issue of evacuating," said the mediator. Someone said, "Of course, we must evacuate. In fact, it might be too late to flee. Since Yeosu was overrun, if we want to flee, we must do so right away."

Another asked, "Then, what should be our manner of evacuation?"

"What's important is to move those in the leadership who would be targeted and singled out easily by others to Busan. Then, I think that it makes sense to evacuate the rest slowly as further opportunities emerge."

"That cannot be so. It is wrong for the leadership to evacuate first and voluntarily. Unless you take the regular members with you, you cannot say that you want to evacuate first. Instead, let us evacuate the parishioners to freedom. We, the staff of twenty four, can die in martyrdom." Once again, Rev. Son sought the answer in martyrdom. In this way, they reached the decision to evacuate as many of the regular members as possible as the meeting was dismissed.

The first thing is martyrdom. The second is martyrdom. The third is martyrdom. Personally, it is martyrdom. Publicly, it is martyrdom. [He talked] martyrdom in his family. [He spoke] martyrdom at the church. [He mentioned in his stories] martyrdom. [He preached about] martyrdom in his sermons. It was all about martyrdom!

Rev. Son said on many occasions, "About my time and place of death, I don't mind I die while I am preaching at a pulpit, or while witnessing [Christ] to others in the streets, or while praying in a quiet place. But I am afraid to die in my sickness." For Rev. Son, there was no greater opportunity to [live into these words] than now.

"Ding, ding, ding..."
It is the sound of the church bells that announces the evening worship service to the far and near.

The sound of the bells floats along the line of the sunset in an evening,
And it rings as far as to the other side of the ocean.
The sound of the bells portends the evening bells,
That express the sanctity of religion, matrimony, and labor.

The sound of the bells portends the heavenly bells,
That give indescribable peace, comfort, and hope,
To people in anxiety, fear, and emptiness.

Furthermore, the sound of the bells portends the quiet bells,
That promises to give the spiritual food at any time,
To those leprosy patients whom were isolated,
From their families, relatives, kinsmen and society,
And who possess resentment, sadness, and disappointment.

If it were in a different time and a different place,
It would be only right to yearn for this sound of the bells again and again.
But these bells are foreboding something ominous.

The sound of the bells in the bell tower of Aeyangwon Church
Shook the evening that dawned on the land without any care.

It was August 23.

A month had already passed since the communist forces invaded Suncheon and Yeosu and set up a world of the red by establishing the communist rule as per their scheme and resolve.

It was a Wednesday night. Even in ordinary days, there would have been a Wednesday worship service. Now that when the hope in this world had been thrashed two or three times over, [not having Wednesday service] in this time of emergency was not a consideration!

Perhaps, it was July 24. The General Assembly publicized that Christians should pray to God to speed up coming of the victory [over the enemy]. Upon getting this announcement, the church rang the bells and organized worship three times a day. Rev. Son conducted a week-long special revival meeting at the end of which he ordered fasting for everyone. Since then, whenever there was a worship service as well as in regular days, he kept urging people to be ready to be martyred. On this day, the bells rang out to announce the Wednesday service and all the people of Aeyangwon began gathering with tenseness in their hearts.

They sang Hymn No. 89 'Hover O'er Me, Holy Spirit' and Hymn No. 204 'A Mighty Fortress is Our God.' They sang these hymns so zealously that it was as if their singing was aimed at shaking down the communist soldiers, leftist groups, women comrades, government officers, and those that are against God as well as destroying Kremlin Palace in Moscow and the foundations of the nation of the devil and household of evil spirits. The accompaniment of an organ was not needed. They did not need someone to lead them in singing the song. All of them seemed like warriors on the front line that were charging straight ahead with bombs on their backs.

The Scripture was from Revelation 2:10. In his mind, he reminisced about a moment when his wife encouraged him at the Yeosu train station.

"Dear my beloved, as you know, the seven churches recorded in the book of Revelation represented the churches in the world whether in the time past or present, whether in the East or West. Of those seven churches, the church of Smyrna symbolizes the church of Korea presently since it is in a time of tribulation and poverty." Rev. Son began preaching his sermon titled 'Obey till death.'

"Concerning this problem, what constitutes as obeying till death? First, the Chinese character for the word obedience (忠誠) is *Chung* (忠) and it is constructed by combining the character for the center of one's being, *Jung* (中), so that there would not be any wavering or movement, and the character for heart, *Sim* (心). Therefore, according to this word, obedience is the sum of thanksgiving, repentance, praise, and prayer. It should reflect the integrity of one's life that demands consistency between what one asks of his or her family or friends and how one lives. If our words and actions are not matched, how can we say that we have obedience?"

These words of Rev. Son carried much weight. It might not matter during the time of peace. But in this urgent situation, it was more than one thing that Rev. Son wanted to put into practice what he had been preaching all along. Several times, people from the security office came to verify Rev. Son's presence. Rev. Son ordered Aeyangwon Church members to dig a bunker and stay there to pray lest they get arrested. On another occasion, he told people to put a box inside the hospital room and hide behind it to pray. But concerning his own safety, he refused to hide to protect himself till the end. He was heard saying, "Why do you make me waver? You are not loving me by doing this, but instead, bothering me. Why would I hide somewhere else when I have the house of God right here?" Knowing these things about Rev. Son, there was no one among the parishioners that Rev. Son did not talk about loyalty in words alone but lived it out in his own life.

"Secondly, doing your best with all your strength is loyalty," said

Rev. Son. Then, he continued, "Therefore my beloved." The tense face
of Rev. Son was glimpsed through the shiny lenses of his eyeglasses
reflected by a dim gasoline lamp. Around one thousand members gazed
into that shiny eyeglasses.

"Thirdly, the courageous faith that does not fear death is loyalty.
The faith that compels you to withstand death, not fear death, not fear
one's own death, and die in order to keep one's trust in Jesus Christ
for the sake of God's kingdom and his righteousness is loyalty. The
result of the heart that loves the Lord resolutely, truly, honestly, simply,
and wholeheartedly leads to the sacrifice that is naturally martyrdom.
Consequently, there was no one among all the martyrs that had
gone before us who had not been ready and who chose to do it on an
impulse."

These words of Rev. Son explicitly endorsed [martyrdom].

Once, there was an incident like this. One day, people from Yulchon-
myeon People's Commission came to visit suddenly with a list of people
including Dr. Lee and nine other and declared that the list showed those
who committed wrongdoings in the past. They said that a minimum of
six hundred people need to sign the petition that was to be submitted
to UN for prosecution. Rev. Son refused it in one word, of course, and
only asked them to pray with him. However, surprisingly, they did not
return on the day that they said to return to retrieve the document with
a seal on it.

On another occasion, when there was no more food within
Aeyangwon, one of the persons who were serving Rev. Son said, "Since
we cannot do anything, let us just have an official worship service and
hoist the red flag as a formality so as to buy their good graces and find a
way out of this difficulty."

Rev. Son struck the desk in rage and said, "How ungrateful are
you? It goes without saying that we cannot accept communism that
advocates atheism. From the time of the 8.15 independence till now,

we have been more than well fed with three *hoppe* a day. How can we commit such travesty just because we are going hungry for a few days? Morally speaking, it can never be. We should live purely and die purely. Until soil gets into my eyes, we can never hoist the red flag." Rev. Son rebuked him in a loud voice.

In this speech, Rev. Son seemed to be speaking out of his own experiences when he endured all kinds of hardship and fears in trying to serve God and follow the footsteps of Jesus and those times when he charged ahead in faith while risking his own bloodletting and death.

"Fourthly, courage to endure till death is loyalty. Loyalty is to persevere in all things that we go through daily. It is the life of taking one step at a time by enduring again and again. At the same time obedience is the life of martyrdom. Loyalty is to work in sweats, pray in tears, and fight against sin till we bleed. This is martyrdom. For this, our sweats become invaluable. For this, our blood becomes precious. Only those who possess the day as theirs and claim this hour as theirs could obey and die as martyrs in each hour of their lives. It means to be loyal unto death while remaining with a joyful heart." There was nothing regarding how the communist soldiers are or the army soldiers of South Korea are in Rev. Son's sermons. His sermons only taught how authentic Christians need to live always for the sake of Lord's glory and how they need to die in order to become the possessors of the glorious crown.

"Elder Shin, Elder, Pastor, Pastor..." shouted a young man as he struggled to catch a breath and it was unclear whom he was addressing.

"Elder, Elder, Pastor, are you sleeping?" The voice called out again after a pause.

"What is it? Who is this?" asked Rev. Son as woke up and sat up.

"Pastor!" The young man lost his words upon hearing Rev. Son's voice.

He thought, "Should I tell him to flee or should I tell him to go over to the church?"

In the wake of the 6.25 invasion, many people came down to visit Aeyangwon from Seoul, Jeonju, and Suncheon. Among them were those who claim to know Rev. Son but whom Rev. Son did not know well. The staffers of Aeyangwon feared that there were leftist partisans among these individuals. This was the reason that they brought Rev. Son's family inside Aeyangwon. After that, whenever he could, he told people, "If anyone comes and looks for me, tell them that I am praying at the church." On several occasions, strangers came to visit Rev. Son. But each time, they turned those people away by telling them that Rev. Son had already fled. On that day, however, the young man, after coming to find Rev. Son, did not know whether to tell him to flee immediately or move to the church and hesitated.

It was September 13. It was passed lunchtime. The chairperson and six departmental heads were watching the passersby vigilantly from office right inside the main gate of Aeyangwon. In that moment, the chief of the Yulchon-myeon branch, the deputy chief, the captain and two other persons from the Yeosu security office came to Aeyangwon armed with weapons.

The six departmental heads represented the departments of executive office, treasury, accounting, medical affairs, religion, education, and industry. But the chairperson was someone chosen without the knowledge of the pastor as a part of the contingency plan who would have to deal with the outside world just in case some unforeseen event happened. In short, he was a bogus chairperson.

"Hey, Comrade Kim, Aeyangwon doesn't receive rations these days?" one of the visitors said in a kind tone of voice as they came into the chairperson's office.

"Yes, we will be there soon."

"Is the roster of the committee set?"

"Yes, here it is," said the chairperson as he gave the list over to one of the individuals.

The man who received the list pored over it carefully for a while and said, "Rev. Son is not listed."

"Even the one who is not here is to be listed?"

"What? Rev. Son is not listed?" said the other as his attitude changed dramatically.

"He has gone away to pray."

"Stop lying. We came because we heard that Rev. Son was here. What do you mean that he went away to pray?" asked the man.

Chairperson Kim was not the only one surprised to hear these words. All of the people who were standing around the room were surprised.

Thinking that they were bluffing, Chairperson Kim said in a shaking voice, "I am telling you that he is not here because he is not here for real."

"I told you not to lie. This is the fourth time. You are trying to lie to us till the end because we have been taking your words at face value. Aren't you?"

Those who were quick-witted tried to analyze their body language to ascertain the truth.

"We did not lie."

"If you did not lie, are you forcing us to lie? What are you going to do now that we are going in to find him here?" One of the men postured to go inside Aeyangwon. The warning made the staffers' hearts to sink. The sound of clicking meant that someone was loading the bullets to the submachine gun.

"Then again, do not be so stubborn and let us know where Rev. Son is."

"..."

Everyone hesitated to give an answer.

"How come you are not saying anything? You cannot even lie now?" Again the man threatened.

"If you don't speak up, I am going to kill all of you lepers. Don't you know that we took care of one of you already?"

Everyone shuddered at these words. His words, "Don't you know that we took care of one of you already?" referred to the incident in the early morning of the first Sunday of August. On that day, the bells rang to announce the early morning prayer meeting as usual. Suddenly, a group of twelve communist soldiers came to Aeyangwon and pointed their guns at the gate and ordered to open the gate which had been closed temporarily. Then, they not only proceeded to shoot the German Shepherd to death but also the young who was startled out of sleep and ran toward Aeyangwon as if to deliver the news of intrusion or he was so scared. He died without being able to utter even one word. When those who were there finally opened the gate, they shouted that they came to arrest the sons of bitches that were hiding out there. In other words, they were looking for South Korean police officers and soldiers. The people of Aeyangwon were able to turn them away only after convincing them only the disabled were there. Knowing about this incident, all the staffers were shocked to hear the man's words, "Don't you know that we took care of one of you already?"

"Comrades, let's go in," said the leader of the entourage as they started to move out of the room. In this moment, a young man ran in and reported, "See here, Pastor has come back from the island. He is at the church praying."

"I knew that was the case. You should not have lied like that," said the leader and stepped in to Aeyangwon.

The staffers seemed to be confused as to what had happened, though some felt relieved to be out of the jam. As they were rebuking the representatives of Aeyangwon, a quick-witted young man slipped out and ran to Elder Park to consult about what to do. When asked, Elder Park spoke after a long pause, "Do you think that they really knew what was happening before they came?"

"Yes, they seemed to know that Rev. Son was here. They were in such a hurry to get inside Aeyangwon. They threatened to kill all one thousand of us, if we do not tell the truth and they find Rev. Son on their own once they are inside."

Elder Park thought about what to do. When he met Rev. Son in the morning, he told him, "Since the number of people coming here and looking for you is on the rise, we cannot remain calm and tell them that you are not here. So, why don't you flee to a safer place?"

Rev. Son replied, "Do not do that but tell them the truth. I am decided and ready to die as a martyr. If God wills and gives me a chance, I would do it anytime. If they ask even now, tell them I am praying here at the church." Park thought it would be God's will to do as Rev. Son wished. That is the reason that the young man said that Rev. Son had just returned after praying. And this was the reason that Elder Park had sent another young man to alert Rev. Son of the danger.

As the young man initially hesitated to speak up thinking whether to tell him to flee or go to the church, Rev. Son said, "Why? Did people come to arrest me?"

"Yes. We told them that you were not here. But they began shouting that they would kill all of us if we lie. They were threatening and like the last time, the submachine gun..." explained the young man.

Starting a few days ago, Rev. Son's back pain flared up, but as usual, he carried on to spend the night praying in tears. On that night, he was lying down to rest a while after working on the draft of his sermon for the Wednesday worship service. Upon receiving the news, however, he got up slowly and quietly. Though his face was pale, he maintained a resolute demeanor. Though his body was fatigued, he got up quietly and weightily like a massive mountain as if his time had come.

He put down the ink pen, watch, and other valuables which he took out of his pocket. He changed into a suit and got ready to leave.

"Where are you going?" asked the young man curiously.

"To the church." He let out an answer that was more of a sigh and leaned on his cane to walk.

Did he mean to follow the trail of the Lord who walked over to Gethsemane on the Mount of Olives while praising God in order to clutch on to a cold rock wet with dew and decide on his end?

"Deaconess Kim, we have trouble, Deaconess Kim" shouted Deaconess Choi from afar.

"What? What happened?" Deaconess Kim stood up with the herbs that she pulled off the soil in her hand.

"This is a big trouble. This is a big trouble. They came to get the pastor, the communists." Then, without giving the other a chance to ask more questions, she ran back to from where she came. Without knowing what had happened, she began moving her legs that were not that responsive since she had been squatting for some time to run in haste to the house of Elder Shin.

Ever since Rev. Son moved into Aeyangwon, several deaconesses have been guarding the vicinity of Elder Shin's house where the pastor had been staying. Since there were several staffers on guard in the direction of the gate, they had been patrolling the side facing the beach fearing that someone would come to spy from that direction. Even the sight of a boat that passed by from a far distance made them apprehensive. Since they could not afford to be seen as guards, they pretended to pull herbs from the ground while keeping an eye on the surroundings. On the other hand, Rev. Son walked around in the plain sight as if nothing bothered him. He did the same in the daylight as well as the nighttime. Contrary to their wish, Rev. Son never stayed inside away from the public view. Fortunately, days passed without an incident and he had been safe for about a month and a half already. Deacon Kim thought that he would be safe as usual on that day and just focused on picking herbs. Deaconess Choi left the words of thunderous impact, "I heard that they came to arrest the pastor," and disappeared right away. When Deaconess Kim reached the house of Elder Shin to find out what was really happening, she found no one around. Tearful Deaconess once again pull herself up the treacherous hill to get to the church thinking that the pastor might be there.

Oh, what was happening? There were elders standing still and crying silently. There was Rev. Son who was walking slowly as he was guarded by the communist soldiers armed with submachine guns! He was walking with his pale face drooped and leaning on his cane. Because she felt fainty as she became tearful, Deaconess Kim grabbled on the nearby pine tree tightly.

The vision of Judas Iscariot standing in front of Roman guards with swords and batons, Peter with his sword drawn, and angels numbering more than twelve passed like a flame in a dark night. Then, Deaconess Kim's head bumped into a branch of the pine tree with a "thump" sound.

When she gained alertness, she saw Rev. Son following the men without saying anything. She wondered what the elders and deacons were doing just standing there and crying. She sighed, "Hey, people, why are you standing there doing nothing," as she walked over to where they were.

Being at a loss for words, she asked Lee, "Why don't you follow him instead of standing here?"

"They said not to follow. They said that they are going to the office and it would only make things worse if we follow them," said Lee.

"...?"

Deaconess did not understand what that meant.

[This is what happened.] The staffers of Aeyangwon who had to confess that Rev. Son was indeed present upon being threatened by the chief of the Yulchon-myeon branch and his cohorts. Then, the staffers led them to the interior of the church sanctuary. They found Rev. Son inside the sanctuary. He was in the deepest part to the inside and back of the sanctuary which was constructed into two levels and praying lying down in the direction of the auditorium.

The chief of the branch walked over to where Rev. Son without taking off his shoes and said, "Hey, comrade, are you Rev. Son?"

Rev. Son continued praying some more. Then, he quietly raised his head and looked at them. His face and attitude could be said to resemble the look of Jesus Christ who faced the mob with swords and bats on the hill of Gethsemane!

"What is it, fellows?"

"Are you Rev. Son?"

"Yes, I am."

"Then, let's go to the office for a little bit. I got things to ask you." After this short conversation took place, Rev. Son began following them without putting up a fight. The parishioners of Aeyangwon Church had already received the news and surrounded the front gate of the church. He leaned on the cane with his weakened body. With his pale face hanging down a bit, he walked out the church door silently. Many in the crowd wanted to block his way while screaming and crying. One of the persons in the branch chief's entourage sensed this sentiment of the crowd and yelled, "Comrades, be quiet and do not follow us. Rev. Son will only go as far as that office at the gate. We have some questions to ask him. If you do not remain quiet, this would work against Rev. Son." That was the reason that people stood there with teary eyes doing nothing.

Not knowing these circumstances, Deaconess kim felt that she might never see Rev. Son again said, "What is this? Let's just follow him," as she began walking with a limp. However, the crowd stood there just looking at Rev. Son and Deaconess.

As the afternoon sunlight at Aeyangwon infiltrated the shadow underneath the tree, everyone stood there frozen like a group of chicks looking at their mother hen being taken away in the grips of an eagle.

The 20th Century Court
Chapter 7

"Hey, what do you think will happen?" An old mister, Jang, asked Shin who was next to him.

"I don't know," said Shin as if he was annoyed.

"If a person like you does not know, then who knows? Please, anyone, tell me what you know, so that I am not so anxious inside!" Jang who was in his old age fought hard to keep his tears from flowing.

"How can anyone know what will happen? These days, even bombing has died down. When I went out to the town to receive my lessons, I saw the poster on a wall that said even Masan was liberated by the communist forces." A student named Kim Chang-Su whispered to Jang, the elderly.

"Masan!" Jang's response to him was loud.

"Yes," said Chang-Su in a weak voice.

"Liberation? What liberation?" Jang said begrudgingly as he cried again.

"Shut up, you dogs! Who told you to speak? If you don't listen to me, you will get a bucket of water poured over you," yelled the jailor who oversaw the center for reindoctrination. For a while, silence prevailed.

"Let's believe in Jesus. Believe in Jesus and go to heaven. Heaven," a voice of an old man echoed throughout the dark and gloomy jail. This voice of an old man witnessing Christ was one sound that could not be blocked out.

After the tragedy in Yeosu and Suncheon Incident, there had been a great loss of life due to the fighting between the leftist and rightist camps. Now that the communist forces swarmed into the south, those zealous leftist partisans who once were active in the wake of the 8.15 independence but were later driven deep into the woods came back and took the control of the Yeosu region once again. As a way to promote themselves, they took into custody police officers, rightist organizations, leaders, rich farmers, businessmen, and government officials. Though many fled to Busan, a great number of people were arrested. Among the arrested were those who did not feel that they would be arrested because they did not do anything wrong. Some of them were arrested while hiding out inside their houses. The jail was still full of people even though many who were charged with serious offenses were swiftly executed. The jail was so crowded that there was no room to sit down let alone lie down. It would have been better if people were allowed to speak. This was also prohibited. However, some carried on their conversations stealthily and intermittently as opportunities presented themselves. At times, they were safe. In other times, they were caught and suffered serious punishments.

The offenders were labeled collectively as dogs. The South Korean soldiers were called 'yellow dogs.' Policemen were called 'black dogs.' Christian were called 'the spies for Americans.' Pastors were called 'the bastards of Americans.' In this way, they were called names in harassment. However, there was a person who was in the old age of seventy three and set on dying as a martyr. Without resting or getting weary, he witnessed Christ to those who were seated next to him or his handlers. His name was Rev. Cho Sang-Hak and he was the pastor of Deokyang Church.

If someone yelled at him, "You, old dog and spy for Americans!"

He answered, "Believe in Jesus."

When someone said, "Why don't you shut up?"

He said, "Yes, let's go to heaven."

"Are you deaf, you old thing?"

"Let's believe in Jesus and go to heaven."

Rev. Cho initially fled when the communist forces entered Deokyang on July 27. But he thought of how he did not have an opportunity to die as a martyr during the years of Japanese rule and came back to Deok-Yang. Then, he watched over the church and led worship there until he was arrested. He began preaching the gospel even to the communist soldiers thinking, "This is the time to hold the scale and measure one's faith on this scale." While preaching the gospel, he awaited for his arrest by taking bath every morning, thereby keeping his body clean. When he was taken into custody, he changed into a new set of clothes and left for Yeosu. Once taken into custody by the Yeosu security office, he kept preaching the gospel without ceasing. Though he dealt with a lot of discomfort in many ways due to his bad hearing since his younger years, he ignored whatever people hurled at him in words and endured all kinds of sufferings and gave all he got in preaching the gospel.

"Hey, give me some water."

"Shut up, there is no water."

"Why no water, I hear the sound of water flowing."

"What you mean, the sound of water? It is only the sound of peeing."

"Please, it is not. Give me some water."

"Shut up, you, son of a bitch. If you could do whatever you want, we would have left you at home. Why would we bring you here? You, crazy? You, son of a bitch. How was it to sit on a swivel chair and suck the blood of your fellow citizens? So, you are thirsty today, huh?"

The one who kept on asking for water said, "Oh," and could not say anything anymore. But after a pause, he started again, "Hey, look, Mr. Comrade, kill me when you ought. But give me water, please. My body is feverish."

"What? Mr. Comrade? When did I become your comrade? You, son of a bitch. I don't want you to call me your comrade."

"Well, do not be so mean. Please give me some water, Mr. Comrade. Water." He acted as if he was gasping for breath.

"All right, if I was like you, would I give you water?" The man brought a cup of water as if he was being greatly charitable. The one who asked for water gulped it down. Then, he acted as if he came back to life and closed his eyes saying, "Oh, now I am alive." There were many who envied him getting the water.

When it was the hottest, they put twenty eight people inside the jail which had the capacity for only twelve people. Every day, they gave out two or three balls of barley in the size of a large duck's egg wrapped with seaweed along with soybean paste or a handful of salt. Six individuals shared a bowl of water when eating their meals. Besides that time, they did not see water at all. It was a terrible situation. Ingesting soybean paste or salt taken with their meals made them all the more thirsty. This posed a great difficulty for someone who suffered from a fever. However, being unable to sleep at night posed another kind of suffering.

One could not expect either the food or the sleeping condition to be good inside a jail. But it was another thing to push twenty eight or thirty persons into a jail that was made for only twelve persons. It was too small to lie down in let alone sit up in. Those who were falling asleep had to fall asleep and those who were awake had to sit quietly while everyone tried to squeeze in. They could talk freely neither. If caught, there would be a hell to pay. But in fact, there was no way that anyone would find it comfortable to sleep in here. Not only were they concerned about what would happen to their lives, but they were also dying to find out about the wellbeing of their families on the outside.

Around midnight, there was a commotion outside and the door to No. 2 jail cell opened. Then, they shoved a person in the jail cell. There were people who looked up to find out who it was that came in to the cell. There were also those who fell asleep while sitting up due to hunger and sleepiness. The new person came inside, sat down, and silently closed his eyes. After a while, he said in greeting, "Fellows, how are you doing?" He seemed very comfortable inside the jail. However, no one cared to reciprocate to greet him as if they felt it was inconvenient to do so. They might have been more concerned about having one more person to fit inside the overcrowded jail.

Early morning on September 15, Chang-Su was surprised when he woke up. The reason was that he found Rev. Son at the corner of the jail sitting and praying in his jacket. Though he wanted to inquire of him immediately, he refrained because he saw Rev. Son closing his eyes again to pray. He felt drawn by something to hang his head down and pray. Though he prayed before, he found renewed strength as his prayers deepened. He could not help but pray and cry at the same time. He thought, "How can a person like that pastor be put in here? What could he possibly have done that was so criminal? He is a saint who even forgave the person who murdered his sons, Dong-In and Dong-Sin, and adopted him as his own. Is he going to meet the same end as Dong-In and Dong-Sin did? Is he going to get the same treatment as all of us get? They are so bad." Then, he thought of Dong-In with whom he used to play and Dong-Sin with whom he used to work for the student association. He remembered visiting Rev. Son to comfort him after the death of Dong-Sin. Rev. Son said, "Dong-Sin? There is no worry for he has gone to heaven. It happened according to God's will. Chang-Su, you should also follow Jesus well!" He could not believe that Rev. Son who comforted him on that day had been arrested and brought into the jail right in front of him. His tears turned into sobbing. There was not even one person who asked him why he was crying or to stop crying. They probably felt that the young student was crying early in the morning because he missed home or was hungry.

On the other hand, Rev. Son was looking back on the last ten years of his life. It was the same month, September in 1940. It was the same weekday, Wednesday. September 25 of 1940 was Wednesday.

September 13 of 1950 was Wednesday, too. It was the same jail. During the Japanese rule, it was the jail of Yeosu Police Department. This time, it is the center for reindoctrination of Yeosu Security Office. Though the events were different and the handlers were different, it was the same battle of faith to Rev. Son.

10 months at Yeosu Police Department

4 months at Gwangju Detention Center

1 year and a half at Gwangju Prison

A short period of time at Gyeongseong Jail

5 years at Cheongju Jail until the 8.15 independence

Though he was released upon the independence, he gave his two sons as the sacrifice of martyrdom during the Yeosu tragedy. Now that he was again incarcerated at the center for reindoctrination, the past ten years seemed like a broken cruel dream!

Perhaps, because the film of the past 10 painful years had finished running through the silver screen inside his head, Rev. Son opened his years one hour after Chang-Su first recognized him.

"Aren't you Rev. Son?" asked Chang-Su.

"Yes," said Rev. Son as he turned his face.

"When did you come in?"

"Last night."

"When did you come?"

"Last night."

"On what day were you caught by these people?"

"On the 13th, but who are you?"

"Yes, I am Chang-Su."

"Who?"

"I am a son of Elder Kim of Yulchon and I used to go to the same school as Dong-Sin did. I am Chang-Su."

"Oh, I see. When did you come here?"

"About ten days ago."

As they were quietly conversing, all of a sudden, from the outside, someone shouted, "Fellows, believe in Jesus. Believe in Jesus and go to heaven."

"Be quiet, you, old man..." Someone rebuked him.

Hearing these words, Rev. Son quietly closed his eyes again. The voice was definitely familiar to him. It was surely that of Rev. Cho Sang-Hak. When he met him some time in the past, he told him, "I am embarrassed of my past that I could not fight as you did, Rev. Son." He heard about Rev. Cho getting arrested when he was on the outside. He realized that Rev. Cho was indeed here in this jail and wanted to meet him. Then, another young man spoke up, "Pastor, I am in this room also."

"Who is it?" He turned to look across the dark room.

"I am Guk-Jin."

"Mr. Choi, is that really you?"

Finally, breakfast came in after a routine roll call. For those who do not know what would happen to their lives each passing day or in the right next moment, breakfast time was one certain occasion that would provide them with the strength that they need to extend their lives to that end. They were served joy three times a day in the form of meals. So called meal was consisted of a ball of barley in the size of a duck egg, half-spoon size of unripe soybean paste, and a bowl of water given for all the people inside the jail. More than half of the incarcerated had been there since more than a month ago. It was not just one or two persons that fell ill seriously due to malnutrition, heat, and anxiety. In fact, they waited for the meal times as if they live only for those moments. Some even prowled with their eyes to see if anyone would not eat his ration in the hope that their portion would become bigger. These people shoved breakfast into their mouth as soon as it was given them. Then, the momentary joy of taking the last bite would extend until the next meal comes in.

But Rev. Son was different. With his share of vegetables on the side, he would give thanks to God at least for ten minutes for the food given him.

"Oh, Lord, thank you." Rev. Son's prayer in tears would make it seem that he had forgotten about eating the food.

"Amen," said Rev. Son as he opened his eyes.

"Did all of you finish eating already?"

"Yes, we did." The person with a long beard who was the unofficial captain among the prisoners answered.

Rev. Son cut the ball of barley in half and gave one half to the most hunger-stricken person in the jail and said, "Eat this. It gets awfully hungry in here."

"Yes," said the man as he put it in his mouth quickly. Rev. Son began chewing the other half hard. Choi Guk-Jin who could not eat when he was being held at the Yulchon police branch could bring himself to eat while here.

"Please, sit."

"Thank you."

"You must be suffering a lot."

"Not at all..."

When Rev. Son was being brought to this place, he passed through the Yulchon police branch. At that time, a command came down from the higherups that he needed to be interrogated at Yeosu Security Office and transported him to Yeosu. Other prisoners had to spend the night inside the center for reindoctrination, the jail, whereas Rev. Son was kept inside a night duty room. Even after he was brought to Yeosu, he was treated fairly. Though once a person threated Rev. Son by saying, "Are you that Rev. Son? You need to confess honestly," he was treated nicely in comparison to others. Having Rev. Son stay within the already overcrowded the center for reindoctrination and eat a ball of barely in the size of a duck egg was an unavoidable necessity. However, after being called out for the interrogation, the person who was in charge was friendly in his words and attitudes toward Rev. Son.

Yeosu Security Office was better furnished than the Yulchon police branch the day before. Inside were arranged in a line a post with a slogan and the portrait of Kim Il-Sung.

"I heard that you suffered greatly in prison during the Japanese reign," said the man as both he and Rev. Son sat down.

"Yes, moderately, uh, just a little."

"How long did you have to suffer?"

"I managed it somehow. It was six years."

"I am sorry for your sufferings. But I am sorry again. Would you fill this out?" The man said as he pushed the confession form to Rev. Son.

"It is all formality. If you fill this out, then I will make sure that you are released soon."

When he examined the form, things such as place of birth, address, name, class, social status, resume, and confession needed to be filled out. He found no problem writing down his place of birth, address, or name. But he did not know what class and social status meant. Then, he got to the place where it said 'resume' and 'confession.' He thought that he could fill out the resume part, but he was clueless about the confession part. So, after reading the form, Rev. Son began to pray. The man might have been annoyed by this, and he pulled out a cigarette and lit it. Even after the prayer, Rev. Son still did not know what to put down in the confession part. He did not know to whom he was to confess. He felt that there was nothing that he needed to confess to his captors, unless it was to God that he was confessing. People were not even worthy to be the hearers of his confession unless it was a report on things that he should brag about. Then, he might have something to write about...

"What do I need to put down in the confession section?" Rev. Son asked unexpectedly.

"Pastor, don't you know what that is? It is for you to make a confession... you made mistakes in the past, don't you?"

"Yes," answered Rev. Son. Then, after thinking for a while, he picked up the pen and wrote something down eagerly.

"You mean this?" Rev. Son handed his confession to the man.

The man read his confession and then gazed at Rev. Son as if he was dumbfounded.

His attitude changed. "You call this garbage your confession?"

"So, this is your confession, huh? You haven't suffered enough yet, huh?"

Rev. Son did not even touch the class and social status. He wrote, "From early on, I was called by God. However, my sin is great for not having evangelized the whole of Korea by sharing God's grace. For my sin of neglecting the blood of the Lord on the cross and failing to teach the truth of the gospel to the modern men who fight violently, I deserve to die. I deserve to die ten times over for my sins. I am so powerless, disloyal, and ignorant to do anything about this predicament where people commit indiscrimate murders and dream about the world domination through violence..." The man was at a loss for words after reading this confession.

"Hey, Rev. Son, my comrade, for what did you serve time in prison during the Japanese rule?"

"Was it because of Shinto worship?"

"It was against God's commandments."

"That's what I am talking about. You are wrong. What God's commandment? That is the commandment of American dogs. You served the anti-Japanese agenda to be a bastard for Americans. What you mean, God's commandment? Where is God?" The man tried to bury Rev. Son with his words.

Rev. Son did not want to deal with him anymore and remained silent.

But the man said again, "Hey, Rev. Son, my comrade, how much did you go around giving bad publicity to communism?"

"…"

"How come you cannot say anything?"

"…"

"Why can you not say anything? Who wrote that book, that *The Atomic Bomb of Love* or something?"

"It was my friend."

"Who told him to write it?"

"I don't know."

"What you mean you don't know? You forced him to do it, right? You also made him to do the production 'Hyang'?"

"…"

Rev. Son felt that it was not even worthy it to deal with him and stayed silent.

"Why can you not say anything? What I said was all true, right? You can never deceive me."

"From where were you taken?"

"I came from Aeyangwon."

"Shut up. Don't you know how many times that we sent people to Aeyangwon? You were hiding somewhere and communicating with the enemies by radio transmission, right? You could no longer hide, so you came out. Am I not right?"

"…"

This accusation was also groundless. Rev. Son did not say anything and hung his head down.

"Raise your head. Why do you put your head down time and time again? You are praying for our ruin again, right? If you wanted to be a pastor, you should have sat around and prayed. Why did you go around as a pro-American activist and serve as a slave to the American dogs?"

"…"

"Why do you go crazy working as a spy for American bastards?"

"..."

"Why can you not say anything? Hey, you, Rev. Son, you call this a confession? You, impudent bastard!" The interrogator pulled out something like a bat and hit Rev. Son with it several times. However, Rev. Son stayed still and did not open his mouth. In that moment, the door opened and someone called the interrogator out saying, "Comrade Cho, there is a call for you from Suncheon Security Office."

Rev. Son laid himself down on the ground in that empty room. He cried and prayed, "Oh, Lord! How can I refuse the beating that you took and how can I resist the misunderstanding that you suffered? How can I not receive the judgment that you received? How can I reject the suffering that you endured? Thank you for giving me the cross that you bore." The clock rang ten times. The portraits on the wall must have known that he would have victory!

On that night, Choi Guk-Jin awoke to a strange noise.

It was a groaning sound. "Argh, argh, argh..." Along with it, "People, I am dying. Argh, argh, argh...! Believe in Jesus, argh, argh, argh...! Revere God to go to heaven. Ah! Argh!" It was the sound of Rev. Son groaning unconsciously in pain. Earlier that day and when he was alert, he witnessed to others by telling them to believe in Jesus so that they could go to heaven. Now, he was in distress and was saying unintelligible things as he groaned in pain. Likely, it was due to the beating he took during the day.

Choi Guk-Jin was shocked to hear Rev. Son preach the gospel even in that unconscious state of being. Chang-Su who was sleeping in the middle of the room woke up to the noise. The two of them went over to where Rev. Son was and tried to nurse Rev. Son somehow. When the morning came, they asked the jailor for a doctor. When he got an injection of medicine, only then his condition got stabilized. In this way, Rev. Son got to be close to Choi Guk-Jin and Kim Chang-Su. As they spent time together, Rev. Son compared his experience of being incarcerated during the Japanese rule to that of his situation at hand. He used to say, "One day in here is as difficult as a month during the Japanese rule," as he gave half of his food to them.

And it was remarkable that Rev. Son prayed, memorized the Bible, and witnessed to others whenever he had time to do so.

"**F**ellows, what shall we do?"

"Well…" No one said anything because they were overwhelmed by the multifarious and urgent nature of the issues facing them.

"If you do not speak up, it would be greatly difficult to resolve them in the future." The demanding words of Elder Park added to the sense of discouragement that was already present.

On September 18, a secret meeting of the staff of Aeyangwon Church was called to discuss the issues at hand and choose how to respond to the challenges ahead. Rev. Son's arrest took place on September 13 which was Wednesday and the day of the Wednesday evening service. The parishioners of Aeyangwon Church mourned Rev. Son's arrest more than they would mourn for being estranged from their parents, spouses, and children. Since God was the only hearer of their petitions, they rang the bells just as they had done in the past to announce the Wednesday evening service. Then, many gathered to pray as cried and cried as they prayed deep into the night. Though they had prayed without sleeping and eating when Rev. Son was arrested during the Japanese rule. However, it could not match the degree to which people interceded for Rev. Son this time. They truly did not know what would happen to him once he was taken into custody. They felt that they should have ganged upon them so as to keep Rev. Son from being taken away! They also felt sorrowful about not having done everything to force Rev. Son to move down to Namhae or Busan. More than that, they thought that they should have let him go when Chorayng Church came to take him away as their new pastor in the wake of the 8.15 independence. People spent that night reminiscing about the past as well as being regretful and praying about many things. The next morning which was 15th, several people came from the police branch and forcefully demanded to know who gave them the permission to ring the bells and what kind of secret meeting that they had organized after sending Rev. Son away. On the other hand, they told them that People's Committee should be organized and to not ever again call for a prayer meeting or worship services.

Another matter pertained to what to do about Rev. Son who is behind the bars. Would it be better if they did not do anything? Didn't they at least organize a movement to free him? They first said that they would take Rev. Son as far as the office right in front of the gate. Then, they said that they needed to take him to the police branch because they could not have the quiet inside the office. Elder Park, then, begged earnestly that they should do it another day due to the ill health of Rev. Son. He also begged that since Rev. Son could not walk well, they would take him on a stretcher. All these appeals were rejected forcefully. They could not do anything but say farewell to him at the gate. Though the memory of feeble Rev. Son being taken away was still vivid in their minds, they continued to remain in the dark about what happened to him after that. They heard that when Rev. Son passed by the village of Guam-ri, he supposedly bid goodbye to the kids who were out in the streets by saying, "Be well, be well." Also, the mother of Bok-Rye who lived near Aeyangwon saw Rev. Son being led away to Yeosu Police Department as she was on her way back home from visiting her daughter. Rev. Son saw her and said that he was on his way to Yeosu and he went hungry without food the night before. This was how they learned that Rev. Son had been transferred to Yeosu. They were clueless about his status after that. This made all the issues to discuss urgent and demanded their attention. These issues were:

1. The issue of organizing a movement to free Rev. Son
2. The issue of organizing the committee for Aeyangwon
3. The issue of discontinuing meetings for Aeyangwon Church
4. The issue of dealing with people remaining in Aeyangwon
5. The issue of making personal decisions about what to do in the future

Besides these issues, there was one sensitive but at the same time lamentable and inconceivable problem of certain individuals within Aeyangwon that were being used as puppets by the elements on the outside. To start with, these individuals did not have a solid foundation of faith. They did not know what kind of trouble that they would have to face for if this staff meeting was somehow leaked to them. The punishment would not be so light. To say it bluntly, even the people present for this meeting seemed to fear that there might be spies among themselves and be cautious in their words.

"Then, let's discuss the agenda item by item. What shall we do to free Rev. Son?" asked Elder Park again.

"..." No one had a response.

Though this issue was of the greatest urgency, they felt that it was an impossible issue to resolve. Though they could very well compete each other about who could pray more to God, it would be almost impossible for the disabled like them to buy others with money or depend on others to wage a campaign to free Rev. Son. That was the reason for the continued silence. It would be like for a mouse to put a bell on a cat's neck.

"If you do not say anything, then what are we going to do about?" Elder Park asked once again out of frustration.

"Since our driver will drive to Yeosu tomorrow, send some money with him. Though it is not clear if they would allow the money in for Rev. Son, let's try it."

"But do you really think that they would honor our demand?" said someone.

"Well, though it might not work. Let's try it anyway. According to someone, there is a person in Yeosu right now who has leftist credentials and who used to be in the same prison as Rev. Son while he was in Gwangju during the Japanese rule. It is said that he regarded Rev. Son as a saint. We could go to him and negotiate with him. It seems that Rev. Son is regarded as a saint even among them. If it does now work, then it is the will of God. But shouldn't we try something that we can try?" The man who made the initial suggestion explained emphatically.

"Let's try that. Regradless whether he would accept our petition or not, there is no point for us to worry in advance and not try."

"Let's do that," people agreed. Then, someone said, "How much money should we use?" "Let's use ten thousand *won*," suggested someone else. Then, with the agreement of everyone, they decided to send the money the next day.

"That's that, but shall we stop at that? How about campaigning for his release?" The question was asked again.

One person suggested, "Why don't we discuss it with the person who is called 'Mr. Noh?'"

"Well, I do not know how to regard him really. It is hard to know if he has really repented or if he has put a mask on?"

"That might be so. But like he said himself, shouldn't we judge him based on what he has done while in Suncheon or here in Aeyangwon? Hadn't he refused to go out to work already even when people from the local government came out here and asked him to do some work?" the one who suggested it initially spoke again.

This so called 'Mr. Noh' was a young man who lived in a village not far from Aeyangwon and who was an earnest member of the communist party. Some time ago, he was in Geomun Island working at an elementary school there. When he was back home because of his sibling's wedding, he met a friend of his. Through his friend, he became a communist party member. At the time of the Yeosu uprising, he became very active as a member of the southern labor party. However, after the three days of uprising passed, he was arrested when the army entered and sentenced to capital punishment. But when his parents went and pleaded desperately for his life, he at least was spared the immediate execution of his sentence. For that reason, he was moved through the prisons of Daejeon and Mapo consecutively while serving his commuted sentence of twenty years. Around October in 1949, Rev. Son had a chance to lead a revival meeting at Seoul Seongdo Church. While he was in Seoul, he visited Mapo Prison to speak there. While there, Rev. Son sought out those prisoners who were from Yeosu, Suncheon, or Yulchon associated the uprising in Yeosu. He also visited Mapo Prison and carried out evangelism and comforted prisoners there. At that time, Mr. Noh had a chance to sit down with Rev. Son. He ate and prayed with him as well. Mr. Noh was influenced by this encounter with Rev. Son and came to respect him. And because of this, he subsequently decided to live a life of faith. From that point on, Mr. Noh asked about the wellbeing of Rev. Son both through writing or his relatives. In addition, he requested to be prayed for by others. Once, Mr. Noh's father came to visit Rev. Son. He told him that his son asked for a hymn book and a bible and inquired about how to get them. Rev. Son bought those books and sent them to him. They kept in touch until the 6.25 invasion happened. Right before the invasion took place, all the prisoners, particularly the leftist sympathizers, were sent to the south. However, Mr. Noh was not one of the prisoners selected for the release. It was only after the communist forces overran Seoul and opened up the prisons that he was able to find his freedom. But since he cleansed himself of his past, he refused his release saying that he was weak. When on his way from Seoul to his hometown, he used his influence to free a certain pastor's wife who was about to be killed by the communist soldiers in Suncheon. Rev. Son welcomed his safe return home and when he was hiding out in Aeyangwon, he allowed him to come along and stay with him. Because of these events, the staffers of Aeyangwon were torn between whether to believe that he had truly repented or been putting up a false front.

"But isn't it easier to know the ten feet deep into the water than a person's heart?" said someone in opposition.

"In seeking Rev. Son's release, shouldn't we ask someone we think is useful regardless of what kind of person he is? Besides, I am saying this because he emulates Rev. Son. Also, even if we try and realize that we were wrong, what would be our loss?" Another person spoke out. At the end, they decided to discuss the matter again the next morning. Though they did not think that Rev. Son would be swiftly executed, they had to urgently work for Rev. Son's release because they thought the counteroffensive of the UN forces were imminent and feared that Rev. Son would be harmed by the bombing by warships or airplanes.

Another issue to address is the organizational structure of the Aeyangwon committee and the discontinuation of all worship services. In truth, these issues were beyond their control. Even if they oppose the establishment of the committee, it would be futile. Even if they decide to keep the church door open, they did not know what would happen and if things would turn out to be the way they wished. However, the issue of secularists within them, those who came into Aeyangwon as refugees and became embedded within the community, was decided as follows. By telling people that since Aeyangwon was no longer a safe haven and they could not stay if any kind of controversy happened, they asked them to move out of Aeyangwon. However each person should act in regards to this issue, because it could not be ratified by the group. The reason was that the staffers were not in the position to dictate to others how they should act and it was only possible to take a passive approach to the issue. While they were to deal with each day as

The Atomic Bomb of Love

it happened, they decided to avoid clashing with malevolent elements among them. This was a resolution that did not resolve anything. Though it was not clear who said it, it was said that dissenters were to be summarily executed and healthy young men were to be conscripted into militias, and patients with serious health conditions were to be sent to Sorok Island, thereby disbanding the entirety of Aeyangwon. The leftist neighbors of Aeyangwon truly wished for this to come true. In this way, the submachine guns of communists were set on wiping Aeyangwon from the face of this earth.

"Mrs. Son, Mrs. Son"

"..."

"Mrs. Son, aren't you there? Yang-Geun, aren't you there?"

"..."

In this way, the voice called for Mrs. Son several times.

Only after a long lapse, Mrs. Son said, "Yes, who is it?" It was Mrs. Son that emerged. Her face showed that she had been praying.

Since Rev. Son was taken into custody, Mrs. Son did not feel the need to stay within the walls of Aeyangwon. Taking into consideration the decision of the staff meeting that requested all the secularists to move out, Mrs. Son came out of Aeyangwon and stayed at her family's house.

After the arrest of Rev. Son, Mrs. Son felt like not dealing with anything and felt intuitively that somehow she would never see him again. For this reason, she wanted to cry out to God while fasting. Furthermore, had something happen to Rev. Son, she had the urge to follow him in death. But when she counted the months, this was the month in which she was expected to give birth. Thinking of the baby within her, she could neither go hungry nor deal with her body in a reckless manner. Even without these conflicting sentiments, her body bore down on her heavily.

"Haven't I been surviving all this time despite losing my two sons,

Dong-In and Dong-Sin? But my husband was there with me, wasn't he? What if I lose even my husband? Then, what? I still have four young children with me as well as this baby within my body now. If something happens to my husband, I do not know what would become of my children and me. But if something happens to me, then, my children would definitely become a den of beggars, wouldn't they? What in the world happened to Dong-Hee who was in Seoul with Ms. Hwang? No. Nothing will happen to my husband. It cannot be..." thought Mrs. Son. In this way, she kept repeating the same thoughts in her agony for several days. That day was not an exception. As usual, she was praying in her tears that evening. In the middle of her prayer, she felt that there was someone who came to see her and came out to see who it was.

"Mrs. Son, I heard that Rev. Son would be released without being found of any crime."

"...?"

"According to Mr. Park who went to plead for his son's release, Rev. Son is likely to be released either tomorrow or the day after tomorrow." The person who came to visit relayed to her a message of vital importance.

"Really?" Only then, Mrs. Son opened her mouth.

"Yes, these are the words of Mr. Park. He thinks that his son will be released along with Rev. Son."

However, Mrs. Son was not readily relieved in her heart. Perhaps, it was November 19. The people of Aeyangwon sent money along with the driver in the hope of buying Rev. Son's release. But to their dismay, the money was not accepted on the ground that there is no such thing as buying one's way out of trouble as it had been the case during the Japanese rule. They also tried to have Mr. Noh lobby go to Yeosu and lobby for Rev. Son's release. However, he, too, was ineffective in his mission and just ended up wasting money. Mr. Noh lamented the fact that he did not have the clout that he used to have. Now, people believed that Rev. Son's captors made it a personal vendetta against him. For this reason, Mrs. Son had been distressed for several days. Furthermore, it was hard for her to believe that they would free Mr. Park's son who used to work actively for congressional campaigns and be on the staff of the rightist organization for young men. Since the communists frequently lied, she thought that they might have deceived Mr. Park in order to calm him down.

"Are you sure that's the case?" Mrs. Son asked again.

"Really. This communist partisan that Mr. Park knew informed him secretly."

Now, these words brought some relief to Mrs. Son. Mrs. Son did not think that, whoever this partisan person was, he gave Mr. Park a misinformation just to make him go away. In one corner of her mind, she remembered hearing about a relative of someone who lived in Aeyangwon who was supposedly a council member of Yulchon-myeon and in constant contact with the authorities in Yeosu. She wondered if Rev. Son's release had been worked out through him.

"Thank you so much."

"Please do not worry so much about it," the person walked away in the direction of Aeyangwon.

She thought, "My husband is going to be released without being found guilty of anything! How could it be? Listlessly, she gazed at the faraway sea that reflected the evening sunset for a long time. What is the reason that they are letting my husband go free?" She did not know if it was true or not, but she heard the rumor that the leftist groups were a little discouraged now that the UN forces landed on Incheon and the south Korean army landed on Gunsan and Pohang around September 15. She wondered, "Is my husband being released because of these circumstances?" She kept on thinking, "I heard that the leader of the leftist groups who used to be at the prison in Gwangju was now in Yeosu. Was it his favor that freed my husband? Or is it that they are releasing my husband because they realized that they could not touch him despite that they are leftists?"

She concluded her thoughts, "Oh, well, I should get dinner ready tomorrow and go out in the direction of Yeosu in the evening. Will he come by car? Will he be walking? It has been ten days already since he was taken away. I am sure that the complexion of his face changed a lot!" Her eyes became filled with tears and the image of the distant sea became blurry. "It is only tomorrow. Today is almost gone. What will tomorrow bring to people?"

Five days passed since that day.

Both inside and outside Aeyangwon, people were excited to hear the good news. The news was that Mrs. Son gave birth to a son in the morning of the 28th without any serious complication. She had waited for Rev. Son since the morning of the 24th, but he never came. Because he could not have come on the same day even he was released on the 24th, she believed that he would be back at least on the 25th. Therefore, as she waited for him, she sent someone out to the vicinity of Sinpung Bridge to wait for him there. The day also passed without the return of Rev. Son. She thought that, had he been released on the 25th, he would return home surely on the 26th. In this way, she waited for another day for him. It happened that the household of Mr. Park also spent the same day in waiting for him. Time to time, she sent a messenger to the house of Mr. Park to see if his son had come back. In the same manner, Mr. Park inquired of the Son's household. The day of the 26th passed also. Now, it was the 27th. That day was also nearing its end. It goes without saying that Mrs. Son continued to prepare food for each meal and a change of new clothes as she waited upon Rev. Son. Her heart seemed to be drying up. For some reason, the frequency of bombing kept increasing. She expected to hear something the next day which was the 28th. As she was spending the night of 27th in that fashion, her body felt different all of a sudden and she gave birth to a son in the morning of 28th. Aeyangwon secretly sent out people so that they could provide post-labor care for Mrs. Son. Mrs. Son, however, could not hide her tears for yet another reason. She felt amiss for not having her husband to celebrate this momentous event. Had he come back the day before or two days ago, he could have shared this joy of the day with her in the place of Dong-In and Dong-Sin.

She wondered, "Would he ever come back to bask in this joy? Or will it not be so? How can I send him this news if he will not be here for some time? It is out of the question that he would be overjoyed to see this baby in person. Even if he just gets to receive the news, he would be overjoyed."

Not knowing how to deliver the news to her husband, it was a matter of profound sadness to her. Even at the sound of a dog barking, she wondered if someone was coming near. Even the sound of a leaf falling sounded like the footsteps of her husband. Even the sound of children shouting outside sounded like someone calling, "Daddy!" The baby did not cry at all after crying a bit when he was just born. This was a docile baby, a good baby, a baby that Rev. Son would find so much joy in. For a moment, she forgot about the whole world as she looked down at the baby. But in that moment, her eyes were filled with tears!

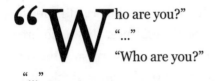

"Who are you?"

"..."

"Who are you?"

"..."

Though there was no answer, a man was drawing closer.

"Who are you?"

"..."

"Look out, a thief!"

"..."

Even at the shout, "... a thief!" the person did not run away. It was certainly a man that was coming closer. In fact, no one would come out to help even if one yelled, "... a thief!" It was a time when people could not walk around comfortably either day or night except the communist soldiers or local militia. Even if there were men around, no one was going to venture out and help the person yelling, "... a thief!" The man who was getting closer might be a thief who knew about this scenario.

"Is it you, Seong-Bae?"

"..."

"Aren't you Seong-Bae?"

The man named 'Seong-Bae' was a person in his fifties and mentally disabled. He traveled from Suncheon to Yeosu anytime he wanted. He was a mentally disabled with a semblance of normality for the fact that he was able to somehow obtain food from people wherever he went. Thinking that it might be Seong-Bae, she called out but there was no reply.

Mrs. Cha, the wife of Rev. Cha, who went out to pray in the quiet backyard before the dawn, was staying at Rev. Son's house for a period of time. She saw a shadow over the fence that was lit dimly by the fading moonlight and was stopped immediately in her track. She got scared, turned around, and ran back into her room.

This unknown owner of the shadow was Kim Chang-Su. He apparently obtained one life from the nine lives, emerged from the place of death alive, and came to Rev. Son's residence. He was covered with mud all over his body and wearing only an underwear. Mrs. Son whose body was beginning to return to normalcy after giving birth called him into her room upon finding out that he came.

"Oh, Mrs., quickly, Rev. Son to Mipyeong... Oh, I am cold, I am scared, quickly..." The young man spoke incoherently and collapsed on the floor. Having intuited what he meant, Mrs. Son thought out loud, "Oh, is that true? My husband has succeed!"

"What happened?" asked Mrs. Son frailly as she looked down on the newborn infant with teary eyes.

"Yes," said the young man. But it seemed like the young man was not alert. Mrs. Son was dying to find out what happened from him. So, she asked again, "Hey, young man, are you alert?"

"..."

Mrs. Son fed the young man who fell unconscious as soon as he ran into the room before sunrise a bowl of gruel. Then, she made a bed on the floor on which he could lie down. She thought about his words, "... Mrs., quickly, Rev. Son to Mipyeong...," but she could not make out what he really meant. Though she thought, "My husband made it," she could not be confident about what made her say so. Furthermore, she wanted to hear more from him. She wanted to verify what his words, "Rev. Son to Mipyeong," meant, whether he meant that he came to Mipyeong along with Rev. Son or whether he meant for her to go to

Mipyeong to meet him or whether he meant that something happened to Rev. Son in Mipyeong. Anyhow, she needed to wait until the young man had woken up in order to know the truth. Only thing she got out of the young man up to this point was only, "Yes." The young man finally gained alertness around breakfast time. He looked around the room and said, "Quickly send someone to Mipyeong. I was locked up in the jail along with the pastor. Last night, I was led to the place of execution along with others. I ran away from them when there was a chance." He began pouring out the details as in the following.

"So called the 'political strategy team' who supposedly came around six in the morning yesterday began arming themselves with weapons. Even those jailers who were in plain clothes armed themselves as well. During the morning session of ideological indoctrination, they said, "Today, all of us, the staff, decided to grant you release, so follow our instructions." Then, they proceeded to give us water and even allowed us to smoke. They seemed genuine in granting us our freedom. But I felt that our release was still in question, so I asked the pastor, "What will happen?" He said, "To us, it is not a question of our release, but of our triumph at the end. Pray more so that your soul does not get destroyed." Mr. Choi who was a member of this village and brought in on the same day as Rev. Son became overjoyed when he heard of the imminent release. He even said to Rev. Son, "Rev. Son, I will carry your bag on the way back home." Rev. Son replied, "Sure? Well, thank you. But I saw Dong-In and Dong-Sin in my dream last night. Do you think it will happen? Really?" When it was evening, they said that they would give us dinner. After counting how many poeple were there and feeding a roomful of people their dinner, there was a loud voice saying, "Do not bring dinner in and make them stop eating." When I looked through the slot through which food used to be brought in, I saw thugs armed with weapons coming near the door. Then, they flung open the door. They yelled, "Everyone, come with your belongings." They lined the men up and tied a rope around them one at a time. At the time, I did not know what to do. Mr. Choi who was speaking to Rev. Son a little while ago said, "I think they are going to kill us all." Rev. Son replied, "Well, they are going to kill us, then. Kill us, then. Pray hard now." He said this as if he was not troubled by the prospect at all and kept his reply short. Then, he got up and put his jacket on and let them tie him with a rope. After tying us all, they pushed us into a spacious auditorium. Then, they addressed us, "If we want to, we can kill you right now right here. But we will not do that. Instead, we will take you with us to Suncheon so that you would not end up being forced to serve Americans." So, you should remain calm and do as we say." The man with a gun strapped around his waist and a Japanese sword in his hand looked around and spoke with authority. Those that were tied up were all patriots and numbered around one hundred fifty or one hundred sixty. Again, he said, "Once we are in Suncheon, we will rehabilitate you ideologically and then release you to your freedom if you are obedient. If you need more rehabilitation, we will turn you over to those that are greater than us so that you would be turned into excellent communists. If you open your mouth or look to the side or try to run away, I will shoot you with this gun mercilessly. Please make a note of that." Not only that, those thugs that had us surrounded were holding Japanese swords, daggers, submachine guns, and pistols. It was a fearful situation." The young man seemed to be having a flashback of that horrendous scene and curled up in fear.

It was Sepember 28. The state of the war turned against the communist forces. After the UN forces landed on Weolmi Island of Incheon on September 15, the whole front line prepared to wage a huge offensive. Then, the UN forces overran Yeongdeungpo, took back Gimpo Airport, entered Seoul, and pushed on with crushing force. The outlook for the south Korean army turned optimistic as the communist forces could not help but retreat. But the communist forces felt it was too lamentable to let these territories slip away from their control for nothing. They also thought that these individuals would become a roadblock when they mount a counteroffensive later on, so they decided to get rid of them when they had the chance. For this reason, it was customary for the communist forces to kidnap and take the patriots along with them or have them killed.

Yeosu was not an exception in this sense. Like other towns and cities, one hundred fifty or so people of rightist persuasions were in the custody of the communist forces. Among them were businessmen, ship captains, the chair and members of the rightist association for young men, former police officers, the director of construction department, pastors, evangelists, the principle of a school and its staff, wealthy farmers, the chief inspector, the chief of a myeon, the director of post office, postmen, and laborers. Kim continued on with his words.

"By the time that we were instructed like this and taken out of Yeosu, it was past 10 o'clock. Since it was around the time of the festival of Chuseok (Hangawi: a major harvest festival and a three-day holiday in Korea celebrated on the 15th day of the 8th month of the lunar calendar), the moon was bright. When people became fearful of night bombing, they made us stop for several times. When I was still in the prison, I wanted to be tied up near Rev. Son. But it was not to be. Rev. Son was tied up next to Kang Dae-Seop who was a former detective and I was tied up next to someone else. When we walked, we walked in a line. There was Rev. Son. After him was a woman. Then, I was the next in line. I did not know what happened, but Rev. Son did not have his shoes on. One of the thugs asked Rev. Son for fun.

"What is your occupation?"

"I do not consider it an occupation, but I am a pastor," replied Rev. Son.

"A pastor? Then, are you the one who evangelized to many people while in prison?"

"Yes, I did."

"Why do you work hard to evangelize others?"

"I witness Christ to others because I want them to believe in Jesus and go to heaven."

"So, comrade, do you believe that heaven really exists?"

"Yes, of course there is."

"You are so vain, what you mean it exists?"

"Surely, there is, if you look it up in the Bible..."

"Ah, ha, ha, ha, heaven? Yeah, so go to heaven and live well there. We will just build our own heaven here on the earth and live well..."

"Forget that and why don't you believe in Jesus also?"

"Shut up. Who are you to witness to me?"

"I witness to everyone..." In that moment, the person who was leading the group ran up to them and yelled, "What are you talking about?" Then, he left the man who started the conversation in the first place alone but began beating Rev. Son with a rifle butt. Even as he was getting beaten, Rev. Son did not say anything. Whenever a gunshot was heard from behind, they said, "Well, a son of bitch is getting shot because he tried to run away," and threatened us that the same thing would happen if we tried to run away as well. After two hours, we arrived at the branch office of Mipyeong. Then, they had us sit down in a line and told us to put our heads down. Then, some of them gathered to one side and began to discuss about something. Afterwards, they told us, "Since bombing has been escalated, it is dangerous for a group of more than two hundred people to move together. Then, they divided the group into several subgroups. Once the division took place, they let the first subgroup leave first. After ten minutes, the sound of guns blasting away was heard from afar. When everyone was greatly shocked by this, the thugs gave out a barrage of cursing which sounded like an excuse, "Those sons of bitches, they tried to run away again! Sons of bitches, that's why you get shot." Then, they let the second group leave. Rev. Son was in this second subgroup. At the time, I was in the third subgroup. After Rev. Son's departure, I still remained where we had first stopped. Then again, the sound of gunshots and people crying out echoed through the air and seemed to shake the mountain. The thugs repeated the same thing in order to deceive us. I thought that something was up and was afraid to die thinking that my end had come. But more than fearing my death, I feared my sins more. If I was to die, I wanted to go to heaven and a prayer slipped out of my mouth involuntarily. Then, I heard, "The third subgroup, move out." They led us into an orchard next to a hill known as Suk Rock. Even before entering the orchard, I was able to hear people screaming and groaning. However, I could hear someone singing hymns even in the midst of cacophony. The smell of gunpowder and blood mixed together was unbearable. At the trunk of a fruit tree were many bodies squirming. Seven men hiding underneath a tree with their guns drawn in my direction suddenly came into my view. I did not know what happened, but I realized that my hands were no longer tied. This realization made me want to run. Then, I turned on my killers and ran past them. I did not know what happened after that or to which direction I ran, but I heard several shots being fired in my direction and I even heard the bullets flying past me. When I finally gathered myself, I was at the bottom of a rock. I climbed to the top of the rock and prostrated myself to pray to God. While I was praying, I was reminded of Rev. Son and said to myself, "What happened to Rev. Son? Was he able to run away like me? Or was he shot to death?" I wanted to know what happened to him and let you know at the same time. That's why I came to this place. On my way here, I thought I saw the communist soldiers and had to hide in the field of beans."

Chang-Su's eyes were filled with tears after telling this long story. Perhaps, the sight of Mrs. Son, a widow who had just lost her husband to endless suffering and the inconceivable reality of an infant that had not seen its father since birth by the matter of just one day might have pushed him to tears. No one knew when the whole family gathered, but they were there listening to the story. It went without saying that all of them were crying. Mrs. Son relayed the rough content of the story to Aeyangwon.

"Deaconess Kim, did you go and see the baby yet?"

"No, not yet."

"Then, who saw the baby?"

"I heard that Mrs. Park, the wife of Elder Park, went over there. The baby looked exactly like Rev. Son." Tears welled up in the eyes.

"I heard that, too. It is unfortunate that Rev. Son never got to see the baby..." The person sighed.

"Hey, go and see if they came," prodded sub-deacon Sung.

"Probably not. They said that they would let us know," said Deaconess Kim whose legs were not strong.

"Come on, go out and see. Who knows? They might have come already."

"Well, they said that they would let us know. For what should I keep going back out there?" She gave in to the persistent request.

After the arrest of Rev. Son, Aeyangwon suffered through its own share of hardships. The community was accused of opposing the communist government of North Korea, hiding of a radio, harboring the soldiers and police officers of South Korea and giving signs to UN among many other charges. In this way, the communists came out to Aeyangwon time to time to give it hard time. It might be reasonable that Aeyangwon was bombed at least once. But surprisingly, it never was bombed even if its vicinity was heavily bombed. No wonder, they felt jaded to come and bother the people of Aeyangwon. At times, they would call out all the staffers of Aeyangwon. Other times, they would call out just six departmental heads. Sometimes, they came and harassed the elders. They singled out Elder Park as a rightist traitor in particular. They would set up People's Court and investigate his wrongdoings. Once, they took him to a riverbank and threatened to kill him with a gun without bullets. For this reason, not a day passed without some sort of trouble.

It was September 28. The communists came to Aeyangwon on that night as well and brought out all the elders and deacons and threatened them as if they would kill them all. Though they made haste in accusing the people of Aeyangwon, since the charges were groundless, they ended up leaving Aeyangwon after telling them to think about what they did wrong and act wisely. They might have been a remnant of communist soldiers on retreat or members of local militia. Nevertheless, they spent that night in fear. However, the next morning, the news of Rev. Son being sent to a guillotine spread faster than a telegram. They heard that the news was based on the words of a certain young man who was also dragged to a killing field but somehow managed to escape alive. The entire Aeyangwon was turned upside down. There was no one who did not mourn. Immediately, the staff meeting was called and it was decided to send three individuals, Jeong Dal-Su, Hong Sun-Bok, and Kim Won-Tae, to the site of killing. It was still inconceivable for people to think that Rev. Son was dead.

The sentiment was strongest for Deaconess Kim and sub-deacon Sung. It was because they remembered the past hardship of living through the problem of Shinto worship. Since they believed that Rev. Son who was arrested during the years of Japanese rule would never falter in his faith, they kept the purity of faith even if they had to live the life of vagrants and beggars. They remembered how Rev. Son came to Okjong-myeon, Bukbang-ri, where they had been residing in order to retrieve Ms. Hwang and Dong-Sin. As God had miraculously kept him safe until they were able to meet him in this way, they believed in the possibility of another miracle. Even though he was dragged to the killing field, they believed that he would return alive. See the young man who was dragged to the place of his death but escaped to his freedom! Since sub-deacon Sung could not move due to her chronic condition of arthritis but was relegated to lying down, she kept on calling on Deaconess Kim to go and inquire of the situation. It was seven o'clock in the morning when the three individuals left. It would take them until four in the afternoon to go and come back even if they made haste. Though it was before noon, they were anxiously waiting to hear something. Then, around two in the afternoon, the rumor that someone saw the body of Rev. Son. It was said that his body was located inside the orchard of the myeon's chief beneath Mount Gwe-Ak in Mipyeong. Furthermore, it was said that his body was not damaged too much. Therefore, some people from Aeyangwon quickly retrieved the medical bag from the hospital, pulled out the bedcover, and put the emergency medications inside the bag, and left for where the body was supposedly while holding out the hope that he was not dead, but merely fainted.

That was the reason that they were so anxious and kept looking out the window. Also, they were not the only ones doing that. All the households, whether across from them, behind them, in front of them, or next them, were waiting for the dispatched party. However, despite their waiting, neither those who were sent out earlier nor those that were sent out much later did not return. This led to all kinds of speculative thoughts in the minds of people. People thought, "Can it be that the pastor was hurt only a little? Can it be that the disputed party could not locate him because he somehow made it to someone's house and is being cared for there? Is that the reason that they have not come back yet? Or can be it that the dispatched party is late in coming because he is hurt and cannot walk well and has to walk very slowly?"

In that moment, a lone voice cried out, "I think they are coming,

Deaconess Kim." People came out without asking in which direction
that the returning party was coming and just ran to the gate. Those that
were running to the gate met a few people that were running toward
them from the opposite direction. Apparently, the returning party was
not coming from the direction of the gate but from the direction of the
levee which was on the left side. From afar, a group of people carrying
a stretcher could be seen coming toward them. As the crowd watched
the returning party, they wished that the distance between them would
instantly vanish away. But they knew that the returning party was still
good forty minutes away in terms of walking distance. In the meantime,
all the people of Aeyangwon were gathered there. They were captivated
by the same thought and their gaze was fixated on the same target.

Six years ago, when Rev. Son was released from Cheongju Prison in
the wake of the 8.15 independence, he returned to Aeyangwon by taking
the same path. The joy they experienced then could not be compared
to the sadness they had now. It was beyond belief that Rev. Son who
walked out of Aeyangwon alive sixteen days ago was returning as a
corpse. If the former was Rev. Son's triumphant return in victory of
faith, then could the latter be described as the procession of a general
returning from a victorious campaign?

Everyone, whether young or old, men or women, healthy or sick, was
there. Except the shut-ins due to serious medical condition, even the
blind patients got to that place with the help of others. Even sub-deacon
Sung who previously depended on Deaconess Kim for information
dragged herself out there despite her painful arthritis in her legs.
The body of Rev. Son on the stretcher passed through the side door,
through the back aisle of the women's quarters, and into the yard of
the sanctuary. It was as if a saint's soul was being brought into the gate
of heaven in the midst of the welcoming of heavenly hosts and angels.
Then came the moment of lifting up the cover sheet! His face was pale
and soiled a bit. His lips were smashed open and showed his white

teeth. However, he looked as if he was peacefully at sleep. The hope of resurrection turned into a storm of grief and brought on a shower of tears. His two palms showed bullet holes. It looked like he was shot while he folded his hands in prayer. There also was a bullet wound on his shoulder. Due to the look of coagulated blood on his shoulder, he probably suffered for a long time before dying of massive blood loss. It was hard to describe the scene of leprosy patients beating their chests, tearing their clothes apart, embracing the corpse, putting their faces against his, crying, and wailing. No one knew how or from whom she heard of the news, but Mrs. Son was walking toward them from afar despite the heaviness in her body due to giving birth just a day ago! Only the fading sunset was guarding the tranquil night sky.

It was 9 o'clock in the morning of October 13.

It was Friday, fifteen days removed from the day of his death as a martyr.

While the rest of Korea was celebrating the takeover of Pyeongyang in addition to the recapture of Seoul, there were two thousand and one hundred leprous parishioners in Yeosu Aeyangwon where a round of commotion had passed through that were filled with grief, the very opposite of joy elsewhere.

They were conducting the funeral of Rev. Son who was a husband, wife, father, son, master, and servant to them.

The day was in the recent past, almost a half century ago.

In 1902, he was born as the eldest son to a poor farmer who lived in a tranquil mountain village in the region of Chilwon.

The gospel of the Lord called him. He lived, walked, and completed the life of a friend to lepers, an apostle of love, and a martyr.

If his hobby was being a friend to lepers,

If the six years of suffering in prison were ordinary to him,

If loving the enemy worthy of immense hatred was simple to him,

Then, it must have been his wish to meet the heroic death of a martyr.

Who would have known that grace, that power, and that providence of God that was borne out of the cleansing by the atoning bloodshed on the cross?

Aeyangwon was where he found the saintly beauty in the faces without eyebrows,

Where he touched eternal life in curled up fingers,

Where he searched for heaven within the flesh that was wasting away,

And what he could not forget even in his sleep and dreaming.

Not only did he teach through his words the kind of faith,

That was more precious than gold,

But he also protected his sheep from the whip of Shinto worship,

And shielded his sheep from ruthless fighting.

The church was where he defended his flock of one thousand one hundred sheep.

In that month of October from three years ago,

He cried out the nine reasons for his thanksgiving in that yard,

As he offered the two sacrifices of martyrdom,

In the manner of Abraham on the top of Mount Moriah.

The day of the 13th from a month ago,

He refused many opportunities to hide away in a shelter,

In the manner of Peter defending Rome.

That was the place where he was taken away by the Nero of the 20th century.

The sky is high and without clouds,

The sea is without waves and spread out with no end in sight.

It is 9 o'clock in the morning calm.

There were six hundred different kinds of funeral odes at the bottom of the funeral bier that had been decorated beautifully for many days.

The funeral was being carried out in a grand and solemn manner in the presence of distinguished guests from all over and one thousand one hundred parishioners of Aeyangwon.

Amid the tears of those in attendance, the program was conducted in the following order.

Opening word		Presider, Rev. Oh Jong-Deok
Hymn	No. 247	All
Prayer		Rev. Jung Gyu-Oh
Scripture Reading	Matthew 23:29–36	Presider
Special Song		Aeyangwon Choir
Sermon	About Martyrdom	Rev. Park Yun-Sun
Chronology of Life		Deacon Huh Young-Sun
Special Song	Duet	Students from Korea Theological Seminary
Eulogy	Representative from Aeyangwon	Deacon Lee Hyun-Cheol
Eulogy	Representative from Presbytery	Rev. Nah Deok-Hwan
Eulogy	Representative from Christian Newspaper	Mr. Kim Bong-Seon
Announcement		
Hymn	No. 252	All Adjournment

It took a great effort to push back those who were crying and clinging unto the corpse of Rev. Son as it was brought in. After washing the blood off the body, it was clothed and laid on a bed and placed inside a school classroom. Then, the body was placed in a casket and brought into the house of the pastor. After three days, the body was shallowly buried. Then, it was dug up again and prepared for the funeral. When Mrs. Son first received the body of Rev. Son, she prayed and cried. When Dong-Ryun who came along with his mother did not want to look at the body of the pastor because he was fearful, she said, "Dong-Ryun, this is your father who used to give you a piggyback. This is your father who loved you very much." When the body was being dressed, while caressing his eyes, Mrs. Son kept saying, "Do not worry about Aeyangwon anymore. Close your eyes in peace. Close your eyes in peace." At one point, she placed her husband's body on the bed and put the newborn baby in his arm and took a picture of them lying down together. The sleeping baby with his eyes closed resembled his deceased father so much. When the body was placed inside the casket, she looked at him through the glass opening and said, "Let go of your love and go. Let go of your love and go. Let go of the love that had been deepened for twenty-six years and go. Why is it so hard for me to let go of you?" In this way, she did not want to leave his side among many other things. I cannot record every single detail about what happened. When Jae-Seon ran in and embraced the corpse, he cried out, "You saved me when I was to die. How come you died before me? How can this be?" His mourning was so intense that it could have brought even the mountains, rivers, and forests to grief. Then, after wearing a mourner's hempen hood and hempen top coat, he carried out the duty that belonged to the eldest son of the family.

Once, before Rev. Son's arrest, Jae-Seon came to Aeyangwon and tried to convince him to flee. But Rev. Son did not heed his request. He, then, decided to defend Aeyangwon from the enemies along with Rev. Son. However, Rev. Son opposed Jae-Seon's decision and convinced him to return home to his family of origin so that he could care for his old parents there. It was because Jae-Seon's family anxiously awaited his return because his older brother had been conscripted into military as a South Korean soldier. And when the family had lost contact with Jae-

Seon's second and third oldest brothers who, before the war, lived and went to school in Seoul, his family dearly wanted to have him return home. When he finally went to visit home after spending several days at Aeyangwon, he was completely cut off from Aeyangwon because the communist forces moved in to the region surrounding Aeyangwon. One of the first things that the communist forces did once taking over a place was to recruit young men to form local militias. Due to the danger of being taken away and made into a militia man, Jae-Seon had to remain hiding inside his house. However, he had been getting the news coming out of Aeyangwon through a deaconess of Sinseongpo Church intermittently. One day, he received the news that Rev. Son was taken into custody. This tore him apart inside and made him vexed about what to do. He wished that he had been arrested along with Rev. Son. But he feared to face the local militiamen on the hunt of [rightists]. He thought about going to Yeosu and trying to win the release of Rev. Son by disclosing what he had done as a former communist. However, he did not think that he would be well received just for revealing his past. So, he discussed with his parents about what to do and yet he did not arrive at a good solution. In the meanwhile, much time went by. He was not satisfied with just sending food and fish to Mrs. Son who was pregnant at the time and for the family. Then, upon hearing that the communists had retreated away on September 30 and the news [of Rev. Son's death], he hastily made his way [to the funeral]. He did his best to fulfill his duty as the elder son from the beginning and to the end of the funeral, doing more than what Dong-Hee, Dong-Jang, Dong-Su, Dong-Ryun, and Dong-Gil could ever do. After the funeral, the body of Rev. Son was buried alongside the graves of Dong-In and Dong-Sin in Dongdo Island.

Several days passed. One early morning when the sun had yet not risen, there was a woman who was praying quietly amid the three graves on Dongdo Island. The waves were gently breaking on the beach and the salty breeze of the sea was blowing over the island. It was Mrs. Son who was, according to some, the most unfortunate person for having sent her two pillar-like sons and her husband ahead of her to heaven and had the responsibility to care for her little ones all alone.

This is how she came to this place.

Even when the funeral was done, she did not want to remain at home all alone. Her heart which first went into shock when Rev. Son was imprisoned due to the issue of Shinto worship became all the more weakened upon receiving the news of the deaths of Dong-In and Dong-Sin. Again, she felt like her heart was ripped apart when Rev. Son was taken into custody by the communists. But it was when the news of her husband's death reached her that her heart's condition took a dramatic turn for the worse. Now, it took only a mere thought about what happened to turn her body feverish and push her to the brink of emotional paralysis. Furthermore, going through the funeral of her husband placed a great strain on her postpartum body. At the time, she was not aware of the worsening physical condition. However, now as the shock of the whole event began to taper off, she felt pain all over her body as if she had been beaten up besides the enormous heaviness in her heart.

Her mental state was such that there would be angry outbursts at the smallest annoyances such as eating food, looking at clothes, and baby crying. If someone happened to say something silly, she would become so upset. Things got worse whenever she closed her eyes. The sight of Dong-In, Dong-Sin, and her husband lingered on in her mind. She was almost able to hear some kind of sound. She longed so much to say something to them. Of course, she could neither fall asleep nor remain sleeping. It seemed almost that the deceased would appear out of this corner and that corner. It seemed almost that they were calling for her from this place and that place. The world extolled her two dead sons as martyrs and praised her husband saying that he was a saint. But for her, being a mother of martyrs or a wife of a saint did not seem that great.

She preferred having her two sons alive to being a mother of martyrs. She would like to have her husband alive than being a widow of a saint. She thought, "Going to heaven as a martyr and being a saint in heaven would be great, but who would know all of my sufferings and pains that I experienced because of that? To whom could I supplicate? What could I do with the little ones that are growing up so fast? Who would guide Jae-Seon who was adopted as a son in faith and love? What would become of Dong-Hee who went to study in Seoul and had not come back yet? Rev. Son, my husband, who possessed great faith told me that he had dreamt of seeing Ms. Hwang and Dong-Hee alive, but even he is dead now. Who could say that seeing someone alive in a dream is the same as having the person alive in real life? Since Jae-Seon went to Seoul in order to find out what happened to them, I have not heard anything yet and I don't feel too optimistic. I know that Mr. An who is in Seoul would care for them well in times of peace. But with the war going on right now, I do not know what happened to them. If they are alive, could it be that they heard the news of my husband's martyrdom? Or could it be that they had not heard? Why would they not send a message if they had heard of the news? Deacon Lee said he heard over the radio that our soldiers kept on defeating the enemy and succeeded in pushing the enemy over to the other side of Daedong River. If this is true, then, it is likely that Mr. An, Ms. Hwang, and Dong-Hee are alive. They would have sent their word to me already..."

The stream of random thoughts flowed through her consciousness endlessly filling her head with noise. It brought comfort to her whenever she looked at her baby quietly sleeping oblivious of all the cares in the world. To think of the baby not being able to see his father and the father who died without seeing his baby was one undeniable cause for her heartache. She could not forget about her concerns and worries. She walked out of the house saying, "Well, I should go outside and get some fresh air!" Though she had not premeditated this, the path had led her to where the father and the two sons were buried.

She almost heard a sound coming from afar through the hazy moonlight. A figure seemed to be walking toward her. As she came in through the gate of Aeyangwon, passed through the single women's quarters, and passed by the sanctuary, she could hear the prayers of church members that were participating in an overnight prayer meeting. The figure of Rev. Son preaching at the pulpit suddenly flashed and disappeared. The sound of him preaching was heard before quickly fading away.

She walked past an unknown grave and walked over a dike to enter Dongdo Island. She felt as if the three persons were emerging out of the three graves saying, "Mother," but it was only the wind blowing through the pines. She thought, "Dong-Sin, you are lying down here. Dong-In, you are lying down there. My dear husband, you are over there. Should I lie down there as well?" The place did no longer look like a gravesite. It was a living room where her beloved husband and two sons were occupying. It was no longer a collection of graves on the ground, but a heaven and a paradise to which she longed to belong. She cried, "My dear! Dong-In! Dong-Sin! My husband! Dong-Sin! Dong-In, Dong-In, My dear!" She bobbled her head to left and right and front and back as she cried out. The words came from deep inside her as she recoiled her body. These words were blurted out of her mouth and the sound of her calling her loved ones turned into a lament. Though she wanted to wail freely, she could only cry, "Lord, what would you do with me?" in her prayer interwoven with her tears as she put her face down in-between the graves.

The three graves, however, did not say a word.

The three graves remained silent even they were called.

The three graves remained silent even they were asked.

The three graves remained silent even when she cried.

The three graves remained silent even when she laughed.

When will the trumpet of the Archangel blow?

The Day of Outdoor Commemoration

Chapter 10

"**A**untie!" She yelled out as she tried to wake up Ms. Hwang who was sleeping next to her.

"What?" she got up surprised.

"My dad did not die," said Dong-Hee happily.

"How do you know," asked Ms. Hwang again.

"Yesterday, in my dream..." Dong-Hee said hastily.

"I know that he did not die either," said Ms. Hwang as she clapped.

"Did you dream, too? Tell me."

"Why don't you tell me first?"

"No, please go ahead and tell me."

"You tell me first."

"Auntie, don't be like that. Just tell me first."

Each wanted to hear about the other's dream.

Even in the midst of the sudden onslaught of the 6.25 invasion, they were able to survive without any major problem until Seoul was retaken on September 28. However, they could not go home to Yeosu due to the lack of transportation. They could neither send a message to Aeyangwon in Yeosu due to the lack of telephone service nor receive news from home. They anxiously had been waiting to hear from home somehow. Whenever they heard someone had returned to Seoul from Busan, they would run to meet that person in the hope of hearing about Yeosu. Sometimes, they skipped breakfast. Other times, they wandered around till late hours to find someone who could tell them the news about their hometown. They heard that there were at least forty five or six pastors and elders belonging to various denominations such as Presbyterian Church, Methodist Church, Holiness Church, and Salvation Army who were either killed or kidnapped within Seoul. Among them was Rev. Kim Dong-Cheol, the pastor of Suhsomun Church where Dong-Hee and Ms. Hwang regularly attended for worship. Even in peaceful times, the household of the pastor was in bad financial situation. Now in the wake of the 6.25 invasion, when the two women went to visit the family, they learned that a greater poverty had befallen the family. This made them worry about home all the more. If Rev. Son were martyred, what had become of Aeyangwon? What had become of Rev. Son's family. These concerns literally drove them to insomnia.

When they visited Rev. Han of Seoul Youngrak Church who had returned from his hiatus in the south on October 8, he told them that he had not heard that Rev. Son fled to Busan. Around October 14, they met a certain pastor who told them that Rev. Son had indeed was martyred at Aeyangwon. However, on the same day, they heard from another person that American Navy had transported Rev. Son to safety either to Japan or America. Since they could not ascertain which story was accurate, they promised each other that they would pray to God to show them the truth in a dream. On the first night, there was no dream. But on the third night, Dong-Hee had a dream about her father. She saw his father in his unkempt appearance and with his pale face. When asked why he was the way he was, he said he had been in a cave fasting and praying and that was why he could not cut his hair. Dong-Hee interpreted this dream as meaning that his father was still alive and woke Ms. Hwang up right away to tell her so. According to Ms. Hwang's dream, Rev. Son came to her in a shiny white garb and his face was radiant. He was holding a Bible and standing with Mr. Jeong Hae-Geum. He said, "You two waited for me, right? You were so anxious thinking that I was dead, right? You see, I am not dead!" She initially did not know what to make of the dream because there was a saying that dreams usually conveyed what was opposite.

She wondered, "Does my dream mean that Rev. Son did not die? We prayed to God to show us the truth. Since he said, "I am not dead!" should I take it as meaning that he is alive?" Though she woke up from her dream, she remained lying down quietly as she tried to verify the veracity of her dream. But Dong-Hee got up first and concluded that her father were still alive. In this way, the two women were encouraged by what they dreamt and encouraged each other by sharing their dreams.

Such an experience attests to the axiom that those who dream are indeed happy.

"Mother, look at that bulletin. It says that Rev. Son died as a martyr!"

"What?" Lady Park was shocked to hear these words. She stopped sewing reflexibly and said, "When does it say he died?"

"It does not say the day but only that a memorial service will be held on Sunday the 29th of this month at 2 p.m."

"Where?"

"At Namdaemun Church."

Lady Park teared up as she conversed with her son. Around June of last year, she attended the revival meeting that Rev. Son led at Shindangdong Central Church and she experienced God's grace greatly then. At that time, she brought her unbelieving husband along to the revival meeting saying that a renowned saint of the world was the speaker. That became a turning point for her husband and he started to attend church regularly. Additionally, her husband who used to harass her for her faith both directly and indirectly for the past eight years stopped his mean ways. Since then, whenever Rev. Son led a revival meeting in Seoul, she would set aside everything and go to hear him speak. The last time that she saw him was at Donam Church's revival meeting and it was April 10 of that year. While she was wondering about where Rev. Son's next revival meeting was, the 6.25 invasion broke out. While she felt fortunate that her family was not harmed, it was shocking and sad to hear the news of Rev. Son's death.

She did not know where to turn for more information regarding the situation of Rev. Son's death. Since Rev. An Gil-Sun, the pastor of her church, was kidnapped himself and those who went south had not returned yet, there was no way of gathering information. Suddenly, she wondered if her neighbor, the wife of Deacon Cho, knew anything and she went over to her house at once. Mrs. Cho, however, did not know anything. Not knowing what to do, Lady Park and Mrs. Cho asked around and found their way to where the bulletin was posted.

The bulletin was posted on a wall right next to a burnt down lot. The bulletin was written in black ink on a white piece of paper which was incapable of answering any question. It was there just like Lady Park's son described.

The Memorial Service for Rev. Son Yang-Won's Martyrdom, the Apostle of Love

October 29, 2 p.m.

Presbyterian Namdaemun Church

They looked at each other and wondered silently, "Had he really gone away?" They saw tears in each other's eyes.

Suddenly, there was a flashback. One day in the past, she asked Rev. Son to write on a piece of paper when his birthday was and what his address was. He wrote his reply on that piece of paper, "My address is the embrace of the Lord. My birthday is the day that I was saved but I am not sure which date it was. Therefore, my life on earth is my life of living in a tent and I shall have my birthday party on the day that I enter heaven." As she reminisced, she thought he would be having his birthday feast in heaven about now. In that moment, she heard a passerby remark, "No! How can it be? Another great man is gone."

On the other hand, Lady Park's husband bought an evening edition of *Yunhap Daily* and was surprised to find the article mentioned right

below. He tried to walk home as fast as he could while reading the
published article.

Defending the Lord's Revelation till the End
The Godly Martyrdom of Rev. Son Yang-Won

Rev. Son who was known as the apostle of love had endured six years of
imprisonment for his refusal of Shinto worship during the Japanese rule
in Korea. In the years following the 8.15 independence, his two sons were
sacrificed as the offerings of martyrdom at the hands of their enemies during
the uprising in Yeosu-Suncheon Incident. Rev. Son had audaciously rescued
the killer of his sons from execution and adopted him as a son in faith. Despite
the communist invasion of 6.25, he remained at Aeyangwon Church in Yeosu
to protect the leprous parishioners with whom he had spent twenty five years
until he was shot to death in the early morning hours of September 29 by the
retreating communists who were fleeing the offensive of the South Korean
army. He was forty nine years old. A memorial service is scheduled at Seoul
Namdaemun Church on October 29th at 2 o'clock in the afternoon.

"Today, we are here for the memorial service of love of Rev. Son Yang-
Won, the apostle of love. When a person departs from this world, it is
conventional to have a memorial service of mourning for the deceased.
The memorial service serves as a forum of mourning and grieving the
death of the person. However, since the death of Rev. Son Yang-Won
could not be an occasion of grief, I believe that it is more fitting to call
this memorial the memorial service of love rather than the memorial
service of mourning."

The one who spoke these words in the opening address was none
other than Rev. Chae Jeong-Min who was seventy years of age and who
was both an elder colleague and a comrade in faith to Rev. Son. His
face evinced the deep emotion welling up inside him. With the green
pasture of the hill of Naksan (Mount 'Nak') in the east and Suam Valley
of Inwangsan (Mount 'Inwang') in the west and ever-green Namsan

(Mount 'Nam'), he stood somberly gazing at Yeonbong (Peak 'Yeon') of Bukhansan (Mount 'Bukhan').

He reminisced that it was just the month of February that year when Rev. Son came to his church in Haebangchon and led a revival meeting so graciously. He regarded the passing of a great servant of the Lord tragic and knew that there would never be another person who could represent the living history of the church of Korea better than he did.

If Joseon Dynasty were but an empty dream of a long spring day and if the period of thirty six years of the Japanese rule were but a sleepy day in summer, then three months of the enemy occupation were a dream of all dreams. The capital city was overrun in the wake of the 6.25 invasion. Seoul was retaken during the 9.28 offensive. The intersection of Namdaemun silently spoke of the things of the old. Now at 2 o'clock in the afternoon of October 29, 1950, on the lot of the church's ruins which was simply decorated with two Chrysanthemums, numerous Christians who lived within the walls of Seoul gathered for a memorial of Rev. Son on the one month anniversary of his death.

The words of the elder apostle continued. "I wanted to comment in the book *The Atomic Bomb of Love* that his sons did the work of God the Son and their father the work of God the Father and the author the work of the Holy Spirit. He even did the amazing feat of adopting the person who killed his two sons as his own. At the end, he died the death of martyrdom. People often speak of martyrdom. But we must make a distinction. Just because a Christian dies, it does not make him or her a martyr. The enemies will make even those who were arrested and killed for slandering into martyrs. However, the martyrdom of Rev. Son is of a completely different sort. As the devil thought it had won the victory when it had Jesus killed, many may have thought that Christianity would disappear from this nation if they killed Rev. Son and his two sons. That is the devil's greatest mistake. It is my wish that all of us become like Rev. Son..."

As people sang Hymn No. 155, "My one wish, Lord, is this alone; to serve Thee all my days, then rise to stand before Thy throne and sing thy deathless praise," many images of Rev. Son leading revival meetings in Seoul passed through their minds.

Not only did the images of Rev. Son preaching the word of truth in early morning, morning, and evening sessions as well as other designated occasions was given expression, but also the images of him speaking against a violent response to the uprising in Yeosu-Suncheon Incident and crying out to God in prayers regarding the issues such as idolatry of Shinto worship and bowing to the flag that were at the root of the nation's decline and visiting those in prison to encourage them by saying, "I am a sinner just like you," and not minding wearing a woman's overcoat and walking down the street in a scarf made of fox fur as if he could care were eulogized.

Then, the prayer of Rev. Lee Hak-In came next.

"Heavenly Father who controls the matters of life, death, disasters, and blessings and who controls the rise and fall of a nation, I cannot understand your divine dispensation in allowing your servant's blood to be spilled. He was the servant who lived solely for you on earth. Not only did he cry out for the sick and ate with the sick, but he also gave his life for you, Lord, at the end. But now, we can no longer hear your gospel preached through his mouth. How could you take him away with all the things that are left to do in this land? Who would do your work? Since you granted us the second liberation, if you had allowed your servant to remain here a little longer, he would have done so much of your work. Now, what? I cannot understand your will in taking him away. However, help us to repent of our lukewarm faith of the past that prevented us from bearing the fruit in our Christian life and offering you our lives. We ask that you help us so that we could offer our bodies and minds in the same manner as your servant had done. Lord, you have been glorified through the passing of your servant. Give us the same grace and power so that we could also be just like him and offer you the sacrifices of martyrdom. Surely, there will be more occasions that demand the blood of your servants in this land which is in a time of great tribulation right now. I earnestly pray that the blood of your servant be a wheat seed that brings forth much fruit in our lives so that we could also bring you great glory. I ask you to preside over this service and grant much comfort to the family of the deceased. Since it is said that the descendants of the righteous do not die of hunger, give them their daily bread. I pray in the name of Jesus Christ whose love is so abundant. Amen."

The prayer was followed by the Scripture reading and sharing of the chronology of the life of the deceased. After these things, Deacon Kim Hong-Bok who fled to the south and visited Aeyangwon in the wake of the 6.25 invasion came up to the podium and gave the report on Rev. Son's death.

"Allow me to speak truthfully and honestly regarding this holy and mysterious event." Then, he proceeded to giving a thorough report on what he saw and heard when he had visited Aeyangwon and what had transpired at Aeyangwon and in Yeosu after he left. His every word made people weep. He spoke of how Mrs. Son gave birth to a son in the morning of September 28, the day before Rev. Son's death. He also described how the leprous patients at Aeyangwon mourned Rev. Son's death by saying, "When our parents abandoned us who had given birth to us and carried out their minimal responsibility by just sending us food, Rev. Son showed his love by sucking on our leprous sores. Now, who can we trust and how can we live?" He also reported how Rev. Son's son in faith and love, An Jae-Seon, carried out the role of the elder son in the place of Dong-In and Dong-Sin and how he cried out in front of the body of Rev. Son, "Didn't you save me? Then, how could you die first?" In describing this sight, Deacon Kim said that it was as if all the land was mourning along with him. Hearing these words of Deacon Kim, the audience could not help but break out in a loud lament.

The next in the order of the service was the sermon by Rev. Kim Chi-Sun who was the senior pastor of Namdaemun Church.

"I thank you greatly for coming and attending the memorial service for Rev. Son today. Though there are many beautiful churches within the walls of Seoul, I consider it a great honor and thank God for being allowing us to host this godly service on the burnt ground of our church. Moreover, I consider it an immense glory that I, an unworthy person, am given this chance to preach a sermon at the memorial service for Rev. Son." The introduction was followed by a sermon on Revelation 2:10 titled "Obey unto death." The sermon made a parallel between Joseph, a faithful servant of God of the Old Testament and Rev. Son. The points of comparison are as of the following.

1. As Joseph was faithful in opposing evil, Rev. Son faithfully opposed evil throughout his entire life.

2. As Joseph was faithful to the word of God, Rev. Son showed his faithfulness to the word of God by testifying truthfully to it.

3. As Joseph was faithful in carrying out his duty, Rev. Son faithfully served Aeyangwon.

4. As Joseph remained faithful through hardships, Rev. Son endured six long years in prison for the church of Korea.

5. As Joseph remained faithful even when in high positions, Rev. Son humbly remained faithful without losing himself in self-admiration even as he was praised greatly by others.

When the preacher was explaining his fifth point, many in attendance remembered how Rev. Son had once vociferously opposed the banner that read "The world's greatest saint, Rev. Son Yang-Won" in advertisement of the revival meeting that featured him as the main speaker. Rev. Son's disdain of self-promotion was such that he objected to preaching until the banner was taken down.

The preacher then proceeded to make his last point.

6. As Joseph obeyed God unto death, Rev. Son also obeyed God unto martyrdom.

The preacher continued, "The basis on which these two great men of faith were able to obey unto death was first their faith, second their love, and third their hope."

In conclusion, the preacher said, "The martyrdom of Rev. Son will greatly contribute to this nation becoming a Christian nation. For this reason, Rev. Son's martyrdom is priceless. As per the words of Apostle Paul, we should run the race and run it till we die. I believe that there will be numerous people in the Korean church who place their hope in heaven following the example of Rev. Son's martyrdom."

In this way, the sermon that spoke of confidence and hope generated by Rev. Son for both the church and the nation of Korea as came to an end.

After being introduced by the presider, Rev. Park Hyung-Ryong went up to the podium, gazed at the audience with a grim face, held up the paper on which his eulogy was written, and began speaking.

"Rev. Son who is the only pride of the Korean church and the standard-bearer of the greatest love had left us and gone away to the afterworld."

"Though he did not intend to leave us on purpose, it already has been a month since he fell tragically to the bullets of the enemies. He had left this world as we know it and become a man of history. Now, we are no longer able to receive teaching from him or witness his actions in person. Only thing that we can do is to open up our spiritual eyes and commemorate his lived life with our words. We, the members of the Korean church, have the obligation to earnestly, wholeheartedly, and continually cherish the memory of Rev. Son who is truly the only pride and the standard-bearer of the greatest love. It is because we would most likely not ever see anyone else like him in the annals of the Korean church again. No, he is indeed a saint of rare renown even in the annals of the world Christianity. Oh, how lamentable is the passing of Rev. Son! The Korean church had sent away a great hero in the annals of its history and Christendom lost a saint rare in the annals of its history. Though I do not know how to describe the greatness of Rev. Son, I will still try to speak of it by pointing out a few remarkable features of his lived life."

After glancing over the audience, he continued. "First, Rev. Son was a great man of godliness. His whole life was a breath of prayer and the Bible became his daily food that provided him with spiritual satisfaction and a full measure of thanksgiving. In this way, despite bone-permeating poverty, he lived as a godly man of uncommon joy and ceaseless praise. His body became shriveled due to six hard years in prison. One time, his family had to subsist on the monthly allowance sent in by their beloved son, Dong-In, which he earned by working hard at a factory. Dong-In used three *won* out of his monthly salary of twenty three won. Then, he would send the rest of it, all twenty *won*, to his family. The poverty in his life was such that a group of his parishioners including Miss Hwang had to go around asking for alms and people of Aeyangwon had to sneak food in to feed the family by saving a portion of tithes. Even in the midst of such hardship, he exhorted his father and his beloved wife and beloved children to be content, endure, and thankful through his letters. On another occasion, as he was following the procession of his two sons' caskets when they were killed, it was said that he was singing the words of Hymn No. 248.

> When all my labours and trials are o'er, and I am safe on that beautiful shore,
> Just to be near the Lord I adore, will through the ages be glory for me.

In his words at the end of the funeral of his beloved two sons, it is said that he listed nine items of thanksgiving. Indeed, there are tens of thousands of godly Christians, but there are not many that can be compared to Rev. Son. Therefore, we should earnestly, wholeheartedly, and continually commemorate this great and godly man in Rev. Son."

The audience waited anxiously to hear what Rev. Park would say next. What kind of commemoration was it...

"Second, Rev. Son was a great evangelist. He spent several decades doing the work of evangelism. Through his efforts, many churches were planted. It is not countable how many times he breathed life into the souls mired in sin as he visited and led revival meetings at churches all across Korea. When he came to the revival meeting at our seminary in April of last year, he said that it was his fiftieth speaking engagement since the liberation. How great would be the fruit of his work of evangelism accomplished through his life-long ministry of revival meetings? Even when he was imprisoned due to his opposition to Shinto worship and when he was interrogated by Japanese judges, he considered them as opportunities for preaching the gospel to government officials. It is said that the interrogation report on him numbered more than five hundred pages because he took time to explain his views on nationhood, divinity, Christianity, the Bible, sin, and the end times. His sermons were based on the biblical truths and articulated the experience of faith and were used powerfully by the Holy Spirit to move the hearts of his hearers. Therefore, we should commemorate Rev. Son earnestly who was a great evangelist."

The audience was busy picturing Rev. Son leading revival meetings in various places.

The sermon continued. "Third, Rev. Son was a great warrior of faith. He kept the commandments of God through a great persecution toward the end of the Japanese rule and maintained the fidelity of his faith and ultimately triumphed by enduring six years in prison. He suffered for a long time as a prisoner under trial. Having completed the sentence of a year and a half at Gwangju Prison, he was prevented from being released due to his lack of compromise on the part of his faith. He was transferred to prisons in Gyeongseong and Cheongju and had to endure many more years of imprisonment. Even among the saints who endured imprisonment in order to maintain their faith, Rev. Son was the warrior of faith par excellence. We should commemorate Rev. Son earnestly who was a great warrior of faith."

Everyone in the audience teared up. Among those in attendance was a certain person with the last name Kim who was moved to tears by these words spoken about the faith of Rev. Son. He was almost fifty years old and repenting of his sins of the past. Due to his family's poverty, he used to work for Gwangju Prison during the Japanese rule of Korea. Not only was he an unbeliever at the time, he acted as a pro-Japanese sympathizer in order to get promoted and be successful. For these reasons, he did not look favorably on Rev. Son who happened to be imprisoned for his opposition to Shinto worship. He was one of many who mistreated Rev. Son in order to break him down. He was reminded of the punishment he dished out to Rev. Son for his stubbornness in doing nothing but fasting and worshipping on Sundays. Rev. Son apparently had refused to work, bathe, and even eat what was a meager food ration on Sundays. This memory made him despise himself greatly.

In the wake of the 8.15 independence, he gave up his job and moved to Seoul with his family. Then, he had become a believer through his wife's family's witness. He now felt the gravity of his sin of mistreating

Rev. Son in the past weighing on him. One incident in particular made him feel guilty. Two years prior to the independence, around January of 1943 when it was blistery cold, an old man in his seventies came to visit Rev. Son at the prison saying that he was Rev. Son's father. He remembered how the old man did not deal harshly with his son in prison but conversed with him regarding his health and the affairs of the family. He regretted not giving the father and the son more time to visit with each other. Once, he thought about going to see Rev. Son in person and confess to him his wrongdoings and tell him about how he came to live a new life. But because he kept on postponing it though he lived in Seoul, he had now lost all opportunities to do so. That was the reason that he could not help but cry.

Rev. Park mustered up his strength and resumed.

"Fourth, Rev. Son was a great friend to lepers. He started his ministry for leprous patients as a young minister-in-training at Busan Hansen's Disease Hospital. He was ordained as a minister and began his parish ministry at Aeyangwon Church in Yeosu. Though there was a time when he ministered at a church of healthy civilians, he spent twenty five years as a friend-pastor to lepers and now he is buried along with his two deceased sons on the grounds of Aeyangwon Church. Though there are many who befriend lepers in the world, there is no friend like Rev. Son. Let's pretend that Saint Francis had ever dismounted from his horse upon meeting a leper on the road to kiss him in greeting. How much would we record that incident as a part of Christian history and praise him for it? Then, how much more should we praise Rev. Son who gave his life to serving lepers in their midst as their friend? We should commemorate Rev. Son earnestly who was a great friend to lepers."

As the story of Rev. Son, the greatest friend to lepers that had ever lived, was being told, there was a man who was crying alone under a tree that was a little removed from the crowd. He had a straw hat on and was dressed in tattered clothes. He could not take his outer coats

off where it was only appropriate to take them off. He could not sit
among the crowd even when he wanted to be close enough to hear
clearly what was being said. It was clear that he was a leper.

Rev. Son had the knack of visiting beggars whether it was in Jinju
or Daejeon or any other region for that matter. Especially, wherever
lepers lived whether underneath a bridge or deep in a forest, Rev. Son
would go and intentionally seek them out there. He worshipped with
them and carried out the work of evangelism among them. He also
exhorted them not to be a pest but contribute to the commonwealth
of their country by turning themselves into a factory of prayer despite
their disabilities. When Rev. Son was released from prison upon the
8.15 independence, he had a chance to stop over at Okjong-myeon
Bukbang-ri on his way home to Aeyangwon. Though he was worn down
in his body, he found some beggars underneath a long bridge in Jinju
Namgang and preached the gospel to them. One of the beggars who
was there kept on wandering around and happened to reach the vicinity
of Seoul. While in Seoul, he stayed over at the temporary shelter for
lepers which was located on the ground of Mangu-ri Public Cemetery
and was associated with Rev. An Gil-Seon of Shindangdong Central
Church. Last year, when Rev. Son came to visit the shelter as per Rev.
An's request, he was able to meet him and worship with him. Even
after that meeting, the man continued to receive news about Rev. Son
through Rev. An. However, in the wake of the 6.25 invasion, the man
could not find out about Rev. Son's situation at all. When he was out
begging the day before, he stumbled upon the bulletin about Rev. Son's
memorial service and learned about his death. In order to seek more
information about Rev. Son's death, he went to Shindangdong Central
Church but nothing was left of it on its burnt down ground. He heard
about the kidnapping of Rev. An and came to a dead end in his search.
He spent the night at what was left of a burnt down house near the
street of Namdaemun and came to attend the service the following day.

While being conscious of his status as a leper and careful as to be not conspicuous, he was paying tribute to Rev. Son in his heart whom he greatly respected. When a certain deaconess cried out, "Now, in whom can we trust with our lives?" he wanted to say exactly the same thing. As he was listening to the eulogy, he was once again amazed by the greatness of the man that Rev. Son was. At the same time, as he thought about how discouraged many lepers would be from now on, he could not help but weep. He opened up the Bible and took another look at the words that read "Luke 17:11–19." These were surely the handwriting of Rev. Son.

"Fifth," said Dr. Park as he hesitated to continue.

"Uh... fifthly, Rev. Son was a great man of love who even loved his enemies. When his two sons were killed during the uprising in Yeosu-Suncheon Incident, Rev. Son sent his emissary, his own daughter and Rev. Nah Deok-Hwan, to the authorities to negotiate for the freedom of the killer of his two sons when he was arrested and about to be executed. Then, after negotiating in all possible ways and rescuing the killer, Rev. Son adopted him as his own son." Dr. Park spoke in a tearful voice. "I heard that Rev. Son rehabilitated him in faith and sent him to a Bible school to be trained as his successor. Rev. Son's actions put him on the top of the list of those who were able to love their enemies. It is truly the glory and pride of the Korean church that Rev. Son's name was spread throughout the world. We should earnestly commemorate Rev. Son who showed his great love even to his enemies."

It was rather comfortable to be under the autumn sun's rays in that evening. Suddenly, an airplane appeared from one side and flew over the place dropping leaflets. The crowd hated the sound of a passing airplane and were eager to hear what the speaker would say next.

"Sixth, Rev. Son is a great martyr who now wears the glorious crown of righteousness. On the third anniversary of the deaths of his two sons, which was September 28, he was shot to death in an orchard by the communist soldiers that were busily retreating out of Yeosu at night.

The crying of the crowd went up a notch. Dr. Park's voice was also tearful.

"Before the communists arrived, he had many chances to evacuate and save his own skin. But he left behind to be with the patients of Aeyangwon. He had the heart of a shepherd that could never desert his distressed and poor flock. Knowing that he was arrested and killed in that manner while keeping watch over the church, I can say that he was a good shepherd that gave his life for his flock of sheep." His voice seemed to have conveyed something to all the pastors in attendance including all the church staff members who had failed to honor their duty.

With strength, Dr. Park once again spoke. "Who among us could doubt that he was crowned with the glorious crown of righteousness in heaven? We should commemorate the great martyr in Rev. Son eternally."

In this way, Dr. Park had listed six reasons for his tribute to Rev. Son. After a pause, he picked it up again.

"We do not have a proper title with which to sum up the godly man, the evangelist, the warrior of faith, the friend to lepers, the lover of enemies, and the martyr in Rev. Son. Perhaps, the title of saint fits him the best. Even the Japanese jailor at Gwangju Prison was touched by Rev. Son's words and deeds to the extent of addressing him as a saint. How much more should we who had access to all facets of his life call him but a saint? Even the world could not avoid addressing him as a saint."

Dr. Park swallowed his tears. Then, he started again. "In my opinion, the history of the Korean church had not seen a saint like him for the longest time. It is also difficult to find a saint like him in the annals of the world Christianity. We call Saint Anthony a saint for his godliness. But he did not have the deeds of an evangelist, a warrior of faith, a friend to lepers, a lover of enemy, and a martyr. Though we admire Saint Augustine and Saint Francis, they also did not have the credentials of having lived with their families and died with them. Justinus, Hus, and Wycliffe gave themselves up as martyrs, but they were no friends to lepers or lovers of their enemies." In this way, after having mentioned the saints of the old, Dr. Park lifted up his teary face, lifted up the manuscript in his hand, and cried out, "Therefore, being compared to other people, it is clear that Rev. Son is indeed a rare saint even in the annals of the world Christianity!"

"Oh! Do you, the world, know this Rev. Son who is the sole saint that the seventy-year history of the Korean church has produced? Do you, the world, know that he is also a saint of uncommon renown in the annals of the world Christianity? Do you or do you not know?"

"You, the godly sons and daughters of the church of Korea! Lament the passing of the great saint, Rev. Son, and make an elegy for him. Let us earnestly and eternally commemorate his distinguished merits! Let us imitate at least one of his many examples. If we do so, the believers throughout the world will also imitate us in commemorating and following the footsteps of this great saint."

2 p.m. October 29, 1950
On the premise of Seoul Namdaemun Church
Rev. Park Hyung-Ryong

Dr. Park descended from the podium amid the cries of the audience.

1. Why has he gone away alone
    Leaving behind the thirty million kinsmen
    In this land that has so much work to be done
    Due to the collapse of the 38 Parallel?

(Refrain)
He dreamed of being a sacrifice of martyrdom all his life.

He dreamed of being a sacrifice of martyrdom all his life.
He sent his two sons ahead of him.
Did he go away in pursuit of Jesus?

2. With twenty five years of caring for the sick,
   With another six years of life in prison,
   With the offering of his two sons,
   Was he done with his mission?

3. He met the sword and rifle with gladness.
   He met the beating and whipping with laughter.
   He met his enemies with love.
   Was he finished with journey?

4. Over the hill of Gethsemane,
   Across the valley of Golgotha,
   To the top of Calvary,
   Did he go away in pursuit of Jesus?

As Ms. Hwang Sun-deok sang the song to the tune of "I Can Hear My Savior Calling," the crowd saw the life of Rev. Son being unfolded like a panorama in their minds and cried.

Especially, it was hard for Ms. Hwang to fight her tears as she sang the song. Ms. Hwang who knew Rev. Son's life better than anyone thought that it would have been better for him to have died during his imprisonment of six years [at the hands of the Japanese] than to have witnessed the uprising in Yeosu-Suncheon Incident, the pitiful in-fighting of church politics, or the eschatological collision of ideologies. Furthermore, she felt, had she known the things would turn out the way they did, she would not have asked [God] so earnestly to give her a dream. She regretted also not taking Dong-Hee home to Yeosu when the 6.25 invasion happened. After learning that Mrs. Son gave birth to a son the very day before his martyrdom, she felt like, if she had wings, she would have already flown over to where Mrs. Son was to find out how she and her infant son were doing.

Next in the order was the memorial address of Mr. Lee In-Jae. Two years ago, Mr. Lee was present at the funeral of Dong-In and Dong-Sin at Aeyangwon. Mr. Lee spoke of how Rev. Son was able to thank God for rejecting his own sacrifice of martyrdom that he himself offered for six years. Instead, he was grateful that God received the sacrifice of martyrdom from two young people who were uncorrupted by the world all at once. Mr. Lee also shared how Rev. Son continued witnessing to others even up to the moment he died.

"Rev. Son and I have been buddies from the same hometown. To summarize what kind of person Rev. Son was, I would say foremost that he was a person who learned to fear sin very early on in his life. He went deep into the woods to pray in order to get rid of the root of sinfulness in his life. He also fasted. Once, in order to kill his lust, he decided to become an eunuch and went down to Busan Railroad Hospital to have the surgery done. The only reason for not being able to follow through with his decision was due to the hospital director's refusal. From this one episode, we could easily know how much he fought against his own sins."

Everyone was surprised to hear this and sighed, "He fought against sin in that manner..." Once, there was an incident like this. Last fall, there was a revival meeting at Seoul Chungmuro Church. A group of young adults were gathered around two o'clock in the afternoon. When Rev. Son went up to the pulpit to lead the meeting, he felt like the Holy Spirit was not working in their midst. So, he said that there might be a sin that either he or those who were present had not repented of and instead of preaching, he led them through a time of praying out loud simultaneously. The audience agreed with the assessment of Rev. Son as someone who fought fiercely against sins.

The speech continued.

"After serving the sentence of a year and a half at Gwangju Prison, he could have returned home. But because Rev. Son understood the gravity of the sin of giving in to Shinto worship, he opposed it even if it meant doing more time in prison. The reason that he asked to be further imprisoned for life and transferred to Cheongju Penitentiary was this. He feared sin. Indeed, he was a rare saint born to the Korean church in the modern times. He was a true disciple of the Lord. Our Lord was a lamb of God that carried the sins of the world away. However, at the same time, he was called the lion of the tribe of Judah. Rev. Son who modeled himself after the Lord was in one aspect a gentle apostle of love. But in regards to fighting against sin and protecting the truth, he was as strong as a lion. In personal encounters with others, he was like a gentle lamb, but whenever he was preaching at a pulpit, everyone got the impression that he was as fearful as a lion. Today, we are commemorating Rev. Son who so fiercely fought against sin."

Out of nowhere, two pigeons appeared and flew over the gathered. The sight gave some comfort to the grief stricken crowd.

The last item in the order of service was the word of thanks from the grieving family. Until then, Dong-Hee had her head down and been crying. Her father who showed more affection to her after her two brothers were killed was now gone. Not knowing of her father's death, she spent the last three months in Seoul anxiously praying to God for her father's safety. She even prayed to God to reveal about her father's situation in a dream. Dong-Hee with a student haircut and dressed in mourning clothes walked up to the podium. People began to weep again at the sight of Dong-Hee. Standing on the stage, she looked down on the crowd for a while before speaking.

"Today, thank you, all the pastors, for providing such a grand..." Her words stopped.

She began to speak again, "... memorial service. I do not know how to thank you all mothers and fathers..."

In a tearful voice, she resumed, "... but I see you, pastors..."

"It is as if I am facing my deceased father in person. Just like when my brothers died in martyrdom three years ago..."

After a short pause, she continued, "... it is the same now that my father died in martyrdom..." Her words that followed swallowed in her tears.

The crowd responded in tears as well. When the service was over, it was around five o'clock in the afternoon. But no one did not leave the site but continued in silent tribute.

That day, a few of the leaflets dropped by an airplane that flew over the church found their way to the ground. They had a picture of the UN flag and the following words printed on them.

"The Symbol of Hope for the Unified Korea"

"The day of complete destruction of communism has come near. Almost all of North Korea is liberated and the UN is busy planning to establish the democratic government for the unified Korea. The goal of this plan is to rescue Korea from the ruins of war as well as to bring in the international aids to help reestablish the economic infrastructure of Korea that has been destroyed by the communists. All of patriotic Koreans are looking forward to the UN aids that will go to help constructing a strong and free Korea."

Would the hope expressed by the leaflets with the picture of the UN flag help unfold the life within the little wheat grain that was produced by the blood of martyrdom?

The Triumphal Song of Martyrdom

The Imposition of Shinto Worship

Red clothes,
Blue clothes.

Hands tied together,
Feet frozen and stiff.
His pale face hidden at least
Inside a criminal's hood.
An innocent criminal.
They say he most certainly poured out his blood.

Indiscriminate Fighting
Plunder and intimidation
Arson and destruction
Curse and murder.

How many souls did fall to the tips of submachine guns?
How many spirits disappeared at the blade of swords?
At the end, the land and rivers became a sea of blood.
The blood to succeed the cross was mixed with that of others.
Who could bury that blood deep in the ground?

If twelve thousand peaks are the pride of Korea,
If the history of half thousand years is the ivory tower of this nation,
Then, numerous martyrs are the glorious crown of Korea.

Mountains might change their shapes,
History might change its course,
But the blood of martyrdom will shine only brighter as time goes on.

Ah,
Dear martyrs,

Oh, you, the shepherd kidnapped and missing,
Your name will ever so brightly shine through thousands of generations,
Like that of Stephen,
Like that of Enoch.

However,
In the morning of the 8.15 independence,
Dark clouds gathered around the 38 parallel.
Then, the fierce wind of the tragedies in Daegu, Jeju, and Yeosu came.
Then, the storm of the student uprising in Shinuiju and the incident in Chodo
came.
Then, the 6.25 invasion of thunderous military power took place.
The rain shower of November 27 poured down,
And turned the land and rivers of Korea into a sea of blood.
What to do with three thousand altars of the Lord that were ruined?

What to do with one million believers without Moses that were pushed back
by the waves of the soldiers of the 20th Century Pharaoh only to ghastly gaze
at the fallen bridges of Red Sea, Daedong River, and Han River and to appeal
to the miraculous waves of water?

The remnant of all the tragedies includes the families with burnt down houses,
orphans without parents, elderly whose spouses and children died,
and mobs of beggars without possessions.
What to do with thirty million Koreans who wait for a Samaritan on the road
to Jericho?

But, more importantly,
What to do with those pastors' wives who used to hold their infants in their
bosoms in wintry evenings and incessantly pray in tears for their husbands in
prison while conjuring the images of their husbands preaching the gospel of
the Lord in the past?

What to do with all the sons and daughters whose parents were taken away
by the communists? They search the treacherous terrains of mountains and

valleys for the corpses of their parents based on baseless rumors.

What to do with the little children on the back of their mother who wanders around after putting her bags down on the ground without having anyone to ask for shelter in a rainy night?

But this is the path chosen by Rev. Ju Gi-Cheol who once headed to the prison after entrusting the care of his elderly parents to the Lord and Lady Oh Jung-Mo, his wife, who threatened him that she would divorce him if he got out of the prison by compromising his faith.

But this is the path chosen by the powerful evangelist of the slogan, "Jesus Heaven," Rev. Choi Bong-Suk, and Elder Park Gwan-Jun, the Elijah of the 20th Century, who was known for crying out, "Japan, a nation of idols, would most definitely collapse."

But this is the path that Dong-In and Dong-Sin took. They were the two slain lambs that cried out, "Why don't you stop and believe in Jesus? Since we are fellow Koreans, let us not fight. Our nation will be blessed only if we live in the spirit of Jesus."

But this is the path that Rev. Son Yang-Won walked. He loved his enemies to the point of adopting the killer who killed his two sons and becoming a sacrifice of martyrdom himself.

But this is the path that Bae Chu-Dal, a believer, walked who was committed to not violating even on iota of God's commandment and observed Sabbath faithfully.

Such is the path walked by the cloud of witnesses in the tradition of the Old Testament and the New Testament.

But, most importantly,

This is the path walked by our Lord Jesus Christ who said that foxes have their holes, birds in the air have their nests, but he did not have a place to rest his head.

How is it not something to sigh about, cry over, and lament about?
Since the imposition of Shinto worship turned him into Jacob, Peter, and Paul of the 20th Century, his red and blue clothes have transformed into the white garment of an angel, his two shackled hands have become the possession of the cross, his swollen two legs have aligned to the direction of the heaven's castle.

Who knew that his pale face with a criminal's hood on his head would become a glorious face with a golden crown on his head!

Since the indiscriminate violence turned him into Stephen, Peter, and Paul of the 20th Century, who knew that [his sacrifice] would make a flower bloom at the tip of a submachine gun, bear a fruit on the blade of a sword, cause the 12,000 peaks [of Korea] into the pillars of the fire of righteousness, unleash the river of love down the history of five thousand years, and turn the land and rivers of this nation into the dwelling of the Lord!

Ah,
Martyrs,
You, the shepherd kidnapped and missing,
Your name will shine brightly through thousands of generations.
Your families would follow your steps.
Young people would rise up as the heirs of your blood.
Over the hill called 'hardship!'
Across the valley called 'trials!'

March 23, 1951
The 1st Service for Memorializing Ministers Who Were Kidnapped and Remain Missing and Comforting Their Bereaved Families.

Betrayal Realized

Chapter 11

W ould some people say that the funeral was carried out hastily? Perhaps, it would have been better for people if at least the funeral had been long. Anyhow, after the funeral, there was a disturbing rumor going around within Aeyangwon. It was speculated that an insider had given Rev. Son over to the communists. Hearing this, who would not have been able to remain calm? On the other hand, how many would have believed it as likely? How ludicrous it was! What kind of preposterous charge it was! Everyone knew that it was the local militias or the security personnel that took Rev. Son into custody. And this was the most plausible account of what took place. But to say that a member of the Aeyangwon family betrayed Rev. Son over to the enemies was a terrible thing!

Furthermore, after the funeral, a revival meeting was conducted for ten days with Park In-Sun as the guest speaker who happened to come to attend the funeral from Busan. If something as speculated had truly happened, why would not have been revealed? After all, many were moved by the revival meeting. This impact of the rumor had begun to destabilize not only the six departmental heads of Aeyangwon and young adults, but also the elementary school students of the church.

"Hey, Bok-Sun, I heard Seong-Sim's mother talking. She said that the person who betrayed Rev. Son was at large within Aeyangwon. Do you know who it was?"

Bok-Sun grimaced in disgust and said, "What you mean by 'do I know who it was?' It is a rumor fabricated by people in the society who hate all of us here at Aeyangwon. Do you really think that there is someone among us who could betray Rev. Son?"

In fact, the society was a fearful place. It was so cruel to know how terribly the patients who ended up at Aeyangwon were treated by their family members and relatives when they were living in their respective homes. The society maintained its spitefulness toward this community of leprous patients and treated them as human parasites. Some of the spitefulness arose in part due to the society's regard of the patients' effort to make something of themselves as in their spiritual life as a vanity and annoyance. This tendency was evinced in the communists' action of ordering bamboo spears to be made with the intention of committing a genocide against this defenseless population.

"Elder, how could be remain calm when he hear something so incriminating?" A young man who lived at Aeyangwon seemed very much agitated when asking this question.

"If not, what do you suggest that we do? We also want to be exonerated, but don't you know that people say what they do because they do not know the truth of what happened?" The elder expressed a concerned look on his face as he gave his reply.

"If then, shouldn't we call in several staffers including the chairperson and try to find out who it was that originated the rumor?"

"Well, if it backfires, then people's feelings would be hurt. Until we have credible evidence, we cannot interrogate people based on a rumor. However, I realize that you cannot go about a fact-finding process without hurting people's feelings..."

It was truly a predicament.

"But can we really remain silent? If there is an evidence, we should get to it. If it was one of the members of Aeyangwon, then we have an obligation to make that person repent."

"I know what you are saying. Do not just talk to us about it. You should call a congregational meeting and let us push this thing in the direction of the decision that the meeting makes."

In this way, a congregational meeting was called and the decision was unanimously reached to investigate the truthfulness of the rumor by first locking up the chairperson and the clerk of the emergency commission and a few others and interrogating them. However, it was not as if the chairperson or the clerk of the commission was without a complaint. Who among the commission members did create the commission because they wanted to? Who among them did volunteer to serve as the chairperson or the clerk because they wanted to? Wasn't it warranted by the circumstances of having to make contact with the outsiders and maintain the duplicity of administration? Wasn't it true that they were forced to bear these responsibilities? Wasn't it done in order to receive food rations? Wasn't this the reason that they took on the roles as the chairperson and the clerk? Wasn't this the reason that they did not have anything else to do internally or even externally? Then, how was it that they were now locked up and being interrogated just because of a baseless rumor? They felt truly victimized.

"Hey, Mr. Kim, just spill your beans."

"What do you want me to say?"

"What you mean?"

"I am asking because I am clueless."

"You know why. It is concerning the person who betrayed Rev. Son over to the enemies."

"Well, I also think that is inconceivable. If I had known who it was, then I would have been the one to confront that person. Since I do not know anything about it, what do you want me to say?"

"If you do not know, then who knows it? You served as the chairperson and you had rapport with them."

"What? Rapport? What can you say that I had rapport with them?

On what base do you make that observation?" Mr. Kim was apparently outraged by the charge.

The young men who were in charge of the interrogation did not have anything specific to put forth as an evidence against them. If they were in the world, they would have resorted to torture in interrogation. However, since it was Aeyangwon where Rev. Son pastored, they could never do anything like that. But like the saying, "It is easier to see ten feet into the water than to peek into a person's heart," it was frustrating for them to not be able to know the truth. After interrogating the suspects for a long time, they put them back in the detention area. They could not think of anything else to do other than restricting their access to food as a way of pressuring them to confession. However, nothing would come of it if the suspects denied any involvement. In this way, the suspects were resigned to their situation and kept praying while waiting to be released.

"Comrades, who are you?"

"We are from Aeyangwon."

"What is Aeyangwon?"

"It is a shelter for patients with leprosy."

It was September 12. A young man with rightist affiliations happened to overhear the conversation. He was being detained for several days at a jail in Yulchon and waiting for his release. The young man's mind was now immersed in listening on the conversation. The conversation continued.

"Ah, I see, the one in Sinpung. Yes, I know. For what business are you here?"

"Yes, we came to petition for food rations for Aeyangwon."

"Listen, didn't the communist council inform you that rations would be given out to you already?"

"Yes, we were informed, but ..." There was a reason for the hesitation.

Since the 8.15 independence, the people of Aeyangwon which numbered one thousand and one hundred had been dependent on food rations given to them through the social services department of the government. Even under the rule of the communists, it was fact that their survival depended on food rations from the outside. The state authorities sent a message through the communist council that food rations would be given out to them on the condition that a communist council was organized at Aeyangwon. However, the people of Aeyangwon did not want to establish [such an intrusive arm of the communist regime on their grounds]. For this reason, a faction of the Aeyangwon staff decided to petition the communist council of Yunchun-myeon for a special permission that would allow them to receive two hundred fifty bags of rice. However, Rev. Son and several influential staff members resolutely opposed this decision.

Due to this development, more than the parishioners with families and female parishioners, it was some people from male quarters that could not withstand going hungry and began venturing out of Aeyangwon to beg for food. However, since people were less inclined now to be generous and give food to the beggars, this solution did not fare well either. A few who did not find the uncompromising position of the faithful too practical. To them, refusing outside help albeit that of the communists did not amount to freedom of faith but unnecessary stubbornness. They thought of submitting their complaint to the six departmental heads but gave up on the plan eventually. However, another idea came to them. They decided to visit the branch office and petition for food rations directly. But when the moment came for them to explain their petition, their words betrayed them.

"We already let you know. Why didn't you come and take them with you?"

While the conversation was continuing, other office workers who had gone out in the morning came in.

One of them asked, "Who are these comrades?"

"Yes, they are from Aeyangwon."

"Aeyangwon?"

"What business do you have here, comrades?" The man asked again.

"They came to ask for food rations," said the person who had been in conversation with them in the first place.

"Food rations? I heard that Aeyangwon refused to take in the rations assigned to them!"

"..."

"What is the reason for it?" asked the man again.

Not knowing how to answer the question, they replied, "Why don't you come and organize the communist council for us?" They answered the question by not answering.

"Oh, I see. We will be there tomorrow."

"However, before we go, we should know certain things about..."

"Those people that used to be there, are they still there?"

"Yes, everyone is there except a small number of people visiting home due to the scarcity of food."

"Are the six departmental heads there?"

"Yes!"

"Are there the elders of the church?"

"Yes!"

"How about Rev. Son?"

They blurted out their reply without thinking and came to regret having said it. However, they rationalized their mistake away by thinking, "Well, what could they do to Rev. Son? After all he is a person of great compassion that adopted even the killer who killed his sons.

"How about Mr. Cha?"

"Mr. Cha is not around."

"I see. In that case, we will be there to organize the council."

"Yes, please do."

When the conversation ended, those who came from Aeyangwon left to return home and the communists broke out into a propagandist song as if they got excited just thinking about what would happen the following day.

He did not know whether if he had been asleep or were dead. He knew for sure that he had been shot and fell to the ground. However, with his eyes open, he could tell it was nighttime by the moonlight and sparkling stars. He thought, "Am I alive? Or am I in the afterworld?" By the sight of things moving in front of him, he realized that he was not dead and tried to move his body a bit. He felt movement in his body. Now, the smell of blood and gunpowder was unbearable. Then, he realized that he was among a pile of dead bodies. Of course, he was. He and five others were dragged away and shot at by seven soldiers. It was just natural that he was found among dead bodies.

So, he lowered his breath and scanned his surroundings and tried to get up in order to run away. But he could not move because his legs were weighed down by dead bodies. Thinking that blood circulation was cut off in his legs, he gave himself some time before trying again. In that moment, he heard voices.

"Should we check it again?"

"Yes, let's do that." There was a sound of people walking. Checking what? How was it done?

"This guy is completely dead."

"This one has a faint pulse."

"He is still alive after spilling so much blood?"

"But still."

Suddenly, a voice cried out, "Ah, ah, you, sons of bitches!"

The young man opened his eyes instinctively and looked in the direction of the cry. He was able to size up a long sword reflected by the moonlight. It looked like a Japanese sword. Though he did not know exactly how many people were there, he could count at least three or four persons. The figures looked like a demon. These men were poking the bodies with their swords one by one. The scene of carnage made him want to run away instantly, but his legs still did not respond. He thought that he was really dead now as he tried to move his legs again. Still, there was no movement. The soldiers kept getting nearer. Without knowing what to do, he dug into the bodies with his head and held his breath. The men came to where he was. He felt a stabbing sensation in his body. He clenched his teeth in order to not make any sound. He withstood the pain of his body being stabbed at and kept himself from crying out in pain.

Then, he fainted. After a short while, he gained consciousness and realized it was a quiet night. Once again, the smell of blood was unbearable. He was able to lift his head up. He looked around to see where he was pierced, but he did not find any part of his body in pain. He lifted his arms up. The two wrists were still bound with a rope. One wrist was almost free. Before cutting the rope, he tried to move his legs, shake his ankles, and bend his knees. It was strange. There was no wound anywhere. He freed his hands by cutting off the rope and touched his body from the head to toes. There was no injury. He felt something mushy in his hands. It was the blood from a corpse next to him that was clotted on his chest. He tried to lift himself up. He thought, "Ah, it is working now." As soon as he got up, he sat down on the ground again. He looked around if there was anyone around. There was no one indeed. He decided to get away by crawling. As he crawled over a body, he thought he heard the sound, "Help me get free!" However, he was not going to stop at the sound. His head and shoulders kept banging into things. They were trees. They were not pine trees for sure. He thought they were some kinds of fruit trees. However, he did not have time or the peace of mind to figure out what kinds of trees these were. After a while, he ran into something sharp. He realized it was a wired fence with sharp metal ends. It was not difficult for him to get through the fence of the orchards. He got himself through the wired fence and to freedom.

These are the accounts of what happened that were reported by the young man who came back alive. He told the stories of what he overheard at the security office and how he suffered in the jail cell along with Rev. Son upon being told that the corpse of Rev. Son was recovered and the funeral was being arranged. He mentioned that Rev. Son would not have been arrested if some of those men who came to visit the security office from Aeyangwon had not been eager to volunteer the information.

No one knows who did it, but these words morphed into a rumor and went around the community that the person who betrayed Rev. Son over to the communists was at large within Aeyangwon. Those who went over to the security office in order to negotiate the release of food rations did not think that they had committed a crime by doing what they did. They felt that they were not guilty because they did not purposefully mean for Rev. Son to be arrested. They hoped that there was someone else who did really betray Rev. Son. However, the situation continued to worsen and turn into a huge scandal. Naturally, those who went to negotiate with the communists in secret were exposed and led to their confession.

However, people including Mrs. Son came to the defense of these individuals who came to understand the wrongfulness of their actions and repented. Even when the government office in Yulchon and CIC heard of their actions and came to arrest and prosecute those who were responsible, everyone defended the guilty parties and shielded them from harm. The underlying principle that guided these decisions was, "If Rev. Son were alive, how would he have treated them?" There was an incident regarding Rev. Son as in the following.

It was one spring day of 1946, one year removed from 1946, the year of liberation. Rev. Son was on a train bound to Gwangju. It was his first visit to Gwangju since liberation. He felt very much different from when he was being transferred to Gwangju after being taken into custody from Aeyangwon and spending ten months at Yeosu Police Station. The train was filled with people. Those that were returning home from Japan and through Yeosu packed the train. Rev. Son thought, "In the past, I was in chains though things were not as hectic as now. However, though I am a free man, I cannot move around because of so many people." He felt a strange sentiment coming over him as he got off the train at Gwangju Station. In that afternoon, Gwangju was a busy place. The sky over Mount Mudung clear and there was not even one speck of cloud to be found. But the streets were chaotic. After moving through the crowd in the direction of the west, he entered the spacious street leading to the courthouse. He remembered how he was escorted in chains by three detectives when he was being led away to Gwangju Prison in the past. It was a road that brought up all sorts of memories. He thought, "Do the people that are walking down the street know this or not?"

After walking for a while, as he neared the front of the courthouse, he suddenly hesitated in his steps. It was because the sight of seeing so many people entering and leaving through the door of the courthouse overwhelmed him emotionally. He sighed, "When would sins cease to exist? When would sinners cease to exist? This is the place where I was sentenced to the prison term of one year and a half. The building continues to remain here. But where have all the prosecutors and judges gone? The courtyard that I saw then is still here. But how many times have the flowers bloomed and withered?" Rev. Son thought about going to Room 5 where he used to be interrogated by detectives. But he decided to forget it. He thought, "What good would it do now?"

He passed by the front door of the courthouse and walked hastily toward the state government building of the South Jeolla Province. When he just entered the front door of the building, he saw a middle-aged man walking toward him. When the man lifted his head, Rev. Son was so surprised to recognize who it was. He was definitely a former detective that used to torture him. His name was Kinjo Hisao. He was a former enemy who made him suffer in prison not one year and a half but six years. What was more surprising was the color of the man's face. It was all yellow.

The man said, "Oh my, how are you pastor? When did you arrive? I should have gone to visit you already. Oh, pastor, please forgive me. I did what I did because it was a wretched time." He showed contriteness in his attitude.

Upon seeing this attitude of his, Rev. Son immediately went on to say, "Oh, no, what do you mean? It is all useless."

Rev. Son then put his hand forward to shake the man's hand. He said, "Mr. Geum, you should relax. I understand two things about the past. First, that was a terrible time. As Japan's power began to wane, they resorted to everything in order to win the war. It was a time when they tried to turn Koreans into Japanese, don't you agree? Secondly, your job was not a good one. Of all jobs, you had the job of a detective. Who would not have done what you had done in your situation? Why would you do the things that you had done to me if you had not been in that occupation? You and I are not enemies. Only that time and that occupation led you to do such things. But for me, it was the greatest test of my faith. It was the time when I had to decide whether to live or die in the presence of God. But since God gave me the strength to overcome the test, it is not a problem for me anymore. I had already forgotten about the things of the past. So, you should relax, too. Of what could I possibly forgive you? Only thing I ask of you is to believe in Jesus." In this way, Rev. Son used the encounter as an opportunity to share peace and witness the gospel to the man.

"Oh, thank you so much. I shall believe. I will believe most definitely." The man was able to move away from Rev. Son in peace. Therefore, how would Rev. Son deal with these men who committed a sin in their ignorance? Most surely, he would have offered them forgiveness. In this way, this incident came to be resolved without any trouble.

8.15, liberation!
It brought us limitless joy and hope.
The 38 Parallel!
It tied us up with a rope of limitless insecurity and terror.

In the morning sky brightened by the 8.15 liberation,
Dark clouds of the 38 Parallel appeared out of nowhere.
The storms of the uprisings in Daegu, Jeju, and Yeosu came.
The fierce winds of the student uprising in Shinuiju and Chodo blew.
The thunder of the 6.25 abomination roared.
The rain showers of 11.27 poured down.
The floods of blood covered all the land and rivers of Korea.
Who knew that the ridges of the five-thousand history turned into hills of the dead!

The seed of the gospel fell on my country and my land.
The seed sprouted and flowers bloomed within my nation and my people.
Elder Son used to pray day and night and Lord called him to be with him when he was in Harbin.
The two sons were preparing for their future and Lord called him to be with Him when they were in the backyard of Suncheon Police Department.
Rev. Son was busy protecting his flock left and right and Lord called

him to be with Him when he was in the orchards in Mipyeong.

Who knew that they would be called away to be with the Lord while they were working so hard to produce the fruit of indestructible eternal life!

If Jesus' betrayal by Judas who was his disciple was according to God's great sovereign will,

If Gandhi, a saint, could be assassinated by his kinsman,

If the assassination of Baekbeom, Mr. Kim Koo, by his fellow Korean marked the glorious end of a revolutionary,

It is not a coincidence that two sons were killed by their fellow student.

It is not a coincidence that Rev. Son was arrested due to the ignorant mistake of some people in his flock.

Who could know the ways of the Lord?

Who knew that a gift was to be given on the day of his martyrdom!

As Mrs. Son was being interrogated by the representatives of CIC, she felt her heart becoming jumping again. In trying to answer the questions posed, she teared up with Dong-Gil who was sucking on her breast and seemed to be oblivious to the world. She could not help but look in the direction of Aeyangwon and picture the graves of her husband and two sons in her mind.

"Am I indeed a fortunate person? Or the most unfortunate of all unfortunate persons? I became the wife of a so-called saint and the mother of so-called young martyrs. Isn't it a blessing that people of the world or ordinary believers could not have? Isn't it a blessing that other countries or nations could take away? But on the other hand, isn't my existence cursed to have sent my two strong sons away ahead of their time, been separated from my husband who was not yet old enough due to death, to have to bear the burden of caring for five little children alone? How did my two sons comfort me with their smiling faces whenever I cried the tears of sadness and breathed out a sigh of weariness! How did my husband encourage me to be strong in faith whenever the alluring temptations of the devil assaulted me! Now that they turned into a handful of dust, would there be a woman more unfortunate than me?" In the midst of these thoughts, she wondered, "Had we moved down to Busan then, I would not be in this situation..." She was reminiscing about the following incident.

Once, after the 8.15 independence, Busan Choryang Church had invited Rev. Son to become its pastor. Though Rev. Son initially refused the invitation, they insisted that he should come and serve as its pastor at least for two years. He considered the invitation as an opportunity to build up the church of Korea in the crucial years following the 8.15 independence. However, he did not make a decision either accepting or refusing. Instead, he told the church that he would pray about it. Hearing of this development, eleven hundred patients of Aeyangwon began earnestly to pray to God that Rev. Son would not leave them even if it was for two years. Even, the former director of Aeyangwon, Dr. Wilson, who came to visit the liberated Korea, pleaded with Rev. Son to "not forsake the downtrodden." These supplications convinced Rev. Son that he should not leave Aeyangwon even for a short period of time and decided against becoming the senior pastor of Choryang Church.

Had Rev. Son moved onto Busan Choryang Church, Dong-In and Dong-Sin might have been spared. Also, Rev. Son might have survived as well. These thoughts of regretfulness tugged at her.

Then, she thought, "But is it all God's will and the way of the cross." In that second, the words of a hymn flowed spontaneously out of her mouth.

The cross borne by my Lord, the people of the world refuse.
There is a cross for each and every person.
There is mine, also. I shall bear and carry my own cross.
I shall go to heaven to wear that crown of glory.

When she had finished singing the hymn, she looked down at Dong-Gil who was sucking on her nipple. He was now fast asleep. Mrs. Son laid Dong-Gil on the floor of the room and moved swiftly to the adjacent room. She emerged out of the room with the handbag in which she usually carried a Bible and a hymnal. Then, she quietly pulled out a few letters of the bag trying not to wake Dong-Gil up. These letters were only second to the Bible in importance and she took them out time to time to read. These letters were written by Rev. Son about ten or fifteen years ago.

The bygone yesterday
Old dream flowed away in time
These are definitely of Rev. Son's handwriting.
But where and what is he doing?
How about me right now?
What am I?

It seemed like the image of Rev. Son's smiling face pass over the letter held in her vibrating hand.

Dear my beloved Yang-Sun

I am sure that you had already received and read my letter that I sent previously. It must be hard for you to care for my aged father and the little ones of ours trying to make ends meet with the little you have. You must be tired and find it weary. I read on the letter sent in by my brother that everyone in the household is doing all right. Thanks to God's grace of protection and your earnest prayers, I am doing well physically and in my studies. However, to know that six households subsist on the harvest of one sack of rice makes me greatly concerned.

1) But I know that God who cared for us in the past would protect us in the future.

2) I know that since we are all God's servants, God would not make us work and keep us hungry at the same time.

3) Since we do not live by rice but by God's word, we would not die due to the lack of grains.

4) I know that since it is said that the righteousness would not die of hunger, we, Christians, would not die of hunger. Since we pray the Lord's Pray to God for our daily bread, I know that we would not die of hunger.

Therefore, what matters is that,

1) we have such a faith [that pulls us through difficult times].

2) and we dutifully carry out our responsibilities entrusted by God.

The money that I passed on to you through my father is already spent. It is the money saved by not buying a winter undergarment or even one book to read. It is money taken out of my tuition and sent to help out my father who is struggling due to famine and to make sure my wife and children do not go hungry. Since the amount of money is little and there were many things for which to use money, I entrusted it to my father who is experienced and my sibling who is good at budgeting things. I hope you would understand. If I come upon some money later on, I will send five *won* in your name. Use two *won* for meat and three *won* as per your needs. Though I am here studying, I share in the financial hardships we have. Since we are one as a married couple, what can we do? Let us suffer in joy. Our suffering is for the Lord and of the hope we share, aren't you joyful? Let's not grumble or whine. Let us not blame anyone and suffer gladly as we do it unto the Lord. Even if we go hungry, let us be hungry in joy. Even if we eat, let us eat together. When we suffer, let us do it in joy. When we cry, let us cry together. Living temporarily in this dreamy world, let us be harmonious in joy.

As she uttered, "Living temporarily in this dreamy world... true, it is indeed a dreamy world!" she changed the letter.

... the angels in heaven could not live on earth. Then, how much more should we, the children of God, live according to the world? Since our kingdom is in heaven, we should live according to the law of heaven and live only for God. In this way, we become the people of eternal life while we are here on earth. When we try to live for material things even a little bit, we immediately face things that cause us misery. Knowing this, we become certain that we are not of the world.

Now, it was a different letter.

I cannot describe how glad and grateful I was to receive your letter for which I waited yearningly. But when I read that you are suffering so much because of coldness, I could not sleep or eat. I was so pained in my heart that I could not even focus on my study. So, not being able to withstand it, I send to you two *won*. Please use it wisely to buy something to keep yourself warm from the cold. Though I want to send you even my muffler, I cannot send it for I am also suffering from cold and do not have anyone to send it with. I can assure you that the money is something that I procured in my earnest. Use it only to get something to keep you warm. We are suffering like this right now, we are suffering for the Lord. We do it in joy and God will bless us. Who knows? We might also live in abundance in the future.

There was a letter like the following.

... When the next year comes, I shall graduate from this school. Two years have already passed. The remaining one year is as good as gone. Do not envy [so and so] for buying rice paddies. Do not even concern yourself with it. Truly, when I see [so and so] buying up rice paddies through my eyes of faith, I am deeply concerned about the person. If he was just like everyone else, then it would be a normal thing to do. I want to admonish him in truth. But fearing that he would think that I am being jealous of him or that I am wrong in my faith, I cannot even admonish him about it. Only thing I can do is to pray to God that somehow he would come to his senses on his own. A minister is an apostle and a servant of the Lord. A minister is someone who imitates the prophets of the old in abandoning even what one owns. And yet, if a minister tries to make money and build one's wealth by saving up and resorting to buying rice fields, isn't that truly a dangerous thing to do? Even when I graduate next year, I will never plan to save up or purchase rice fields. Aren't we short in money even to help and support our parents and siblings? Though my father and children go hungry due to our family's meager situation brought on by my tuition, I do not plan on eating, wearing, and living well by disobeying the truth of God... however, instead of becoming destitute intentionally or squandering money without a budget, if we entrust it to the father and live according to the Lord's will... Since you will be the wife of Rev. Son next year, prepare yourself for it by praying a lot and having conviction...Rather than enjoying all kinds of pleasure of the world and living in sinfulness and discontent, how happy would it be for us if we become a family that enjoys the contented life of truth? This would turn into many blessings in the life to come. Even if there is no blessing for us in this world or the next, shouldn't we live with dignity and according to God's will?

One letter read like the following.

... Do not send Dong-In to school on the days of Shinto worship and make him not to bow before the Shinto temples. Tell him not to bow even if his school finds out it and threatens to or does indeed expel him. Since it concerns the second commandment, we could never do it. Please explain the situation to my dear father.

Suddenly, she was startled to find herself reading the letter in a tearful voice. Dong-Gil was awake with his sparkling eyes open. He might have awakened by her reading of the letter out loud. He seemed to think, "Why is mommy crying? What is she reading?" Looking at Dong-Gil, a thought occurred to her. "What if he asks me about his father when he is all grown up, what am I going to do? Will I point to the sky or in the direction of the grave in Dongdo Island?" It came to her as a dilemma. Another dilemma was, "What am I going to do on his birthday? Should I throw a birthday party for him or have the memorial service for his father?" She resolved the matter in her heart by thinking,

"Well, I should say to him that it is his birthday here on earth, and it is his father's birthday in heaven."

Here I would like to introduce one more letter to the readers as a way of reflecting on Rev. Son's journey of faith.

Dear father, mother, and my wife

All the signs point to the imminent return of Jesus. The fact that our faith is becoming weaker or that each church's situation is dire seems to attest that the Lord's return is near. That day will bring joy to those who live according to the Lord's will and love Christ, but it will be a day of fearful judgment for those who know only the world. How joyous would the Lord's return be for those who live for righteousness on earth and in truth for the Lord? Father and mother, since we decided to devote all our material possessions and even children to the Lord and live in truth, how great would it be for us if we live without complaining but only joyfully and gratefully? Job was a righteous man who was innocent and lived according to the will of God. But didn't God give him great trials and tragedies so as not to punish for his sins but to give him greater blessings? How blessed are we going to be if we live each day on earth for the truth and the Lord with persevering and patient hearts? If we live our lives daily striving to overcome trials through our true faith, it is said that though our exterior might age, but our interior would become renewed day by day. Though we experience the shortage of things and our bodies suffer greatly, don't we have the comfort of God and the joy and contentment of the hope that comes from looking forward to the future blessings and heavenly eternal life? If things are peaceful and good all the time, then who would not fail to believe and could we honestly call that a true faith? If we are able to keep faith that endures all hardships and sufferings, then how would we not think of heaven that we are promised? When I pray for you, my parents and my wife, I first pray for your health and the comfort in your hearts. Then, I pray earnestly that you do not become discouraged in your faith due to the physical pain and material needs. Since we have to go through this suffering, let us pray that we would live for the truth and in faith. I cry my tears in my supplication to the Lord more about the possible loss of faith and reduction of great future blessings due to current hardships than your physical pain. We might lose all our possessions, but we should never lose our faith. We might lose our health, but we should never lose the power of prayer.

Since we committed everything to the Lord, wouldn't he take care of it? God said that whosoever gave up his parents, wife, brothers, and children for his kingdom will be blessed on earth and receive eternal life in the life to come. God also said that we would receive persecution along with blessings and it is blessed to suffer for the Lord. Therefore, let us be joyful knowing that we are suffering for the Lord.

The joy that we have in bearing the cross is different from the joy that people in the world have. People in the world are happy when they have money, they are healthy, and their family affairs are in good order. However, the joy that Christians have is one of unconditional nature. They are joyful in all things even when in sickness, hardships, persecution, and suffering. Reading the letters from my father and wife, I see that you are spending these days lonely, saddened, and shedding tears. Personally, I am deeply anguished and at the same time feel guilty. However, if the household of Elder Son with three of its sons being servants of God which has the hope of eternal life and reputation of renowned faith could not endure hardships and be comforted in faith, then what does it mean to be blessed to believe in Jesus? How can we preach to unbelievers in the pulpits and out in the streets that to believe in Jesus is to live a blessed on earth and receive the gift of a peaceful heart? Even when in poverty, should we not have the abundance of spiritual grace? Even when our exterior age, shouldn't our interior become joyful and renewed each day? Dear beloved father or mother, I am not faulting you however. Every person in flesh is bound to become weakened temporarily when faced with hardships. But, I ask you to pray and be comforted by the Lord and look to the kingdom of our hope.

Even if we, your three sons, happened to be rebellious, wasteful in using up your wealth, and make you suffer, you should still be comforted in faith. How much more should you, my parents and wife, be gracious and deal with things in faith, since we serve the Lord and had given up everything in order to minister unto others? For those who stepped up to serve the Lord and nation, suffering is only temporary and joy and blessings are eternal.

In the old, Moses left behind the glory of the life in royal palace and went out to the wilderness. Also, had Paul not abandoned the riches and glory of the world and received suffering gladly? People do not understand that to suffer like this is indeed a great blessing and take it for granted. Many are afraid to suffer even a little bit and fail to endure anything. For it is a great blessing, ordinary people cannot receive it. I am so thankful and moved to tears because God had allowed us who are so feeble both in mind and body this great responsibility and blessing.

Come to think of it, knowing that hardships and trials facing our family is are getting more intense, I am sure that God knows that our faith is weak and is trying to train us. Each member of our family should realize this and examine one's faith and draw closer to the Lord. Though I am looking for opportunities to work for a church in order to alleviate the burden on you, my parents and wife, I find it strange that the Lord has not allowed it yet.

I know that we will be blessed both here on earth and in heaven only if we become resolute in our faith. I also know that God will help us immediately when our family have material needs. Therefore, do not worry that God is not helping us materially or be concerned that you are suffering in your body. But only think and pray how you can live your lives in faith and truth. Be ready to receive the Lord in flesh for the Lord's return is surely imminent.

I wish that you carry on the family devotion time and even if you are tired, do not fail to do your diligence in attending the church and reading the Bible. Let us cast all our burdens upon the Lord and live in faith. Everything works together for the good of those who live by faith. Also, those who live by faith receive the comfort of heaven.

May you enjoy peace in God and never change in faith.

April 2, 1936
Son Yang-Won

P.S. To my wife, I did not mean that Yun Byung-Hun will get off at Pyeongyang Station, but that I will meet him inside Pyeongyang Station and on its platform if you let me know when and in what train he will be arriving. So, just let me know the time of the train's arrival.

If He were Alive Today
Chapter 13

I n examining Rev. Son's faith both in expansive and in-depth manners, I wanted to ask the question, "If he were alive today, what would he do as he is faced with the nation that has lost its bearings as to where it needs to go, the church that has lost its ability to address sinfulness critically, and the ecclesial breakdown that allows for the continual expose of its past, thereby leading to sinning twice and three times over. This question led me to the following assumptions of mine.

First, he would have died all over again being shriveled and famished as he cried out in prayers for this nation and the church of Korea day and night. He led a pray life which made him to cry out in constant supplication whether in gratitude or in sadness. Only if we could remember Jeremiah of the old who never stopped crying for the doomed future of his nation, who of us would not cry at the reality of this nation and the church of Korea?

As I was penning this commentary, I happened to read the sermon of Rev. Kim Chang-Geun, the vice moderator of the Holiness Church of Korea, titled "Tears borne out of my love for the nation." He wrote,

> Tears are the noble result of one's emotions and the solemn expression of one's heart. Tears are never borne out of a convictionless heart. Also, tears from an upwelling of emotions could never be blocked off... Jesus, the Son of Man, cried out for his nation and kinsmen on the Mount of Olives. If we may examine his reasons for this,
> 1. He cried for the future of his nation. Because the nation of Judah betrayed the laws of God and walked the path of wickedness, the shadow of destruction

was drawing ever so near. Surely, the holy citadel, Jerusalem, was destroyed on September 8, 70 A.D. While Jerusalem had been in siege for four months, countless people died of hunger and some even committed the travesty of eating their own children. On the day of the fall of Jerusalem, seven hundred thousand died and ninety seven thousand were taken into captivity. Foreseeing the tragic future of his nation, Jesus wept.

2. Jesus wept for the past of his people (Matthew 23:37). For what reason, did they seek the fearful curse and pitiful end? It was the consequence of their killing of prophets and stoning whom God sent and disobedience to God. It's like the saying, "Beans sprout where beans are sowed and cucumbers are produced where cucumber seeds are sowed." As in the natural laws, the wages of sin is death. Looking back on the part of his people, Jesus wept.

3. Jesus wept for the present condition of his people dancing in sin. Whilst the invading hands of Roman Empire were upon them, the fate of the nation was in grave danger, the public was mired in misery, and morals had fallen to the ground, they turned their religion into legalism, leaders and those in power misused their authority and status to commit all kinds of evil, and rich people became obsessed with money making and pleasure, thereby being intoxicated in the present of wickedness. It was as if the fish in the water preyed upon the weak without seeing the net of the fishermen closing on them. It was a pathetic sight where people gave themselves up for play and pleasure without realizing the calamity upon their throat. They failed to heed the warning of justice.

I was deeply moved by this sermon. If the Lord wept for seeing the cause and the result of the predicament that was at hand and the future, then would he cry or laugh at the state of the Korean nation and the Korean church which is supposed to be the heart of its nation? Consequently, how would Rev. Son not weep if he were to deal with the current situation? I heard this about Rev. Son once. There was a contentious debate surrounding the issue of bowing to the national flag and the 36th General Assembly in the months of March and April, 1950 in reference to the problem of Gyeongnam Presbytery. As Rev. Son left for Seoul, he told his wife that he would fight till the end regarding these matters and that she should not think that he would return home in one piece. If he treated those issues that seriously, how much more indignant would he be concerning the pitiful situation of today? The end of the Korean nation! The tragic state of the Korean church! If the democratic bloc is defeated in the war, what to come in the future is so obvious. However, even if the democratic bloc wins the day, looking at the present state of this nation, it would not escape the same fate that India suffered at the hands of England which for several hundred years exploited and oppressed India. It would not escape the same irreparable end that American Indians met even after having their treasure house plundered. The reason for this is not because the foreign nations would be so mighty or ready to invade Korea. Rather, it is because my nation and my people are choosing the path of self-destruction.

Rev. Son said, "If we continue on this path, our land will become like that of Sodom and Gomorrah. And if we continue on this path, God will give us a greater whipping and the day of annihilation on the face of the earth will surely come for the nation of Korea." These words echo like a fearful prophecy. Therefore, wouldn't Rev. Son at the end collapse from the exhaustion of weeping and crying day and night?

Second, we can think of how he would have dealt with the church. I often hear people trying to add credence to their positions by saying, "If it were for Rev. Son, he would not have done this but that." The same happens whether it has to do with the problems of the presbytery or the church or the seminary.

"Rev. Ju Gi-Cheol or Rev. Son Yang-Won would not have done this but that." These are the words of those who try to strengthen their own positions. Many times, people push for the resolution of things by speaking to the urgency of the times. In these situations, if Rev. Son were alive today, on whose side would he be? In my opinion, before being on this side or that side, he would most definitely be on the side of Jesus.

After committing to the title of this chapter, I became deeply concerned. It was because I feared that it would end up being my subjective criticism. However, while I was writing the second half of Rev. Son's biography, the original file of Rev. Son's sentence of one year and a half in prison which contained Rev. Son's honest confessions before the detective and the prosecutor assigned to him happened to come into my possession. Upon receiving it, I became as excited as having gotten my hands on a star in the sky. Though I included the sentencing record in Chapter 3: Six Years of Imprisonment, I did not introduce the actual file and all the records found in it.

The file contains a written opinion, a criminal report, a report on the criminal suspect, an investigation report, a report of confiscation, a list of the confiscated items, an interrogation report (No. 1–3), an interview report, a report on witnesses (Kim Gyung-Ho, Shin Gil-Su, Huh Ok, Jeong Wal-Sun, Jeong Gi-Jae), and a report on suspect's conduct. All these records were from Yeosu Police Department and the detective from the police department of the South Jeolla Province.

The records from the attorney general's office of Gwangju District Court included an interrogation report (No. 1–4), an investigation report (2 witness reports... Kimura Michio, a witness report (Kim Gyung-Ho, Shin Gil-Su, Huh Ok), a request for a court hearing).

The records from the investigation department of Gwangju District Court included a file on Attorney Seon Jeong-Gye, a notice from the local administration office, a request for release, the record of a court hearing (the 2nd, sentence, a request for an appeal).

I pored over these records overnight and in a solemn mood. Certainly, these included personal accounts of Rev. Son. I cannot include the records in their entirety in this book, but I hope that in the next opportunity I will be able to introduce them to the world. Here, however, I introduce to the readers a part of the deposition that took place with a detective.

The Suspect Interrogation Report (The 1st Session)

Suspect: Daechon Yang-Won

The suspect is hereby interviewed by a detective regarding the suspect's violation of the Peace Preservation Law in front of Kinjo Hisao, a police officer of the South Jeolla Province of Governor-General's Office, on October 22, 1940, at Yeosu Police Department.

Q: What is your name and age?

A: My name is Daechon Yang-Won and thirty nine years old.

Q: What is your class and occupation?

A: I am a commoner and a Christian minister-in-training.

Q: What is your address and hometown?

A: My address is Yeosu-gun, Yulchon-myeon, Sinpung-ri, Aeyangwon. My hometown is Gyeongnam, Haman-gun, Chilwon-myeon, Guseong-ri, No. 685.

Q: Have you received any pension or award money or been a government official?

A: No.

Q: Have you ever received a criminal proceeding, suspension of indictment, or release with a warning up to this point?

A: No.

Q: Will you truthfully answer all the questions regarding the incident?

A: I will be honest in my answers.

Q: What is your level of education?

A: (Omitted)

Q: What is your work experience?

A: (Omitted)

Q: Through whose introduction, were you employed by Aeyangwon?

A: (Omitted)

Q: How is your health?

A: I don't have a particular illness.

Q: Tell me about your family.

A: (Omitted)

Q: How about your possessions?

A: (Omitted)

Q: What is your old name?

A: My name is Son Yang-Won, but I had an old name, Yeon-Jun, when I was a child.

Q: Tell me about your conversion to Christianity and background of your faith.

A: (Omitted)

Q: What are your views about the Bible?

A: There are the Old Testament and the New Testament in the Bible. The Old Testament mainly contains prophecies about the coming of Jesus Christ and the narrative of faith that runs through the coming of Jesus Christ. The New Testament deals with the fulfillment of the prophecies about Jesus Christ and exposits eternal life gained through faith and the doctrines about how to live according to the will of God as well as the end times and resurrection. There are in total sixty six Old Testament and New Testament books in the Bible that starts with Genesis to Revelation. What is written in the Bible is the word of God, Yahweh, and to me, it is a record of absolute authority that could never be changed or altered by anything. I made it my life-long goal to believe in the doctrines and receive the eternal life that is promised. God, Yahweh, is the father of Jesus Christ and Jesus Christ is the father of all believers. As I said already, flesh dies and returns to dust, but Jesus' grace of atonement on the cross allows for those who trust in him to be saved from hell and enter heaven to enjoy eternal life. Upon Jesus Christ's return, all the believers will undergo the union of their flesh and spirit and resurrect and enjoy eternal life with him. Therefore, the

Bible is the only guide for my life and bedrock of my faith. I believe that everything recorded in the Bible is true and will come to fruition.

Q: For Christians, what is God?

A: Christians believe the following about God.

1. God is love.

2. God is righteous.

3. God is light.

4. God is spirit.

5. God is the Creator of all things.

6. God is sovereign.

7. God is the Judge that will judge all people at the end.

If I may explain each item in depth,

1. God is love... It means that God sent his only Son, Jesus Christ, to the earth so that he could bear the cross and save all people who were condemned to death because of their sin. Jesus propitiated for the sins of all people on the cross.

2. God is righteous... God sets what is righteous and unrighteous for all people. God awards those who are righteous and punishes those who are unrighteous. Then, what is righteousness? Being righteous means being right and we find the standard of righteous in the Bible. Everything the Bible condones in it is righteous. Everything that is outside the boundary of the Bible is unrighteous.

Q: What do you think of the imperial edict for education?

A: If it is in agreement with the principles of the Bible, then it is all right. However, if it does not, then it is not right.

3. God is light... God teaches what sin is to people who do not know what it is. In short, God awakens one's sensitivity to sin. Next, God teaches about heaven and hell to which people will be assigned at the

end. In this way, God teaches people about who is truly God. God gives light to all people.

4. God is spirit... Though God is not visible to human eyes, God exists even in the heart. We call this God's omnipresence and almightiness. Omnipresence refers to the fact that there is nowhere God is not. Also, there is nothing that God cannot do.

5. God is the Creator... Everything in the universe was created by God, Yahweh. It says in Genesis 1:1, "In the beginning, God has created the heavens and earth." Furthermore, it says in Acts 17:24 that God created the universe and everything in it and there is nothing that God had not created with his hands. Of course, even Japanese Empire along with all the nations in the world was brought into being by God. Therefore, all the nations are being guided according to God's will. Though Amaterasu is said to be the divinity of Japan, it was all done under the sovereign command of God. Therefore, not only God, Yahweh, is the origin of the human race, but also Amaterasu was allowed its authority by God, Yahweh.

6. God is sovereign... God controls the three sources of light: sun, moon, and stars. The cycles of year, month, and day are under God's control. The matters of life and death of a life and the fate of a person are also under God's control. The emperor of Japan is a human being. Acts 17:25 says, "And he is not served by human hands, as if he needed anything, because he himself gives all men life and breath and everything else." Likewise, the emperor himself received his life, breath, and everything else from God including the land, people, wealth, the status as the monarchy, and even the authority to rule.

7. God is the Judge who will judge all people at the end... The Bible in its entirety, the sixty six books from Genesis to Revelation, reveals the will of God about the end of the material world. We call this eschatology. (Omission). The end time refers to the period of time from the first coming of Jesus to his second coming. This is Year 1940 according to

the western calendar. Though we do not know the return of Jesus would occur today or in a few years, it is certainly imminent. As an evidence, we can list all kinds of wars, droughts, floods, and outbreaks of serious diseases that affect the humankind harmfully and these are the manifestations of the end time. As we, Christians, wait earnestly for the return of Jesus Christ, we prepare ourselves to be ready for it and this is our faith. Upon his return, everything in the material world as in the present age, nations, people, power, status, and other things will be destroyed and the spiritual world will be established. The spiritual world is unlike the present age and refers to a world without sins. Here, those without faith in the present age will receive the wrath of Jesus and be punished and those with faith will attend the wedding banquet with Jesus. As wedding epitomizes the life's moment of greatest joy, the wedding banquet here symbolizes the apex of joy that believers are to enjoy with Jesus. The length of this wedding banquet is supposedly seven years. After the wedding banquet, the kingdom of thousand years will come. In the kingdom of thousand years, Jesus will reign as the king of all kings and those with great faith will be installed as princes and those with lesser faith or no faith will become the subjects of the princes. If the king of the present age is of great faith, then he shall be a prince. If he does not, then he will be a subject of a prince. Of course, the emperor of Japan will not escape this reality. The length of the kingdom of thousand years is one thousand years. In its aftermath, an eternal world will come. By an eternal world, it is conventionally referred to heaven and it is attested in Revelation 21 and 22. When this world comes, there will be 1) the transformation of material things, and 2) the resurrection of body. In heaven, there are twelve castles decorated with twelve jewels and twelve pearly gates. There will be no a) tears, b) suffering, c) illness, and d) death. Truly, this blissful world will continue eternally and people will enjoy this happy existence eternally. However, in this eternal world, the last judgment will be rendered by

Jesus Christ. Previously in the kingdom of thousand years, those with weak or no faith were made the subjects under the princes. But in the eternal world, unbelievers will be punished severely and exiled to hell by Jesus. Only true believers will be allowed to remain in this world. This is the Christian doctrine about God.

Q: Then, do Christians continue to criticize the rule by the emperor of Japan?

A: It says in Romans 13:1–7, "Everyone must submit himself to the governing authorities, for there is no authority except that which God has established. The authorities that exist have been established by God. Consequently, he who rebels against the authority is rebelling against what God has instituted, and those who do so will bring judgment on themselves. For rulers hold no terror for those who do right, but for those who do wrong. Do you want to be free from fear of the one in authority? Then do what is right and he will commend you. For he is God's servant to do you good. But if you do wrong, be afraid, for he does not bear the sword for nothing. He is God's servant, an agent of wrath to bring punishment on the wrongdoer. Therefore, it is necessary to submit to the authorities, not only because of possible punishment but also because of conscience. This is also why you pay taxes, for the authorities are God's servants, who give their full time to governing. Give everyone what you owe him: If you owe taxes, pay taxes; if revenue, then revenue; if respect, then respect; if honor, then honor." In speaking of authority, people were given authority depending on their social class from God. The authority of the emperor to rule the Japanese empire, the authority of the Governor-General to rule over Korea, the provincial governor to rule the province, the district magistrate to rule the district, and the town chief to rule the town were all given by God, Yahweh.

Likewise, all the kings in the world received the authority to rule their respective kingdom from God, Yahweh. As aforementioned, everything in the universe was created and is sustained by God. Since God, Yahweh, sustains even the emperor and has preserved the land of our nation by entrusting it to the hands of the emperor under God's rule, God can just as easily take our land out of the hands of the emperor and give it to someone else. Therefore, the success and failure of Japan depends on the thoughts of God. Acts 17:26–27 says, "From one man he made every nation of men, that they should inhabit the whole earth; and he determined the times set for them and the exact places where they should live. God did this so that men would seek him and perhaps reach out for him and find him, though he is not far from each one of us." This refers to the length of time for each nation's existence. When it says, "He determined the times set for them," it refers to not only each nation but also each province, each district, and each town. Therefore, God, Yahweh, has designated the length of time for each nation's existence. This proves what John 1:3 said, "Through him all things were made; without him nothing was made that has been made."

Q: Then, does it mean that God, Yahweh, rules over all the nations in the modern world?

A: Yes, that is right. Even the war in Europe and Chinese-Japanese War are being unfolded under the sovereign will of God and those who go against God's will be destroyed. The outcomes of both the war between Great Britain and Germany and the war between China and Japan will be dictated by the will of God. There seems to be all kinds of war, flood, drought, and earthquake presently happening in the world, more so this year and these seem to be the signs of the end time. These signs are also being given according to God's will. Surely, these signs will not cease until the return of Jesus Christ in not-so-distant future. Until the eternal world is established on earth, we cannot hope for the happiness of the mankind. Therefore, we, Christians, are awaiting the return of Jesus Christ and the establishment of the eternal world even before Jesus comes back.

Q: For what Christians criticize the privatization of wealth?

A: If there is a Christian critique of the right to hold possessions, it refers to the wrongfulness of the current policy of privatization. In terms of the right to own possessions, there can be three owners.

1. Since God sustains all the created order, we can speak of God's right to own.

2. In the present, we can speak of the government's right to own. It is because the government can keep its possessions securely in custody.

3. Then, there is the individual's right to own. In this case, possessions are acquired through the individual's hard work.

However, there is not a qualitative difference among these three kinds of ownership. They are essentially the same. It is not God's will that the individual wastes his possessions anyway he sees fit. Also, it goes against God's will that the government unilaterally turns the money of its people into weapons in order to go to war. Therefore, the current policy of privatization of wealth is fundamentally at odds with God's will and has to be ousted from the world. Summarily, any policy concerning the wealth of the nation or the wealth of individuals can only be arbitrarily and temporarily applicable from the time of Jesus' first coming thru his second coming. Upon the return of Jesus, these things become extinct and only the eternal world becomes actualized.

Q: What is the ultimate end of Christianity?

A: The end of Christianity is to see the return of Jesus Christ and the passing of the present age and the establishment of the eternal world with Jesus as its sovereign ruler. The goal is to teach believers well so that when that time comes, they would carry out the rule righteously.

Q: The place of the return?

A: Since Jesus will return in the body of a human being, it is assumed that it will be somewhere in our world. However, the place was not designated and I do not know where it will be.

Q: When will the return take place?

A: As aforementioned, now is the end time. I believe that recent famine and wars suggest the imminence of his return. It might take place tomorrow, but the day or the hour is certainly unknowable.

Q: Isn't it greatly irresponsible on the part of the citizens to undermine the rule of the emperor of the Japanese empire and seek to establish the eternal world as Jesus Christ as its ruler?

A: Though it might constitute unfaithfulness, as I said before, since it is written clearly in God's word that Christians will be given a more blessed life in the eternal world than in the present age, it is the duty of Christians to work hard to follow the will of God.

Q: If so, about what do you have to complain and be discontent?

A: For example, it is the imposition of Shinto worship. Shinto is the temple where Amaterasu, all the past emperors, and distinguished honorees are worshipped. I consider it a form of idolatry. Christian doctrines forbid idolatry. Christians are the children of God and not the children of Amaterasu. In Christianity, it is forbidden to even worship one's ancestors. It is written in Deuteronomy 5:7 and Exodus 20:3, "You shall have no other gods before me." This means that,

1) One should not worship any other god except God, Yahweh.

2) One should not worship any other god along with God, Yahweh.

Deuteronomy 5:8–10 and Exodus 20:4–10 say, "You shall not make for yourself an idol in the form of anything in heaven above or on the earth beneath or in the waters below. You shall not bow down to them or worship them; for I, the Lord your God, am a jealous God, punishing the children for the sin of the fathers to the third and fourth generation of those who hate me, but showing love to a thousand generations of those who love me and keep my commandments." Therefore, the policy of the government in forcing Christians to observe the worship of multiple gods which is unrighteous constitutes the greatest violation of God's will and surely will bring about the great punishment at the time of God's judgment.

Q: What about regarding the emperor as being divine?

A: It says in Isaiah 45:5–6, "I am the Lord, and there is no other; apart from me there is no God. I will strengthen you, though you have not acknowledged me, so that from the rising of the sun to the place of its setting men may know there is none besides me. I am the Lord, and there is no other." Based on this passage, I cannot say that the emperor is divine.

Q: Then, it seems to me that your evangelistic work can be construed as having the destruction of nation of Japan as its intended goal. What do you think?

A: The return of Jesus Christ will bring about not only the destruction of Japan but also that of every nation in the world. To depend on the nation of Japan and be destroyed at the end could not be an option for Christians who look forward to eternal life. To depend on the nation of Japan makes them too insecure. Furthermore, one must think about these things from the perspective of a higher calling. To love people that are in the world is to bring them to salvation through faith in Christ. We should strive to add one more person unto the community of believers each day. This is to allow as many people as possible to enter the eternal world and enjoy eternal life there. When there are many Christians in Japan, then the policies of the nation will automatically change and evil laws such as the imposition of Shinto worship will disappear, thereby transforming Japan into a nation based on Christian principles. Therefore, for that reason, I am doing the work of proselytizing and expanding the community of faith as a minister in order to prepare for the actualization of the eternal world.

Q: Let's suppose that the return of Jesus Christ is indeed possible. However, it will not be able to bring about the ruin of Japan that has been modernized and militarized to a great extent. What do you think will be the manner in which what you say will come to fruition?

A: You are right. Even when Jesus returns in the body of a human being, he will not resort to cannons or guns. These weapons are for the use of human beings. If there is no one to use them, they become useless. When the number of Christians is greatly increased and almost all of the humankind has become the children of God, then weapons are not needed to change the policies of our nation, thereby transforming it into a Christian nation.

Q: I believe that your evangelistic work is to bring about radical changes in our nation. Do you have any objection?

A: I have no intention to resort to violence directly. However, when the citizenry becomes Christianized, then Japan can no longer maintain the status quo. And as result, fundamental changes in the Japanese society might occur.

Q: Who are your co-conspirators?

A: I do not have anyone whom you can label as my co-conspirators.

Q: Where do you carry out this work of evangelism?

A: (Omission)

Q: Is it correct that you stirred up civil disobedience regarding Shinto worship?

A: Since the topic of Shinto worship is gravely important after 1938, I do not know all the instances when I discussed this problem. However,

1) I talked about it with the patients at Yulchon Aeyangwon about three times.

2) I also talked about it in Namgyeong Yangsan-gun (Omission).

3) I also talked about it at Gyeongnam Mulgeum Train Station (Omission).

On these instances, I explained how Shinto worship violates Christian doctrines and urged people to refuse it.

Q: Do you have anything more to say?

A: No, there is not.

Based on this interview, if Rev. Son were alive today, we can be certain that he would continue to walk the same path and maintain his allegiance to Jesus. From the deposition, we know that Rev. Son never blamed anyone or caused anyone to suffer with him. He lived a life that was based on the Bible and single-mindedly focused on confessing and sharing his faith publicly even with his life on the line. In other matters, he lived a simple life. On the contrary, from the witness testimonies of Lee and Kim, we can see how some people blamed and criticized Rev. Son's conduct in order to defend themselves.

Q: Have you ever listened to Rev. Son's sermons?

A: Yes, as Rev. Son already mentioned, he served as an itinerant preacher for the province of Busan under the auspices of Joseon Presbyterian Church and went around the churches in the places such as Shichal-gu, Busan-bu, Yangsan-gun, Gimhae-gun, and Haman-gu. It was around October in 1938. After the sermon, he met with me and Kim in the church office and explained to us about the problem of Shinto worship. At the time, I realized his views were different from mine and I had to report it to the person in charge of the region of Busan.

Again, there was this conversation.

Q: That night, what do you think he meant by saying to the twenty members that they did not have to believe inside the church?

A: Well, I do not know what he exactly meant by it. But I assume that those who practice faith inside the church are targeted and forced by the police to participate in Shinto worship. However, those who practice outside the church are not found out by the police and thus, are not forced to participate in Shinto worship.

It would have suffice for the person to stop here, however he went on to add,

A: The doctrinal position advocated by Son Yang-Won is the same as that of Rev. Choi Sang-Rim, Han Sang-Dong, Ju Nam-Seon, and Yun Sul-Yong who are being interrogated currently for their involvement in the Christian incident in Busan. Therefore, I know that he went around the churches in the region of Busan and carried out the work of proselytizing.

At the end, the man heaped further accusation onto Rev. Son with an empathic ending to the conversation.

Q: Do you have anything else to say?
A: No, I don't have much except to say that people like Son Yang-Won who preach unpatriotic doctrines must be punished to a great extent.

On the other hand, according to the deposition record of a group of twenty one pastors and elders, which was included among the collected records of other persecuted Christians, who were arrested and interrogated simultaneously in reference to an incident involving a certain presbytery, there was something so unbelievable going on at the time.

They said things like, "The names, Yahweh, and Amaterasu, are the two names of the same god. For this, it is not a violation of Christian doctrines to do Shinto worship." "Amaterasu is the creator god of Japan and God, Yahweh, is the creator of all things. Though it constitutes a violation of Christian faith to do Shinto worship, we do it as if we are doing to God." "God, Yahweh, is the one who created the universe and everything in it. But in Japan, Amaterasu is regarded as the defending deity of Japan and as such treated as the supreme god which is worshipped at Shinto temples. Therefore, the difference between the creation of God, Yahweh, and the creation of Amaterasu is that of the extent of creation. The work of creation is essentially the same. Within this frame of reference, God, Yahweh, is called Amaterasu by the Japanese. The essence of Amaterasu points to God, Yahweh. In this sense, the spirit of worshipping God, Yahweh, at the church is the same as the spirit of worshipping Amaterasu at Shinto temples. As such, it does not constitute a violation of Christianity's monotheistic orientation." With these words, many acquiesced to Shinto worship. However, the Japanese regarded this theological rendition to be a blasphemy against Amaterasu, their founding deity, and the dignity of the emperor and charged them with defamation. Those pastors are still alive and in practice. Though I do not know whether they still have the same thoughts or not, from what I see, I can assume which is the case to some degree by looking at all the things that are appearing in the present nation and outside the present church. In urgent times, they switch God, Yahweh, with something else and serve that thing as if it is God himself. They are masters at changing their colors depending on the time and situation. There are numerous examples of this. People did the same thing with Dangun, Stalin, Truman, dollar, atomic bombs, and espionage. However, Rev. Son in his foolish stubbornness never knew how to switch his allegiances or even blame others. Despite changing times and public opinions, I believe he would have been steadfast in his adherence to the word of God and living the life of faith by being on the side of Jesus.

Perhaps, he would have been on the side of the camp that supported the General Assembly. In the wake of the 8.15 independence, he was approached by Mr. Choi Deok-Ji of so-called the reconstructionist camp.

He said, "It goes without saying that you should not associate yourself with the secularized practical church. And you should not even go there to preach. Instead, if you belong to the reconstructionist camp and stand firm with us, then the church of Korea will be righted... etc."

At the time, Rev. Son replied in the following manner. "Even the Lord came to earth for a sinner like me. Then, how can I forsake this world? He was the Lord who even abandoned the world to go find the Samaritan woman. How can I then call the church a den of demons and turn my back on it? When the temple in Jerusalem was corrupt, Jesus entered it and cleaned it out. How can I not follow the footsteps of the Lord? I seek to do as my Lord, a friend to tax collectors and sinners, had done." However, it does not mean that he indiscriminately sided [with the General Assembly] just because it represented the majority or the General Assembly of the Presbyterian Church.

Those who heard his sermons at the 36th General Assembly which was held in Daegu from April 21 thru 25 of 1950 would surely have known this about him.

1st Day: "Let's recover the ark."

2nd Day: "Who is the enemy of the cross?"

3rd Day: "Let's be baptized by the Holy Spirit."

4th Day: "The Christian way to be victorious"

5th Day: "The subject of daily living"

Rev. Son indeed preached true repentance.

In a work published posthumously, he wrote in a chapter titled 'For whom do you work?,'

"Am I not a person who was predestined by God before all creation to live and die for the new nation? However, when I examine my interior life of faith, my life as a pastor, it seems that I am living for myself. Knowing that I am obsessed with my work and activities each day,

1) I seem to be working for my stomach,

2) for my fame,

3) and for my ideology.

Though it is the Lord who brings everything into my hands and guides me to work for him and his flock,

1) I make clothes out of sheep's fur for myself,

2) I fill my stomach with the milk of sheep,

3) I run amok as the leader of the flock.

Since I do not give my whole heart and best effort for the sheep even a little, woe is me."

From this, we realize how Rev. Son strove to find reasons for repentance before God and work faithfully in carrying out the work of the Lord entrusted to him. I believe there is a lesson for the current church leaders to take away from him.

He may have belonged to the ultra-conservative faction (Kosin) after all. He was undoubtedly the clerk of trustees at Korea Theological Seminary. However, I doubt that he became a member of the ultra-conservative faction just because of his background as an imprisoned conscientious objector of Shinto worship. Furthermore, he must have not become a member just because he was a presbytery member of Gyeongnam Buptong Presbytery. In fact, right before he was martyred, he moved his membership to Suncheon Presbytery which belonged to the General Assembly. It was not because he viewed that just because a person had been an imprisoned Christian, he or she neared perfection as a person or just because a person belonged to the ultra-conservative faction, he or she neared perfection as a believer. Rather, he must have not wanted to be pulled into anything factional. What is certain is that he must have had fellowship with any individual or group that wanted to draw near to the Lord through repentance and life in truth. These connections were brought on by the Lord and Rev. Son must have made them his comrades in faith from whom he could never separate himself even if he tried. His principle was unchangeable. He could never become a comrade in faith with those who were interested in causing factions with outside influence whether in a time of peace or a time of war. Perhaps, it would have been very easy for others to make a commitment to belong to a faction. It would have been possible in a social organization, school, military, or any other group. However, how could anyone walk the path of hypocrisy within a religious organization let alone a Christian community? How much more could one espouse an errant view of the Bible or change one's views to those of new theology or compromise with the changing times and circumstances? One should not think twice about rejecting such a faction. Rev. Son did not oppose Shinto worship just because he was a Korean. If this was the case, then when the issues of Dangun temple worship or bowing to the national flag emerged in the wake of independence, he should not have been interested in these... because these were being done by fellow Koreans. Rev. Son did not proclaim that the Japanese emperor would go to hell because he hated him for who he was. If this was the case, why would he busily travel throughout South Korea with the Lord's gospel on his back? Did he do this because they were fellow Koreans and he could not hate them? But whether before or after independence, whether with the Japanese or the Korean, he worked as a servant of God with an unchanging attitude. He did the work he should do and walked the path that he should walk. How do those who accused Rev. Son during the Japanese rule by saying, "People like Son Yang-Won who preach unpatriotic doctrines must be punished to a great extent," act like patriots before Korean officials now that the times are different? Those who said, "People like Son Yang-Won who preach unpatriotic doctrines must be punished to a great extent," might be able to take up the facade as patriots now. The key is not whether to insist on the faith that has become arrogant or to follow the resolution passed by the majority at the presbytery or the General Assembly. The real key is whether to thoroughly cleanse the past or not, whether to begin again with the heart that is born again. In this sense, I can say emphatically, before Rev. Son would be on this side or that side, he would be on the side of Jesus. Accordingly, whether this side or that side, Rev. Son would side with those who put the Bible as the standard of unchanging truths and strove to draw near to Jesus. Furthermore, he would forcefully cry out to the present church and this nation to repent.

Lastly, if he were alive today, he would faithfully prepare his way for the future. What do I mean by, "he would prepare his way for the future?" It can be gleaned from his deposition with the detective that he did not speak of his opinions but what the Bible taught faithfully. And he spoke boldly and truthfully.

Q: Then, does it mean that God, Yahweh, rules over all the nations in the modern world?

A: Yes, that is right. Even the war in Europe and Chinese-Japanese War are being unfolded under the sovereign will of God and those who go against God's will be destroyed. The outcomes of both the war between Great Britain and Germany and the war between China and Japan will be dictated by the will of God. There seems to be all kinds of war, flood, drought, and earthquake presently happening in the world, more so this year and these seem to be the signs of the end time. These signs are also being given according to God's will. Surely, these signs will not cease until the return of Jesus Christ in not-so-distant future. Until the eternal world is established on earth, we cannot hope for the happiness of the mankind. Therefore, we, Christians, are awaiting the return of Jesus Christ and the establishment of the eternal world even before Jesus comes back.

And he boldly proclaimed the following.

Q: Isn't it greatly irresponsible on the part of the citizens to undermine the rule of the emperor of the Japanese empire and seek to establish the eternal world as Jesus Christ as its ruler?

A: Though it might constitute unfaithfulness, as I said before, since it is written clearly in God's word that Christians will be given a more blessed life in the eternal world than in the present age, it is the duty of Christians to work hard to follow the will of God.

He espoused the hope that ignored the reality and only looked to the future. However, he dealt with each problem that came his way faithfully for the glory of God and to help bring about the will of God. Even if it meant that he was to be misunderstood or fall into a disadvantageous situation, he did not care and steadfastly went about to deal with the problem. For this, he walked his path even when faced with the problem of Shinto worship; he continued to walk the same path after Korea's independence; he maintained his course during the Yeosu-Suncheon Incident; he walked the path steadfastly even when the 6.25 invasion occurred. When faced with the issue of Shinto worship, he did not even think about retiring to somewhere. When the independence occurred, he did not act arrogantly or hoard attention. When the Yeosu-Sunchen Incident happened, he did not mourn the deaths of Dong-In and Dong-Sin too terribly. When the 6.25 invasion happened, he did not worry too much about himself or his family but watched over his flock and voluntarily embraced martyrdom. We can know from the sources that he ignored the reality of things, but he was never unfaithful in carrying out his responsibilities. Had he retired due to the issue of Shinto worship or had he extended his life by fleeing to Busan in the wake the 6.25 invasion saying, "It is not to keep myself safe but to insure the future," would we look at him the same today?

We can read from his diary or his collection of sermons this feature about him. He wrote under the title 'Today is my day,' "Since yesterday is gone, what I like or dislike about it is no longer of interest to me. Since tomorrow is a day in the future, I do not know what will happen. In this sense, only today truly belongs to me. People are easily deceived by the past and end up in failure because they brag about what they did well in the past. Also, people are easily deceived in life because they tend to postpone things to the future. Christians are those who seek satisfaction, gratitude, duty, faithfulness, and truth that each day brings." Besides his writings, it is his life that showed his commitment to preparing himself for the path that he would take in the future oblivious to whether his environment or situation changed or not.

On January 15, this year (1951), experienced something unforgettable and was moved to my tears in Busan. It was none other than the arrival of Jeon Young-Chang, my friend, by airplane whom I thought was in the United States of America. It was when Busan was in the danger of being overrun by the Chinese soldiers that were pushing the offensive southward. The rumor was going around that the UN forces would give up on Korea evidenced by their perpetual retreat. It was when both the refugees and natives of Busan sought so desperately to flee Korea if at all possible. It was when not only foreigners but also Koreans wanted to flee to America, Japan, Taiwan, Jeju, and Geoje Island to save themselves. The government as well as other organizations and associations sought their places of refuge. Even pastors of those church that were known for the commitment to caring for their flocks sought to find ways to save themselves. Pastors and parishioners alike looked for the ways to survive. In fact, this was the time when those with abilities and money used to move their families to places such as Japan and America. I don't know why my friend decided to leave America which was the safest place and the most enviable place and come back to Korea in this dangerous time. Nevertheless, he arrived by plane in Suyoung Airport. He said, "I return to my country in haste to live through the predicament facing my countrymen. If the Lord allows it, I shall live. Or if the Lord's will is otherwise, I shall gladly die. If I waited just one more week, I would have been able to attend the graduation ceremony. But I heard that flights to Japan would cease after one week. So, I left behind my graduation and diploma and came here." I was so happy that I patted him on the back in excitement. Perhaps, it was God's blessing. The Chinese forces began to retreat. However, what was remarkable was not the retreat of the Chinese forces. It was the attitude of Mr. Jeon that was remarkable.

Faith that ignores the reality and condones irresponsibility is the faith of hypocrisy that should never be allowed. However, one could see the true kind of faith in the lives of Rev. Son, those leaders who belonged to the reconstructionist camp, the ministers who served in the region of Geochang and a few brothers in faith. The true path for the Korean church lies in not neglecting the reality of the present though it is grossly unjust and being faithful to one's duty. I don't like people saying, "The ultra-conservative camp is this" or "I cannot follow the decision of the General Assembly" or "I don't like it because so-and-so is behind it." I wish that this type of mindset is uprooted from the church.

Here, I want to address one problem in the present that I am facing which cannot be taken for granted. I believe that there is one thing that the Korean church must do in the wake of the 8.15 independence. I am disappointed because the church has not done one of the most important things that the church should do for some reason. I am speaking about the attitude of the Korean Christians towards the fifty martyrs and their surviving families. I believe that addressing this issue has the potential to restore the church from its failure during the Japanese rule and at the same time bring glory to God. Though the martyrs entered the annals of history, we still have their surviving families with us who suffered with the martyrs in their campaigns of faith both directly and indirectly. Except the effort of some members of Sanjeonghyun Church in trying to shore up support for the family of Rev. Ju Gi-Cheol, there is nothing done at the Presbytery level or the General Assembly level. Due to the establishment of the 38 parallel, there were differences as to what had actually transpired, but it is true that there has not been any systematic planning. In the meanwhile, the

6.25 invasion transpired. I don't know if I was fortunate or unfortunate, but I spent three months hiding out in Seoul behind the enemy lines. Upon the recovery of Seoul from the enemy forces on September 28, I realized that just in the region of the capital about forty five or forty six pastors from all different denominations were either martyred or kidnapped. This added to my interest in the surviving families of the martyred or missing pastors. So, I made it my ministry to visit these families with a few friends in faith and tried hard to push for some kind of relief program for them. However, due to the southward push by the Chinese forces, I could not see the plan materialize and ended up moving down to Busan. In Busan, I was captivated by the same desire and tried my best to support these families. When I received some support, I was able to organize the very first revival meeting in support of the surviving families of the martyred or missing ministers. People came together around fifty households and one hundred ninety persons and shared great comfort with each other. Among the surviving family members were some who said they would follow the footsteps of their fathers and fight the fight of faith at the forefront of the battle. Among them were also those who had been weakened in faith due to the hardship stemming from the martyrdom or kidnapping of their loved ones and who later experienced the joy of renewal. It must have been one month after the revival meeting. I felt that an organizational structure was needed for the relief work of these families and it led to the organization of the association of the families of martyrs. Furthermore, the organization identified seven goals of which the most urgent task was the education of the children of the surviving families.

The things began to move quickly in Busan and the members who were interested in supporting the education of the children of the surviving families began to be recruited among individuals and churches. Along with this, a plan for the relief was being put together. In the meantime, there were many who readily signed up for the cause, but there were several churches and individuals who were resistant to the idea. The biggest reason for the resistance was the conflict between the ultra-conservative camp and the General Assembly camp regarding their efforts to expand their respective membership. Many pointed to the churches affiliated with the ultra-conservative camp that signed up for the cause as the reason for their nonparticipation. They intimated that, despite the good intention of the cause, it could be used as a marketing campaign tool by the ultra-conservative camp. According to them, they could not participate in such an effort because it might weaken the influence and foundation of their ecclesial body. When I visited a certain church in the vicinity of Busan City five or six times, I explained to its leadership that this relief effort did not have as its motive to recruit people for any denomination or faction but to provide relief to the families of those who died for the name and glory of the Lord. I asked the representative of the church to support a few children and help make their future brighter if unable to become a full member of the association. However, the representative refused to even consider it. What was the reason? He said that it did not concern his faction and his situation was not conducive to this kind of work.

Right now, the educational expenses for about eighty children are being currently supported by fourteen Presbyterian and Holiness congregations in the vicinity of Busan City. However, it is still the case that calling for aid for many is going unanswered. Only then, I realized how foolish I was in thinking that this relief ministry would easily find success with the Korean church. I believe that this project was a litmus test for the Korean church of the present in deciding in which direction it should go. How in the world did I think that such project would happen so easily! I thought the failure of this project showcased something so obvious about the state of the church. If this where the church is, to emphasize the spirit of martyrdom and speak of the cross at the pulpit of the Korean church is of absolute hypocrisy. Rather, they should stay with the sermons are humanistic, ecumenical, diplomatic, social, moral, and practical in orientation.

Recently on the anniversary of 9.28, I visited Yeosu Aeyangwon thinking that there would be a memorial service for Rev. Aeyangwon. Contrary to my expectation, the church told me that it decided to cancel the one year anniversary event of Rev. Son's death. Personally, I wanted to arrange a memorial service in Busan, but I decided against it due to extenuating circumstances. But I wanted to know why Aeyangwon had to cancel its service. They listed several reasons for the cancelation. They are,

1) In the wake of the 8.15 independence, memorial services for martyrs tended to become indistinguishable from the ancestor-worship rites of unbelievers.

2) If Rev. Son were alive today, he would have prohibited such practice.

3) The household of Rev. Son never emphasized memorial services.

4) There is no biblical ground for such practice.

5) There is no precedence in the history of Christianity about such practice.

There is some ground here for further exploration of the appropriateness of memorial services. Just because they did not have a memorial service, it does not mean that they did nothing for the day. They brought Rev. Jeong Gyu-Oh as the guest speaker and had a revival meeting. On the last day of the revival meeting, they did a special offering for the surviving family of Rev. Son. The offering on that night amounted to 3,500,000 *won* and was used to set up a foundation for the family. I felt that this arrangement was one hundred times better than a memorial service with a festive atmosphere. Should I say that this was a true memorial service without a structure? Through this experience, I was comforted by the fact that the Korean church's heart was still vibrating. There was definitely a significant gap between the attitude of the status quo of the Korean church and the people of Aeyangwon regarding the welfare of the surviving families of deceased or missing ministers.

I truly wish that the leadership of the Korean church moves away from the empty faith that rejoices in abusing the law and power to confiscate church buildings from other people or to deny other churches from opening their doors. Instead, I wish that we can truly seek the better tomorrow for this nation and empower individual members to prepare their own path. I wish that we can walk as true saints the path that Rev. Ju Gi-Cheol and Rev. Son Yang-Won walked. If not careful, I am afraid that we would become the guide that turns the Korean nation into slaves of a foreign nation. Therefore, I beseech the Korean church to not succumb to the evil of selling out its nation, race, flock, and God. Whenever I do not know what to think, I turn to the essay titled 'The argument for atomic bombs' by Cho Young-Am which was published on Seoul News in the beginning of December last year and read it alone in sighing. A part of the essay is like the following.

... If the retreat of the UN forces out of North Korea ends up being just that, a retreat, then our boldness would be in vain. Who will guarantee the safety of our fellow pro-democracy militias in the provinces of Pyeongan and Hamgyeong? Whenever I think of it, my sight becomes filled with darkness. I know and believe that God will not be unsympathetic towards us. What can we do about the sad fate of our nation in having all the right conditions both temporal and spatial for the destruction by atomic bombs that are the greatest in power in the world? The atomic bomb that used to have the efficacy of forty *li* in radius terms of destructiveness is now ten times more destructive. Then, wouldn't it destroy the area of four hundred *li* with one shot? If one can over four hundred *li*, then twelve atomic bombs can wipe out the entire land of Korea from the face of the earth. Please drop twelve bombs on us! Then, there will be no one left in this land that is full of sin and empty of blessing... Both China, the puppet of Russia, and North Korean communists will also become a handful of ashes before this fire of destruction. Afterwards, powerful rays of radiation will make even our greatest ghosts joyfully wander around in air.

Future historians will call these atomic bombs the atomic bombs of Mugungwha (Rose of Sharon). Out of the ashes the atomic bombs of Mugungwha, a nation without evil schemes, double-crossings, envy, jealousy, laziness, and idiocy will rise. Let us dream about this field of the beautiful atomic bombs! We will be sorrowful about nothing. We will only wail bitterly about the love that never materialized, the love of one person.

I only wish that this longing painted by the brush of a mere writer would forever remain as an essay and nothing more!

Judgment

Oh my!
Thunder, lightening, clouds, angels, ten million saints, trumpet sound... judgment!
This shall be the momentous judgment that the Lord promised.
The judgment of growth continues until we become the good grains and the empty heads of grains are left behind.

Sheep on the right,
Goats on the left,
Is this the judgment of one's work that one receives without one's awareness?

"Teacher, how are you?"
This is the prelude of death by hanging for Judas Iscariot who made a big fortune.

"Then, what should I do with Jesus that is called Christ?"
This is the cry of Pilate at the judgment seat.

"Crucify him. Crucify him."
This is the war cry of self-destruction for the nation of Judah who thought it
received the chance of a lifetime.

"For if their purpose or activity is of human origin, it will fail. But if it is from
God, you will not be able to stop these men; you will only find yourselves
fighting against God."
This was the wisest prophecy of all generations by Gamaliel, the Pharisee.

After mankind had made its dwelling on earth,
After history had settled on time,
After heroes had risen up and established their nations,
After nations had risen up and expanded their territories,

When wealth is spent, there is no trace of it.
When power is spent, there is no trace of it.
Though military might conquers, there is no legacy.
Though human work triumphs, there is no acquisition.
Though life is oppressed, it does not lose its strength.
Though truth is overshadowed, it does not lose its luster.

Snow storm swooped down on the infant body in a manger.
Power drove out the shivering baby to Egypt.
The grim realities of life made him spend his youth as a carpenter.
The society's views turned the Son of God into a crazy person.
The religious placed the Messiah under the death sentence.
The laws of the land crucified an innocent man.
The devil tried to bury eternally the great feat.
However, life defeated all these things.
And truth resurrected all these things.

Riches and glory, fame and status,
No, I can never exchange this life with anything, even the whole world!

Hardships and persecution, curse and massacre,
No, this truth can never be hidden even if the whole universe forces upon it!

If this whole land is this nation's abode,
If five thousand years are this nation's pride,
If thirty million countrymen are one ancestor's decedents,
If one million Christians are this nation's heart,
If three thousand altars are this nation's holy of holies,

The Korean race [the race of *Baedal*] should be the rightful hero of this land.
The white-clad folk should be the rightful ivory tower of this history.
The people of the north and south should be the rightful descendants of the ancestor.
One million Christians should be the rightful possessors of the blood of this heart.
The holy altar of the Lord should be the rightful source of eternal bliss.

But the land has been cut in half and become the battlefield of foreign nations.
But the whole land of Korea has become scorched and its history incinerated.
But Koreans have sold other Koreans and dug the grave of self-destruction.
But the flocks of sheep have lost their way and were unable to find the path of blood.
But the holy altars became desecrated and turned into the palaces of curse.
How could this be?

The judgment of a nation is brought about as the result of the total settlement of accounts of that nation in that age.
The judgment of a race is the Babel Tower of that age's leaders.
The judgment of leaders is the shadow of that age's religious people.
The scale of judgment is upon the shoulders of religious people.
A pandemonium of fire,
A live hell of life,
A clot of white blood cells,
A great accusation of Satan,
Who could be spared from this charge?

Olives are born of an olive tree.

A cluster of grapes is on a grave vine.

Fig fruits are under the leaves of a fig tree.

A thistle is on a thistle plant.

Thorns are of a thorny tree.

The self-trap of the 38 Parallel is the harvest at the end of the Japanese rule.

A human being of despair, a disabled veteran is the gift of selfish ambition of heroes.

Living corpses, citizen reservists are the mirror of pleaser-seeking high government officials.

The grave of the world, the land of blood are the blueprint of the world's current thoughts.

The wild hair and blood-stained lips of the UN princess are the disgraceful flowers of civil war.

Inflation-driven hardships reflect the greed of profiteers and money mongers.

The mobs of young beggars in the street are the new face of Korea.

The fight over the altars that were abandoned by the Holy Spirit is the epitome of the religious profiteering.

When will be the day of judgment?

Where will be the seat of judgment?

What will be judged?

Who will be judged?

Do not ask these questions.

The Lord will come and carry out the last judgment.

The Lord will bring in the good grains as well as the empty heads of grains.

The Lord will separate the sheep from the goats.

Joseon's judgment was issued at Pyeongyang Sumoonbak Church when the resolution for Shinto worship was passed.

South Korea's judgment was issued at Seoul Saemoonan church when the committee with *carte blanc* was organized.

The enemy forces' judgment was issued at Daegu First Church when a special council was appointed.

The future of Korea's judgment was issued at Busan Central Church when the moderator of Buptong Gyeongnam Presbytery was buried.

The final victory lies in life.
The ultimate triumphal return is in truth.
Evergreens put down deep roots due to the northerly.
Isn't the fragrance of a Japanese tree in snow beautiful?

"Teacher, how are you?"
This is the prelude of death by hanging for Judas Iscariot who made a big fortune.

"Then, what should I do with Jesus that is called Christ?"
This is the cry of Pilate at the judgment seat.

"Crucify him. Crucify him."
This is the war cry of self-destruction for the nation of Judah who thought it received the chance of a lifetime.

"For if their purpose or activity is of human origin, it will fail. But if it is from God, you will not be able to stop these men; you will only find yourselves fighting against God."
This was the wisest prophecy of all generations by Gamaliel, the Pharisee.

The End

After Putting the Pen Down

While I was penning the '*Atomic Bomb of Love*,' I had never dreamed that Part I and Part II would be finished consecutively in a very short period of time. Now that Part II is successfully completed, I felt regretful and fearful in thinking that what I wrote in a prayer in Chapter 18: Prayer of the Martyr of Part I might have come true.

I am extremely grateful that this book is being published only a year and a half after it was written and in time for the very second memorial service for Rev. Son's martyrdom. But I still cannot help but fear that I might not have prepared it as much as possible for the publication and for this, I am sorry to the servant of God that had already gone to be with God. The publication was delayed because I suffered from appendicitis on two separate occasions and I started my new position at the ministry of commerce and industry since April of this year. At the same time, these circumstances, I believe, have helped the publishing process. I believe that everything has worked toward the good of this project. Furthermore, I hope and give thanks to God that this book benefits the nation of Korea which, it seems, suffers from a never-ending cycle of war and calamity.

I am truly sorry that I have not fulfilled my responsibilities at Korea Theological Seminary, Korean Christian Gyeongnam Relief Council, and Korean Christian Relief Committee for the Surviving Families of Martyrs satisfactorily while I was writing this book. I have never felt so powerless in my life regarding my own duties and those that were asked of me.

It goes without saying that the materials that Rev. Son Eui-Won generously made available to me has been instrumental to writing this book. Also, it is nothing short of a miracle that I came to be in possession of the original interrogation record that led to the prison sentence of one year and a half for Rev. Son. I say this is a miracle that something like could happen in Korea where times have changed and a war had taken place. For this, I am deeply indebted to Elder Won Tak-Yun at Gwangju District Court.

I also would like to thank my dear brothers, Son Chang-Sup and Kim Byung-Bo, and Oh Jun-Il of Goryo Publications.

I apologize for many typographical errors and omissions and I ask for your understanding since these were due to all kinds of business related circumstances, imperfect conditions in the environment, and the pressure of the deadline.

For my last words, I would like to say that I do not wish for this book to be sold in a large quantity so fast. On the contrary, even if it means that I have to deal with a financial shortcoming, I wish that it does not become a book that produces a blind following or is sensationalized. In this sense, I am once again faced with the realization that the ultimate gift for those who strive to spend their lifetime for the glory of God and the victory of Jesus Christ rather than individual or ecclesial success or prosperity is nothing but the cross.

To be treated as heretics for just being in the Kosin camp is utterly ridiculous! It will be better to call it Kosin (孤信派) in the sense of being alone in earnest faith!

Jesus was branded a religious blasphemer by the religious Pharisees, a political rebel by the occupying Romans, and a traitor by the people of Judah. Shouldn't it be the same for those who try to live righteously today as the end time dawns and the return of the Lord draws imminent?

September 28, 1952

The Memorial Service for the 2nd Anniversary of Rev. Son's Martyrdom